RETHINKING WORK AND LEARNING

UNESCO-UNEVOC Book Series
Technical and Vocational Education and Training:
Issues, Concerns and Prospects

Volume 9

Series Editor-in-Chief:
Dr **Rupert Maclean**, *UNESCO-UNEVOC International Centre for Technical and Vocational Education and Training, Bonn, Germany*

Associate Editors:
Professor **Felix Rauner**, *TVET Research Group, University of Bremen, Germany*
Professor **Karen Evans**, *Institute of Education, University of London, United Kingdom*

Editorial Advisory Board:

Dr **David Atchoarena**, *UNESCO International Institute for Educational Planning, Paris, France*
Dr **András Benedek**, *Ministry of Employment and Labour, Budapest, Hungary*
Dr **Paul Benteler**, *Stahlwerke Bremen, Germany*
Ms **Diane Booker**, *TAFESA, Adelaide, Australia*
Mr **John Budu-Smith**, *formerly Ministry of Education, Accra, Ghana*
Professor **Michel Carton**, *NORRAG c/o Graduate Institute of International and Development Studies, Geneva, Switzerland*
Dr **Chris Chinien**, *Workforce Development Consulting, Montreal, Canada*
Dr **Claudio De Moura Castro**, *Faculade Pitágoras, Belo Horizonte, Brazil*
Dr **Michael Frearson**, *SQW Consulting, Cambridge, United Kingdom*
Dr **Lavinia Gasperini**, *Natural Resources Management and Environment Department, Food and Agriculture Organization, Rome, Italy*
Dr **Peter Grootings**, *European Training Foundation, Turin, Italy*
Professor **W. Norton Grubb**, *Graduate School of Education, University of California, Berkeley, United States of America*
Dr **Dennis R. Herschbach**, *Faculty of Education Policy and Leadership, University of Maryland, College Park, United States of America*
Dr **Oriol Homs**, *Centre for European Investigation and Research in the Mediterranean Region, Barcelona, Spain*
Professor **Phillip Hughes**, *Australian National University, Canberra, Australia*
Professor **Moo-Sub Kang**, *Korea Research Institute for Vocational Education and Training, Seoul, Republic of Korea*
Dr **Bonaventure W. Kerre**, *School of Education, Moi University, Eldoret, Kenya*
Dr **Günter Klein**, *German Aerospace Centre, Bonn, Germany*
Dr **Wilfried Kruse**, *Sozialforschungsstelle Dortmund, Dortmund Technical University, Germany*
Professor **Jon Lauglo**, *Department of Educational Research, Faculty of Education, University of Oslo, Norway*
Dr **Alexander Leibovich**, *Institute for Vocational Education and Training Development, Moscow, Russian Federation*
Professor **Robert Lerman**, *Urban Institute, Washington, United States of America*
Mr **Joshua Mallet**, *Commonwealth of Learning, Vancouver, Canada*
Ms **Naing Yee Mar**, *UNESCO-UNEVOC International Centre for Technical and Vocational Education and Training, Bonn, Germany*
Professor **Munther Wassef Masri**, *National Centre for Human Resources Development, Amman, Jordan*
Dr **Phillip McKenzie**, *Australian Council for Educational Research, Melbourne, Australia*
Dr **Theo Raubsaet**, *Centre for Work, Training and Social Policy, Nijmegen, Netherlands*
Mr **Trevor Riordan**, *International Labour Organization, Bangkok, Thailand*
Professor **Barry Sheehan**, *Melbourne University, Australia*
Dr **Madhu Singh**, *UNESCO Institute for Lifelong Learning, Hamburg, Germany*
Dr **Manfred Tessaring**, *European Centre for the Development of Vocational Training, Thessaloniki, Greece*
Dr **Jandhyala Tilak**, *National Institute of Educational Planning and Administration, New Delhi, India*
Dr **Pedro Daniel Weinberg**, *formerly Inter-American Centre for Knowledge Development in Vocational Training (ILO/CINTERFOR), Montevideo, Uruguay*
Professor **Adrian Ziderman**, *Bar-Ilan University, Ramat Gan, Israel*

For other titles published in this series, go to
www.springer.com/series/6969

Rethinking Work and Learning
Adult and Vocational Education for Social Sustainability

Edited by

PETER WILLIS

University of South Australia, Mawson Lakes, Australia

STEPHEN McKENZIE

University of South Australia, Mawson Lakes, Australia

ROGER HARRIS

University of South Australia, Mawson Lakes, Australia

Editors

Dr. Peter Willis
Centre for Research in Education,
Equity and Work
(Hawke Research Institute for
Sustainable Societies)
School of Education
University of South Australia
Mawson Lakes Blvd.
Mawson Lakes SA 5095
Australia

Dr. Stephen McKenzie
Centre for Research in Education,
Equity and Work
(Hawke Research Institute for
Sustainable Societies)
School of Education
University of South Australia
Mawson Lakes Blvd.
Mawson Lakes SA 5095
Australia

Prof. Roger Harris
Centre for Research in Education,
Equity and Work
(Hawke Research Institute for
Sustainable Societies)
School of Education
University of South Australia
Mawson Lakes Blvd.
Mawson Lakes SA 5095
Australia

ISBN: 978-1-4020-8963-3   e-ISBN: 978-1-4020-8964-0

DOI 10.1007/978-1-4020-8964-0

Library of Congress Control Number: 2008933599

© Springer Science+Business Media B.V. 2009
No part of this work may be reproduced, stored in a retrieval system, or transmitted
in any form or by any means, electronic, mechanical, photocopying, microfilming, recording
or otherwise, without written permission from the Publisher, with the exception
of any material supplied specifically for the purpose of being entered
and executed on a computer system, for exclusive use by the purchaser of the work.

Printed on acid-free paper

9 8 7 6 5 4 3 2 1

springer.com

Foreword
Rethinking a Sustainable Society

Alan Mayne

The world has already passed the midway point for achieving by 2015 the eight Millennium Development Goals for a "more peaceful, prosperous and just world" that were set by the United Nations in the wake of its inspirational Millennium Declaration in 2000.[1] These goals range from combating poverty, hunger, and disease, to empowering women, and ensuring environmental sustainability. However Ban Ki-Moon, the United Nations Secretary-General, conceded in 2007 that progress to date has been mixed. During 2008 the head of the United Nations World Food Programme cautioned that because of the surge in world commodity prices the program had insufficient money to stave off global malnutrition, and the World Health Organization warned of a global crisis in water and sanitation. Depressing news accounts accumulate about opportunities missed to achieve a fairer world order and ecological sustainability: the manipulation of election results in Africa, human rights abuses in China, 4000 Americans dead and another nation torn apart by a senseless and protracted war in Iraq, and weasel words by the world's political leadership in the lead-up to negotiations for a climate change deal in 2009 that is supposed to stabilize global carbon dioxide emissions.

It is clear that the parameters of the debates that drive progressive policy change urgently require repositioning and energizing. As is shown by the contributors to *Rethinking work and learning*, experts in the humanities and social sciences (HASS) could have an important role to play in this process. However two things are required in order for their input to have real value. First, HASS researchers must "cut to the chase." Public debate has already moved beyond establishing that sustainable development requires as strong a social agenda as it does economic functionality. HASS researchers must take the next step and help to delineate and actively assert that social agenda. As Nobel Prize winner and former World Bank chief economist Joseph Stiglitz puts it, "Development is about transforming the lives of people, not just transforming economies. Policies for education or employment need to be looked at through this double lens: how they promote growth and how they affect individuals directly" (2006, p. 50). Stiglitz argues that the processes of globalization since the

---

[1] *United Nations Millennium Declaration*, United Nations General Assembly, 55th session, Resolution 55/2, 18 September 2000.

late 1970s have resulted in "a democratic deficit" that can be corrected only through "a greater concern both for the poor countries and for the poor in rich countries, and for values that go beyond profits and GDP" (2006, p. 276). Rectifying that deficit provides HASS researchers with their best opportunity to contribute substantially to knowledge building for a just and sustainable world.

The second challenge facing HASS researchers, if they really are to reposition public debate about social sustainability in this way, is to distance themselves clearly from the jibe that "the emperor has no clothes." Such is the magnitude and the urgency of the sustainability crises that face human society in the twenty-first century that the HASS sector must dispense with the baggage of conventional academic and professional process and focus instead on developing practical protocols for sustainable living. Now is not the time to indulge in obtuse jargon and abstract word play (neither of which should be confused with the need to maintain benchmarks for action that are anchored in core ethical or spiritual values). We need the clear and active engagement of HASS researchers in order to fashion a just and sustainable world. Since it is easy to throw stones at others, I will instead direct this criticism at myself. I have been an academic historian for thirty years, and for all of those years have written and taught about the imbalance between urban wealth and poverty which sustained city growth during the first wave of globalization during the nineteenth and early twentieth centuries. It was easy for me to deplore social injustice in the past, because in adopting the perspective of a would-be social reformer of equity imbalances in the past I was really only tilting at shadows in the present. The situations I studied had passed, and the participants in them were long dead and buried. But parallel social imbalances are accumulating around the world today, and as a result of continuing rapid urbanization half of humanity now lives in urban areas. The social inequality that has become entrenched in cities is a major impediment to achieving the Millennium Development Goals. I see the "slums" stretching below me whenever I fly into Mumbai, and I see them when I travel to work in Delhi at JNU. How should historians respond to the present-day outcomes of social transformations whose development they have comfortably traced in the past? And how, more generally, should HASS researchers translate their technical expertise into effective social action in support of the Millennium Goals?

"Slum" is an outside construct that misrepresents the complicated social, economic, political, and environmental specifics that perpetuate urban inequality in diverse places. It is a label based on fear, misunderstanding, and indifference. It endures and continues to skew public policy reform because of a mixture of cynicism and ignorance by public regulators and private developers. The sad result is evident in the decision by the Maharashtra state government in 2008 to demolish Dharavi, the heart-shaped mosaic of dirty and smelly neighborhoods—but nonetheless functional and resilient communities—that has long existed in the center of Mumbai. Journalist Dan McDougall argued recently that careful investigation of

> Mumbai's labyrinthine Dharavi slum [reveals] one of the most inspiring economic models in Asia. Dharavi may be one of the world's largest slums, but it is by far its most prosperous—a thriving business centre propelled by thousands of micro-entrepreneurs who have created an invaluable industry—turning around the discarded waste of Mumbai's 19 million citizens.

> A new estimate by economists of the output of the slum is as impressive as it seems improbable: $1.4bn a year. (2007, p. 29)

Juxtaposing the competing visions of Dharavi, McDougall noted that "For Dharavi's detractors, mainly Mumbai's city fathers and real estate developers, keen to get their hands on the prime land, the shanty is an embarrassing boil to be lanced from the body of an ambitious city hoping to become the next Shanghai. But for a growing number of environmental campaigners Dharavi is becoming the green lung stopping Mumbai choking to death on its own waste" (p. 29).

Kalpana Sharma exposed the sham about Dharavi when in *Rediscovering Dharavi: stories from Asia's largest slum* she rejected outsiders' characterizations of the district's brutality, crime, and dysfunctionality and instead described the reality of day-to-day community life. One of Sharma's strengths, and it is replicated by the contributors to *Rethinking work and learning*, is her immersion in society's "grassroots." The preface to her book begins: "This book would not have been written if the people of Dharavi had not welcomed me into their homes, extended their hospitality, and shared their stories and their dreams with me" (2000, p. xi). Potentially one of the most important contributions of HASS research to policy debate about social sustainability is its sensitivity to and respect for local knowledge systems that have been disregarded and discountenanced by policy makers. Building knowledge for sustainability should no longer entail (as it has too often in the past) talking down to disempowered constituencies; it must engage with them in order to understand local concerns and where necessary reinforce local action and the informal support networks that already attempt to mediate community health, education, and work issues.

Rethinking sustainability requires real understanding of subaltern knowledge systems and support networks, and enduring partnerships that build upon this knowledge and which harness and develop grassroots energies. Too much public policy has faltered in the past because it ignored or snubbed local experience and the vernacular processes that articulate them. As Sharma said of the inhabitants of Dharavi, they are "people like us who can think out and plan their own future" (2000, pp. xii, xvii). Genuine social justice and social inclusion programs for the new millennium need to tap into this "savviness," rather than be superimposed upon it. HASS inputs are well suited to help us achieve this goal. As a historical illustration of what I mean, Mumbai's urban planners may have done better in Dharavi if they had reflected upon Robert Darnton's historical accounts of eighteenth-century France. Darnton's interest lies less in the lives of philosophers and the well-to-do than in those of peasants and urban workers, and in *The great cat massacre* he reminds his readers that the historian's job is to uncover

> the way ordinary people made sense of the world. He [sic] attempts to uncover their cosmology, to show how they organized reality in their minds and expressed it in their behavior. He does not try to make a philosopher out of the man in the street but to see how street life called for a strategy. Operating at ground level, ordinary people learn to be "street smart"—and they can be as intelligent in their fashion as philosophers. (1985, pp. 3–4)

Darnton's point of view in studying the past resonates with Sharma's purpose in writing about the inhabitants of Dharavi today. It also overlaps with the wide variety of social science perspectives that are presented here in *Rethinking work and learning*.

These intersections remind me of the British social historian J. F. C. Harrison, whose works encouraged me, when an undergraduate, to think deeply about social justice and social inclusion. Harrison wrote many books, but one is especially relevant to the concerns that are shared by Willis, McKenzie, Harris, and their collaborators. It is called *Learning and living, 1790–1960: a study in the history of the English adult education movement* (1961). Old-style historical narratives such as Harrison's, and the best of present-day social science research, have one key element in common: they value storytelling. Sharing stories expands relationships because it tends to build mutual respect and to foster conciliation. It assists social inclusion and cohesion by providing sounding boards for diverse social relationships and experiences. It accelerates reform programs by pinpointing social justice issues where policy intervention cannot be gainsaid. Stories about conflict and reconciliation in Africa are a good example. Another example is provided by the subaltern voices that have been relayed from shantytowns in places such as Dharavi. Storytelling can nowhere guarantee better social outcomes because progressive policy take-up is invariably contested and often ultimately denied, but at least the rethinking and repositioning has begun.

Storytelling takes many forms. It can be expressed through text, voice and song, play and performance. It is expressed in art. During my research collaboration with Indigenous artists at Borroloola in the Northern Territory of Australia my hosts demonstrated the power of storytelling to remedy enduring wrongs. Remote Aboriginal settlements and outstations are regularly characterized in the mainstream Australian media as brutal and dysfunctional places. Borroloola is ridiculed as being the furthest and most marginal place that an Australian citizen can go to without a passport. But local artists construct storylines in both paint and "whitefella" language about the history of their country, its spiritual pathways, and its ecological rhythms, which are starting to win outside appreciation for their homelands, cross-generational bonding within their community, and a new source of shared learning, work, and income for local people.

Sharing stories, and drawing moral lessons and practical blueprints for action from them, is an essential starting point for rethinking the key planks of sustainable communities in the new millennium. Although there is now little time remaining to meet the Millennium Development Goals for 2015 of a socially just and sustainable world order, rapid and large-scale social progress is nonetheless still feasible and achievable (see United Nations, 2007).

References

Darnton, R. (1985). *The great cat massacre and other episodes in French cultural history*. New York: Vintage Books.

Harrison, J. F. C. (1961). *Learning and living, 1790–1960: a study in the history of the English adult education movement*. London: Routledge and Kegan Paul.

McDougall, D. (2007). Success in a slum. *Guardian Weekly*, 16–22 March, p. 29.
Sharma, K. (2000). *Rediscovering Dharavi: stories from Asia's largest slum*. New Delhi: Penguin Books India.
Stiglitz, J. (2006). *Making globalisation work: the next steps to global justice*. London: Allen Lane.
United Nations (2007). *The Millennium Development Goals Report, 2007*. New York: United Nations.

Introduction by the Series Editor

Rupert Maclean

Promoting skills development for employability, through means such as technical and vocational education and training (TVET), has been an important feature of education in all societies, regardless of their level of economic and social development, since the beginning of time. This is to be expected, since work is fundamental to human survival, and work-related skills need to be passed onto each new generation of learners.

The main difference over history, and between countries, has concerned which modes of delivery have been dominant: that is, whether skills development for employability has been mainly through formal, non-formal or informal means. In practice each of these modes of delivery has to varying degrees had a role to play, although in earliest times the modalities mainly concerned informal and non-formal means of learning.

In modern times TVET has become an increasingly important part of formal education systems. The very first World Bank loan for education, granted in 1963, was for TVET; and TVET accounted for about 40% of all educational loans in sub-Saharan Africa until the early 1960s. In 1991 the Bank reversed gears, partly due to a World Bank policy paper which argued that TVET was not a good investment when compared to general education. This led many experts and policy-makers to conclude that training is best left to the workplace. This view was promoted by a major policy change by the World Bank, which was earlier considered to be one of TVET's staunchest supporters.

Over the past five years or so, TVET has again been attracting increasing attention from governments, and is very much back as a key part of the development agenda.

There are several important reasons for the return of TVET to become one of the priority areas in education. The world of work – those who create employment opportunities, the employees and workers themselves, and the educators and trainers who provide the skills needed for employability – is regarded as being central to achieving sustainable development and so is of great importance with regard to the United Nations Decade of Education for Sustainable Development (ESD),

---

Rupert Maclean (✉)
UNESCO-UNEVOC International Centre for Education, Bonn, Germany

2005–2014. At its most basic level, achieving sustainable development means achieving the targets set in the Millennium Development Goals, as agreed by all countries in the world at the special September 2000 session of the General Assembly of the United Nations. Skilled workers are central to achieving all eight goals and associated targets in the Millennium Development Goals. In this sense, TVET underpins every single one of the MDGs.

In addition, TVET is regarded as being very important if Education for All (EFA) is going to be achieved, since skills development for employability is a major motivator for people to become literate, and to engage in lifelong learning.

Making gains in poverty reduction, job creation, health or environmental concerns, and achieving EFA and ESD, is not possible without a focused TVET policy, which can lead to huge improvements in education, gender equality and living conditions.

Achieving the MDGs therefore requires the development of strong and effective TVET, in terms of equal access for all, and programmes with high relevance and quality assurance. As a strategic vision, the Millennium Development Goals are steps towards a longer-term vision of building human, social, economic and environmental capital, especially in developing countries. However, maintaining and building social, economic and environmental capital depends upon human capital, and upon the institutions for TVET that develop work-ready human capital that is the engine for sustainable development over the long run.

In this regard there are several main concerns that need to be addressed, such as:

- The acquisition of skills for work, and for citizenship and sustainability, is crucial for economic and social development because 80% of the world's workforce use technical and vocational skills in their work.
- TVET should be relevant to the needs of the labour market, be of high quality, and broadly accessible to all. However, this ideal is often not being met, particularly in developing nations, economies in transition, and those in a post-conflict situation.
- There is a need to assist UNESCO's 193 member states to improve and integrate TVET as part of the global Education for All Campaign, and also to assist the alignment of TVET with the tenets of sustainable development, with particular reference to promoting best and innovative practices.

This timely, cutting edge book explores ways of rethinking work and learning with particular reference to adult and vocational education for social sustainability. The authors argue that Human Resource Development is of key importance if sustainable economies and societies are to be achieved. They also argue that when policy makers examine sustainability their main area of focus or emphasis tends to be the economic dimension of sustainability. However, they believe that there is a need to rethink the concept of sustainability, placing a greater emphasis on social sustainability including notions of peace-building, the central importance of values and ethics, and importance of social justice and social cohesion and the role of religion and spirituality. In all of these areas, TVET is regarded as being important to achieving both economic and social sustainability.

This book makes an important contribution to examining the meaning and significance of sustainability, and encourages the reader to rethink this important concept.

Acknowledgments

The completion of this project has been made possible through the support and encouragement of Rupert Maclean from the UNESCO-UNEVOC International Centre at Bonn, the editor of the series to which this volume belongs. We would also like to mention with appreciation the support from Natalia Matveeva at UNESCO-UNEVOC and the kindly and flexible assistance we received from Harmen van Paradijs and Marianna Pascale at Springer in The Netherlands.

In Australia, our "AVE for Social Sustainability" project which has come to fruition in this volume was enriched and energized by an early symposium at the University of South Australia that many of our chapter writers, international and national, attended in April 2006. This gathering was sponsored by a seed grant from the Hawke Research Institute for Sustainable Societies (HRISS) and the university's Division of Education, Arts and Social Sciences, for which we express much appreciation. We also want to thank Bernie Lovegrove from the Asian South Pacific Bureau of Adult Education in Canberra who connected us to scholars/educators in the Asia–Pacific region.

Our thanks go to supportive colleagues from the University of South Australia at the Hawke Research Institute for Sustainable Societies: Alan Mayne, the then director, who wrote the foreword to this collection; Barbara Comber, the present director, and Gerry Bloustein, who has overview of editing and publishing support at the institute. In addition we, the editors, especially thank colleagues in the Centre for Research in Education, Equity and Work (CREEW), one of the institute's research concentrations: Tom Stehlik, Alan Reid, Michele Simons, and Miriam McLean.

The complex processes of linking and negotiating with international and national authors and creating a critical and creative dialogue with them was possible only with the enthusiastic and skilful assistance of the CREEW/HRISS editorial team: Anne Morrison, Kate Leeson, and Paul Wallace. The editors wish to thank them especially for their kindly and valuable help with keeping the exchanges with authors alive and with the detailed editing, proofing, and formatting that have given this book its fine finish.

We would like to thank finally and especially our partners who have shared our work: Eileen with Peter, Louise with Stephen, and Susan with Roger.

Peter Willis, Stephen McKenzie, and Roger Harris

Contents

1 Introduction: Challenges in Adult and Vocational Education for Social Sustainability 1
Peter Willis, Stephen McKenzie and Roger Harris

Part I Social Sustainability Perspectives in Adult and Vocational Education

2 Advancing Social Sustainability Through Vocational Education and Training 13
John Fien and David Wilson

3 An Ecology for the Fourth Pillar: Imaginal Learning for Social Sustainability in AVE 25
Peter Willis

4 The Historical Contribution of AVE to Social Sustainability in Australia 45
Roger Harris

5 The Language of Longing: Rationality, Morality, and Experience in Education for Sustainability 63
Aidan Davison

Part II Foundations for Social Sustainability in Adult and Vocational Education

6 Educating for a Sustainable Democracy 83
Michael Newman

7 Transformative Learning and AVE for Social Sustainability 93
Patricia Cranton

8 Education, Religion, Sustainability, and Dialogue 107
   Chris Provis

9 The Role of Religion in Education for Social Sustainability 119
   Heather Foster

Part III Creating Spaces for Social Sustainability in Adult and Vocational Education

10 Claiming Sustainable Space: Families, Communities, and Learning,
   an Auto/Biographical Perspective 133
   Linden West

11 Health Literacy and AVE for Social Sustainability 145
   Kay Price

12 Education in Post-conflict Environments: Pathways to Sustainable
   Peace? 155
   Rebecca Spence

13 Social Sustainability and Activation Strategies with Unemployed
   Young Adults 163
   Danny Wildemeersch and Susan Weil

Part IV Adult and Vocational Education for Social Sustainability in Action

14 Chasing the Vultures Off the Roof: AVE for Living in Sierra Leone .. 181
   Astrid von Kotze

15 The Contribution of Non-formal Adult Education to Social
   Sustainability: Policy Implications from Case Studies
   in the Asia-Pacific Region 193
   Richard G. Bagnall

16 Community Adult Learning Contributions to Social Sustainability
   in the Asia-South Pacific Region: The Role of ASPBAE 211
   Bernie Lovegrove and Anne Morrison

17 Birds Learn to Swim and Fish Learn to Fly: Lessons from the
   Philippines on AVE for Social Sustainability 225
   Edicio dela Torre

18	**Breaking the Silence: Exploring Spirituality in Secular Professional Education in Australia** .... 237 Joanna Crossman	
19	**Waldorf Schools as Communities of Practice for AVE and Social Sustainability** .... 249 Tom Stehlik	
20	**Conclusion. AVE for Social Sustainability: Where to from Here?** .... 261 Stephen McKenzie	

Name Index 265

Subject Index 271

Contributors

Richard G. Bagnall   Dr. Richard G. Bagnall is Professor in Professional and Vocational Education at the Hong Kong Institute of Education. His scholarly work is in the social philosophy of lifelong and vocational education, with particular emphasis on the ethics of educational theory, advocacy, and policy. He has published over 100 books and papers in that field, including *Cautionary tales in the ethics of lifelong learning policy and management: a book of fables* (Dordrecht: Kluwer Academic, 2004) and *Discovering radical contingency: building a postmodern agenda in adult education* (New York: Peter Lang, 1999). His teaching is centered on the philosophy of lifelong learning and he has supervised to graduation the doctoral studies of 25 candidates.

Patricia Cranton   Dr. Patricia Cranton received her PhD in 1976 from the University of Toronto in Canada. Patricia's primary research interests have been in the areas of teaching and learning in higher education, transformative learning, and, most recently, authenticity and individuation. She is currently a Visiting Professor of Adult Education at Penn State University in Harrisburg, Pennsylvania. Patricia Cranton's most recent books include a second edition of *Planning instruction for adult learners* (2000), *Becoming an authentic teacher* (2001), *Finding our way: a guide for adult educators* (2003), and the second edition of *Understanding and promoting transformative learning* (2006).

Joanna Crossman   Dr. Joanna Crossman is a lecturer in the School of Management at the University of South Australia. Her research interests lie in spirituality in learning and organizations, emotions and relationships in learning and work, assessment, international and cultural leadership, as well as intercultural communication. She teaches communication and supervises a number of doctoral candidates in research areas allied to her own interests. Joanna chairs an International Education in Business research group and is co-editor of a new online journal, *Journal of International Education in Business*. She has held a number of management and academic positions in Norway, England, the United Arab Emirates, Malaysia, and Australia.

Aidan Davison Dr. Aidan Davison is a lecturer in the School of Geography and Environmental Studies at the University of Tasmania, and formerly Program Chair of Sustainable Development at Murdoch University. After a brief career in biochemistry, Aidan has worked in environmental studies, venturing from this base into philosophy, sociology, politics, and human geography in search of good explanations of technology, nature, and sustainability. The author of *Technology and the contested meanings of sustainability* (SUNY, 2001), Aidan has published many articles and book chapters on topics ranging from public perceptions of biotechnology to Australian urban history to environmentalism.

Edicio dela Torre Edicio dela Torre served as a chaplain and educator of farmer leaders and youth leaders in the Philippines, and was an activist during the years of martial rule. After spending some years as a political prisoner, he worked in popular education among local and migrant Filipino communities in the Philippines and Europe. For three years he was the head of the government agency for technical education and skills development. Presently, Edicio is involved with grassroots leadership development as the President of the Education for Life Foundation in the Philippines.

John Fien Dr. John Fien is Innovation Professor of Sustainability at RMIT University in Melbourne, where he is responsible for catalyzing research teams to address issues of sustainability across the broad fields of business and economics, design and fashion, education and training, and social and environmental planning. He has supported UNESCO and UNEP in developing plans for the United Nations Decade of Education for Sustainable Development and was the author of the UNESCO multimedia teacher education program *Teaching and learning for a sustainable future*. He was co-moderator, with David Wilson, of the 2004 International Experts Meeting on "Learning for Work, Citizenship and Sustainability" in Bonn.

Heather Foster Dr. Heather Foster teaches religion studies and education at the University of South Australia. After completing her undergraduate studies in anthropology and history at the University of Adelaide, she worked on various research projects at the University of South Australia and the University of Adelaide, including working in the northwest of Thailand. Her PhD explored the practice of Hinduism in the diaspora, focusing specifically on Hindu women. Most recently she has served on the executive of the Australian Association of the Study of Religions (AASR), presented an invited Charles Strong Trust lecture, and convened the 30th anniversary conference of the AASR.

Roger Harris Professor Roger Harris has had extensive experience in teacher training and research in adult and vocational education. He is currently a key researcher in the Centre for Research in Education, Equity and Work, Hawke Research Institute for Sustainable Societies at the University of South Australia. He has had a keen research interest in national training reform over the past 18 years. His recent work includes a number of nationally competitive funded research projects on workplace trainers, VET staff development, VET professionals' work, apprenticeships and traineeships, training packages, learning cultures, workplace learning, private training providers, and intersectoral student movement, as well as two Australian Research Council projects on workplace learning in SA Police and notions of continuous improvement in the automotive industry. He is a member of the Australian VET Research Association (AVETRA), and currently is editor of the *Australian Journal of Adult Learning*. He is also director of a national research consortium on "Building the capability of VET providers for the future," funded by the Australian government, and Program Leader (Education and Training) in the Australian Cooperative Research Centre for Rail Innovation.

Bernie Lovegrove   Bernie Lovegrove works as Program Manager for the Asian South Pacific Bureau of Adult Education (ASPBAE) and has been with the organization for the past 12 years. His diverse work involves program coordination and networking among ASPBAE's broad membership, which comprises over 200 member organizations, workshop design and facilitation, regional liaison, and resource mobilization. He has a Masters in International and Community Development and has worked in the development and education fields for over 20 years. Earlier he worked as an Education Officer for the then Australian Council for Overseas Aid (ACFOA, now ACFID) and as Canberra Coordinator for Community Aid Abroad (now Oxfam Australia).

Alan Mayne   Professor Alan Mayne has a Research SA Chair at the University of South Australia, and is Professor of Social History and Social Policy in the University's Hawke Research Institute for Sustainable Societies. He also holds a Visiting Professorial Fellowship in the Centre for the Study of Law and Governance at Jawaharlal Nehru University. His core interests revolve around sustainable communities in urban and rural society. His publications include *Fever, squalor and vice* (Brisbane, 1982), *The imagined slum* (Leicester, 1993), *The archaeology of urban landscapes* (with Tim Murray, Cambridge, 2001), *Hill End: an historic Australian goldfields landscape* (Melbourne, 2003), *Eureka: reappraising an Australian legend* (Perth, 2006), *Beyond the black stump: histories of outback Australia* (Adelaide, 2008), and *Building the village: a history of Australia's Bendigo Bank* (Adelaide, 2008).

Stephen McKenzie   Dr. Stephen McKenzie was awarded a PhD in English from the University of South Australia in 2000. His doctoral research focused on conceptions of Asia in the medieval and early modern periods. Between 2002 and 2005 he worked as a research officer at the University of South Australia and undertook research on the social aspects of sustainability, which generated numerous publications and presentations at several international sustainability conferences. He is developing an interest in the intersection between religious ethics and social sustainability and has published in that area. He now lives in the Solomon Islands where he cares for his two young children.

Anne Morrison Dr. Anne Morrison's PhD focused on interest-driven language learning, where adults are learning for interest or pleasure rather than for academic or vocational reasons. She recently joined the Centre for Research in Education, Equity and Work, Hawke Research Institute for Sustainable Societies at the University of South Australia, as part of a team investigating the relationship between vocational skills and training opportunities across regional Australia.

Michael Newman Michael Newman worked as an adult educator for some forty years in both the UK and his native Australia. He was a community outreach worker, the principal of an adult education college, a trainer in the Australian trade union movement, and a university lecturer. He has written a number of books on adult education and social action, his most recent being *Teaching defiance: stories and strategies for activist educators*. He is retired, but continues to write and occasionally speak on activism and learning.

Kay Price Dr. Kay Price is a Senior Lecturer within the School of Nursing and Midwifery, University of South Australia and has expertise in qualitative research, specifically critical analyses and political methodologies (critical, post-structural, and cultural studies). Her interests include analysis of systems and interfaces within systems, analysis of health care and health services, and managing complexity. Her research has focused on exploring and evaluating service delivery and creating opportunities for the provision of appropriate health services and a health workforce in the global marketplace. She particularly enjoys theorizing differently and challenging taken-for-granted views or assumptions so as to advance health care and health services.

Chris Provis Dr. Chris Provis studied and taught philosophy, then worked for some years in industrial relations and now is Associate Professor in the School of Management at the University of South Australia, and Deputy Director of the Ethics Centre of South Australia. He has published articles about industrial relations policy, principles and practice of negotiation, applied ethics, and other topics. His book *Ethics and organisational politics* appeared in 2004.

Rebecca Spence Dr. Rebecca Spence is the Director for the Centre for Peace Studies, University of New England in New South Wales, Australia. She is the designer and lead trainer in an adult education training consortium, specializing in training in peace-building processes for the Asia-Pacific. She has worked as a consultant for government and non-government organizations, specializing in peace and conflict impact assessments. She has published books, manuals, articles, and chapters. Her most recent publications are to do with engaging the community in peace-building activities in Timor.

Tom Stehlik Dr. Tom Stehlik is a former school teacher and currently Senior Lecturer in the School of Education at the University of South Australia. He teaches and conducts research in the areas of change management, organizational learning, student engagement, and vocational education and training. He has had a particular interest in Steiner education for many years as a parent, educator, musician, and member of a Waldorf school community.

Astrid von Kotze Astrid von Kotze is a Professor in the Community Development Programme at the University of KwaZulu-Natal, South Africa. Her work in adult education and community development began as a member of an experimental theater company that created and performed political plays in apartheid South Africa. Since the 1990s she has been engaged in various forms of popular education and community development, with a particular emphasis on culture and the arts and on disaster mitigation and risk reduction. She has a particular interest in livelihood studies and social movements and extensive experience in the production of participatory teaching and learning materials particularly for people living in oral cultures.

Susan Weil Dr. Weil is Emeritus Professor for Systemic Action Inquiry at the University of the West of England. She is the founder of the SOLAR Center: Social and Organisational Learning as Action Research (University College, Northampton) and from 1996 to 2002 she served as its director. Since 1991 she has been a fellow in organizational learning and development at the Office for Public Management. Dr. Weil has authored, co-authored, and edited numerous books and published extensively in scientific journals.

Linden West Dr. Linden West is Reader in Education in the Department of Educational Research at Canterbury Christ Church University, UK and Co-Director of the Centre for International Studies of Diversity and Participation. His books include *Beyond fragments*, *doctors on the edge* and he is lead editor of a new volume from Peter Lang: *Using biographical and life history approaches in the study of adult and lifelong learning*. Linden coordinates the Biographical and Life History Research Network of the European Society for Research on the Education of Adults. He is presently working on families and their learning, using auto/biographical perspectives. He is also a qualified psychoanalytic psychotherapist.

Danny Wildemeersch Dr. Wildemeersch is a Professor of Social, Comparative and Intercultural Education at the University of Leuven in Belgium. He is head of the Centre for Research on Lifelong Learning and Participation. His research focuses on a variety of themes such as intercultural learning, learning and social participation, intercultural dialogue, education and citizenship, environmental learning and education, transitions from school to work, and participation in development cooperation. He has published widely on these topics in various languages.

Peter Willis Dr. Peter Willis is senior lecturer in education at the University of South Australia, specializing in the education and training of adults. His main research areas at present concern transformative and "second chance" learning among adults and the relationship between religion, spirituality, and civil society. Before his academic career, he worked first as a religious missionary priest and then an adult educator in community development and cultural awareness education with Aboriginal and non-Aboriginal people in the outback Kimberley area of Northwestern Australia and in Central Australia. He wrote about these and subsequent experiences in two books: *Patrons and riders: conflicting roles and hidden objectives in an Aboriginal development program* (Queensland: Post Pressed) and *Inviting learning: an exhibition of risk and enrichment in adult educational practice* (London: NIACE). Recent edited publications include: *Lifelong learning and the democratic imagination* (with Pam Carden; Post Pressed); *Pedagogies of the imagination: mythopoetic curriculum in educational practice* (with Timothy Leonard; Springer); *Wisdom, spirituality and the aesthetic: mythopoetic foundations of lifelong learning* (with Leonard, Morrison, and Hodge; Post Pressed).

David Wilson Professor David Wilson was Professor Emeritus at Ontario Institute for Studies in Education, University of Toronto and Senior Consultant with the UNEVOC-UNESCO International Centre for TVET. He served twice with UNESCO, once with the ILO and as Project Officer (TVET) with the Asian Development Bank. David undertook consulting projects in over sixty countries with bilateral and multilateral aid agencies, and published articles and books on comparative and international education, TVET, educational planning, HRD, knowledge management, ICTs, and the future of technology and work. David was co-editor (with Rupert Maclean) of the UNESCO-UNEVOC International Library of TVET. David passed away in late 2006.

Chapter 1
Introduction: Challenges in Adult and Vocational Education for Social Sustainability

Peter Willis, Stephen McKenzie and Roger Harris

How can adult and vocational education (AVE) systems help to create social sustainability? The chapters in this volume approach this question from a range of methodological and geographical positions, but all share the concern that current AVE systems are failing to adapt to the changing nature of work and society and are thereby missing a crucial opportunity to enable the growth of more sustainable and equitable communities. In various ways, our contributors call for the reorientation of current AVE systems to include the use of ethical, philosophical, and imaginal teaching styles to complement the technical and professional pedagogical modes that currently predominate in those systems.

We use the word "reorientation" as a deliberate echo of the recent work undertaken by UNESCO-UNEVOC on the current and potential role of technical and vocational education and training (TVET) in sustainable development. UNESCO-UNEVOC has generated much discussion internationally around the opportunities and challenges facing TVET providers in reorienting their training systems so as to embed skills for sustainable development in the workforce. The argument is powerful and straightforward: social cohesion and environmental protection will remain distant ideals for many people unless they can be linked with the everyday livelihood activities that people must pursue in order to achieve economic or food security. In order to forge these links, new types of knowledge will be required, including values and attitudes as well as new technical skills. TVET settings are the obvious places for this new type of learning to occur.

We refer to this new kind of knowledge generally as "knowledge for sustainability." In this book, many of our contributors explore models of education that position this "knowledge for sustainability" alongside the more specific technical skills that are taught in settings that focus on preparation for work. It is through the development of new types of knowledge within the workforce that are both vocationally relevant *and* contribute to sustainability that the distant ideal can become a reality. Although this agenda is widely recognized as important, little cohesive research has been undertaken on *how* TVET providers are beginning to develop these skills within the workforce. We have no clear conceptual models of how the process can

P. Willis (✉)
University of South Australia, South Australia, Australia

work, or case studies to inform the design of such models. This picture is true of TVET research worldwide, despite continued calls from UNESCO-UNEVOC to step up activity in this area. The Bonn Declaration on Learning for Work, Citizenship and Sustainability describes TVET as the "master key" for sustainable development.[1] Yet, at present, we do not know how this key can be turned to best effect or in what kinds of locks it can best be used.

In this introduction, we wish to alert the reader to key distinctions in terminology and thereby introduce some important themes of this volume. Such distinctions are important; in a field as large and complex as sustainability (or adult and technical education, for that matter), key terms differ greatly in their meaning according to context, and a lack of clarity results in words becoming buzzwords and concepts becoming catch-all phrases. The three main distinctions we wish to discuss here are the difference between AVE and TVET; the difference between sustainable development and social sustainability; and a final distinction regarding the meaning of "education for social sustainability."

This book focuses on the pairing of the twin concepts of adult and vocational education (AVE) and social sustainability. AVE differs from TVET partly through its inclusion of adult and community education as an important setting for imparting knowledge and skills for sustainability. We cast this wider net because we do not think that TVET alone—especially as it is currently practised—can be the master key to sustainable development or social sustainability, and we must turn to other education sectors for ideas on how to reorient it.

We see adult and community education as an adaptable vehicle for community development in areas where early schooling and post-compulsory education have been inadequate. Further, unaware of adult education methods, many TVET providers struggle when dealing with retrenched adult workers looking to re-skill or indeed with adult learners in disadvantaged areas who have never received initial formal training. Finally, adult and community education (in Australia, at least) has traditionally concerned itself with precisely the kind of issues we are describing by the term "knowledge for sustainability"—knowledge that is concerned with making a better society as a whole, not simply a better livelihood for the individual.

The second distinction we need to make here is between the general field of sustainable development and our more specific focus on "social sustainability," because social sustainability is very different in kind from its counterparts in the triple bottom line: environmental and economic sustainability. When we speak of environmental sustainability, we know what it is that we wish to sustain, and our task is simply to manage existing ecosystems as best as we can. To a lesser extent this is true of economic sustainability as well: the task at hand here is to ensure that our economy is sufficient to sustain a decent standard of living. When we come to social sustainability, however, we are playing another game. As many communities

---

[1] The Bonn Declaration was the product of an International Experts Meeting on Technical and Vocational Education and Training held by UNEVOC in October 2004. A further meeting on TVET for Sustainable Development—Opportunities and Challenges was held in Ho Chi Minh City in June 2006.

can lack elements of viable structure and appropriate social and decision-making processes, social sustainability cannot simply refer to keeping what exists alive and flourishing, but must encourage necessary changes while also ensuring the continuity of communities and their values.

A sustainable society, as put forward in the volume, is one in which the demands of the economic sphere do not predominate over the needs of the social. In a sustainable society, all citizens would be encouraged to imagine and create futures in which their own means of economic and social security contributed to the sustainability of society as a whole. Thus, a "socially sustainable society" is a more useful term for describing the chapters in this volume than "sustainable development," a term that can be—and often is—used to describe any development that is economically viable and will create employment, even if its implementation causes or perpetuates social and environmental problems.

While there is a wide variety of definitions for sustainability as a whole, and its environmental and economic branches, social sustainability is rarely defined on its own. We offer the following criteria not as "the final word" on social sustainability but simply as an initial point of reference.

Social sustainability refers to a positive and long-term condition within communities and a process within communities that can achieve and maintain that condition. The following features are indicators of the condition, and steps toward their establishment and implementation are aspects of the process:

- equity of access to key services (including health, education, transport, housing, and recreation)
- a system of cultural relations in which the positive aspects of disparate cultures are valued and protected and in which cultural integration is supported and promoted when it is desired by individuals and groups
- widespread political participation of citizens not only in electoral procedures but also in other areas of political activity, particularly at a local level
- mechanisms for a community to fulfill its own needs, where possible, through community action
- mechanisms for political advocacy to meet needs that cannot be met by community action
- mechanisms for a community to identify collectively its strengths and needs
- *equity between generations, meaning that future generations will not be disadvantaged by the activities of the current generation*
- *a system for transmitting awareness of social sustainability from one generation to the next*
- *a sense of community responsibility for maintaining that system of transmission.*

The last three points are in italics to emphasize that this truly is a definition of a sustainable society, as well as simply a "good" one. Sustainable is more than "good." It is a powerful concept precisely because it focuses attention on the mid- to long-term future, and evokes consideration not only of how people's ideas and actions in the present are going to contribute to the improvement of society, but also of *how we are going to ensure that these improved conditions are maintained.*

This second point is critical when we are thinking about developing new policies and practices in education. By adding sustainability to the equation, we are forced to consider issues of resources, community acceptance, and the transmission of our ideas to future generations. It is no longer enough to simply say "this action will have a positive result." We must begin to consider how the result may be sustained.

This brings us to the third and final distinction in terminology: the distinction between "education for social sustainability" and "education for a sustainable workforce." By "education for social sustainability," we mean the development of teaching and learning styles that allow students to gain knowledge and skills that will enable them to become more socially and environmentally responsible citizens. By "education for a sustainable workforce," we mean the positive effect that education (particularly technical and vocational education) has on bolstering employment levels and therefore creating greater financial security in a particular region. The first is about creating a better society; the second is about obtaining and maintaining employment.

Our volume is focused on these different relationships between the terms "education" and "social sustainability"—and particularly on any form of education that specifically seeks to forge links between them. While technical and vocational training is clearly vital the world over, it must be paired with other styles of education that foster social and environmental harmony. It is no longer enough to train people to do today's jobs tomorrow and argue that this has contributed to sustainable development because the recipients have been given livelihood security. A true reorientation of the TVET system and the workforce will come about only when people are trained for the work of the future—work that not only provides security, but is also socially just and environmentally responsible.

To summarize the previous sections, AVE for social sustainability as a theoretical model refers to teaching and learning within adult and vocational education settings *that contributes to social sustainability*. This means that it

- actively contributes to the economic welfare of individuals by enhancing their career skills
- actively enhances the economic stability of communities by improving the skill pool
- actively enhances the social sustainability of communities by imparting knowledge and values associated with strong and open democratic societies
- is easily embedded into the fabric of communities and therefore is easily perpetuated
- contributes in some way to its own perpetuation into the future.

Much work remains to be done in collecting a body of case studies on AVE for social sustainability—or, to put it another way, examples of "education for social sustainability" within TVET and adult and community education settings. Many of the examples provided in this volume (outlined in the following part of this introduction) do not describe themselves as social sustainability projects. Some do not even refer to social sustainability overtly, but instead talk about creating safe spaces for personal therapy, spirituality development, peace education in post-conflict settings, or the development of community health centers. This alerts us to the possibility that other suitable case studies might not be conveniently labeled as "education for social sustainability" either. We hope therefore that this volume, as well as providing an initial landmark, will also highlight the wide possibilities for further research. What other areas of activity might provide us with models for reorienting the TVET system? TVET alone cannot be the master key to sustainability; it requires lessons from adult and community education in order to understand how to use it.

The chapters that follow are clustered in four parts. The first, "Social sustainability perspectives in adult and vocational education," provides an overview from a number of different angles. John Fien and David Wilson in Chapter 2, "Advancing social sustainability through vocational education and training," apply a systems approach to thinking about the possible functions of technical and vocational education to foster a strong inclusive relationship between sustainable development as a scientific goal and a culturally directed search for ecological balance. Such concern for balance can promote equity between different countries, races, social classes, and genders but it requires appropriate curriculum that invites learners to reflect upon the values and principles that guide human actions. AVE has to focus on its responsibilities in general education, especially in relation to learning for work as part of citizenship and sustainability. Such programs can provide opportunities for learners to develop knowledge, skills, and values appropriate to helping create a fairer and less troubled world for all.

Peter Willis in Chapter 3, "An ecology for the fourth pillar: imaginal learning for social sustainability in AVE," explores appropriate pedagogic ways to evoke and nourish social sustainability's "fourth pillar," namely "cultural life," or more accurately "cultural vitality and life enthusiasm." This life enthusiasm can be seen as a key factor in the health of a society and its ecology, which can be called its social ecology. The author focuses specifically on pedagogic ways in which AVE, in addition to logical and rational approaches, can evoke and foster social ecological learning imaginally.

A third perspective is provided by Roger Harris in Chapter 4, "The historical contribution of AVE to social sustainability in Australia." The chapter examines the dominance of the economic over the social in the historical development of AVE in Australia. The author draws attention to the traditional person–job relationship that has underpinned many approaches to TVET: "the dominant ethos of productivism." This affords precedence to economic interests, and thus subordinates the needs of individual learners to those of industry, privileging work and employability over noneconomic outcomes. As a consequence, AVE's contribution to social sustainability, he argues, has been largely submerged and thus neglected, under-resourced, and to a large extent under-valued.

The final perspective in this section is provided in Chapter 5 by Aidan Davison, "The language of longing: rationality, morality, and experience in education for sustainability." He argues that sustainability is a preoccupation that simultaneously engages powers of reason, belief, and feeling, mixing up any neat separation of descriptive and normative claims. It is also a preoccupation that unsettles a long-standing dualism of theory and practice on which so much in education has been built. Current initiatives such as the United Nations Decade of Education for Sustainable Development promote the embedding of universal ethical principles of sustainability in curricula as the basis for creating more sustainable attitudes, values, and behaviors. The author contends that such approaches are, at best, only partially effective and, at worst, politically dangerous. The chapter concludes that, in its most fundamental and pre-institutional forms, education for sustainability is best understood as a capacity for critical and reflexive encounters with the reciprocity of sustenance that constitutes self and world.

From these broad-ranging overviews in the early chapters, the four chapters in Part Two, "Foundations for social sustainability in adult and vocational education," focus on some of the educational bases for social sustainability. In Chapter 6, "Educating for a sustainable democracy," Michael Newman points out that social sustainability cannot exist without justice and that resistant anger against injustice can be one of social sustainability's more powerful tools. Those of us with the opportunity to help ourselves and others learn can examine the ways to help people express their anger and then respond to that anger. We can teach ourselves to think clearly, that is, to think critically and independently. We can teach ourselves to think imaginatively, that is, we can open ourselves to insight. We can teach ourselves to choose to act. And we can teach ourselves to act well. We can help ourselves and others become thinking, imaginative, active, moral beings in a socially sustainable way.

Patricia Cranton in Chapter 7, "Transformative learning and AVE for social sustainability," explores approaches to transformative learning and its links to social sustainability. She shows first how the traditional "cognitive" approach enriched by critical reflection can lead to revised habits of mind about the self and the world. She then describes how "relational" theorists who favor "connected knowing" over "autonomous knowing" pay attention to the role of relationships in learning and understanding others' points of view. She refers to the extra-rational dimensions of transformative learning linked to the power of so-called imaginal and emotional learning. Imaginal and emotional learning relates to a contemplative way of thinking and reflecting using the power of human imagination, which differs markedly from logical rationality. Social sustainability needs its own stories and story-tellers and these need to be discovered and celebrated.

In Chapter 8, "Education, religion, sustainability, and dialogue," Chris Provis claims that sustainability is looming larger in regard to the social world as well as the natural environment. The author asks what role moral education can have in promoting dialogue among groups. The main point developed here is that dialogue takes different forms depending on what is at issue. Less well developed are processes for dialogue where differences between people tend to be cognitive differences rather than differences of preference or interest, but where issues do not centrally revolve around truth or falsity. This may be the sort of dialogue required where people are separated by religious differences. It may be approached as different "ways of seeing" or "ways of framing." In education, we need to become clearer about this sort of dialogue.

In Chapter 9, "The role of religion in education for social sustainability," Heather Foster examines the manner in which religions create symbolism, meaning, and values through their adult educational and teaching practices. Through an understanding of the connection between religion and the creation of meaning and values within communities, strategies can be developed for workplace education which could incorporate education on religions, religious assumptions, and cultural differences. This could also lead to a more harmonious functioning of multicultural workplaces and global networks.

Part Three, "Creating spaces for social sustainability in adult and vocational education," contains four chapters that illustrate various spaces/domains for social sustainability. In Chapter 10, "Claiming sustainable space: families, communities, and learning, an auto/biographical perspective," Linden West moves the focus to smaller units. He seeks to link notions of learning, families, and intimate aspects of human relationship with issues of sustainability, both personal and social. This includes strengthening the social fabric and invigorating democratic processes with reference to marginalized communities. The chapter draws on studies of groups of parents and the professionals they had to deal with when they were involved in family support and learning programs in several sites in England. The author chronicles and illuminates the meaning and impact of particular interventions through parents' eyes, as well as those of workers on the ground, in what is deeply contested territory.

Kay Price in Chapter 11, "Health literacy and AVE for social sustainability," points out that, in a world characterized by consumerism, any education format focusing directly or indirectly on influencing the health status of a person constitutes a product that is premised on what is "sold." She clarifies a need for health educators to attend to how people think and make decisions about their health and for this to be integrated into their health literacy learning. This chapter addresses how AVE providers could develop appropriate programs in this area.

Rebecca Spence in Chapter 12, "Education in post-conflict environments: pathways to sustainable peace?," queries whether formal and non-formal education processes can act as catalysts for peace. Recognizing that education is one of the main tenets of any peace-building process, she suggests how educational policy and practice could and has been shaped so as to integrate key peace-building and reconciliation principles. Using examples from a variety of conflict-affected countries, the chapter explores the benefits and challenges associated with educating for longer term peace.

Chapter 13, "Social sustainability and activation strategies with unemployed young adults," is by Danny Wildemeersch and Susan Weil, who carried out research on education, training, and guidance of the young unemployed in Europe. It is concerned with revealing, understanding, and resisting hidden inequity that is emerging from government policies of self-help and personal responsibility. The authors are particularly critical of the current policy emphasis on "activation" strategies which emphasize self-responsibility and entrepreneurship. They point out that such policy tends to focus on and even blame the socially excluded rather than social exclusion itself. They then demonstrate how this type of activation discourse operates in a restrictive way. They finally sketch "reflexive activation" as an alternative that does not conceal policy ambivalences and complexities, but rather takes them as a point of departure for practices of AVE for social sustainability.

Part Four, "Adult and vocational education for social sustainability in action," analyzes several applications in a variety of contexts and, in so doing, illustrates some of the limits and barriers to AVE being a force for social sustainability. Astrid von Kotze in Chapter 14, "Chasing the vultures off the roof: AVE for living in Sierra Leone," examines community health clubs in Sierra Leone. She suggests that "work" needs to be understood not just as jobs/employment, but in terms of activities executed to maintain and create life. She then seeks to clarify what a more inclusive notion of vocational education and training might look like. For people who spend so much of their time and energy struggling to maintain life and living and who diversify their daily livelihood activities in order to reduce risk and enjoy some measure of dignity, what would constitute really useful AVE? Finally the author questions whether "social sustainability" is useful as an overarching theme or whether "social change" would be a more appropriate term.

Chapter 15 by Richard Bagnall, "The contribution of non-formal adult education to social sustainability: policy implications from case studies in the Asia-Pacific region," draws on five case studies of the contribution of non-formal adult education (NFAE) to vocational learning for income generation. The democratic, participative, community-based, and humanistic nature of traditional and holistic NFAE provision has a strong commitment to social justice and inclusion. NFAE courses in wealth creation have also sought to promote a more informed, active, and responsible citizenship. This general benefit could be seen to encourage productive self-employment or cooperative enterprise, rather than the emigration of labor from disadvantaged regions.

In Chapter 16 Bernie Lovegrove and Anne Morrison reflect on educational work for social sustainability under the title of "Community adult learning contributions to social sustainability in the Asia-South Pacific region: the role of ASPBAE." The Asian South Pacific Bureau of Adult Education has a strong role in teaching advocacy skills to educators and community activists in the Asia-South Pacific region. It is a regional association largely of civil society organizations and individuals engaged in both formal and non-formal adult education. Many of these organizations have been able to impart a more holistic approach to learning that includes values and citizenship education, community-building ethics, and education about traditional cultures and practices, while at the same time imparting skills useful for income generation. Much more needs to be done in terms of researching, analyzing, and advocating their valuable impact in contributing to social sustainability and in arguing the case for more substantial and secure funding support for them to play this role and expand their work.

Edicio dela Torre in Chapter 17 entitled "Birds learn to swim and fish learn to fly: lessons from the Philippines on AVE for social sustainability" reflects on the relationship of adult community education and technical education and training, and the interplay between development workers, technician/extension educators, and grassroots leaders. He explores this through two stories from his own life experiences. The first is about the promotion of technology for productivity (the Green Revolution) and the farmers' prioritization of a change in land tenure as a precondition for adoption of technology. The second is from post-conflict educational programs for Muslim rebels and their families. The Technical Education and Skills Development Authority developed a program of "community-based training for enterprise development." But it needed an accompanying program of "education from life, for life."

In Chapter 18 by Joanna Crossman, "Breaking the silence: exploring spirituality in secular professional education in Australia," there is a considerable change of pace and area of interest. Following an exploration of the concept of secular spirituality, she argues that there are compelling reasons for including spiritual perspectives in student learning. She explores how the concept of secular spirituality relates to ideas about social sustainability and demonstrates the usefulness of social sustainability in "situating" discussions and providing a framework for addressing spiritual values in adult education and ultimately the workplace.

In the final chapter in this part of the book, Chapter 19 entitled "Waldorf schools as communities of practice for AVE and social sustainability," Tom Stehlik points out that Waldorf schools seek to be cooperative learning communities of parents and teachers. While the "core business" of a Waldorf school is to educate children, the author also shows that engagement with the educational philosophy and the school community promotes formal and informal learning for adults in a range of areas, including parenting, relationships, family dynamics, and personal development. He also puts forward the concept of "parenting as a vocation" as a valid and important aspect of contributing to social capital through a considered and informed approach to raising children for a socially sustainable future.

In conclusion, the global task of re-thinking work and learning for social development and its links with social sustainability in various arenas around the world presents equally as urgent and as challenging, a point highlighted by Stephen McKenzie in his concluding Chapter 20, "Conclusion. AVE for social sustainability: where to from here?" There is a pioneering "feel" to much of the AVE for social sustainability work analyzed in the following chapters, as adult and vocational educators, with an awareness of the importance of social sustainability in the societies in which they are working, seek to respond as effectively as they can to the changing circumstances of work and social life. In so doing, they stimulate us to *re-think our notions of work and learning*.

Part I
Social Sustainability Perspectives in Adult and Vocational Education

Chapter 2
Advancing Social Sustainability Through Vocational Education and Training

John Fien and David Wilson

Abstract This chapter explores the implications for technical and vocational education of viewing sustainable development not only as a scientific goal but also as a culturally directed search for a dynamic balance in the relationships between social, economic, and natural systems. Such a balance would promote equity between the present and the future, and equity between countries, races, social classes, and genders. As a focus of learning and cultural change, sustainability requires a conscious commitment by all to *reflect upon the values and principles that guide our actions*. Such a view challenges technical and vocational educators to focus on their responsibilities in general education, especially in relation to learning for work as part of citizenship and sustainability. This approach would mean that programs provide opportunities for students to learn how to reflect upon their own values, how they affect workplace practices, lifestyle choices, and the social, economic, and environmental impacts that would result if everyone in the world believed and acted as they did. Such programs would also provide opportunities for learners to develop knowledge, skills, and values appropriate to help create a fairer and less troubled world for all.

Toward a Sustainable Future

The major challenge in the world today is to find ways of living and working sustainably, so that the reasonable needs and wants of people from all walks of life and in all countries can be satisfied without over-exploiting the natural resources upon which all life depends and without threatening the ability of future generations to meet their wants and needs.[1]

J. Fien (✉)
RMIT University, Melbourne, Australia

[1] This chapter is adapted from *Orienting technical and vocational education and training for sustainable development* (UNESCO-UNEVOC 2006), which the authors prepared for UNESCO-UNEVOC and is revised here with the permission of Dr. Rupert Maclean, Director, UNESCO-UNEVOC.

Moving toward the goal of sustainable development requires fundamental changes in human attitudes and behavior—in our personal lives, in our community activities, and in our places of work. Successfully making these changes is critically dependent on education and training. The concept of sustainable development is not a simple one, and there is no road map to prescribe how we should proceed. Yet time is short, and we must act without delay. We must move ahead now, in a spirit of exploration and experimentation and with the broadest possible range of partners, so as to contribute through education and training to a sustainable future. Taking incremental steps in both developed and developing nations now is preferable to waiting for larger measures to be realized.

An Opportunity to be Taken

In October 2004, UNESCO hosted an International Experts' Meeting on Learning for Work, Citizenship and Sustainability[2] as a 5-year review of progress since the Second International Conference on Technical and Vocational Education (TVET) which was held in Seoul, Korea, in April 1999. Discussions on the central theme of the Seoul Conference—lifelong learning and training for all, a bridge to the future—led to the conclusion that we need new paradigms of both development and TVET. As the preamble to the recommendations in the final report stated:

> We have considered the emerging challenges of the twenty-first century, a century that will be an era of knowledge, information and communication. Globalization and the revolution in information and communication technology have signalled the need for a new human-centred development paradigm. We have concluded that Technical and Vocational Education (TVE), as an integral component of lifelong learning, has a crucial role to play in this new era as an effective tool to realize the objectives of a culture of peace, environmentally sound sustainable development, social cohesion, and international citizenship. (UNESCO, 1999, p. 61)

The "new human-centered development paradigm" was elaborated at the Millennium Summit of the United Nations General Assembly in September 2000, which agreed to a set of Millennium Development Goals (MDGs).[3] The MDGs include: halving extreme poverty and hunger, achieving universal primary education and gender equity, reducing under-five mortality and maternal mortality by two-thirds and three-quarters respectively, reversing the spread of HIV/AIDS, halving the proportion of people without access to safe drinking water, and ensuring environmental sustainability. They also include the goal of developing a global partnership for development, with targets for aid, trade, and debt relief. As a strategic vision, the MDGs are steps toward a longer-term vision of building internal capacity in all,

---

[2] The International Experts' Meeting was organised by UNESCO in collaboration with the German Federal Ministry of Education and Research (BMBF). The meeting was held in Bonn, Germany, on 26–28 October 2004.

[3] See http://www.un.org/millenniumgoals/.

especially developing, countries such that all institutions for education and training can act as engines for sustainable development.

Achieving the MDGs necessitates action on issues such as poverty, hunger, education, gender equality, child and maternal mortality, HIV/AIDS, safe water, upgrading slums, and global partnerships for development that include technology transfer. Effective Vocational Education and Training (VET) is integral to finding and implementing solutions to all of these issues. In this way, VET underpins every one of the MDGs and the achievement of sustainable development. It is impossible to think of making gains in poverty reduction, job creation, health, or environmental concerns without a focused TVET policy, and it is equally true that a well-articulated and focused TVET policy can lead to huge improvements in education, gender equality, and living conditions. Much of the improvement in human welfare over the last century in both rich and poor countries is due to technological innovation in the fields of public health, nutrition, and agriculture. These improvements have led to reductions in poverty and mortality rates, and improved life expectancy, for example. Similarly, improvements in areas such as environmental management increasingly rely on the generation and application of new knowledge. In essence, one important aspect of achieving the MDGs requires developing appropriate forms of vocational education and training.

Reflecting such imperatives, the Seoul conference looked to an innovative paradigm of technical and vocational education based upon "a learning culture" that encourages and educates people "to be productive and competitive, and to care for the well-being of its people." It was agreed that "a vibrant training culture is a key factor in attaining that goal ... and empower[ing] youth and adults to play a part in the new development paradigm" (UNESCO, 1999, p. 54). As a result, the final report of the conference is replete with statements about the contribution of technical and vocational education to a sustainable future. For example:

> Technical and vocational education, as an integral component of life-long learning, has a crucial role to play in this new era as an effective tool to realise the objectives of a culture of peace, environmentally sound sustainable development, social cohesion and international citizenship. (pp. 1, 61)
>
> [T]he TVET of the future must not only prepare individuals for employment in the information society, but also make them responsible citizens who give due consideration to preserving the integrity of their environment and the welfare of others.(p. 27)
>
> TVET can play an instrumental role in developing a new generation of individuals who will face the challenge of achieving sustainable socio-economic development. A number of new subjects (issues) therefore need to be incorporated into TVET teaching and learning or be further emphasised for the sake of the future of all of us as we struggle to learn throughout life. A well trained technical workforce is essential for any country's efforts to achieve sustainable development. (p. 29)
>
> [T]here is an urgent need to renew TVET. This should be the top ... priority for every country ... This is a task that can only be accomplished if a country can succeed in articulating TVET with its system of education within a framework of an overall sustainable development strategy. (p. 89)

These statements represent a broadening of TVET from the narrow task of providing training for industry- and occupation-specific skills to the broader task of workforce development and lifelong learning for sustainable development and citizenship. A related initiative that impacts upon TVET is the International Labour Organization (ILO) Decent Work Agenda:

> Decent work means productive work in which rights are protected, which generates an adequate income with adequate social protection. It also means sufficient work, in the sense that all should have full access to income-earning opportunities ... Decent work also means a way out of poverty, allowing economic growth to benefit from competition, and workers' from economic growth ... The evolving global economy offers opportunities from which all can gain, but these have to be grounded in participatory social institutions if they are to confer legitimacy and sustainability on economic and social policies.[4]

International fora have reiterated the important role of TVET in achieving sustainable human development. For example, the international "Education for All" program emphasizes vocational preparation within a context of social and environmental responsibility. Thus, Goal 3 in the Dakar Framework for Action includes a call to "ensure that the learning needs of all young people are met through equitable access to appropriate learning and life skills programmes." This goal emphasizes the importance of skills development for employment and for effective citizenship, and the important relationships between them. In like vein, the 2002 Youth Employment Summit in Cairo called for educational approaches that empower youth, especially young women and the disadvantaged, to face the future with hope and optimism, secure in the knowledge that they have the human capabilities to care for themselves and their families and contribute to sustainable human development (Fien, 2002).

Similarly, the final report of the 2002 World Summit on Sustainable Development emphasized the need for all countries and international agencies to meet "capacity needs for training, technical know-how and strengthening national institutions in ... economically viable, socially acceptable and environmentally sound" development (2002, para. 19) in order to eradicate poverty, improve human health and access to safe water and hygienic sanitation, conserve the natural resource base upon which social and economic development depends, and foster the use of technologies for cleaner production and renewable energy. As a result, the joint 2002 ILO and UNESCO Recommendations on Technical and Vocational Education for the Twenty-First Century state that, as "a vital aspect of the educational process in all countries," TVET should:

(a) Contribute to the achievement of the societal goals of greater democratization and social, cultural and economic development, while at the same time developing the potential of all individuals, both men and women, for active participation in the establishment and implementation of these goals, regardless of religion, race and age

(b) Lead to an understanding of the scientific and technological aspects of contemporary civilization in such a way that people comprehend their environment and are capable of acting upon it while taking a critical view of the social, political and environmental implications of scientific and technological change

---

[4] International Labour Conference, 89th Session, Geneva, June 2001.

(c) Empower people to contribute to environmentally sound sustainable development through their occupations and other areas of their lives. (UNESCO & ILO, 2002, p. 9)

More a Moral Precept than a Scientific Concept

These three goals are central to orienting TVET for sustainable development. Finding approaches to development that balance economic and social progress, address cultural differences, conform to global, national, and local needs, and respect ecological values and limits is the key to sustainable development. However, efforts to define exactly what sustainable development is must reflect the varying conditions in different parts of the world and their impact upon national and cultural priorities and values. For example,

> to an individual living in rural poverty in the developing world, "sustainable development", if it is to make any sense, must mean increased consumption and a higher living standard. By contrast, to an individual in a wealthy country, with a closet full of clothes, a pantry full of food and a garage full of cars, "sustainable development" could mean more modest and carefully considered consumption. (UNESCO, 1997, para. 25)

Thus, sustainable development is not a fixed concept; rather it is a culturally directed search for a dynamic balance in the relationships between social, economic, and natural systems, a balance that seeks to promote equity between the present and the future, and equity between countries, races, social classes, and genders. The interdependence of people and the environment requires that no single development or environmental objective be pursued to the detriment of others. The environment cannot be protected in a way that leaves half of humanity in poverty. Likewise there can be no long-term development on a depleted planet.

This makes sustainable development more a moral precept than a scientific concept, and links it as much with notions of peace, human rights, and fairness as it does with theories of ecology or global warming. Indeed, while sustainable development involves the natural sciences, policy, and economics, it is primarily a matter of culture: it is concerned with the values people cherish and with the ways in which we perceive our relationship with others and with the natural world (UNESCO, 2002).

TVET and Social Sustainability

As a focus of learning and cultural change, sustainability requires a conscious commitment by all to reflect upon the values and principles that guide our actions. All cultures, communities, individuals, and workplaces have their own views on what such values and principles should be and, given the need for sustainable development to be locally relevant and culturally appropriate, it is not possible to outline specific values to be encouraged in VET.

However, programs should provide opportunities for students to learn how to reflect upon their own values, how they affect lifestyle choices and the social, economic and environmental impacts that would result if everyone in the world believed and acted as they did. Such programs might also provide opportunities to reflect upon the relevance and likely impacts of the values held by other communities and cultures, and the applicability to consumption and production choices of the values in an ethic such as the "Earth Charter." These include:

- respecting Earth and life in all its diversity;
- caring for the community of life with understanding, compassion, and love;
- building democratic societies that are just, sustainable, participatory, and peaceful; and
- securing Earth's bounty and beauty for present and future generations.[5]

While termed an "Earth Charter," such principles are central to social sustainability and are embedded in the concept of "sustainable livelihoods," which embraces existing concepts of work and employment but widens them to include the multiple forms of economic and noneconomic activities through which people create opportunities to sustain themselves, their families, and their communities. The United Nations Development Program defines livelihoods as "the assets, activities and entitlements which people utilize in order to make a living" (UNDP, 1997, p. 6), with assets including local natural resources (i.e., land, water, common-property resources, flora, fauna), but also social (i.e., community, family, social networks), political (i.e., participation, empowerment), human (i.e., education, labor, health, nutrition), physical (i.e., roads, clinics, markets, schools, bridges), and economic resources (i.e., jobs, savings, credit).

The wide view of resources and abilities in the concept of sustainable livelihoods raises questions about the traditional "person–job" relationship that forms the foundation of many approaches to VET. While education, particularly VET, has important roles in developing the social, human, and physical capital needed for a sustainable livelihood, it is perhaps a very different form of VET that is required (see Lawrence and Tate, 1997). This makes it imperative to ensure that young people receive the best education possible to prepare them for a life of productive employment—and to have the entrepreneurial skills not only to develop work opportunities for themselves and others but also the commitment and initiative to contribute to the social, economic, and environmental well-being of their communities.

Thus basic education is central to effective VET. Literacy and numeracy are vital here. The health and safety of workers often depends upon their ability to read instructions (e.g., on fertilizer bags) and to make accurate calculations (e.g., of mixing and application levels). The wider skills of scientific and social literacy are also important, for example, for equipment maintenance and repair and understanding technological change (scientific literacy) and for group work, dialogue, and negotiation with colleagues and supervisors, gender and ethnic tolerance, and other skills

---

[5] See www.earthcharter.org

needed for harmonious relations in the workplace (social literacy). The application of such literacy to the world of work and active citizenship needs to become a core dimension of VET if it is to respond to the imperatives of social sustainability.[6]

Thus, Quisumbing argues for an "holistic and integrated human resource development program for TVET" that "aims to prepare the individual to become a responsible, free and mature person, equipped not only with the appropriate skills and knowhow of the latest technologies, but also with deep human and spiritual values and attitudes—a sense of self worth, self esteem and dignity" (2001, p. 2). Central to the development of knowledge, skills, and attitudes for social sustainability, she argues, are the abilities

- to work by oneself and with others in teams, with integrity and honor, with honesty, punctuality, and responsibility;
- to adapt to varying situations; to know and understand problems and issues; to work out solutions creatively;
- to resolve conflicts peacefully;
- to have a good grasp of the reality of the world, of oneself, and of others;
- to possess some general knowledge with specialization in some field or area of work; and
- to continue learning and pursue lifelong education in a learning society.

A focus on the knowledge, skills, and attitudes for social sustainability can develop all the powers and faculties of the individual—cognitive, affective, and behavioral—and from them can flow such "work values and attitudes as creativity and adaptability, productivity, quality and efficiency, patience and perseverance, loyalty and commitment, freedom and responsibility, accountability, the spirit of service, a futures orientation, and a genuine love for work itself" (Quisumbing, 2001, p. 2). The UNESCO DeSeCo Initiative sets a global standard for generic, psychosocial, and key transferable skills, which will further social sustainability.

This view places ethics at the heart of developing social sustainability through TVET. Wonacott (2001) notes that the literature on ethical issues in TVET is most often concerned with dilemmas in teaching and the use of technology related to questions of power, access, control, intellectual property rights, privacy, equity, speech, etc. Ethical and legal issues for specific occupations are also often addressed. There are also definite ethical and moral implications associated with social sustainability, including the following:

- **Respect for cultural diversity** is a core value in social sustainability. All people have the right to employment regardless of their ethnic or racial heritage and their religious beliefs. The rights to employment of indigenous peoples are especially important. This applies also to opportunities for further training and promotion. The internationalization of the workforce through globalization and

---

[6] The role of basic education in promoting sustainable livelihoods is discussed in Lawrence and Tate (1997).

labor migration also emphasizes the importance of developing respect for cultural diversity in all TVET programs (see Pegg, 1997; Brown, 2002).
- **Gender equality** is also a core value in social sustainability. The rights of women to equality of outcomes from education and training (as well as access) and to equality of employment opportunities, working conditions, access to further training, and promotion are important human rights that need to be enshrined in TVET programs. The vital importance of freedom from discrimination and sexual harassment, associated monitoring, reporting, and disciplinary processes also need to be taught. These are matters for both male and female students and workers: women need training in ways to protect their rights and freedoms in the workplace while men need training in their obligations to respect and honor all their work colleagues (Scott, 2003), Sustainability will be difficult to attain without equal access, participation, and remuneration of women.
- **Inclusion** of other excluded groups, for example, disabled people and ethnic minorities, is essential for sustainability in TVET and workplaces. Without the inclusion of all groups in a society sustainability will not be achieved.
- **Workplace relations**: One positive result of the reduction in levels of management and the increase in workers' levels of educational attainment has been the empowerment of workers to advise management of better ways to operate or produce finished goods. This reduction from as many as eight to as few as three levels of management has improved communications between labor and management. Historically, communications between employers and employees has been mainly top-down. Increasingly it has become the practice of enlightened employers to elicit ideas from their employees that improve production and lessen waste. The same holds true for the creation of sustainability, both in TVET and in the workplace. Relations *between* coworkers also benefit from improved communication, plus tolerance of others' differences. It goes without saying that a contentious workplace is not likely to be a sustainable one.
- **Teamwork at the workplace**: A harmonious workplace is one in which teamwork is both valued and practiced. While teamwork was important during the agricultural and industrial ages, it appears to have taken on new importance in the emerging information age. Many writers exhort TVET institutions at all levels to concentrate upon the training of "knowledge workers," defined as those "who use *logical-abstract thinking* to diagnose problems, research and apply knowledge to propose solutions, and design and implement those solutions, often as a member of a team" (Wilson, 2001, p. 21). The restructuring of assembly lines during the industrial age, and the maintenance of many assembly line principles and practices in the emerging information age—in particular the assembly of electronic equipment of all types—necessitate the enhancement of teamwork principles to ensure sustainability. Productivity issues, for example, the failure rate of assembled equipment, highlight the importance of teamwork. Therefore, it is incumbent upon TVET institutions to foster the necessary climate and/or "culture" of teamwork right from the initial

entry of students and trainees into TVET institutions. It is also imperative that TVET teachers and instructors set a correct example by functioning as a team.

- **Relations between employers and employees**: Conflict between labor and management has been a long-standing impediment to harmonious relationships between employers and employees. However, in some countries enlightened employers recognize that harmony is directly related to improved productivity, reduced spoilage, and even innovations suggested by employees. Many collective agreements now include mechanisms for continuing TVET, delivered either at the workplace or by means of released time for employees to attend off-site seminars, workshops, and courses. In some instances employers pay or reimburse tuition fees. In Japan, Career Development Grants are made by the government to employers to promote TVET and/or sponsor HRD leave (Cummings & Jecks, 2004). The contribution of such initiatives to employee retention constitutes yet another sustainable innovation. The effective introduction of technological innovations is usually accompanied by various forms of continuing TVET. Regrettably, studies have shown that most employer-sponsored training in industrialized countries is provided to sales and managerial personnel, rather than to those responsible for production and service delivery. In order for on-the-job learning to become sustainable it will be necessary for larger numbers of employers to recognize the benefits of continuing TVET.

- **Safety**: Considerations of safety are of prime importance in TVET and in the workplace. Employers bear responsibility for the working conditions and well-being of their employees. Employees are responsible for actions that might place their peers in peril, produce dangerous or sub-standard goods, or damage property. This suggests that another aspect of safety is the protection of TVET students/trainees and employees at the workplace. Making TVET more sustainable in the safety domain involves continuous attention to safe working conditions in all types of education and training, as well as in the workplace. Safety considerations should be prominent in the design of TVET facilities and the procurement of equipment. Safety is often given the highest priority in TVET curriculum development. However, one caveat during training is that there are limits to openness and participation because the teacher or instructor is responsible for the safety of the learners, and at times must exercise firm control.

- **Citizenship:** Social sustainability depends upon the willingness of people to cooperate in building and safeguarding a fair and democratic society. Reciprocal rights and responsibilities are important in a democracy, where the collective voice of citizens is the source of all legitimate authority. These rights include: equality before the law and the freedom to vote, to speak freely on public issues, and to participate in public interest groups. The duties of responsible citizenship include: paying taxes, obeying laws, demonstrating commitment and loyalty to democratic ideals, constructively criticizing the conditions of political and civic life, and participating to improve the quality of national and community life (Klusmeyer, 1996). The rights and responsibilities of citizens extend to the workplace also. This is why respect for gender and cultural differences and skills for developing harmonious workplace relations and teamwork and negotiating improvements in work practices are so important to social sustainability. TVET has key responsibilities to ensure that these civic disposition and participation skills are developed, and experience suggests that this can perhaps best be done through the following kinds of learning experiences:

- student participation in democratically conducted student organization;
- college-facilitated community service that is connected directly to the curriculum and classroom instruction; and
- cooperative learning activities in which groups of students cooperate to pursue a common goal, such as inquiring about a public issue or responding to a community problem (Patrick, 1999; Battersby, 1998).

Conclusion

The values of cultural diversity, gender equality, inclusion, and citizenship together with practices for safety, teamwork, and mutual employee–employer respect underpin the integration of social sustainability into technical and vocational education and training. They have the potential not only to promote more productive and humane workplaces but also to develop the knowledge, attitudes, and skills that are conducive to a fairer, less troubled, and more sustainable world—and surely that is what education should be all about.

References

Battersby, M. (1998). Education for citizenship: service-learning and the reflective citizen. *Learning Quarterly*, 2, 3–6.
Brown, B. L. (2002). *Global mobility of workers*. Trends and Issues Alert No. 35. Columbus, OH: Clearinghouse on Adult, Career, and Vocational Education.
Cummings, S. I., & Jecks, N. (2004). *Skills development and productivity through social dialogue*. Bangkok: International Labour Office, Subregional Office for East Asia.
Fien, J. (2002). Addressing youth employment issues through TVET. Discussion Paper presented to Special Interest Group on Technical, Vocational Education and Training, 8th UNESCO-APEID International Conference on Education, Bangkok, 26–29 November.
Klusmeyer, D. B. (1996). *Between consent and descent: conceptions of democratic citizenship*. Washington, DC: Carnegie Endowment for International Peace.
Lawrence, J., & Tate, S. (1997). *Basic education for sustainable livelihoods: the right questions*. Discussion Paper presented to the United Nations Development Program International Working Group on Sustainable Livelihoods, Pearl River, New York, 18–21 November.
Patrick, J. J. (1999). The concept of citizenship in education for democracy. http://library.educationworld.net/a10/a10-145.html. Accessed 24 April 2008.
Pegg, L. C. (1997). Diversity training and education in the workplace. *Journal for Vocational Special Needs Education*, 19(2), 62–66.

Quisumbing, L. R. (2001). *The importance of values education for TVET and its economic and human resource development program.* Paper presented at the UNESCO Asia Pacific Conference, Adelaide, 25–29 March.

Scott, M. L. (Ed.) (2003). *Equity issues in career and technical education.* Information Series No. 390. Columbus, OH: Clearinghouse on Adult, Career, and Vocational Education.

UNDP (1997). *Adult education and jobs, or sustainable livelihoods?* Paper presented to UNESCO CONFINTEA V Panel on Changes in the World of Work, Hamburg, Germany, 12 July.

UNESCO (1997). *Environment and society: education and public awareness for sustainability. Background paper prepared for UNESCO International Conference, Thessaloniki, Greece.* Paris: UNESCO.

UNESCO (1999). *Final report. Second International Conference on Technical and Vocational Education.* Paris: UNESCO.

UNESCO (2002). *Education for sustainability: lessons learnt from a decade of commitment from Rio to Johannesburg. Report to the World Summit on Sustainable Development.* Paris: UNESCO.

UNESCO & ILO (2002). *Technical and vocational education for the twenty-first century: ILO and UNESCO recommendations.* Paris: UNESCO.

UNESCO-UNEVOC (2006). *Orienting technical and vocational education and training for sustainable development.* Discussion paper no. 1. Bonn: UNESCO-UNEVOC.

Wilson, D. N. (2001). Reform of TVET for the changing world of work. *Prospects, 31*(1), 21.

Wonacott, M. (2001). *Ethics: the role of adult and vocational education.* Trends and Issues Alert No. 24. Columbus, OH: ERIC Clearinghouse on Adult, Career and Vocational Education.

World Summit on Sustainable Development (2002). *Plan of implementation.* World Summit on Sustainable Development, Johannesburg, 26 August–4 September.

Chapter 3
An Ecology for the Fourth Pillar: Imaginal Learning for Social Sustainability in AVE

Peter Willis

Abstract This chapter explores an "imaginal" curriculum for social sustainability in adult and vocational education. This imaginal curriculum seeks to find appropriate pedagogic ways to evoke and nourish what Jon Hawkes calls social sustainability's "fourth pillar," namely "cultural vitality and life enthusiasm" (2004, p. 263). This life enthusiasm is a key factor in the health of any society as it interacts with the biological and social world. Drawing on the concept of "social ecology," I discuss the importance of humans being aware and respectful of their location in their social eco-system as embodied, aesthetic, rational, and finally technological beings, where each of these dimensions is interdependent. I then focus on pedagogic ways in which adult and vocational education can evoke and foster social ecological learning imaginally. This involves aesthetic processes that call learners to explore their "life myths" and link them to the myths implicit in social sustainability. Two approaches are described: *reciprocal storytelling*, through which learners are invited to develop responsive dispositions toward aesthetic experiences, and *evocative portrayal*, in which artistic creations and performances linked to elements of social sustainability are presented and a range of responses invited and explored.

Introduction

Human sustainability is conventionally understood in terms of three dimensions: economic, social and environmental. This chapter is concerned with a less familiar dimension: the cultural. Within this cultural dimension, I argue for an "imaginal curriculum." The imaginal curriculum seeks to foster social sustainability by drawing attention to and nourishing what Jon Hawkes (2004, p. 263) calls sustainability's "fourth pillar," namely "cultural life" or more accurately "cultural vitality." Hawkes writes

> This is why I support the application of a fourth, a cultural perspective to stand alongside the standard triangle of social, environmental and economic "pillars". It is through cultural action that we make sense of our existence and the environment we inhabit, that we find

P. Willis (✉)
University of South Australia, South Australia, Australia

common expressions of our values and needs, and, it is through cultural action that we meet the challenges presented by our continuing stewardship of the planet. (2004, p. 263)

And

Cultural vitality is as essential to a healthy and sustainable society as social equity, environmental responsibility and economic viability. (p. 261)

Vitality encompasses the qualitative elements by which a society is perceived to be flourishing. People in a culturally vibrant society are perceived to be "onto something." This life enthusiasm, along with the more prosaic economic, social, and environmental indicators, is a key factor in the ecological health of a society.

Ecology is the study of the relationships between organisms and their environment. However, human acts are not often noted or catered for in conventional ecological studies, and this neglected "social" dimension is the focus of some scholars and activists. Accordingly, the term "ecology" can refer to an *ideal* being pursued in relation to caring for such human environmental and social systems. This "social ecology" is what Hill calls

the study and practice of personal, social and environmental sustainability and change based on the critical application and integration of ecological, humanistic, community and spiritual values. (1999, p. 13, following Bookchin, 1993)

Thus, social ecology has a kinship with social sustainability and is taken here to represent in a holistic way the work that is needed to support social sustainability, in other words, to support human social and biological life as an integrated whole. From this perspective social ecology represents a blueprint for sustainability, focusing on ways to support Hawkes' social, environmental, economic, and cultural pillars.

In reflecting on the general notion of social sustainability as "a positive and long-term condition" (McKenzie, 2004, p. 16), I am interested here in ways in which aesthetic education, a specific pedagogic approach to the cultural part of social ecology and its related life enthusiasm, can resist the entropy, the loss of interest, and motivation that can afflict the organic, interactive, and longitudinal nature of human social life. Social ecology suggests the importance of people being aware of their location in key dimensions of their social ecosystem as *embodied, rational, aesthetic*, and *technological* beings, where each dimension is interdependent and interactive with the others.

The *embodied* dimension of the social ecosystem refers to the interactive biological dimension of human life through sensation and various bodily functions: eating, breathing, defecation, and the like. As Todres (2007) explains, bodiliness carries and shapes almost every kind of human experience.

The *rational* dimension of the social ecosystem refers to the human power for abstract and rational thought applied in empirical and social science and in law and human ethics.

The *aesthetic* dimension involves the human capacity to be moved by beauty and its opposite, and is linked to the power of the imagination to think via images. While the imagination can involve the human creative power of fantasy, there is another more contemplative aspect known as "imaginal knowing." Imaginal knowing (Hillman, 1981) refers to the human power to think in images and to dwell on them, thus complementing the logical rational dimension of conceptual thinking. This imaginal dimension of human social ecology has a direct link to desire and can provide an ongoing foundation for enthusiasm and sustained commitment to chosen action.

Finally, the *technological* dimension of the social ecosystem refers to the capacity of people as tool makers and inventors to harness and exploit natural resources according to their priorities. But of course these priorities need the stabilizing influence of other dimensions to be safe, sustainable, and convivial.

Social ecology, with its emphasis on holism and the complementarity of different elements, can thus be offered as a useful way to think about the multiple challenges of social sustainability. This would support the view of Adebowale that

> Sustainability has always been linked to a core concept of human need so it is a fundamental contradiction to believe it can be achieved without improved social equity and social progress. (2002, p. 5)

Two pedagogic agendas can be drawn from this more human meaning of ecology. The first is to explore more deeply the four significant and complementary agendas in the life of human groups relating to the sustainability of their social ecosystem. The second is to focus particularly on educational ways of fostering the aesthetic and imaginal dimension required for energizing human interest in and commitment to the ideals of social sustainability.

Social sustainability in human organic and social life can be envisioned as having vertical (or life through time) and horizontal (or concurrent life with other persons and things) dimensions. The quality of social sustainability attached to the ecology of human groups is manifested in its capacity to maintain its social and environmental relations both in and through time.

A significant element in the sustainability of a group through time is its capacity to relate creatively and authentically to the lateral challenges of new people and circumstances. This can mean integrating new people and ideas, working toward acceptance and celebration of difference. It can also mean enduring internal and external diminishing processes by generating and nurturing visions and dreams of betterment, which can create a mood of life affirmation and resilience.

Diminishments can be expected to occur from time to time in every society. Internal diminishment can occur though different forms of attrition brought about by changes to the physical environment or by human acts of violence, forms of illness, guilt, woundedness from unjust acts, and other forms of entropy. External diminishment comes from outside the group. These forces can be sudden, such as a tidal wave, cyclone, or human acts of invasion, or they can be gradual, such as drought, migration, or pressure from hostile groups. Against these recurrent diminishments, human visioning, desire, and choice can provide a foundation for ongoing recovery, reconciliation, and healing. These seem to be essential requirements for a sustainable social ecology in changeable and turbulent circumstances.

Dimensions of Sustainable Social Ecology

Sustainable social ecology refers here to ways of purposively seeking to shape and conserve the interdependent processes characterizing social groups and their members within their physical and social environment. The general aim is to encourage positive outcomes in the middle of processes of growth and decline, wounding and healing, conflict and reconciliation in and through time. This enterprise has utopian dimensions and is pursued knowing the difficulty of attempting intervention into such systems while seeking to safeguard life, autonomy, and resilience.

It is suggested here that an approach to adult and vocational education for social sustainability can be enriched by building on John Heron's heuristic idea, which he first elaborated in 1992, that human consciousness has four modes of knowing, each building on the one before. These seem to have considerable similarities to the elements in a human ecology mentioned above. According to Heron, *sensation*—direct somatic experience of the world—lies at the basis of human consciousness. Imagination and *imaginal reflection* build on this, and in turn support *conceptional classification, analysis*, and *calculation*. Finally there is *praxis*, which is the reflective knowledge accompanying purposive action. Building on Heron's matrix, appropriate and balanced ways of building a socially sustainable society can be developed by acknowledging and fostering the complementary synergies of these four modes of conscious action.

Accordingly, since people's actions at different times can show the influence of one or other of these modes of consciousness, and equally their lack, a useful approach to adult and vocational education for social sustainability might be to explore the nature of these four modes of knowing and the balance between them. In other words, ways of living usefully, honestly, and sustainably need to be pursued through a *conscious social and sustainable ecology* by which people come to recognize, deliberately participate in, and sometimes seek to shape the interplay of different forces at work in their personal, physical, and social worlds. This social ecology can be understood to apply to the four significant and interacting life arenas mentioned above to which Heron's four different patterns of consciousness mentioned above apply, namely:

- *bodily, physical consciousness* with its sense-awareness forms of knowing;
- *imaginal consciousness* with presentational, image-awareness forms of knowing and their related feelings and moods;
- *rational, analytical consciousness* with the rational conceptional awareness form of knowing;
- reflective action with its *praxis* awareness form of knowing.

And so the argument of this chapter can be rephrased. I suggest that, by recognizing and honoring the multiple forces and dimensions of human life that are made visible through attention to the different kinds of human awareness and attempting to engage consciously and critically in these modes of knowing and shaping the world, people concerned with social sustainability have a clearer opportunity to develop and refine a more holistic and nuanced pedagogy.

3 An Ecology for the Fourth Pillar

But for human social life to have such depth, honor, energy, and sustainability, people need to be constantly aware of and engaged in reflective activities drawn from these four genres of consciousness and knowing according to a kind of "quest map" both through time (the vertical, diachronic world), and in the physical here and now (the horizontal, synchronic world). Each of the four ways of knowing alluded to above thus need to be acknowledged and shaped to form a more holistic sustainable ecological awareness and practice.

The first dimension of knowing relates directly to the bodily arena: sensations, physical environment, and space—sensations linked to the five senses, to emotions, and to the capacity for pleasure and pain. A sustainable ecological awareness would cater for and deepen people's awakeness and awareness of the sensate world. The five senses would provide messages of health and environmental richness or might trigger alarm in toxic smells, polluted rivers, and unsavory food and drink.

The second, imaginal consciousness is treated more fully below.

The third dimension is that of logic, rationality, and science. Humans, particularly in western cultures, have tended to depend on science to provide accurate information and ways of being with the so-called objective, factual world. In many ways, humans have been both the beneficiaries and the victims of this powerful form of consciousness. On the one hand, science has given us the benefits of computers, telephones, and medicine, yet on the other hand, the scourge of nuclear weapons and greenhouse gasses. The technical, logical dimensions of social ecology need to use the very tools of logical and empirical rationality to encourage the energy of science and logic, while at the same time remaining aware of its limits and the tendency of certain people and cultures to overvalue its usefulness by seeing it as the only valid source of human wisdom and betterment.

The fourth is the dimension of reflective action or praxis. This mental process is linked to human agency. From an ecological and sustainable perspective reflection around action needs to become critical, prudent, and holistic. Planned and executed actions need to be reflectively examined for their long-term effects, their costs and benefits and the possibility of so-called collateral damage or side effects. The previous mention of technology with the dazzling enrichment of its tools and inventions, which can so easily disguise its limitations and perils, is a key reminder of the importance of an ecological dimension in rational empirical thinking to be aware of, critique, and shape human purposive activities according to social ecological guidelines.

And so what is needed is an energetic complementarity between the four modes of knowing, each with their windows into different dimensions of human social ecology. But of course it is one thing to become aware of the need for limits and changes to various elements of human life, and quite another to find the commitment, resolution, and tenacity to make the necessary choices—even when they are uncomfortable—and carry them to completion. The direction and energy of human choice has one of its key foundations in the human capacity for enthusiasm by which the imagination is captured and the heart moved. Ways of evoking and shaping this imaginal dimension, with its links to Hawke's cultural fourth pillar of social sustainability, forms the main theme of the following section.

Imaginal Learning for Sustainable Ecology

The concept of the "imaginal," developed by Hillman (1981), draws extensively from the writings of Henry Corbin (1969). Corbin had interpreted the pioneering work of Ibn 'Arabi, a Sufi mystic, to refer to the human power of image making and its links to the so-called "knowing of the heart," the knowing linked to a person's sense of her or himself and her or his position in the world. The "imaginal" (cf. Bradbeer, 1998, p. 14) differs from the "imaginary," which contains the notion of fantasy. For Hillman (1981), the imaginal has nothing to do with fantasy but much to do with the knowing and reflecting linked to the heart.

Halling, quoting from his personal journal (2005, p. 221), writes of coming to a state of forgiveness:

> My anger and hurt vanished as I was thinking about Heather, but this time as another human being who was struggling, and who basically did not mean me any harm. It is not accurate, I am realizing, to suggest that I just thought that; it was more like an image that emerged for me, an image that was not as much seen as felt. I felt healed; blame and anger vanished. (2008 p. 82)

In Halling's writing, the power of the image reaches to the feeling part of the person. From this perspective it is possible to see imaginal knowing as involving more than the logical rational mind and encompassing gut-level knowing and feeling.

Imaginal awareness can be understood to have two learning dimensions. The first learning dimension is a visioning process requiring an *idealizing* curriculum, by which citizens invent and develop ideals of a society committed to balance the ideals of good management and enterprise with equity and inclusivity. The other learning is a grounding process of attentive compassion requiring an *empathetic* curriculum, through which learners are invited to try to imagine themselves in the shoes of others, sharing in some small way their feelings and experiences. As Greene says of the imagination, "it is what, above all, makes empathy possible" (1995, p. 3).

The visioning curriculum builds on the work of the democratic futurists to envisage possible worlds and the real challenges that inclusivity and equity bring to human life together, particularly when looking at local, national, and global scenarios. The empathetic curriculum has the task of creating scenarios evoking compassionate understandings and feelings for others in the local, national, and world community.

The challenge has always been to discover ways in which adult and community education can develop and promote an appropriate curriculum to foster the imaginal dimension of life. Compared to the curriculum involved in assisting learners to take on accurate information or precise and well-developed skills, the imaginal curriculum is divergent and less bounded and confined. Whereas the instructional curriculum tends to look in a convergent way to measurable objectives and performance outcomes, the imaginal curriculum speaks more obliquely to the imagination and the heart and looks to resonance rather than replication, and to evocation or enchantment rather than to compliance with specified outcomes. Even though a general personal stance or orientation is what is aimed at, such dispositions may be difficult to identify in performative or behavioral terms, and changes of performance specifically linked to an evocative curriculum even harder to measure.

In adult education courses on politics, drama, art, history, and citizenship, imaginal dimensions of human cultural life are often acknowledged but not necessarily fostered in the actual curriculum. It is possible to run historical and cultural courses in a didactic way, speaking strongly to the interests of the logical rational mind but leaving the heart unmoved. An imaginal curriculum directed toward social sustainability awareness needs to have the capacity to capture the ecological imagination and move the heart toward conservation and inclusivity.

So, how can the power of the imagination be evoked to feed the imaginal curriculum? Pattenden represents this challenge well:

> The imagination is the world of the artist, poet and prophet. The imagination is more permissive and tolerant of experiment, in limping metaphors and erased drawings. Its forms allow a recovery of feeling, desire and even of ecstasy in the process of lived existence. These "exhilarating" moments are the ones that are often held under strict quarantine within institutional situations ...
>
> Images form a horizon of choices that awakens a community to change and growth. The power of images is potentially disruptive to institutions concerned with limits on behaviours and ... social contracts. The arts create both attraction and repulsion. (Pattenden 2002, pp. 29, 30)

One such imaginal curriculum has been developed by Maxine Greene, with her work on what she calls "aesthetic education." It builds on the particular power that surrounds many great works of art, on the one hand, and specific receptive dispositions that learners can be assisted to acquire, on the other. It is the second element—the inviting and shaping of dispositions—that Maxine Greene's pedagogy seems specifically to address.

Aesthetic Education: Inviting and Shaping Imaginal Dispositions

People in the right mood, hearing a poem from Seamus Heaney, or a blues song from Nina Simone, or looking at a beautifully designed Japanese garden or Matisse's *Icarus* painting, can be transported through the very process of engagement into a space of enchanted possibility of time out of time. The capacity to be smitten by such works requires predispositions that Maxine Greene (1995) calls "wide-awakeness" and "attention," and it is her belief that people can be assisted to learn how to be moved through the catalytic process of what she calls "aesthetic education."

According to Greene, the human contemplating eye and engaged heart can be encouraged to become compassionate and discerning through appropriate nonintrusive educational activities that assist learners to adopt receptive contemplative aesthetic dispositions toward works of art; to become oriented and receptive to their aesthetic powers; to "listen" to them and allow them to take up residence in their mind and heart.

Aesthetic Education: An Example

In the summer of 2001, I joined a group of educators attending Greene's course on aesthetic education at New York's Lincoln Center Institute for the Arts in Education. Given the advertised social justice and aesthetic themes, I wanted to learn how to be more aesthetically appreciative of artistic work in the context of the challenges of human social and political culture and more awake to the needs and challenges of human life and citizenship. At the same time, I was hoping to learn something of how she does what she does. I was surprised, enchanted, and disappointed. Although not admitting it consciously to myself, I had hoped to learn how to replicate something of Maxine's pedagogic technique in my own work. My expectations were not directly met since Maxine's pedagogy is not a formal structured technique but more a kind of embodied and infectious dialogic life stance. My learning agenda shifted in the course of the program and under its influence and I later realized that I had dismissed ideas of copying her technique in the interest of being part of her dialogic project. I wanted to look with Maxine at the world of art into which she had invited us. I wanted to engage dialogically with her in as deep a way as I could around the aesthetic project she was pursuing with us. I wanted to feel an imaginal, resonative shift in my psyche and I was to learn as well that such resonative moments—particularly intense ones—are not always forthcoming even to those most earnestly prepared and disposed.

The key seemed to be her dialogic "pedagogy of awakening" in the curriculum of her workshop. We spent considerable time at a range of performances that were taking place at various parts of the summer arts program at the Lincoln Center. We were briefed about the artistic work and its general genre as poetry, drama, dance, orchestral music, and song. We became part of the audience and then reconvened to debrief with Maxine. Under Maxine's tutelage—one could hardy call her oblique suggestions "directions"—I found myself paying attention to the artistic event in an intensely aware, mindful way and, synchronous with Maxine, picking up what could be called attention tips. These tips were not directed to the sequence of ideas or arguments of a drama piece or poem but to its aesthetic presence, which I slowly allowed to fill my horizon. A special example of this was Maxine's reading of different poems with her strong Brooklyn accent. This was artistry echoing artistry and I can hear her still. I remember her reading one poem, stopping and asking listeners to attend to it as she read it again with a different cadence. She kept asking what we were hearing, what images did the poem evoke, and, painfully, the question of ways it might have "spoken" to us. The room of forty people, silent and intense, listened to three voices at once: Maxine, the poet being read, and each of us as an attuned listener. The point to be made is that the knowledge I gained and the learning I engaged in had little to do with different representational genres and their intellectual and technical structure but more to do with taking on and developing a habit of aesthetic attention—a kind of imaginal mindfulness.

Imaginal Learning for Social Sustainability in AVE

At first sight evocative, imaginal pedagogy would seem a long way from the kind of convergent and measurable instructional precision required in TVET programs. At the same time much vocational education is perceived by learners and employers to have a transformative dimension so that the trainees are invited into the community of practice of the trade in which they are being instructed and to take on the persona and values of the trade they are learning. When trainees take pride in belonging to their professional or semi-professional work groups and understand where the different parts of their work fit into a broad picture of society, their learning and knowledge has moved a long way from purely technical, instrumental learning. The more holistic arenas of community of practice membership are appropriate locations for imaginal learning around workers' lives and their ideals. Trade union education programs concerned with occupational health and safety and enterprise bargaining are logical sites for deeper exploration of themes relating to social sustainability.

The question then concerns appropriate curricular approaches in adult and vocational education that can address questions of imaginal knowing and learning directly and indirectly in formal and informal settings in classrooms, workplaces, and community meeting places such as learning centers, churches, gymnasiums, and libraries. There are two major tasks already hinted at in the brief description of Greene's idea of aesthetic education. The task is to cultivate appropriate learner disposition toward artistic experiences. The second task is to engage the learner with appropriate art performances and exhibitions in an aesthetically attentive and mindful way. Mythopoetic consciousness can be cultivated in learners by such techniques as reciprocal storytelling and evocative portrayal, which I will now describe.

Reciprocal Storytelling

Reciprocal storytelling is a reflective contemplative process in which an individual person's imaginal consciousness, with its own private powerful images and archetypes, is shared with the imaginal consciousness of fellow learners through a range of reciprocal storytelling and related aesthetic art forms that are accessible to people who may not necessarily possess highly developed artistic skills and capabilities. This is the arena of the yarn spinner, the storyteller, the bush poet, the sculptor with clay and plasticine, the singer, the improvising raconteur or actor. It is in the moments of reciprocal reflection and performance that the aesthetic disposition can be evoked and the individual attuned and oriented to the aesthetic world originally very much local and personal, but sensitized as well to the larger and more generic power of so-called great artistic works that have reached and shaken subsequent generations.

Story-telling as a form of pedagogy has an ancient tradition drawing from practice surrounding fairy tales, myths, legend, fables, and the like. Karen Armstrong writes:

> Human beings fall easily into despair, and from the very beginning we invented stories that enabled us to place our lives in a larger setting, that revealed an underlying pattern, and gave us a sense that, against all the depressing and chaotic evidence to the contrary, life has meaning and value. (2005, p. 2)

As well as the role of explanation contained in some stories, there is also the function of developing and promulgating moral judgment about actions and practices. Arthur Frank notes in his significant work, *The wounded storyteller*, that Coles, who wrote a book called *The call of stories* (1989), emphasized that a moral life can be lived as the "call of stories," specifically literary stories that become woven into one's own life (Frank, 1995, p. 194). In the same volume, Frank refers to certain stories as "a way of redrawing maps and finding new destinations" (p. 53). This is the mythopoetic power of stories to capture the imagination and move the heart to differing degrees depending on the quality of the writing and possible performance on the one hand, and the attention and connectedness of the listener on the other. Thus story-telling from this moral perspective can be said to have a mythopoetic influence or "reach."

Reciprocal Storytelling: An Example

One classic example of reciprocal storytelling is found in the New Testament whereby Jesus used stories to illustrate and "present evocatively" his message to his disciples. From these stories, the disciples developed an open disposition, were freed from the constraints of their personal limitations, were moved to adopt personal change, and attempted to create new life stories of their own. The full power of this imaginal process required a reciprocal reading and intertwining of stories, not just a passive and courteous listening. Jesus waited to hear the reciprocating narrative. The story of the disciples meeting Jesus on the road to Emmaus (Luke 24: 13–35) is a powerful example of the reciprocated narrative, with Jesus listening to the disciples and subsequently replying with further modification and invitations. The gospels in fact represent the long incubation of the stories of those who had heard Jesus' stories and sought to mesh their own with his. There is an artistry attached to the verbal telling and celebrating as these stories entered the realm of oral art. However, their aesthetic power was not in the detached aestheticism of an exquisite piece in the art gallery, but in the framing of the hearts of followers and their subsequent transformed lives.

Evocative Portrayal

The agenda of Maxine Greene's aesthetic education builds on attuned dispositions and invites people to become members of that smitten cohort transformed by great art, whose hearts and minds have been struck and opened. Exposure to works of art has been used in forms of "evocative portrayal" for social sustainability. My notion and practice of evocative portrayal has evolved from my previous work on mythopoetic evocation developed in writings and practices I have been engaged in over the last few years (cf. Willis, 2005).

Evocative portrayal in the context of education for social sustainability is pursued by inviting students to dwell on images of desirable practices, such as inclusivity and reconciliation, around the theme of social sustainability, as represented in pictorial art, film, fiction, and poetry. The educator seeks to create a catalytic process via works of art, in and through which people become attuned to evocations of honor, beauty, friendship, and reconciliation, as artist and beholder or audience, and allowing the "attentive, contemplating heart" to do its aesthetic work. Over some years of practice the following evocative portrayal sequence has emerged as four major stages: (1) dramatic presentation, (2) role-play interview, (3) textual composition, and (4) uptake reflection. The approach is briefly described here, followed by a specific example using an excerpt from a popular film.

(1) Dramatic presentation

Dramatic presentation has two elements: context delineation and drama enactment. Context delineation provides the background, such as setting or circumstances, to an episode taken from film, fiction, artwork, or poetry. The significant moments under investigation are then viewed or performed in the drama enactment. The more the scene is skillfully created by talented actors with the support of appropriate music and scenery the better. The dramatic presentation has the capacity to draw out the curiosity and empathy of the audience, who engage emotionally with the main characters and the challenges they face. This engagement tacitly invites the audience into Hillman's imaginal knowing and feeling, where judging processes of the rational intellect tend to be suspended.

(2) Role-play interview

Once the dramatic presentation is finished, the facilitator recruits two role-players. One person plays the role of an interviewer; the other takes the role of the character that was the focus of the film clip or snippet of drama. Two oral process ("narrative describing" and "questioning interruption") and two textual processes ("textual composition" and "uptake reflection") are now employed.

Narrative describing: Here the role-taker is invited by the interviewer to retell the story of the moment(s) just viewed by the participants. The experience itself is then distilled into a more compressed form.

Questioning interruption: The interviewer then interrupts the flow of the story and asks the narrator to focus on the phenomenon as a lived experience, bracketing any received interpretations and bringing the mind to bear on it directly.

In this negotiated reflective process, the interviewer asks the role-taker to reflect on the specific moment in the event being explored to discover what it was like as an experience. This can be done several times. The interviewer asks the role-taker two sets of questions. The first set recalls van Manen's (1990, p. 103) idea, drawing on Merleau-Ponty (1962), of the "existential coordinates" of an experience. The interviewer asks the role-taker what the experience was like as a bodily experience, a temporal experience, an experience in space, and in social relations. In the second set of questions, the interviewer invites the role-taker to complete some of what Michael Crotty (1996, p. 279) calls "sentence stems," each carrying ingenious variations of the basic phenomenological question: "What is x like as a lived experience?"

The following sentence stems use "action for social sustainability" as the phenomenon in question. Of course, the phenomenon could just as easily be some other form of practice in education, nursing, or counseling. The challenge is to maintain attention on the phenomenon itself and not to focus too much on the feelings that may be associated with it:

Action for social sustainability is like...
Action for social sustainability sounds to me like...
Action for social sustainability strikes me as being...
What I discover in action for social sustainability is...
What I see in action for social sustainability is...
What shows up when I think of action for social sustainability is...
Action for social sustainability can be described as...
Action for social sustainability looks to me like...
Action for social sustainability presents itself to me as...
I picture action for social sustainability as...
What I detect in action for social sustainability is...
I recognize action for social sustainability as being...
Action for social sustainability feels like...
Action for social sustainability seems to be...
I depict action for social sustainability in graphic form as...
What comes to light when I focus on action for social sustainability is...
When I gaze at action for social sustainability I see...
I depict action for social sustainability in poetic terms as...
The metaphor(s) that best convey action for social sustainability is (are)...

Not all of these prompts will be generative, but at least some should bring the portrayed experience alive in the consciousness of the interviewee and those in the group and leads to the next step of "textual representation" in which the experience is reproduced in textual form using three linked processes: distilling, drafting, and display.

(3) Textual composition: distilling, drafting, and display

The *distilling* process is a search for phenomenological themes. This requires a mixture of insight and lateral grouping. The advantage of the Crotty sentence stems is that the phenomenological "eye" makes a series of passes over the experience, letting it present itself in the variety of "windows" created by the different sentence stems. It is then possible to collate these sentences so that revealed elements of the phenomenon can be grouped or clustered around recurrent perceptions named in the various textual representations. Again the agenda is a matter of discernment. Ultimately, one wants to ask the participants to identify one or more themes that they see as central to the phenomenon, and whether an experience encountered in the phenomenon could retain its integrity if a particular theme were absent.

The distilling process leads to the *drafting* process, in which a text is crafted from the distilled images. The researcher/facilitator who has performed or been privy to the distilling process attempts to render the experience now portrayed by many observers in a few sentences. The inquirer here needs to illustrate artistry through the creation and manipulation of representative text. Working a text—the writerly craft of summarizing, grouping, writing, rewriting—is a process whereby one human attempts to convey meaning through the intersubjectivity of language to other people.

Finally, in the *display* process, the researcher is challenged to find the most appropriate way to craft this in a readable expressive text. Such a text might be a poem, a painting, a dance—some form of expressive writing that takes readers back into the lived experience of the phenomenon. Here, the researcher's tool is not the surgeon's analytical scalpel but the poet's pen or artist's brush, called upon to produce focused expressive work. Its quality is to be judged not by the more positivist canons of validity and reliability, but by its degree of verisimilitude and integrity. Display gives the writer a free rein to ask in what way an episode of practice in that particular time spoke to her or him. This genre gives room to move, to express feelings and ideas surrounding, and generated by, the phenomenon. The "poetic" reflection, which is to be understood more as a reflection in verse with poetic features of metaphor and direct image without necessarily possessing the crystalline character of the fully crafted poem, can be in the form of a poem, a short piece of carefully crafted prose, a multimedia presentation, or a piece of artwork. It allows the author once more to represent a more holistic gestalt of her or his experience of the episode of practice. Such a genre can include feelings, fears, joys in the presentation of the phenomenon, and to tell at least a little of her or his reactions to, and interpretations of, the experience. In such verse all the sensations surrounding the event can be named and celebrated as elements of what the episode has invoked in her or him and as such can be seen as elements of the phenomenon. This final text attempts to find the most expressive way to carry the intuited phenomenon.

The oral processes of depicting and distilling and the written processes of drafting and display are structured attempts to foreground the phenomenon itself. There is a conscious attempt to move from the contextualized and dramatized accounts of the experience to "the phenomenon itself"—that which presents itself in the experience. The question then remains: to what extent can such processes foster attitudes that value and promote the phenomenon?

(4) Uptake reflection

The effect of describing lived experience in the way outlined above can bring its intrinsic implications into sharp relief. Phrases like "Now I know what it's really like" reflect a strong realization of what can be called the unavoidable dimensions of a lived experience. Whereas reflective practice traditionally challenges practitioners to resolve contradictions between espoused theories and theories in use, expressive description can generate another related challenge. This is to resolve contradictions, which beginning practitioners might not have been aware of, between the expectations they may have about a form of practice and the actual reality of it as experienced.

When people involved in human service work such as nursing, educating, and counseling reflect on significant incidents linked to social sustainability practice of which they were a part, they may notice that these lived experiences, by their nature, seem to demand a measure of self-revelation from the practitioner and some readiness to be influenced by them. The realization that this is a necessary dimension of the lived experience (rather than just the incidental feelings of the nurse, educator, or counselor at the time) may threaten certain people, while being a source of great interest, even consolation, for others. This experiential reflection gives people the opportunity to go back over an experience, to "taste what something is like."

On a more personal note, the augmented processes in the describing phase, as outlined above, can generate considerable self-appraisal against the inexorability and verity of its portrayal. In one of these reflective exercises, I ended up being virtually forced to confront my orientation toward education, or what Bradbeer (1998, p. 14) would call my "heart," as well as the things I actually do in learning facilitation. I have thus ended up being led more deeply to more composite and multidimensional processes of reflection, with deeper and more thought-out choices for change and improvement, both in stance and action. I suspect that educators who follow this expressive phenomenological path in their reflective practice may find similar challenges and invitations.

Evocative Portrayal: Action for Social Sustainability

The following example of this form of evocative phenomenological portrayal is from an adult educator training session on action for social sustainability through creative engagement with adult learners. The facilitator shows a significant excerpt from the film *Good Will Hunting*, which concerns the challenges and experiences of pedagogic action that seeks to promote social sustainability by fostering inclusivity and reconciliation. The four-part process described above (dramatic presentation, role-play interview, textual composition, and uptake reflection) is used to evoke a range of responses. These responses may concern feelings, critical and discerning thoughts, and subsequent decisions to engage more (or even less) enthusiastically in activities supporting and fostering the elements of social sustainability.

(1) Dramatic presentation

Context delineation: Good Will Hunting tells the story of a brilliant, turbulent, and selfish young man who comes to maturity and some form of social responsibility. Will Hunting (played by Matt Damon) awakens to his authentic self and his social responsibilities largely through exchanges with counselor Sean Maguire (played by Robin Williams), whom he must visit under penalty of serious punishment following acts of violence. Maguire approaches counseling work through a robust challenge interwoven with respectful inclusivity and capacity for reconciliation. This film can be used to illustrate elements of social interaction that have considerable relevance to social sustainability. This is particularly in relation to the balance between individual contribution to the good of the group, and personal fulfillment in work, family, and social relationships. The practice of education for social sustainability (ESS), portrayed in the humanly flawed prophetic challenge and reconciliation work of Sean Maguire' counseling practice, is represented as in some way heroic and admirable. At the same time it is revealed as difficult, challenging, and risky and requiring a kind of sustained and respectful skill and kindness, the portrayal of which is offered to enchant and challenge professionals in adult and vocational education.

A clip of this exchange is played to participants in an AVE setting where there is a presumption that the work of adult and vocational education has always involved relational challenges for learners somehow to become different within the often more technical syllabus of many AVE courses. The question concerns ways in which these relational exchanges between educator and learner can be informed by a concern for elements of social sustainability, particularly those fostering inclusivity and reconciliation. It is a classic case of attending to the non-formal curriculum—the learning that takes place in the informal exchanges, debates, arguments, jokes, and the like that accompany structured educational programs.

Drama enactment: In their first encounter, Hunting is resisting the obligatory therapy and taunts Maguire about his deceased wife. Maguire responds by seizing his client by the throat and threatening him with violence. At their second scheduled meeting, the one of most interest here, Maguire pursues his commitment to education for social sustainability initially by rebuking Hunting in a prophetic and open-ended way, pointing out that his intellectual brilliance is devoid of the wisdom and compassion that comes from embraced and accepted life blessings and wounds.

(2) Role-play interview

Afterwards, two people are invited by the facilitator to role-play an imagined interview with Maguire. The role-play has three parts: narrative describing, interrupting questioning, and phenomenological depicting.

Narrative describing: The interviewer (I) asks the person taking the role of Maguire (M) to describe what happened in his practice of education for social sustainability (ESS) in the second scene.

M: I had arranged a follow-up session with Hunting and when he arrived I grabbed my jacket and cap and told him to follow me. I chose a favorite bench by the lake and after we sat I told Hunting how much his remarks had wounded me until I realized that his knowledge was abstract, rational book knowledge not the sweet knowledge that comes from life choices, commitments, and the real risks of acceptance and rejection.

Questioning interruption: The interviewer interrupts at different points of the narrative and asks "What happened there?" "What was that like?" "How did you feel?":

I: What was education for social sustainability (ESS) in that second session like for you?
M: ESS in that second session was like clearing the air. It was like reclaiming the ground. It was like making the work clear and worthwhile.

I: How did you feel?
M: I felt calm and even loving toward Hunting now that I had worked out a road to travel and he didn't say anything—might even be listening.

The interviewer then invites M to look at the event as a phenomenon—as a lived experience—using scheduled phenomenological prompts to create a more extended phenomenological depiction of the experience using Merleau-Ponty's existential coordinates and then Crotty's sentence stems:
Phenomenological depicting: M is invited to describe the action for social sustainability as a bodily, temporal, spatial, and social experience:

> *Bodily experience:* As a bodily experience ESS for me at that time was stillness and closeness. As a bodily experience ESS for me was minimal body, only eyes and voice.
> *Time experience:* ESS at that moment as a temporal experience was my time. ESS as an experience in time is like seizing and holding the moment.
> *Spatial experience:* ESS in the second encounter with Will as a spatial experience is about stillness and closeness in open space, no walls.
> *Social experience:* ESS practice at that moment as a social experience is like holding Will with my rebuke and challenge.

Naming: Using Crotty's sentence stems, a series of sentences are completed by the participants:

> ESS in this event seems to be *taking the risk of rebuke.*
> I depict ESS practice in this event in graphic form as *like a priest giving a key sermon that had to be heard.*
> What comes to light when I focus on ESS practice in this event is *risky openness in honest challenge.*
> What is uncovered when I focus on ESS practice in this event is *do or die.*
> What unfolds for me as I dwell on ESS practice in this event is *like being caught up in the karmic netting from the previous encounter.*
> I depict counseling practice in this event in poetic terms as *like giving an invitation to come to solid ground.*

The metaphors that best convey the experience of ESS practice in this event are

> *inviting adventure of conversion;*
> *the Guru claims the working wisdom for his/her disciple.*

(3) Textual composition: distilling, drafting, and display

It is then possible to collate these sentences using a distilling process, where insights about the phenomenon can be grouped or clustered around recurrent perceptions named in the various textual representations. Again the agenda is a matter of discernment, since one eventually wants to ask how central a particular theme is to the phenomenon and whether an experience such as the social sustainability processes in counseling, for example, could retain its integrity if a particular theme were absent.

Distilling

>claiming enrichment even in loss and diminishment
>taking the risk of rebuke
>like a priest giving a key sermon that had to be heard
>risky openness in honest challenge
>do or die
>like being caught up in the karmic netting from the previous encounter
>like giving an invitation to come to solid ground
>inviting adventure of conversion
>the Guru claims the working wisdom for his/her disciple

Drafting

Themes of openness and reconciliation, enrichment, risk, and invitation are distilled and arrayed in draft form which then turns into the following reflective verse that sums up the experience.

Display

>Even as he landed that blow
>That brought my hand to his throat
>There something I could feel
>In his innocent cruelty
>
>And now I call to him in the life language
>buried in his hurt and
>now summoned by a glimmer of hope
>And underneath I hear his fear of falling further
>
>And for his eyes and ears alone,
>Run up my flag of life thanks for blessings offered,
>received and made into great life blocks of memory
>and at least some good Karma
>And call him to make his own

(4) Uptake reflection

Finally, the adult, vocational, and workplace education practitioners are invited to reflect on ways in which the portrayed educative exchange spoke to their hearts, and whether they could see ways in which they might want to promote similar inclusive and reconciliatory elements of social sustainability in their educational practice.

This holistic educational agenda needs careful reflection to see where such ideals can be integrated into what have currently become pretty functionalist educational agendas. There is no doubt in this writer's mind that integrating such big ideas into a strongly practical and functional curriculum is overdue. Hopefully some of the approaches mentioned in this chapter can at least sow the seed for a more holistic thinking in AVE programs.

Conclusion

In this chapter I examined ways in which a curriculum for social sustainability in adult and vocational education could be developed in order to attend to the fourth pillar of social sustainability and its links to the imaginal and aesthetic dimensions of human social life. Having drawn attention to the close links between ideas of social sustainability and those of social ecology, I then suggested an appropriate curriculum that might promote this highly human and moral dimension of social sustainability. This involves entering the enriching and challenging world of imaginal knowing, phenomenological inquiry, and aesthetic education and seeing ways in which these powerful reflexive tools might be applied to themes connected with social sustainability, such as inclusivity and reconciliation. I have described two pedagogic strategies. One, *reciprocal storytelling,* aims to evoke caring and reflexive dispositions from potential learners. The other, *evocative portrayal*, offers a way of inviting learners to engage with artistic work relating to the altruistic themes that underpin social sustainability. In both cases, although satisfactory outcomes can never be guaranteed, the road chosen and the pedagogic processes employed seem to be appropriate for the transformative work required in building and maintaining social sustainability.

References

Adebowale, M. (2002). Towards a socially inclusive sustainable development research agenda. In M. Eames & M. Adebowale (Eds.), *Sustainable development and social inclusion: towards an integrated approach to research* (pp. 4–16). York: Joseph Rowntree Foundation.
Armstrong, K. (2005). *A short history of myth*. Edinburgh: Canongate.
Bookchin, M. (1993). What is social ecology? In M. E. Zimmerman (Ed.), *Environmental philosophy: from animal rights to radical ecology* (pp. 354–373). Englewood Cliffs, NJ: Prentice Hall.
Bradbeer (1998). *Imagining curriculum: practical intelligence in teaching*. New York: Teachers College Press.
Coles, R. (1989). *The call of stories: teaching and the moral imagination*. Boston, MA: Houghton Mifflin.
Corbin, H. (1969). *Creative imagination in the Sufism of Ibn 'Arabi*. Princeton, NJ: Princeton University Press.
Crotty, M. (1996). Doing phenomenology. In P. Willis & B. Neville (Eds.), *Qualitative research practice in adult education* (pp. 272–282). Melbourne: David Lovell Publishing.

Frank, A. (1995). *The wounded storyteller: body, illness and ethics.* Chicago: University of Chicago Press.

Greene, M. (1995). *Releasing the imagination: essays on education, the arts and social change.* San Francisco: Jossey Bass.

Halling, S. (2005). On growing up as a premodernist. In G. Yancy & S. Hadley (Eds.), *Narrative identities: psychologists engage in self-construction*(pp. 208–227). Philadelphia: Jessica Kingsley.

Halling, S. (2008). *Intimacy, transcendence and psychology: closeness and openness in everyday life.* London: Palgrave Macmillan.

Hawkes, J. (2004). Culture and democracy. In P. Willis & P. Carden (Eds.), *Lifelong learning and the democratic imagination: re-visioning justice, freedom and community* (pp. 281–293). Flaxton, Qld: Post Pressed.

Heron, J. (1992). *Feeling and personhood: psychology in another key.* London: Sage.

Hill, S. (1999). *A sociology journal.* Richmond, NSW: University of Western Sydney.

Hillman, J. (1981). *The thought of the heart.* Dallas, TX: Spring.

McKenzie, S. (2004). *Social sustainability: towards some definitions.* Working Paper No. 27. Magill, South Australia: Hawke Research Institute, University of South Australia.

Merleau-Ponty, M. (1962). *Phenomenology of perception*, Trans. C. Smith. London: Routledge and Kegan Paul.

Pattenden, R. (2002). In bed with the lights on: the whispering of God talk in public *places. Eremos, 80*, 29–34.

Todres, L. (2007). *Embodied inquiry: phenomenological touchstones for research, psychotherapy and spirituality.* Hampshire, UK: Palgrave Macmillan.

van Manen, M. (1990). *Researching lived experience: human science for an action sensitive pedagogy.* New York: SUNY Press.

Willis, P. (2005). Re-enchantment education for democratic educators. In P. Heywood, T. McCann, B. Neville, & P. Willis (Eds.), *Towards re-enchantment: education, imagination and the getting of wisdom* (pp. 79–94). Flaxton, Qld: Post Pressed.

Chapter 4
The Historical Contribution of AVE to Social Sustainability in Australia

Roger Harris

Abstract The International Experts Meeting on technical and vocational education and training (TVET) in Bonn in October 2004 claimed that TVET was "a most effective means for society to develop its members' potentials to respond to the challenges of the future," yet "not much information and documentation on TVET for sustainable development is currently available." In this chapter I begin with the assumption that this claim is particularly applicable to the third pillar of sustainable development—social sustainability—and I set out to explore historically the contribution of AVE (defined here as embracing activities in what are now known as the VET and ACE sectors) to social sustainability in Australia. I argue that the contribution of adult and vocational education (AVE) has been largely submerged and invisible, and thus neglected, under-resourced, and under-valued. Economic interests, except for a few moments in Australia's history, have always been afforded precedence over social concerns. Nevertheless, AVE has continued to play an important role in promoting social sustainability. I outline the role played by various AVE agencies over the years, highlight several key initiatives particularly in the second half of the twentieth century, and then analyze eight main contributions to social sustainability.

Introduction

From 2005 to 2014 is the United Nations Decade of Education for Sustainable Development. The International Experts Meeting on Technical and Vocational Education and Training (TVET) in Bonn in October 2004 defined sustainable development as having three principal aspects: economic, environmental, and social. The "third pillar" was explained as follows:

> On both the global and local scale, social sustainability involves ensuring that the basic needs of all people are satisfied and that all, regardless of gender, ethnicity or geography, have an opportunity to develop and utilise their talents in ways that enable them to live happy, healthy and fulfilling lives. (UNESCO-UNEVOC, 2004b, p. 78)

R. Harris (✉)
Hawke Research Institute for Sustainable Societies, University of South Australia,
South Australia, Australia

This significant meeting proclaimed that TVET was "a most effective means for society to develop its members' potentials to respond to the challenges of the future. Schools and other institutions of the formal education system alone cannot achieve education and training for sustainable development" (UNESCO-UNEVOC, 2006, para. 5). Yet it was acknowledged that "not much information and documentation on TVET for sustainable development is currently available" (UNESCO-UNEVOC, 2006, para. 18). One would surmise, given the long and strong preoccupation with economics and the rapidly increasing fascination with and recognition of the environment, that such a conclusion is particularly pertinent to the *social* pillar. The notion of sustainable livelihoods was considered "central to social sustainability" (UNESCO-UNEVOC, 2004c, p. 4) and meaningful work was perceived to play an important role. The wide interpretation of sustainable livelihoods raised questions concerning the traditional person–job relationship that has underpinned many approaches to TVET.

This perspective of TVET has been labeled "the dominant ethos of productivism" (Anderson, 2003, p. 16), which, in giving precedence to economic interests, subordinates the needs of individual learners to those of industry and privileges work and employability over non-economic outcomes of education and training. This in turn has resulted in TVET being seen only as a "training-for-growth" and "skills-for-work" sector, to such an extent that the broader general education needed for personal autonomy, citizenship, and sustainability has been largely overlooked (UNESCO-UNEVOC, 2004b, p. 13).

In this chapter I contend that the contribution of adult and vocational education (AVE) to social sustainability has been, and continues to be, largely submerged and invisible, and thus neglected, under-resourced, and under-valued. I argue further that, despite this historical legacy, AVE nevertheless continues to play a significant role in promoting and enhancing social sustainability.

AVE is used in this chapter as a general term to embrace activities in what are known in the Australian context as the two sectors of adult and community education (ACE) and vocational education and training (VET). Both sectors are predominantly post-school (though vocational education is increasingly also offered in schools) and not university. They are difficult to define precisely. Generally however, ACE provides education and training opportunities and personal development programs for people of all ages in communities across Australia—in short, "organized adult learning in community settings" (Clemans, Hartley, & Macrae, 2003, p. 7). Through networks of providers, ACE offers a wide variety of community-based programs for adults that are often characterized as user-pays, flexible, open, and non-compulsory (for the complexity in definition, see Golding, Davies, & Volkoff 2001, pp. 39–46). VET focuses on education and training for work and is more formal and industry-led. It provides people with the skills and knowledge they require to enter or re-enter the workforce, or upgrade their skills. It is provided by public and private providers, which offer a range of nationally recognized qualifications, from certificates through to advanced diplomas. In 2006, 11.4 per cent of Australia's population aged between 15 and 64 years participated in government-funded VET, with 30.4 per cent of those aged 15 to 19 years undertaking some form of VET (NCVER, 2007a, p. 5).

A Historical Snapshot

The tale of Australian AVE over its two centuries is primarily economic, particularly considering the vocational education component; it was an instrumentalist tool for the advancement of the country's economy. In terms of Anglo-European settlement, Australia is a relatively young, small, and developing nation, and the strong economic emphasis of AVE can be both readily understood and acknowledged as critical to its nation building. Yet in the shadows behind the economic façade may be seen, albeit dimly, another edifice standing firm and also of great import to the nation and particularly to its well-being. The social contributions of AVE are well worth exploring and highlighting.

A key influence on AVE in the nineteenth century was the English educational ideal of the liberally educated person, what Whitelock famously headlined as the "great tradition" (1974, p. 12). Liberal adult education was to "assist in the maturation of the individual as an individual—not simply as a factor in the economic equation or as a political citizen, but as a Man ... more concerned with helping men *to be*, than *to be something* ..." (Grattan, 1955, quoted in Whitelock, 1974, pp. 8–9). From the vantage point of the late twentieth century, this perspective can be strongly criticized (e.g., Foley & Morris, 1995, pp. 108, 112) for being narrow and excluding many other forms of learning, particularly related to study circles, trade union and labor education, education associated with social action, and the self-education efforts of workers, women, and Indigenous Australians. This tradition could also be critiqued for focusing too heavily upon the individual and thus downplaying the communal, and for spotlighting AVE's function in personal development while neglecting its contribution to the social good and by implication social sustainability.

In the nineteenth century, there was indeed a diverse range of AVE activity that played a substantial role in promoting social sustainability. For example, public libraries, museums, galleries, botanic gardens, and zoological gardens "developed as centres of self-directed learning, providing ... opportunities to combine leisure with informal and incidental learning ... and the people with means for individual self-improvement. At the same time, they cultivated civic values and promoted the colony's economic growth" (Fennessy, 2007, pp. 3–4).

More formally, mechanics institutes and schools of arts were among the earliest AVE establishments, set up for the "education" of the working person to have a broader view of the world and to think critically on issues of the day. The first mechanics institute was established in Hobart in 1827, and by 1851 institutes were established in each of the major capitals as well as in a number of country towns (Hermann, Richardson, & Woodburne, 1976, p. 27). They dominated Australian AVE for most of the nineteenth century (Whitelock, 1974, p. 127). Foley and Morris claim that they "rapidly moved from vocational and practical to liberal and cultural education" (1995, p. 109) and control over their activities moved from the working class to the middle class. They maintain that it would be a mistake to assume these technical institutions excluded learning of a general nature. Scientific subjects were often the most popular and many people attended largely out of interest and a desire to better understand their world. Thus these institutes had more beneficial and widespread educational effects than allowed for by the "great tradition" view (Candy & Laurent, 1994).

The mechanics institutes eventually became cultural centers; their libraries and reading rooms helped to maintain and extend literacy levels, and appear to have been especially effective as a source of informal education for women (Penglase, 1988, p. 39). Originally excluded from academic secondary schools and universities, women could obtain some elements of higher education at mechanics institutes and schools of arts (Richardson, 2005, p. 229). In this way, not only did these institutions serve to educate the working and middle classes more broadly, but they also made a very important contribution to gender equity.

Moreover, adult learning was encouraged by the increasing population and wealth brought about by the gold rushes, and the mechanics institutes played an important role in distributing learning geographically into country regions. In Victoria, for example, there were three institutes by 1851, over 100 by 1870 and 600 by 1929 (Barraclough & Watt, 1994, cited in Richardson, 2005, p. 231). Classes established in 1856 and subsequently were in English, French, Latin, mathematics, physics, and chemistry. Participation in the institutes came mainly from the lower middle class (shop assistants, clerks) and middle class. The mechanics institutes were valued as agencies of social and moral improvement along with their educational function. For example, there were close links between the mechanics institutes and the temperance movement, and they were generally welcomed as "a kind of educational pesticide" (Whitelock, 1974, p. 125). They were especially popular in country towns where they quickly became all-purpose centers for books, companionship, recreation, and culture, and did much "to soothe the rawness of frontier life" (Whitelock, 1974, p. 129) in a developing country whose population was so small and geographically widely scattered.

By the later nineteenth century, the multiple roles of mechanics institutes and schools of arts—as libraries, centers of formal technical and scientific education, promoters of respectable entertainment, and havens of civilized leisure activities—had to a large extent been channeled into a number of more specific agencies (Candy & Laurent, 1994, p. 118). Many of these establishments evolved into "schools of mines" and technical colleges, at which apprenticeships, even in the traditional trades, included non-technical studies. As in Britain, the technical colleges established classes in three broad streams: occupational education (of which apprenticeship was a major part), general education, and adult education (Hermann et al., 1976, p. 28). Richardson (2005, pp. 207, 238) has noted that the speeches of philanthropists were resplendent with references to the curriculum needing to be more liberal than simply technical studies, such that many of these institutions offered art, drawing, sculpture, foreign languages, and music in the curriculum.

Another successor to the mechanics institutes and schools of arts was the Workers' Educational Association (WEA), which by 1914 had been established in all Australian states but one, and had become the principal form of adult education. The WEAs formed local classes and arranged for the universities to provide extension lectures. Very often these local classes used mechanics institute or school of arts buildings as classrooms.

Through the first half of the twentieth century, the flame of adult learning was kept flickering through the WEAs (only two now remain—in NSW and SA), the Country Women's Association, arts councils, agricultural extension departments, evening colleges, trade unions, church organizations, university extension (begun in the 1890s), and the library movement. A notable development was the Australian Army Education Service, which during World War II provided lectures, discussion groups, craft and hobby classes, concerts, publications, and an extensive library service for the army (Dymock, 2001, p. 20), all of which gave "a spectacular demonstration of how effective and popular adult education can be, given the resources and leadership" (Whitelock, 1973, p. iii). Despite its success during wartime, however, Warburton (1973, p. 198) pointed out that its centralized direction and hierarchical chain of command made it an unsatisfactory model for a democratic community.

In technical education, liberal studies became embedded after World War II in curricula, following initiatives in the United Kingdom. Bailey and Unwin labeled this trend in the United Kingdom as a "curricular and pedagogical phenomenon" which was "perceived to be in some ways a peculiar and uncharacteristic development" (2008, p. 61). This development was fuelled in practice by burgeoning student numbers in technical and commercial courses and by greater proportions being released by employers for one day a week for study, making more hours available for teaching. But it was also a reaction to the utilitarian view of post-school education, and a deliberate attempt to "widen [students'] cultural interests and help to develop their sense of social responsibility" (National Institute of Adult Education, 1955, cited in Bailey & Unwin, 2008, p. 63). In a 1956 White Paper, the Ministry of Education stated that "a place must be found in technical studies for liberal education ... We cannot afford either to fall behind in technical accomplishments or to neglect spiritual and human values" (cited in Bailey & Unwin, 2008, pp. 63–64). Such developments were echoed in Australian AVE after the war, though in both countries these studies later metamorphosed into versions of communication studies and then generic skills, and eventually succumbed to the pressures of policy desiring to tie education very closely to the demands of the economy.

Despite all of these initiatives, generally Australian AVE around this time was "a threadbare, inadequate chronically poverty-stricken affair that affected only a tiny minority of the population, ... in Sir Robert Madgwick's words, ... 'a thing of shreds and patches' ... [and] adult education was very much at the bottom of the educational pecking order" (Whitelock, 1973, p. iii). Long before the Senate inquiry of the 1990s, Wilson dubbed Australian adult education "a Cinderella-like existence in the back kitchen of education" (1973, p. 152), Nelson described it as "almost unbelievably barren" (1973, p. 164) and Bone labeled it "the sterile field" (1973, p. 170). And, postwar, adult education "remained a crazy pavement, with provision and ideas differing across each border" (Whitelock, 1973, p. vi). Allsop believed that it "urgently require[d] a fresh and fundamental reappraisal in the light of recent world thinking around the concept of integrated lifelong education" (1973, p. 185).

Fresh and Fundamental Reappraisals of AVE

There were a number of significant initiatives postwar that can be viewed as attempts to make such a "fresh and fundamental reappraisal" of AVE. Here, four are highlighted. The first landmark was the formation of the Australian Association of Adult Education in 1960. It promised a more national (and international) profile, built around a national clearinghouse, assisting overseas visitors, channeling requests for information or assistance, maintaining a national library, liaising with government and non-government departments and other bodies, and assisting members traveling overseas (Robertson, 1973, p. 163). While it may not have acted upon many of these functions in its early years, it was very successful with respect to publications and conferences (Brennan, 1988, p. 35). Hutchinson wrote in the association's journal:

> the association emerges at a time when it is impossible for intelligent men and women not to be aware that the well-being of their fellow countrymen is inextricably interwoven with the well-being of all men [sic] everywhere. (1961, p. 19)

By 1989, the organization had been renamed the Australian Association for Adult *and Community* Education (my emphasis), and in 1998 Adult Learning Australia, acknowledging that adult learning occurs almost everywhere and not simply within the ACE sector, and reflecting that the learner was the central focus of attention rather than the institutional form of delivery.

The second landmark in the history of postwar AVE was the publication of two important documents, first the Kangan (1974) report, *TAFE in Australia*, followed by the Williams (1979) report, *Education, training and employment*. The highly influential Kangan report established technical and further education (TAFE) as a distinct educational sector, and established a broader educational and social role based on the principles of access, equity, primacy of the individual learner, and the need for continuing vocational education. Arguably for the first time, the social became officially enshrined as the equal of, if not more important than, the economic. The addition of the word "further" was highly significant, for it signified an explosion of non-technical courses and the renaming of many institutions as "community" rather than technical colleges. An influential textbook (Hermann et al., 1976) published soon after the report's release claimed that it was "probably the most significant single event in the history of Australian [AVE]", as the report when implemented would "give a new look to [AVE]" and was seen as "redressing the traditional neglect from which [AVE] has suffered" (p. 225). In particular, it rejected "the manpower orientation that has plagued [AVE] in favour of an educational and social emphasis which underlines a commitment to the development of the potential of individuals within the realities of the demands of the world of work" (p. 228). Twenty years later, Schofield noted again how the Kangan report had shifted traditional notions of AVE: "the positioning of technical education as a narrow training institution responsible for providing industry with a suitably qualified workforce was challenged by the release of the Kangan report" (1994, pp. 57–60). Five years after the release of Kangan, the Williams' report, though having a wider brief than AVE and being more closely linked with labor market issues, reiterated some of Kangan's themes.

In particular, it considered how postsecondary education related to individual needs, and recommended strategies for broadening access to TAFE and for making greater provision for pre-employment training.

The third landmark was the formation of the TAFE National Centre for Research and Development in 1981. The idea for this organization was first raised in the Kangan report (1974), and again in the Williams report (1979). While it was initially to be a center researching the role of technology in vocational education (TAFE National Centre, 1982), the TAFE National Centre for Research and Development quickly broadened its ambit to incorporate a wide range of research topics. Later changing its name to the National Centre for Vocational Education Research, the organization has continued to fulfill an excellent role in furnishing AVE with a much-needed research base, helping to lift the status and visibility of AVE research and promoting Australian VET research via an internationally renowned electronic database (VOCED).

The fourth significant landmark for Australian AVE was the publication of the two so-called "Cinderella" reports in the 1990s. The first report, *Come in Cinderella* (Aulich, 1991), was widely recognized at the time as a watershed in the development of adult and community education. It officially recognized ACE as "the fourth sector" in contrast, structurally and operationally, to the more familiar schools, universities, and VET sectors. This report represented, arguably for the first time, official government acknowledgement of the adult and community education sector as distinctive and valuable, pursuing a commitment to lifelong learning and the creation of a learning society through a range of educational programs. The second report, *Beyond Cinderella* (Crowley, 1997), reiterated and reinforced the messages of the first report, in recognition that there was still much to be achieved in embedding notions of lifelong learning into policy and securing adequate recognition and funding.

Policy Reform in AVE

The challenging philosophy within these various reports, however, was relatively short-lived, if not so much in ideal, then certainly in policy. The policy and funding climate that emerged around the late 1980s and early 1990s privileged the development of vocational training. Indeed, the training reform agenda that commenced in the late 1980s was "more fundamental and significant than at any other time in the history of [AVE], where the needs of the learner came to be subsumed by industrial and economic priorities" (Comyn, 2005, p. 24). By the close of the twentieth century, Ferrier and Anderson could conclude that there was "considerable evidence to suggest that [social goals] have lost ground to economic goals" (1998, p. 1), despite Seddon's (1998, p. 244) warning that the neglect of the former ultimately threatens the achievement of the latter. The key elements of this shift were the rise of economic rationalism, development of an open training market, changes to youth labor markets, and the operation of federalism within Australia's education system (Comyn, 2005). Also contributing was the rise of new vocationalism

(Chappell, 2002), which emphasized the needs of industry and economic growth through encouraging competition, increasing choice, and raising standards by market competition. These elements drove a number of initiatives that collectively reflected the policy pendulum swing back in favor of economic imperatives.

This swing was mirrored in the names of government agencies. The word "employment" was given first priority when, in 1987, education was formally subsumed within a national "Department of Employment, Education and Training" and its partner the "National Board of Employment, Education and Training." Three years later in 1990, the National Training Board was formed with its key emphasis on "competencies." These competencies became the foundation for all national curricula, and then from the mid-1990s for training packages based on national competency standards (meaning what is required in order to perform in the actual workplace to industry-agreed standards). And in 1992 the Australian National Training Authority was established with its "narrow concept of vocational education" (claimed by Senators Carr, Denman, Forshaw, & Bell in the Australian Senate, 1995, p. 74). The very strong emphasis was now on economic imperatives in the face of national skill shortages, increasing global competition, and the desire to lift productivity.

TAFE, after its idealistic beginning from the Kangan report and its echo in the Williams report, gradually retreated under the pressures of economic rationalism back into the shell of technical training, justified as its core business. Even the colleges of advanced education, which were institutions of higher education at that time in Australia, progressively began to dismantle or at least amalgamate their liberal studies departments. The broader meanings of educational and economic inequality were steadily eroded in equity policy. The national training reform brought an industry-driven approach that led the state systems to abandon the community college model and its charter to meet local and regional needs (McIntyre, 2000, p. 31). Institutions progressively shed their community college tags, returning to or becoming TAFE colleges/institutes, and some in fact seized the opportunity to rebadge as institutes of technology. Recent government actions concerned with skills shortages (meaning traditional male trades), the establishment of federally funded Australian Technical Colleges specifically for training in selected trade areas, incentives of free toolboxes for apprentices, and the shortening of the time taken to complete apprenticeships can all be construed as expressions of the reassertion of the economic over the social.

The Contribution of AVE to Social Sustainability

Through these ebbs and flows in education and training reform in AVE's history, is it possible to delineate the contribution of AVE to social sustainability? Hanna wrote in 1965:

> Adult Education is regarded as a marginal activity stuck on to our education system somewhere between our leaving primary school and our going senile; we have to run it with

meagre budgets, leftover facilities and other people's spare time. British adult education from which our ideas and systems derive was substantially a lower class, self-help movement meant to make up for the lack or deficiencies of primary education, and later of secondary and technical education systems ... adult education has not achieved a recognised standing in this country. (p. 3)

With regard to technical education, a similarly low profile was highlighted by Partridge in 1968 in the following manner:

Technical education has been strangely neglected in public and popular thinking ... for many Australians the technical colleges and schools have not really belonged to the educational system at all but have been devoted to a necessary but lower form of activity. It is a rather strange situation ... [its colleges] have not enjoyed anything like the prestige of the universities ... they have not been nearly so well provided for ... paradoxical in a country often accused of being unusually attached to utilitarian or economic values ... high schools and universities have enjoyed the greatest social prestige and been most carefully tended; as a result ... the provision of technical education has not kept pace with other types of education. (pp. 145–147)

It could be argued that not much has changed over the past four decades! Government funding and certainly public perception have always lurched heavily in the direction of schools and universities. Philanthropy has also always been directed more toward these mainstream sectors than to AVE, with a few notable exceptions mainly in Victoria where a number of technical institutions were established by and/or have worn the names of their benefactors, such as William Angliss, George and Ethel Swinburne, Emily McPherson, Francis Ormond, Hugh McKay and David Beazley (Richardson, 2005, p. 3). One component of AVE—vocational education and training (VET)—has continually been perceived by the public as the path from school for the less academic, where one can emphasize the use of hands over heads and hearts. The other component of AVE—adult and community education (ACE)— has been variously perceived as the remedial sector, "Cinderella at the Education Ball," and the fourth sector, perhaps where one can emphasize the use of hearts over heads and hands. The critical question is: do these perceptions of diminished status vis-à-vis schools and universities also mean a diminished contribution to social sustainability?

A robust case can indeed be constructed for a crucial role for AVE in social sustainability. For example, the Australian Council of Deans of Education has recently proclaimed that it "has consistently highlighted the centrality of vocational education and training (VET) to national prosperity and *social cohesion*" (2006, p. 1, my emphasis). To highlight the theme of social cohesion, it is worth ruminating over the following questions: What would society be like with only schools and universities? What would the 70 per cent who do not proceed from one to the other do? From whence would the technician strata of society, the middle level between the unskilled or semi-skilled and the professional, come (a problem that many other countries have faced and are facing)?

So what are some of these contributions? The value-adding effects of AVE are often very difficult to disentangle from other factors, such as structural and employment barriers in society. They are also notoriously difficult to evidence, as conventional measures of attainment and progression are often less relevant or not applicable. However, the acknowledgment of different frameworks for measurement, such as

> longer time scales, the recognition of "pathways" ... and enrichment of lives of individuals, families or communities ... has allowed the identification of a wider set of important and often unexpected social, economic, community and national outcomes and contributions through [AVE]. (Golding et al., 2001, pp. 10, 95)

(a) **AVE caters for a very diverse range of people** at the post-compulsory levels of education. It provides education and training for (a) larger numbers and (b) a wider range of learners than universities. As Murray-Smith once claimed, it "has usually been voluntary, part-time and in many ways a more democratic stream of education than the others" (1971, pp. 313–314). Adult and community education in particular has always been highly decentralized and local, its openness and non-selectiveness enabling it "to be accessed by a wide range of individuals [such that] its cumulative or aggregate impact on communities is therefore potentially very significant" (Golding et al., 2001, p. 11).

In accommodating such learner diversity, AVE has had and is continuing to have a critical role as the *second-chance* sector in providing opportunities to overcome skill deficiencies and remedy shortcomings in previous formal education and training. This label has recently been tested for the public VET system, defined as all activity delivered by TAFE institutes, other government providers, and community education providers, as well as publicly funded activity delivered by private providers (Karmel & Woods, 2008, p. 10), and found to be fully justified. According to Karmel and Woods, the proportion of VET learners who can be categorized as second chance is "very substantial": 41 per cent in 2004 (2008, p. 10). So, too, is the proportion of the eligible second-chance population that undertakes VET. It is estimated that approximately half of early school-leavers (55% of males, 51% of females) access VET by the age of 24 years (p. 16), and that the "overwhelming majority" (82% of males, 97% of females) of eligible adults participates in second-chance VET at some stage between the ages of 25 and 49 years (p. 18). The challenge appears to lie, however, in increasing the rate of completion of qualifications, particularly those above the level of certificate II (p. 8).

(b) **AVE contributes to obtaining jobs and furthering careers**. It provides technical expertise, which contributes to "national prosperity" (ACDE, 2006. p. 1) and, by implication, promotes the well-being of individuals and families and thus social harmony. Work is one "source and measure of social worth" (UNESCO-UNEVOC, 2004a, p. 3) and provides income, which promotes sustainable livelihoods through greater economic sufficiency. AVE often takes place in workplaces, thus providing learning opportunities for newly recruited employees such as apprentices and trainees, and also opportunities for existing workers to have their skills assessed and formally recognized within a national qualifications framework. Survey evidence indicates a high level of course satisfaction on the part of learners in AVE (Golding et al., 2001, pp. 10, 112; NCVER, 2007b, p. 3).

4 The Historical Contribution of AVE to Social Sustainability in Australia 55

(c) **AVE offers learning for individuals that can enhance self-esteem**, sense of well-being, empowerment, happiness/satisfaction, self-confidence, and self-worth, which can lead to not only more dignified lives as citizens (for example, through enhancing social skills) but also increased employment chances (for example, through developing interview-responding skills, curricula vitae and teamwork skills).

(d) **AVE offers alternative ways in which learning might be accessed and experienced** and thus has a significant outreach to those groups that are under-represented or under-serviced by mainstream providers. It can change dispositions toward learning, provide a sense of purpose and promote a sense of achievement through offering small steps toward "success." It can develop learning skills, literacy and numeracy, employability skills, English as a second language, information technology skills, working with others, negotiation skills, and tolerance. All of these enhance self-confidence and increase the likelihood of bonding into society, developing as a responsible citizen, and increasing the desire to contribute to society. Adult and community education in particular can provide a "softer" introduction to learning than that offered within mainstream education, and this is very helpful to those who have limited education, have been out of learning for some time or have had previous unhappy learning experiences (Saunders, 2001). Adult and community organizations are usually able to provide greater flexibility in venues, times, delivery modes, and learning climates. Their generally smaller size and their localized focus enable them to customize offerings to match the needs of local communities and companies.

One important alternative pathway for learning is via traineeships, which are similar to apprenticeships but taken over shorter periods. A traineeship involves paid employment under an appropriate industrial arrangement, a training contract registered with the relevant state department of education and training, and training that leads to a nationally recognized qualification. There are over 600 traineeship vocations introduced to provide employment and training opportunities in a range of areas, including multimedia, information technology, sport and recreation, hospitality, retail, and primary industries. Developed from the mid-1980s, they have dramatically increased the proportion of women and girls in training, as well as providing learning opportunities for many members of equity groups, as new areas of training have opened up in industries that hitherto had not had any tradition of training.

(e) **AVE contributes to social inclusion** by providing opportunities for employment and access to further learning to so-called "equity groups" (in Australia, these are defined as people from low socioeconomic backgrounds; people from rural or isolated areas; people with a disability; people from non-English-speaking backgrounds; women, especially in non-traditional areas of study; and Indigenous people). Currently there are a greater number of women than men taking advantage of these educational opportunities. AVE promotes opportunities for new arrivals, in offering all types of arrangements for developing or improving English language capability, which is so important in a multicultural society like Australia. AVE also provides learning opportunities for older citizens through activities conducted by the University of the Third Age and the Workers' Educational Association, as well as through book clubs and reading networks, all helping to keep minds active and facilitating social interaction. AVE also contributes to geographical access and equity, with centers very widely scattered across the nation, offering education and training and therefore opportunities for employment to rural and remote people.

AVE indeed has had a long history of providing "working-class pathways," as the mechanics institutes, schools of arts, schools of mines, trade schools, business colleges, and technical colleges have always fulfilled this social equity role. A recent study by Foley (2007) found that there was an over-representation of students from low socioeconomic areas in the public VET sector in Australia. According to Foley (2007), VET participation was greatest in low socioeconomic areas (12.7 students per 100 population), a figure significantly higher than the national participation rate (10.8%). In contrast, high socioeconomic status areas recorded a significantly lower participation rate of 8.7 per cent (p. 8). Such over-representation of students from low socioeconomic areas is partly due to the high participation of students from regional areas. Students from remote (16.4%) and rural (13.8%) regions, in comparison with those from non-capital metropolitan areas (10.6%) and capital cities (9.5%), have significantly greater VET participation (p. 8).

(f) **AVE contributes to social and cultural capital** in providing opportunities to further leisure and recreational interests and pastimes (for example, through WEA courses and field activities, or through community and neighborhood centers). In so doing, AVE provides spaces and opportunities for participants to form networks with others, to develop skills of working together, to foster "social literacy," and to enhance feelings of connectedness to community. Due to its close links with communities, AVE is sensitive to small-scale demand that arises from local needs, and thus plays a significant role in providing access and thereby contributing to the development of social capital in communities (Butler & Lawrence, 1996; Falk, Golding, & Balatti, 2000). Clemans et al. have highlighted the community development role that ACE plays through fostering social capital, the "cement of society's good will ... which provides the social infrastructure support for our lives as we move about in a web of elastic networks connecting home, work, learning, leisure, and public life" (2003, p. 33). Likewise, the contributions of VET to social capital in communities have been well analyzed by Kearns (2004).

(g) **AVE offers a complementary pathway through tertiary education**, thereby providing the opportunity for "reverse swing": far more people in Australia with a university education move to AVE than from AVE to university (though the latter may be the common perception, especially with strong policy visibility through articulation arrangements). People move to the vocational education sector, for example, to gain a practical edge to their broad base from university, to help in changing their career, to upgrade with new skills and knowledge, and to develop a second string to their occupational bow (Harris, Sumner, & Rainey, 2005; Harris, Rainey, & Sumner, 2006).

Furthermore, AVE is often a leader in using innovative methodologies, for instance study circles, situated learning in workplaces, non-formal learning, one-to-one coaching, person-centered facilitation, experiential learning, cooperative learning, and e-learning. Its commitment to learner-centered practices through its staff facilitation, program development and management practices offers an environment and orientation that is attractive to learners, especially those for whom previous schooling has been off-putting, and provides an alternative to more bureaucratized settings of formal education institutions.

(h) **AVE promotes active citizenship**. It does this through fostering critical thinking and discussion (via seminars, courses, study circles, and public activities) on significant socio-political issues such as reconciliation, peace, land care, participatory decision making, cross-cultural education, respect for cultural diversity, worker empowerment, and similar non-formal activities that are not normally taken up by other agencies, including educational ones.

Other research has traced outcomes from AVE including: making a contribution to learning cultures within communities; improving learning skills; transforming openness to learning and community involvement; building connections to communities; and improving social and economic well-being of families, communities, and regions (NCVER, 1999; Falk et al., 2000; Golding et al., 2001; Harris and Simons, 2003; Clemans et al., 2003).

All this is not to say that there is no room for improvement! There remains much work to be done in AVE if the definition of social sustainability in the first section of this chapter is to be realized. From the UNESCO International Experts Meeting of 2004 came suggestions for action in education for sustainable development, including enhancing values as well as cognitive and skill education, emphasizing "education of the heart" by putting action at the center of TVET education, and reviewing and evaluating curricula and learning materials on learning for work, citizenship, and sustainability. At the very top, the United Nations recognizes that

> Education is the primary agent of transformation towards sustainable development, increasing people's capacities to transform their visions for society into reality ... The international community now strongly believes that we need to foster—through education—the values, behaviour and lifestyles required for a sustainable future ... Building the capacity for such futures-oriented thinking is a key task of education. (UNESCO, 2008, para. 4)

The task of building such capacity is just as important at the local level as it is at the top level.

Conclusion

This chapter has explored the historical contribution of AVE to social sustainability in Australia. AVE has received attention at various times, most notably following the major reports and reforms outlined above, but the predominance of productivity rhetoric has tended to dampen enthusiasm and respect for educational endeavors that do not readily appear to contribute to the national economy.

While the vocational component (VET) of AVE does *prima facie* retain some favor and governmental patronage for its visible contribution to the skills base, its major effort lies at the lower levels of the qualifications spectrum and its overall status remains low, as it has historically been, in public perception. This is gradually being acknowledged, and there are now fervent and frequent cries for the higher order vocational qualifications to lift the skill base of the nation, seen to be of the utmost importance given the ageing of the present working population and impending skill shortages in critical areas of the economy.

The adult and community component of AVE, however, remains relatively submerged and not particularly in favor with governments. Despite the recognition of social inclusion in the political landscape, reflected for example in the recent establishment of a social inclusion unit in the federal structure (albeit separated from education), its contribution remains largely invisible. First, its enabling and bridging functions go relatively unnoticed when it is completed qualifications and accredited programs that are officially "counted" in national statistics and on the political agenda for funding. Second, its lower status brought about by its concern for the under-privileged and disadvantaged, and its provision therefore of lower level qualifications to cater for these populations, counts against it in the cutting of government funding cakes. Third, it lacks a solid research base to be able to compete effectively in a competitive tendering and evidence-based environment. And fourth, its diverse and disparate character, so often considered a strength in the local arena, works against it in the political arena when it cannot so readily be defined or defended as the more formal sectors of school and university.

The VET and ACE sectors—considered together as AVE in this chapter—have contributed to social sustainability in various ways throughout Australia's history. These contributions have been and continue to be crucial. However, such contributions still remain largely submerged and invisible, and therefore neglected, under-resourced, and under-valued.

References

Allsop, J. (1973). The continuing education of women. In D. Whitelock (Ed.), *The vision splendid: adult education in Australia* (pp. 183–185). Adelaide: University of Adelaide.

Anderson, D. (2003). VET and ecologism: charting the terrain. In J. Searle, I. Yashin-Shaw, & R. Roebuck (Eds), *Enriching learning cultures* (pp. 16–23). Brisbane: Australian Academic Press.

Aulich, T. G. (Chair), Senate Standing Committee on Employment, Education and Training (1991). *Come in Cinderella: the emergence of adult and community education*. Canberra: Commonwealth of Australia.

Australian Council of Deans of Education (2006). *ACDE submission to the review of the National Centre for Vocational Education Research Ltd*. Canberra: Australian Council of Deans of Education.

Australian Senate, Employment, Education and Training References Committee (1995). *Report of the inquiry into the ANTA*. Canberra: Australian Government Publishing Service.

Bailey, B., & Unwin, L. (2008). Fostering "habits of reflection, independent study and free inquiry": an analysis of the short-lived phenomenon of general/liberal studies in English vocational education and training. *Journal of Vocational Education and Training*, 60(1), 61–74.

Bone, M. H. (1973). Comments by a state adult educator. In D. Whitelock (Ed.), *The vision splendid: adult education in Australia* (pp. 170–173). Adelaide: University of Adelaide.

Brennan, B. (1988). A history of the AAAE: the first decade. *Australian Journal of Adult Education*, 28(2), 31–38.

Butler, E., & Lawrence, K. (1996). *Access and equity within vocational education and training for people in rural and remote Australia: summary paper*. Adelaide: Techsearch Business Service.

Candy, P., & Laurent, J. (1994). *Pioneering culture: mechanics institutes and schools of arts in Australia*. Adelaide: Auslib Press.

Chappell, C. (2002). Researching the pedagogies of the new vocationalism. In J. Searle & R. Roebuck (Eds), *Envisioning practice—implementing change* (pp. 193–199). Brisbane: Australian Academic Press.

Clemans, A., Hartley, R., & Macrae, H. (2003). *ACE outcomes*. Adelaide: National Centre for Vocational Education Research.

Comyn, P. (2005). *The rise and fall of the key competencies*. PhD thesis, University of Technology Sydney, Sydney.

Crowley, R. (Chair), Senate Employment, Workplace Relations, Small Business and Education Committee (1997). *Beyond Cinderella—towards a learning society: inquiry into the developments in adult and community education since 1991*. Canberra: Commonwealth of Australia.

Dymock, D. (2001). *"A special and distinctive role" in adult education, WEA, Sydney, 1953–2000*. Crows Nest, New South Wales: Allen & Unwin.

Falk, I., Golding, B., & Balatti, J. (2000). *Building communities: ACE, lifelong learning and social capital: an anthology of word portraits reporting research conducted for the Adult, Community and Further Education Board*. Melbourne: Adult, Community and Further Education.

Fennessy, K. (2007). *A people learning: colonial Victorians and their public museums, 1860–1880*. North Melbourne: Australian Scholarly Publishing.

Ferrier, F., & Anderson, D. (1998). Introduction. In F. Ferrier & D. Anderson (Eds), *Different drums, one beat? Economic and social goals in education and training* (pp. 1–6). Adelaide: National Centre for Vocational Education Research.

Foley, G., & Morris, R. (1995). The history and political economy of Australian adult education. In G. Foley (Ed.), *Understanding adult education and training* (pp. 108–120). St Leonards, New South Wales: Allen & Unwin.

Foley, P. (2007). *The socio-economic status of vocational education and training students in Australia*. Adelaide: National Centre for Vocational Education Research.

Golding, B., Davies, M., & Volkoff, V. (2001). *A consolidation of ACE research 1990–2000: review of research*. Adelaide: National Centre for Vocational Education Research.

Hanna, I. (1965). The adult student and language. *Australian Journal of Adult Education*, 5(2), 3–9.

Harris, R., Rainey, L., & Sumner, R. (2006). *Crazy paving or stepping stones? Learning pathways within and between VET and higher education*. Adelaide: National Centre for Vocational Education Research.

Harris, R., & Simons, M. (2003). *The community sector and skill formation*. Paper No. 10, written for SA Skills for the Future Inquiry. Adelaide: Government of South Australia.

Harris, R., Sumner, R., & Rainey, L. (2005). *Student traffic: two-way movement between vocational education and training and higher education*. Adelaide: National Centre for Vocational Education Research.

Hermann, G. D., Richardson, E., & Woodburne, G. J. (1976). *Trade and technician education: principles and issues*. Stanmore, New South Wales: Cassell.

Hutchinson, E. M. (1961). The international importance of a national association. *Australian Journal of Adult Education*, 1(1), 12–19.

Kangan, M (Chair), Australian Committee on Technical and Further Education (1974). *TAFE in Australia: report on needs in technical and further education*. Canberra: Australian Government Publishing Service.

Karmel, T., & Woods, D. (2008). *Second-chance vocational education and training*. Adelaide: National Centre for Vocational Education Research.

Kearns, P. (2004). *VET and social capital: a paper on the contribution of the VET sector to social capital in communities*. Adelaide: National Centre for Vocational Education Research.

McIntyre, J. (2000). Equity and local participation in VET: policy critique and research directions. *Australian and New Zealand Journal of Vocational Education Research*, 8(1), 31–52.

Murray-Smith, S. (1971). *A history of technical education in Australia*. PhD thesis, University of Melbourne, Melbourne.

National Centre for Vocational Education Research (NCVER) (1999). *Overview of Australian personal enrichment education and training programs 1997*. Adelaide: National Centre for Vocational Education Research.

National Centre for Vocational Education Research (NCVER) (2007a). *Australian vocational education and training statistics: students and courses 2006: Summary*. Adelaide: National Centre for Vocational Education Research.

National Centre for Vocational Education Research (NCVER) (2007b). *Australian vocational education and training statistics: student outcomes*. Adelaide: National Centre for Vocational Education Research.

Nelson, A. J. A. (1973). The role of the universities. In D. Whitelock (Ed.), *The vision splendid: adult education in Australia* (pp. 164–169). Adelaide: University of Adelaide.

Partridge, P. H. (1968). *Society, schools and progress in Australia*. Oxford: Pergamon Press.

Penglase, B. (1988). Hunter Valley readers and adult education in the nineteenth century. *Australian Journal of Adult Education*, 28(2), 9–42.

Richardson, E. (2005). *Philanthropy and the provision of technical education in Victoria, 1860–1940*. PhD thesis, University of Technology Sydney, Sydney.

Robertson, D. S. (1973). A national adult education association. In D. Whitelock (Ed.), *The vision splendid: adult education in Australia* (pp. 162–163). Adelaide: University of Adelaide.

Saunders, J. (2001). ACE VET linkages: provider, student and industry views. Paper presented at the 4th Australian VET Research Association Annual Conference, Research to Reality: Putting VET Research to Work, Adelaide, March. www.avetra.org.au/2001%20conference%20pages/PAPERS%202001/J%20Saunders.pdf. Accessed 5 February 2003.

Schofield, K. (1994). The clash of the Titans. In P. Kearns & W. Hall (Eds), *Kangan: 20 years on* (pp. 57–77). Adelaide: National Centre for Vocational Education Research.

Seddon, T. (1998). Different drums, different drummers: but whose beat is authorized? In F. Ferrier & D. Anderson (Eds), *Different drums, one beat?* (pp. 240–244). Adelaide: National Centre for Vocational Education Research.

TAFE National Centre for Research and Development (1982). *First annual report: 1981–1982*. Payneham, South Australia: TAFE National Centre for Research and Development.

United Nations Educational, Scientific and Cultural Organization (UNESCO) (2008). *Education for sustainable development: quality education*. http://portal.unesco.org/education/en/ev.php-URL_ID=27542&URL_DO=DO_TOPIC&URL_SECTION=201.html. Accessed 30 March 2008.

UNESCO-UNEVOC International Centre for Technical and Vocational Education and Training (2004a). From productivism to ecologism. *UNESCO-UNEVOC Bulletin*, 9, 1–16.

UNESCO-UNEVOC International Centre for Technical and Vocational Education and Training (2004b). *Orienting technical and vocational education and training (TVET) for sustainable development: a discussion paper*. Prepared for the UNESCO International Experts Meeting, Bonn, 25–28 October.

UNESCO-UNEVOC International Centre for Technical and Vocational Education and Training (2004c). Technical and vocational education and training and the "triple bottom line" of sustainable development. *Supplement 4 to the UNESCO-UNEVOC Bulletin*, 9, 1–6.

UNESCO-UNEVOC International Centre for Technical and Vocational Education and Training (2006). *Learning for work, citizenship and sustainability*. http://portal.unesco.org/education/en/ ev.php-URL_ID=30498&URL_DO=DO_PRINTPAGE&URL_SECTION=201.html. Accessed 30 March 2006.

Warburton, J. W. (1973). The Duncan Report: thirty years after. In D. Whitelock (Ed.), *The vision splendid: adult education in Australia* (pp. 198–203). Adelaide: University of Adelaide.

Whitelock, D. (ed.) (1973). *The vision splendid: adult education in Australia. W. G. K. Duncan's 1944 report with commentaries*. Adelaide: University of Adelaide.

Whitelock, D. (1974). *The great tradition: a history of adult education in Australia*. St Lucia, Queensland: University of Queensland Press.

Williams, B. R. (Chair), Committee of Inquiry into Education and Training (1979). *Education, training and employment: report of the Committee of Inquiry into Education and Training*. Canberra: Australian Government Publishing Service.

Wilson, L. (1973). Cinderella. In D. Whitelock (Ed.), *The vision splendid: adult education in Australia* (pp. 152–155). Adelaide: University of Adelaide.

Chapter 5
The Language of Longing: Rationality, Morality, and Experience in Education for Sustainability

Aidan Davison

Abstract The idea of sustainability has become indispensable to a wide and growing array of discourses about positive social futures. Yet this idea is essentially contested and inherently ambivalent. Especially unclear is the relationship between facts and values in narratives of sustainability. Presented as the handmaiden of sustainability since its first steps on the international stage, education has been delegated the task of clarifying this relationship and of aligning ethical aspirations and pragmatic objectives. Emerging agendas of education for sustainable development, in particular, have presented sustainability as a predetermined theoretical end to be reached through the use of neutral practical means. Such instrumentalist agendas have shown little interest in the modern history of education for unsustainability. In contrast, in this chapter I recast education for sustainability as an agenda for the reinvigoration of skills of practical moral reasoning. Such reasoning understands the relationship between ends and means dialectically and sheds light on the interaction of unsustainable realities and sustainability ideals. I suggest that the educational value of sustainability talk lies in its ability to bring education itself into question, and I explore how education for sustainability can better accommodate difference, uncertainty, and ambiguity.

The Introduction of Sustainability

Sustainability is a term whose birth and first forty years have taken place in the glare of international politics. The conception of this term was, of course, far from immaculate. It has general western antecedence in the Latin *sustinére*, from which is derived the English verb "to sustain," and particular heritage in the centuries-old concept of sustained yield found in European traditions of forest and fishery management (Glacken, 1967; Worster, 1993). The contemporary utility, conceptual freight, and grammatical contrivance of the word "sustainability" are nonetheless novel. It has given voice to a peculiarly post-Second World War fall from innocence.

A. Davison (✉)
University of Tasmania, Hobart, Tasmania, Australia

For, despite their overtly positive intent, discussions about sustainability derive their trajectory and their force from historically specific anxieties about unsustainability. That pre-modern indigenous cultures apparently lacked any comparable term yet are now often lauded as examples of sustainability is a useful reminder that language more often betrays longing than it confirms achievement.

Scientists, economists, engineers, and planners have led the way in pursuit of sustainability, in the form of techno-economic agendas for sustainable development. The defining characteristic of these agendas, according to their proponents, is thorough integration of socio-cultural, economic, and environmental objectives. Yet those forging a techno-economic path toward sustainability have also consistently presented sustainability as a personally and collectively transformative ideal, one whose ultimate meanings are ethical, spiritual, and metaphysical (Davison, 2001). Sustainability constitutes a secular normative language for making sense of mortality and morality through narratives of a global human community occupying a finite and fragile planetary home. Animated by fear of a future both endangered and dangerous, narratives of sustainability tell of longing for a future made secure by human stewardship of the earth that sustains them and by fair dealing within the human community.

The relationship between high-tech fixes and ethical awakening, between science and politics, between hegemonic and transformative forces, has always been unclear in narratives of sustainability. The opening page of the United Nations' (UN) manifesto for sustainable development, the 1987 Brundtland Report, *Our common future*, suggests that "our cultural and spiritual heritages can reinforce our economic interests and survival imperatives" (WCED, 1987, p. 1). The report goes on to detail an agenda for directing technological innovation, economic growth, and institutional reform toward sustainability. In the final chapter, however, the focus abruptly returns to normative concerns with the authors' proposition that "[w]e have tried to show how human survival and well-being could depend on success in elevating sustainable development to a global ethic" (WCED, 1987, p. 308).

Much of the challenge of uniting techno-economic and ethical approaches to sustainability has fallen to education. Presented as the handmaiden of sustainability since its first steps on the international stage, education has been delegated prime responsibility for raising awareness, shifting attitudes, and changing voluntary behavior, and in contexts spanning private life, school life, vocational life, economic life, social life, and cultural life. Present understandings of how education can best serve the goal of sustainable development have, in part, grown out of earlier efforts in the field of environmental education to link practical problems, global perspectives, and ethical aspirations. The UN Educational, Scientific and Cultural Organization's 1975 Belgrade Charter for Environmental Education, for instance, presented education as a tool for "building" a new "personal and individualised global ethic" of planetary care (UNESCO, 1975, p. 2). The 1980 World Conservation Strategy of the International Union for the Conservation of Nature, which brought the concept of sustainable development onto the international stage, similarly linked education to ethics:

5 The Language of Longing

> A new ethic, embracing plants and animals as well as people is required for human societies to live in harmony with the natural world on which they depend for survival and well-being. The long-term task of environmental education is to foster or reinforce attitudes and behaviours compatible with this new ethic. (IUCN/UNEP/WWF, 1980, sect. 13)

By the early 1990s, however, under the influence of the Brundtland Report, it was widely recognized that environmental education provided far too narrow a platform on which to rest educational agendas for a new global ethic of sustainable development. An ethic professed to unite social justice with care for the earth, social sustainability with environmental sustainability, necessarily called for education capable of integrating many different types of knowledge. Such integration is no trivial matter. It challenges not just the existing division of educational labor into the physical sciences, social sciences, and the arts, but also the founding modern western metaphysics that divides the world into nature and culture, objects and subjects. The 1992 UN Earth Summit action plan, Agenda 21, articulated the resulting challenge for education from sustainability in this way:

> Both formal and non-formal education are indispensable to changing people's attitudes so that they have the capacity to assess and address their sustainable development concerns. It is also critical for achieving environmental and ethical awareness, values and attitudes, skills and behaviour consistent with sustainable development and for effective public participation in decision-making. To be effective, environment and development education should deal with the dynamics of both the physical/biological and socio-economic environment and human (which may include spiritual) development, [and] should be integrated in all disciplines. (UNCED, 1992, para. 36.3)

To education for sustainable development (ESD), as it is now branded by the UN, has thus fallen the task of integrating description with prescription. ESD is expected not just to increase scientific literacy about earth systems, but to cultivate respect and activate stewardship for the living earth. ESD is charged not simply with disseminating knowledge about the sources of poverty, inequality, and conflict, but with advancing a universal human franchise and the unalienable human rights flowing from it. ESD is required not only to raise awareness about long-term consequences of present actions, but to extend ethical horizons to encompass unborn generations.

In this chapter, I work toward a different account of the relationship between descriptive and normative tasks in education for sustainability than that found in Agenda 21 and the many national and regional ESD programs currently implemented under the auspices of the first UN Decade of Education for Sustainable Development. My account works up from basic propositions about the nature of education, as well as from basic propositions about the nature of sustainability, to challenge instrumentalist assumptions about the relation of means and ends in education for sustainability. I first sketch out the postwar history of sustainability discourse, so as to clarify some common misconceptions, before offering a critical account of the relationship between knowledge, value, and action in agendas for ESD. I then embark on an alternative journey of discovery toward education for sustainability. Steering clear of universal prescriptions and aiming toward possibilities that attend the inevitable ambiguity and ambivalence of the quest for sustainability, I place my trust in the educational possibilities of practical rather than instrumental reason.

Conceiving Sustainability

Any presumption that the parentage of the idea of sustainability is environmentalist and that it rose up from the grassroots to hold the floor of the UN General Assembly is misleading, on both counts. Early postwar environmental movements focused on the need to set limits to human enterprise (including population growth) rather than on the qualities of human development itself. Formed almost exclusively out of the urban middle classes of affluent western societies, the most prominent of these movements focused on the loss of a romantic past rather than on the design of better futures, championing the values of what was thought to lie beyond the limits of modern humanity and its technology; chiefly, the values of nature, wilderness, and tradition (Davison, 2001). It was only later that these movements embraced sustainability as a way of articulating the social values conducive to their accounts of the values of nature and of history.

The gestation of the present preoccupation with sustainability in fact took place within the postwar project of global development—a project of resurrection in the aftermath of global warfare and western colonialism famously summed up by Harry Truman in his 1949 declaration that "greater production is the key to prosperity and peace" (Rist, 2002, pp. 71–72). Not for nothing did the UN launch its first Development Decade in 1961 with the claim that development is "progress toward self-sustaining growth of the economy" (UNDP, cited in Weiss, Forsythe, & Coate 1994, p. 184). From these beginnings, the trajectory of discourse about sustainability has been downwards from the new planetary consciousness being shaped by universalizing discourses of science, the quasi-science of economics, and the globalizing action of technology. In any photograph album of the life and times of sustainability, the Apollo images of earth from space, a product of the super-powered space race of the 1960s, deserve to be on the first page.

The UN's Brundtland Report, Earth Summit, and 2002 World Summit on Sustainable Development mark crucial stages in growing reliance on sustainability as a framework for synthesizing socio-cultural, economic, and environmental understandings of social development. Since the early 1980s, ideas of sustainability have spread far and wide, propelled by mounting evidence that the postwar resurrection of progress through production was having paradoxical results. This includes evidence, for example, that although Truman's vision of greater production was realized, with the world economy growing sevenfold in the second half of the twentieth century, his expectation of prosperity for all was not, with the gap between the wealth of the richest 20 per cent and the poorest 20 per cent also increasing in this period, reaching a ratio of 74 to 1 by 1997 (UNEP, 2002, p. 35). This is evidence, in effect, that the paradox of loss in gain so characteristic of the modern history of science, technology, economics, and education had, if anything, escalated to new heights.

5 The Language of Longing

This is not to say that the increased volume of sustainability talk reflects growing agreement about the causes of and cures for unsustainable patterns of development. Sustainable development has risen in institutional prominence over the last two decades to become one of two goals that jointly define the latest version of the modern project of progress, the other goal being that of economic neo-liberalization (Raco, 2005). Yet, during the period in which it has become an indispensable carry-all for policy makers and a widening coalition of business leaders, sustainability has also been adopted as the *raison d'être* of a chaotic variety of social movements and local projects around the world. Academics have, predictably, also found a great deal to say about sustainability. Life scientists (e.g., IUCN/UNEP/WWF, 1980) and economists (e.g., Pearce, Markandya, & Barbier, 1989), in particular, have played a leading role in the genesis of this concept and then in its translation from abstractions into action. These and related disciplines have worked hard to contribute to the list of published definitions of sustainability, a list tallied at over three hundred, a decade ago (Dobson, 1998, p. 33).

An emphasis on definition remains prominent in policy discourse about sustainability. Take, for instance, the 2007 Australian parliamentary inquiry into the establishment of a national Sustainability Charter. The report of this inquiry, *Sustainability for survival*, concluded the following:

> If Australians are to embrace a national Sustainability Charter, they first need to understand the concept (and reality) of sustainability. However, to date there is no single, universally accepted definition of sustainability or sustainable development and, as evident in this inquiry, any discussion about definition quickly generates debate. (Parliament of Australia, 2007, p. 7)

The politicians conducting the inquiry countenance no positive role for such debate, and put their faith in the possibility of a compelling, unambiguous definition:

> Australians must begin a journey preceded by an agreed definition of sustainability and sustainable development, in order to reach an agreed destination. The important task of developing the definitions of sustainability and sustainable development should be one of the first tasks of the proposed Sustainability Commission. (Parliament of Australia, 2007, p. 12)

Once the ends of sustainability are agreed, assumes the committee, all differences can be put aside in the task of designing "a technical implementation agreement ... aligned with the objectives of the Charter and used primarily by government and industry to advance tangible sustainability outcomes through self-initiated strategies, tactics and tools" (Parliament of Australia, 2007, p. 24).

In addition to those who try to place sustainability on a firm theoretical footing, there is no shortage of academics lamenting the vacuity of the idea of sustainability and warning against conflation of the terms sustainability and sustainable development. Many point out that sustainability is a motherhood statement, benign but meaningless, whose role as a social compass can be revealed to be absurd simply by asking who is prepared to advocate the virtues of unsustainability or, for that matter, forms of sustainability not conducive to survival (e.g., O'Riordan, 1988). The idea of sustainable development, in contrast, is regarded by many of these critics to be malign, a dangerous oxymoron capable of smuggling the *status quo* into negotiations over the design of new futures and of creating an illusion of solidarity between rich and poor (Redclift, 2005; Sachs, 1999). Sharachchandra Lélé's early parody of this illusion is memorable:

> Sustainable development is a "metafix" that will unite everybody from the profit-minded industrialist and risk minimizing subsistence farmer to the equity-seeking social worker, the pollution-concerned or wildlife-loving First Worlder, the growth-maximizing policy maker, the goal-oriented bureaucrat, and therefore, the vote-counting politician. (1991, p. 613)

With good cause, then, Richard Norgaard observed in 1988 that, with the concept meaning "something different to everyone, the quest for sustainable development is off to a cacophonous start" (1988, p. 607). Since this time, the diffusion of sustainability talk across an ever-greater range of social fields and its use in support of an ever-greater range of political objectives has increasingly exposed sustainability to be an essentially contested concept: a concept whose meanings are multiple, contextual, shifting, slippery, and dissonant (e.g., Connelly, 2007; Kemp & Martens, 2007).

In the face of the growing complexity of contests about sustainability, Michael Jacobs (1999) has proposed a distinction in these contests between a first order of principled agreement and a second order of contested translation of principles into practice. As is evident in the example of the Australian *Sustainability for survival* report, Jacobs' assumption that there is a linear, one-way movement from principles to practices undergirds much sustainability talk. This assumption rests on an instrumentalist dualism that seeks to hold theory and practice apart, relegating practical means to the status of servants in the employ of coherent and autonomous ideas. In this way, the rethinking of worldviews, cultural paradigms, and ethical principles in the name of sustainability has been effectively uncoupled from the implementation of new technologies, economic blueprints, and institutional mechanisms (Davison 2008a). As noted earlier, education has been assumed by many to have the capacity to rejoin objective knowledge and ethical aspirations, facts and values, in the search for sustainability. However, to the extent that agendas of education for sustainable forms of development retain an instrumentalist desire for predetermined ends and neutral means, so I argue in the next section, they only contribute to the decoupling of facts and values in the first place.

Education for Sustainable Development (ESD)

At the 1992 UN Earth Summit, Agenda 21 was billed as a global action plan for sustainable development having the endorsement of an unprecedented coalition of national leaders. By the time of the 2002 World Summit on Sustainable Development, however, it was widely acknowledged that, despite impressive techno-economic declarations of fidelity to the ideal of sustainable development, the practical goals set by Agenda 21 were even further out of reach than they had been a decade earlier (UNEP, 2002). In the context of the despair and cynicism carried with this acknowledgement, the mandate of the World Summit was to urgently shift the register of sustainability from one of awareness to one of implementation.

Education has been prominent in this shift from knowledge to action in the form of a proposed transition from education *about* to education *for* sustainable development (Tilbury, 2004). The World Summit Plan of Implementation declared education to be "critical for promoting sustainable development" (UN, 2002, p. 51). Following decades of awareness-raising about sustainability, this advocacy of ESD rests on four assumptions. It is assumed that there exists objective consensus about: (1) evidence of unsustainability; (2) causes of unsustainability; (3) sustainable development as a cure for unsustainability; and (4) the nature of sustainable development. Built atop these assumptions, ESD is predominantly conceived as a tool for cultivating the social conditions in which sustainable development can take root.

It was decided at the World Summit to declare the period from 2005 to 2014 the first UN Decade of ESD, as an important step toward creating "a world where everyone has the opportunity to benefit from education and learn the values, behavior and lifestyles required for a sustainable future and for positive societal transformation" (UNESCO, 2005, p. 6). The organization entrusted with overseeing the translation of the Decade of ESD into reality, UNESCO, argues that the modern concept of universal education, which it has itself championed since it was enshrined in the 1948 Universal Declaration of Human Rights, has emerged in "parallel" with the concept of sustainable development. Indeed, it claims that education is so "central to sustainability ... [that] the distinction between education as we know it and education for sustainability is enigmatic for many" (UNESCO, 2005, p. 27).

I count myself among the many here, but, unlike UNESCO, not because I think the postwar project of universal education as inherently sustainable, and thus the phrase "education for sustainability" effectively tautological. ESD has been built upon unshaken confidence that modern educational institutions, ideals, and pedagogies are inherently progressive. As a result, there has been scant interest shown in the history and contemporary manifestations of education for unsustainability. There has been little acknowledgement that "the content and methods of most education and training ... are currently socializing us to live unsustainably" (Calder & Clugston, 2005, p. 7). Nor has sufficient account been taken of "the difficulty in carrying out socially reconstructive teaching within institutions which reproduce existing social relations" and of the possibility that "the concept of sustainability has become part of that reproductive mechanism" (Chapman, 2004, pp. 93–94). As a result there has been insufficient interest in what could be learnt about education itself in the search for sustainability. In my view, the literature on ESD has generally paid only lip service to the question of the extent to which education for sustainability requires the transformation of existing educational praxis.

It is true that accounts of ESD acknowledge the importance of the creation and transfer of new forms of knowledge and call for a reorientation of education (e.g., McKeown, Hopkins, Rizzi, & Chrystalbridge, 2002). In place of reductionist and homogenizing forms of knowledge, ESD stresses the importance of knowledge that is simultaneously holistic and contextual (e.g., UNESCO, 2005, 2006). The many ambitions that flow from this emphasis include a demand for knowledge that: is of a global and intergenerational scale yet tailored to particular times and places; is steadily cumulative yet attuned to uncertainty; is produced by disciplines yet supports transdisciplinarity; and is founded on public participation yet relies on scientific expertise. Confidence that the inherent tensions in such knowledge can be resolved by ESD, enabling new pedagogical paths to be forged within existing educational frameworks, is strong, if implicit, for such tensions are rarely acknowledged. This is not to say that ESD is claimed by its proponents already to possess all of the knowledge and techniques necessary to promote learning about sustainability. On the contrary, many advocates of this agenda accept that, because "no country is sustainable or has come close to becoming sustainable," and there is, thus, "no proven recipe for success . . . sustainability is essentially *an on-going learning process*" (Tilbury and Cooke, 2005, p. 2).

Commonly encapsulated in the twin catch-cries of "learning by doing" and "learning to learn," this process is now championed in sustainable development vocations such as environmental management, which seek to establish *"policy-as-informing-system* in itself" (Dovers, 2003, p. 5). In these vocations, learning by doing is regarded as central to the process of constituting sustainable development as an adaptive, integrative, and participatory endeavor, one built on institutional and personal capacity for ongoing, systemic learning. Such aspiration for lifelong and lifewide learning has implications that reach well beyond formal schooling. Agendas for sustainable development aspire to create societies made resilient by their capacity to learn from feedback from the dynamic, complex, and unpredictable systems in which they are embedded. Yet this aspiration, especially as it has been shaped by the Brundtland Commission's vision of sustainable development, continues to hold to the modernist faith that scientific, technological, and economic endeavor is inherently emancipating. The ultimate end of sustainable development takes the form of a vision of human maturity through materialist progress that looks uncannily like Francis Bacon's vision of Atlantis, articulated at the outset of the modern project of progress.

The juxtaposition of contingent means and predetermined ends in ESD raises two obvious questions. First, how are theoretical ends to be translated into action? Second, once translated, how is learning by doing to be steered to ensure it does not veer off track? The first question has long preoccupied academic literature about environmental education and, more recently, about ESD in the form of discussion about a knowledge–behavior gap (e.g., Kollmuss & Agyeman, 2002). In discussion about environmental education, instrumentalist explanations of how a perceived gap between knowledge and behavior can be bridged rely upon the idea of nature as a transcendent source of wisdom, one imparted through direct experience as well as through scientific study. In ESD, explanations of how this gap is to be bridged rely upon the idea of a transcendent moral force in the human condition, one expressed in the form of a set of universal and unalienable values. In such explanations, it is the values held by individuals and the ethics legitimated by society that generate the personal commitment and political will necessary to translate the ideal of sustainability into reality, and that act as a moral compass, by which to guide learning by doing along the way. "A holistic or systemic view of sustainable development," argue prominent ESD advocates John Fein and Dianella Tilbury, "sees it as a process of change guided by a number of values or principles" (2002, p. 4). In articulating a pedagogical framework for the Decade of ESD, UNESCO makes a similar claim: "ESD is fundamentally about values, with respect at the centre.... Along with a sense of justice, responsibility, exploration and dialogue, ESD aims to move us to adopting behaviours and practices that enable all to live a full life without being deprived of basics" (2006, p. 4). UNESCO then explains the relation of education to values in this way:

> education constitutes the central pillar of strategies to promote such values. Alongside positive spiritual motivations, education is our best chance of promoting and rooting the values and behaviours which sustainable development implies. As others have noted, "transformative education is needed: education that helps bring about the fundamental changes demanded by the challenges of sustainability. Accelerating progress towards sustainability depends on rekindling more caring relationships between humans and the natural world and facilitating the creative exploration of more environmentally and socially responsible forms of development." (UNESCO, 2006, p. 16)

Such emphasis on transformative education and on creative and exploratory paths toward sustained progress is appealing. Who, after all, would not welcome the prospect of more caring human relationships and greater human care for the earth? Yet the longing for care to be rekindled by ESD is translated into didactic injunctions rather than channelled into courageous inquiry about human history and about the inevitable variety of uncommon human futures. The determinedly up-beat mood of ESD does not countenance perspectives that recognize "persistent and otherwise inexplicable tragedy and suffering in history, and in history to come—even in a world that is otherwise sustainable" (Orr, 1992, p. 18). The central narrative of ESD—namely, that learning by doing sustainable development can be harnessed to universal principles, guided by the transcendent hand of values and applied in science and technology—is inherited uncritically from instrumentalist epistemologies themselves deeply implicated in unsustainable forms of development. Reasserting the hegemony of scientific knowledge and technological efficiency, agendas for ESD cling to the instrumentalist hope that science and technology will be the well-behaved servants of good intentions and lofty aspirations. They thereby perpetuate a modern history of imagining progress as techno-scientific flight from the past; a flight that aims, paradoxically, to reclaim a state of original human innocence (Davison, 2008b).

Unconvinced by instrumentalist claims about the transformative power of ESD, I aim in the remainder of the chapter to recast education for sustainability as an agenda for the reinvigoration of skills of practical moral reasoning in educational institutions and in everyday life more generally. Such reasoning offers no illusion that we head toward the certain destination of sustainability with certain mastery of powerful tools. Rather, practical reason acknowledges only the existence of what John Dewey (1969, p. 106) called ends-in-view, those moral purposes visible from inside the messy, dangerous, and precious complexity of moral experience. This approach does not evoke sweeping vistas of brand new futures. Nor does this approach imagine tectonic shifts in cultural paradigms, nor seek to transcend the ambiguity and ambivalence of ideas about sustainability, nor claim to pick winners in the contests that grow around these ideas. My contention, however, is that practical reason is more likely to aid navigation on the ground toward transformative ethical possibilities in the name of sustainability by enabling more attentive and empowering description of the unavoidable messiness of essentially contested efforts to enact sustainability.

Education for Contesting Sustainability

I noted earlier that the wide uptake of sustainability discourse has made it increasingly apparent that sustainability is an essentially contested concept. Yet the shift from education *about* to education *for* sustainable development has created a demand for sustainability to be represented as a stable, self-evident, and fixed goal. This goal is encapsulated in references to holistic paradigms, whole-of-curriculum implementation, and lifelong learning, and is set up as a pedagogical target for which unambiguous indicators of progress can be measured (e.g., Tilbury & Janousek, 2006). The contestability of sustainability concepts, and of related concepts such as nature and culture, emerges within ESD literature as a problem to be overcome by an appeal to shared values laid over the top of didactic assertion and delegation to experts, albeit experts espousing the virtues of holism.

Welcoming the essentially contested nature of concepts of sustainability, my interest here is to consider the ways in which the educative value of the search for sustainability may be found more in the character than in the content of sustainability talk; more in the exploration of uncommon than of common ground. That is, this value may be found not so much in agreed goals as in new ways of encountering disagreement, inconsistency, incoherence, multiplicity, contingency, and ineffability. What makes sustainability such a potentially valuable prompt for learning is its capacity to hold apparently competing concerns, different modes of knowledge, and social antagonists in dialogue while resisting any authoritative declaration of winners and losers. Like other essentially contested concepts, such as freedom and democracy, the theory and practice of sustainability derives its educative function not from definitive meaning, but from an ability to create and keep open broadly accessible arenas of rational inquiry and debate on matters of immediate, intensely felt, and lived concern. The political theorist William Connolly has argued that such concepts make

> mutual understanding and interpretation ... possible but in a partial and limited way ... The realization that opposing uses [of contested concepts] might not be exclusively self-serving, but have defensible reasons in their support could introduce into these contests a measure of tolerance and a receptivity to reconsideration of received views. (1983, pp. 140–141)

As Connolly recognizes, the encompassing nature of essentially contested concepts is at once a strength and weakness. They are unavoidably prey to co-optation by entrenched ideological and economic interests, dominant discourses, and empowered institutions. The mere presence of governing forces and actors can be enough to set default terms of reference for inquiry into sustainability. The value of discussion about sustainability is thus always in danger of being lost. The transformative power of this discussion is not wisely taken for granted, but has to be constantly re-established through the meaningful encounter of as wide a diversity of interests, perspectives, disciplines, beliefs, experiences, and assumptions as possible. Such encounter is, of course, immensely difficult to sustain in any form of social life, and not least within social institutions, including educational institutions, shaped by instrumentalist ideals of universality and objectivity.

I am arguing, in effect, that contemporary longing for sustainability is itself a form of education, although I have already suggested that the inverse proposition does not necessarily hold true. Unlike ESD literature, I do not regard education— either in the form of institutionalized teaching and learning or more generally in the form of personal and social capacity for the gaining and sharing of understanding— to be a neutral instrument with which to achieve predetermined ends. For a start, the relationship between awareness, attitudes, and behaviors is far from linear, one-way, or predictable, as assumed in these agendas. More importantly, I take from history the lesson that education is as potentially hegemonic and totalitarian as it is transformative and liberating. The possibilities of education are as ambivalent as is the human condition itself. These ambivalent possibilities are at once political, moral, and ontological: education is always political activity, laden with interests that belong to specific socio-cultural contexts; it is always moral activity, bound up in narratives of the good life; and it is always ontological activity, working to bring into being a particular vision of the human condition. Such interests, narratives, and visions are necessarily partial and any theory and practice of education is as contestable as is any theory and practice of sustainability. Understood in its broadest sense as the individual and social possibilities for human learning—possibilities expressed in proficiency in everything from military strategy to meditation techniques—education is not a tool for building sustainability, nor is it a component of sustainability. Education is a complex and contested social field, one vital to any prospect of social sustainability and yet constantly at risk of itself becoming unsustainable. Following this line of thought, it makes more sense to speak of sustainability for education than it does to conceive of education for sustainability. The educative value of sustainability rests on its ability to serve as a framework for personally and collectively reflexive inquiry that enables dialogue across difference. Put another way, this value lies in the way pursuit of sustainability leads to transformative encounters with the radically other. These include new forms of imaginative encounter with long-dead and yet-to-be born human generations; with fellow humans who share our time on earth but little else; with fellow non-human mortals whose destiny is now inextricably bound up with our own; and with the prospect of earth's mortality itself.

Instrumentalist approaches to education for sustainability such as ESD are preoccupied with trying to align action with concepts and to build a bridge of universal values between them. My preoccupation is with how the search for sustainability can resist the disintegration within education of ambivalent human experience into practice and theory, and related attempts to quarantine matters of fact from matters of value, in the first place. Strategies by which to articulate the dialectics of sustainability are vital to this resistance (Davison, 2008a). Such strategies expose the relationship of unsustainable pasts to longed-for sustainable futures, of the world as inherited to the world as desired, of real to ideal. Such strategies locate the transformative power of the search for sustainability in a two-way, open-ended and dynamic interaction between the need for something to be urgently done and the desire for things to be done differently. Such strategies accept that the problems of unsustainability and the solutions of sustainability cannot be neatly separated out; that they are thoroughly entangled in modern scientific, technological, economic, and educational institutions. And such strategies seek to prevent ideas of sustainability from being too easily co-opted within entrenched patterns of power by holding hegemonic interests, dominant discourses, and empowered institutions accountable to the paradox and ambiguity that runs through lived reality.

Sustaining Lessons in Life

Dialogue capable of sustaining a dialectical attraction of opposites has thus far rarely been achieved in contests about sustainability in general, and in agendas of ESD in particular. In exploring the neglected possibilities of ambivalent dialogue in educational encounters with sustainability, I rely upon a twentieth-century resurgence of western philosophical interest in embodied and evaluative expressions of rationality (Bernstein, 1972; Bourdieu, 1977: see Davison, 2001). Originally described as *phronésis* by Aristotle, and often referred to as practical reason today, this intellectual faculty is, at root, a capacity for wise judgement and virtuous character in the face of the overwhelming moral and material complexity of lived experience (Dunne, 1993; MacIntyre, 1984). In contrast to instrumental accounts of neutral means in the service of universal ends, accounts of practical reason emphasize the coproduction of moral ends and practical means. Moral ends, contends Alasdair MacIntyre, "cannot be adequately characterised independently of a characterisation of the means" (1984, p. 184) through which they are realized.

Reflecting the mutually constitutive relationship of narratives of the good life and the practices of everyday life, practical reason resists any ambition for absolute knowledge or complete control. Like scientific (or theoretical) and technical (or applied) modes of logical thought, practical reason is inherently educational in character, which is to say that it is explicable and communicable. Like these instrumental forms of reason, practical reason is a powerful agent in ordering, reproducing, and transforming social realities. All three modes of reason have unique competencies and particular contributions to make to education, and all three are potentially compatible in social life. Unlike instrumental reason, however, practical reason does not decompose human experience into matters of fact and matters of value. Practical reason is not in any way separate from the embodiment and enactment of everyday life, with its incumbent, ceaseless challenge of being good and doing right.

Developed and expressed in the relations and rhythms of everyday life, practical reasoning enables learning that is inductive in its trajectory and intersubjective in its force. Gaining momentum from circumstance, this is the capacity of individuals and societies to bind experience cumulatively into reflexive awareness of wider histories, patterns, narratives, rules of thumb, and possible futures. This is a mode of "learning by doing," a capacity for lifelong and lifewide learning, but not one that can be understood by regarding experience deductively, as if it were a field on which to test the hypotheses and conduct the experiments of pure reason. Practical reasoning is not a capacity of learning applied to the circumstances of life, but one made possible by those circumstances: a capacity simultaneously rational and relational; simultaneously analytical and animated by desire and fear. Attuned to the logical relations of cause and affect, this is a capacity exercised in the towering presence of birth and of death. This is a capacity for sorting and reassembling experience into meaningful and communicable lessons. Articulated in the context of action, these lessons conform not to ideals of consistency, universality, and lawfulness, but to experience of particular yet shared worlds. While finite, these worlds are infinitely changeable. Occupied only locally, and thus learnt only in fragments, these worlds are nonetheless seamless in their relationality. Immensely confusing, inconsistent, and heterogeneous, these worlds are nonetheless meaningful in their ambivalence. Saturated with love and with hate, these worlds are always teacherly. Full of beauty and of ugliness, these worlds are undeniably worth sustaining and worth transforming in the name of sustainability.

Once bound up with theocratic institutions in pre-modern western societies, practical reason has been discredited, misrepresented, and marginalized in secular modern societies through the dominance of instrumentalist ideals of scientific enlightenment and technological control. These are societies bewitched "by the dream of an ethical algorithm—a universal and invariable code of procedures capable of providing unique and definitive answers to all our moral questions" (Jonsen & Toulmin, 1988, p. 7). Thus, while instrumental reason is a powerful driver of agendas such as ESD, practical reason has gained little recognition in approaches to education for sustainability as an equally powerful faculty of navigation. Sharing the longstanding modern suspicion of emotive experience as a parochial, manipulable, and arbitrary basis on which to organize social life, ESD aspires to the detached clarity that gives the astronaut access to a truly global worldview.

Michael Bonnett is one of a number of articulate and perceptive critics who have questioned "the sufficiency of pure rationality" (2006, p. 266) in education for sustainability (see also Chapman, 2004; Calder & Clugston, 2005; Gough & Scott, 2006; Selby, 2006). I agree with him that education for sustainability requires "a perspective which is both theoretical and practical in that it is essentially concerned with human practices and the conceptions and values that are embedded in them" (Bonnett, 2006, p. 270). Yet, while Bonnett's recognition of a "sense of sustainability whose denial would involve alienation from our own essence and therefore from our own flourishing" (2006, p. 275) is welcome, his advocacy for "*non-rational* aspects [of sustainability] ... such as empathy, identification and a broader spiritual dimension" (2006, p. 266, emphasis added) is strangely limiting. In a similar way, so too is this suggestion from David Selby:

> Recognizing the power and persuasiveness of the sustainability case, we can sidestep and compensate for the mechanistic residues within the concept [of sustainability] by also fostering an ethic valuing the short-lived, the unfathomable, the unquantifiable, the indefinable; that which we feel and intuit but which defies easy description. (2006, p. 362)

Despite putting forward valuable counter-agendas of education for sustainability, both Bonnett and Selby perpetuate a disjunction between rational and non-rational phenomena that implicitly reasserts the claim of pure, instrumental reason to define the techno-economic contours of everyday life. Spirituality, empathy, aesthetics, love, and other intensely colored, if indefinable, expressions of human subjectivity do not constitute an attractive foreground set against a gray, all-too-definable, backdrop of mechanistic social order. Every aspect of the project of rational progress is shot through with the colors of desire, myth, and mystery, just as expressions of spiritual, aesthetic, empathetic, and moral understanding themselves help constitute any rational ordering of human worlds. The ineffable and the effable inhabit each other, making each other possible. The modern claim that pure reason has ended the grip of myth on social life is itself mythic, investing science with the resonance of omnipotence, technology with the power of transcendence, economics with the devotion of worship, and education with the moral certitude of a missionary (Davison, 2008b).

A great deal of energy has already been expended in the search for sustainability on widening the ambit of scientific inquiry into nature, in improving technological eco-efficiency, in sending new market signals to consumers and, as we have seen, in making education attempt to tie all this techno-economic activity to a set of universal ethical principles. Yet little has so far been learnt in the search for sustainability about the mythic energies that run through the rational order of sustained progress. It seems to me, though, that if the search for sustainability through education is to be ennobling as well as enabling, as official rhetoric insists it must be, the legitimacy of the modern barriers that arbitrarily divide reason from emotion, science from myth, and the life of the body from the life of the mind has to be challenged. Practical reason has an indispensable role to play in meeting this challenge. This role is as much in constituting and questioning the founding desires and assumptions of education for sustainability as it is in implementing any particular educational agenda.

My core aims in this chapter, then, have been to expose the limitations of instrumentalist accounts of the relationship between education and sustainability, and to catch sight of some of the new directions that can be forged in this relationship with the help of practical reason. In my view, these twin tasks were a precondition for reconfiguring the relationship of education and sustainability as nothing less than a challenge to dominant assumptions about the relationship between reason, morality, and experience. I have, inevitably, managed to offer only the merest beginning on only one of many ways of imagining a practice of learning the world that is at once a practice of sustaining the world. I have given expression to my own longing to grasp sustainability as the precious and all-too-rare essence of education. Happily, the challenge of sustainability can never be taken up whole by any author—monologue being entirely inadequate to the task—and I am content to report that I finish this chapter, if anything, more ambivalent about the possibility of education for sustainability than I was when I started out.

Acknowledgments The author thanks Peter Willis for encouragement, opportunity, and example, and Kristin Warr for generously sharing her knowledge of education for sustainability.

References

Bernstein, R. (1972). *Praxis and action.* London: Duckworth.
Bonnett, M. (2006). Education for sustainability as a frame of mind. *Environmental Education Research, 12*(3), 265–276.
Bourdieu, P. (1977). *Outline of a theory of practice*, Trans. R. Nice. Cambridge: Cambridge University Press.
Calder, W., & Clugston, R. (2005). Editorial: education for a sustainable future. *Journal of Geography in Higher Education,* 29(1), 7–12.
Chapman, D. (2004). Sustainability and our cultural myths. *Canadian Journal of Environmental Education, 9,* 92–108.
Connelly, S. (2007). Mapping sustainable development as a contested concept. *Local Environment, 12*(3), 259–278.
Connolly, W. (1983). *The terms of political discourse* (2nd ed.). Oxford: Martin Robinson.
Davison, A. (2001). *Technology and the contested meanings of sustainability.* Albany, NY: State University of New York Press.
Davison, A. (2008a). Contesting sustainability in theory-practice: in praise of ambivalence. *Continuum: Journal of Media and Cultural Studies, 22*(2), 191–199.
Davison, A. (2008b). Myth in the practice of reason: the production of education and productive confusion. In T. Leonard & P. Willis (Eds.), *Pedagogies of the imagination: mythopoetic curriculum in educational practice* (pp. 53–63). Dordrecht: Springer.
Dewey, J. (1969). *The early works 1882–1898, Vol. 3 1882–1892.* Carbondale & Edwardsville: Southern Illinois University Press.
Dobson, A. (1998). *Justice and the environment: conceptions of environmental sustainability and dimensions of social justice.* Oxford: Oxford University Press.
Dovers, S. (2003). Processes and institutions for environmental management. In S. Dovers & S. Wild River (Eds), *Managing Australia's environment* (pp. 3–12). Sydney: Federation Press.
Dunne, J. (1993). *Back to the rough ground: 'phronesis' and 'techne' in modern philosophy and in Aristotle.* Notre Dame, IN: University of Notre Dame Press.
Fein, J., & Tilbury, D. (2002). The global challenge of sustainability. In D. Tilbury, R. B. Stevenson, J. Fien, & D. Schreuder (Eds),*Education and sustainability: responding to the global challenge* (pp. 1–12). Gland, Switzerland: Commission on Education and Communication, IUCN.
Glacken, C. (1967). *Traces on the Rhodian shore: nature and culture in western thought from ancient times to the end of the eighteenth century.* Berkeley: University of California Press.
Gough, S., & Scott, W. (2006). Education and sustainable development: a political analysis. *Educational Review,* 58(3), 273–290.
IUCN/UNEP/WWF (1980). *World conservation strategy: living resource conservation for sustainable development.* Gland, Switzerland: IUCN.
Jacobs, M. (1999). Sustainable development as a contested concept. In A. Dobson (Ed.), *Fairness and futurity: essays on environmental sustainability and social justice* (pp. 21–45). Oxford: Oxford University Press.
Jonsen, A., & Toulmin, S. (1988). *The abuse of casuistry: a history of moral reasoning.* Berkeley: University of California Press.
Kemp, R., & Martens, P. (2007). Sustainable development: how to manage something that is subjective and never can be achieved? *Sustainability: Science, Practice, & Policy, 3*(2), 5–14.
Kollmuss, A., & Agyeman, J. (2002). Mind the gap: why do people act environmentally and what are the barriers to pro-environmental behaviour? *Environmental Education Research, 8*(3), 239–260.

Lélé, S. M. (1991). Sustainable development: a critical review. *World Development, 19*(6), 607–621.

MacIntyre, A. (1984). *After virtue: a study in moral theory* (2nd ed.). Notre Dame, IN: University of Notre Dame Press.

McKeown, R., Hopkins, C. A., Rizzi, R., & Chrystalbridge, M. (2002).*Education for sustainable development toolkit, version #2*. Knoxville: Waste Management Research and Education Institute, University of Tennessee. http://www.esdtoolkit.org. Accessed 29 April 2008.

Norgaard, R. (1988). Sustainable development: a co-evolutionary view. *Futures, 20*, 606–620.

O'Riordan, T. (1988). The politics of sustainability. In R. K. Turner (Ed.),*Sustainable environmental management* (pp. 29–50). London: Belhaven.

Orr, D. (1992). *Ecological literacy: education and the transition to a postmodern world*. Albany, NY: State University of New York Press.

Parliament of Australia. House of Representatives Standing Committee on Environment and Heritage (2007). *Sustainability for survival: creating a climate for change: inquiry into a sustainability charter.* Canberra: House of Representatives Publishing Unit. http://www.aph.gov.au/house/committee/environ/charter/report.htm. Accessed 10 December 2007.

Pearce, D., Markandya, A., & Barbier, E. B. (1989). *Blueprint for a green economy*. London: Earthscan.

Raco, M. (2005). Rolled-out neoliberalism and sustainable communities. *Antipode, 37*(2), 324–346.

Redclift, M. (2005). Sustainable development (1987–2005): an oxymoron comes of age. *Sustainable Development, 13*, 212–227.

Rist, G. (2002). *The history of development*. London: Zed Books.

Sachs, W. (1999). *Planet dialectics: explorations in environment and development*. Halifax: Fernwood Publishing.

Selby, D. (2006). The firm and shaky ground of education for sustainable development. *Journal of Geography in Higher Education, 30*(2), 351–365.

Tilbury, D. (2004). Rising to the challenge: education for sustainability in Australia. *Australian Journal of Environmental Education, 20*(2), 103–114.

Tilbury, D., & Cooke, K. (2005). *A national review of environmental education and its contribution to sustainability in Australia: frameworks for sustainability—key findings*. Canberra: Australian Government Department of Environment and Heritage and Australian Research Institute in Education for Sustainability.

Tilbury, D., & Janousek, S. (2006). *Development of a national approach to monitoring, assessment and reporting on the United Nations Decade of Education for Sustainable Development*. Canberra: Australian Research Institute of Education for Sustainability & Department of Environment and Water Resources.

UN (2002). *Plan of implementation of the World Summit on Sustainable Development*. New York: United Nations. http://www.un.org/esa/sustdev/documents/docs.htm. Accessed 1 January 2008.

UNCED (1992). *Agenda 21: Chapter 36*. Rio de Janeiro: United Nations Conference on Environment and Development. http://www.un.org/esa/sustdev/documents/agenda21/english/agenda21chapter36.htm. Accessed 2 January 2008.

UNEP (2002). *Global environmental outlook 3: past, present and future perspectives*. London: Earthscan/United Nations Environment Program.

UNESCO (1975). *The Belgrade Charter: a global framework for environmental education*. Paris: United Nations Educational, Scientific and Cultural Organization. http://portal.unesco.org/education/en/file_download.php/47f146a292d047189d9b3ea7651a2b98The+Belgrade+Charter.pdf. Accessed 2 January 2008.

UNESCO (2005). *United Nations Decade of Education for Sustainable Development (2005–2014): international implementation scheme*, ED/DESD/2005/PI/01. Paris: United Nations Educational, Scientific and Cultural Organisation. www.unesco.org/education/desd. Accessed 23 November 2007.

UNESCO (2006). *Framework for the UNESD international implementation scheme*. Paris: United Nations Educational, Scientific and Cultural Organisation. http://unesdoc.unesco.org/images/0014/001486/148650E.pdf. Accessed 23 November 2007.

World Commission on Environment and Development (1987). *Our common future* (Brundtland Report). Oxford: Oxford University Press.

Weiss, T. G., Forsythe, D. P., & Coate, R. A. (1994).*The United Nations and changing world politics*. Boulder, CO: Westview.

Worster, D. (1993). The shaky ground of sustainability. In W. Sachs (Ed.), *Global ecology: a new arena of political conflict* (pp. 132–145). London: Zed Books.

Part II
Foundations for Social Sustainability in Adult and Vocational Education

Chapter 6
Educating for a Sustainable Democracy

Michael Newman

Abstract Irrespective of the subject or the context, adult educators can contribute to the creation of a sustainable democracy by taking every opportunity to teach people to think clearly, to think imaginatively, to act, and to act wisely.

Introduction

Are we sliding inexorably toward fascism? Some of the so-called liberal democracies are displaying disturbing features. The self-proclaimed protector of freedom, the United States of America, is responsible for the horror that is Guantanamo Bay. Australia, land of the "fair go," has detention centers in which it has incarcerated asylum seekers and their children for months and even years while investigating their claims. In the United Kingdom, whose system of justice is based on the principle that an accused person is innocent until proven guilty, security personnel stalked and then summarily executed an innocent man on the London Underground. And all three countries invaded Iraq on the basis of flawed information and against the will of a large number of their own citizens.

There is a terrible irony in all this, which makes one wonder at the intelligence of our leaders. They are throwing out the baby with the bathwater. They are abandoning essential aspects of a free and democratic society in order to protect their free and democratic societies.

Clearly it is incumbent on all of us to protect our democracies. And if we are going to do so genuinely and decently then we need to do so within, and not outside, the principles and ideals of democracy. I am writing this for activist educators, but the questions I ask are equally valid for any and everyone in every walk of life: How can we work toward a sustainable and genuine democracy? How can we contribute to creating a population that is capable of arriving at critically informed opinions? How can we contribute to creating a leadership capable of responding to its citizens with integrity? In the language of this book, how can we help create the conditions essential for social sustainability?

M. Newman

To address these questions I am drawing upon and, I hope, developing ideas that I have written about elsewhere. In a recent book (Newman, 2006a) I argued that we should teach ourselves and others how to defy anyone laying out an unwanted future for us. And in a recent paper (Newman, 2006b) I suggested that we teach and learn how to be fully human in the Rogerian sense; how to be conscientized in the Freirian sense; and how to be free, to use a word given the sense I want by the life and example of Nelson Mandela.

In both texts I go on to say that, irrespective of the subject or the context, and irrespective of whether we are community, adult, vocational, or university educators, we can help ourselves and others learn the following processes: to think clearly, to think imaginatively, to act, and to act wisely. In doing so, we will be teaching and learning how to take control of our own lives and how to resist those people trying to take that control away from us. We will be contributing to the struggle to shore up our democracies against the witting and unwitting forces undermining them.

Teaching People to Think Clearly

To think clearly we need a reasonably tidy mind, and as activist educators we can take any opportunity in our teaching to encourage ourselves and others to order our thoughts. I like to draw on the ideas of A. J. Ayer (1971) and suggest that we develop the habit of distinguishing between statements, speculations, opinions, and injunctions. Ayer uses other language, distinguishing between analytical propositions, empirical hypotheses, and two forms of what he calls "literally senseless propositions."

So Ayer argues that an analytical proposition describes one symbol in terms of another. The statement "A spanner is a tool" would be an example. He makes the point that analytical propositions are like equations. They are ways of describing or equating objects or concepts and *they do not need to start from evidence*. Analytical propositions are no more than associations of symbols, and so are in effect tautologies. We are actually saying: "A tool is a tool." Analytical propositions are statements of what is and is not, and they have a finality about them, an implied stasis. They lock things into place. So in justifying Guantanamo Bay our leaders may tell us: "The war on terror is a struggle for justice." But are they really saying anything more than: "The war on terror is the war on terror"?

Ayer does not dismiss analytical propositions because of their tautological nature. Analytical propositions can excite us because they relate ideas and concepts to one another in new ways. So a mathematical argument can excite mathematicians because no one has expressed these equations of symbols in this way before. But Ayer also alerts us to the fact that many claims to incontrovertible truth by authorities, experts, leaders, and the person next to us at the bar in the local pub are simply the juggling of symbols, descriptions of one thing in terms of another thing: tautological statements without reference to evidence and so taking us nowhere.

An empirical hypothesis describes the world in terms of what is likely to be the case. It is empirical in that it derives from our "sense experience." So we might say: "A painter uses a brush to apply paint to the canvass." What we are actually saying is that given the right or normal circumstances we can be pretty sure that this is what a painter would do with a brush. And we can verify this by observing the painter. But *the statement remains a hypothesis* because we can never be sure that this will always be the case. Ayer in effect warns us that all empirical evidence, no matter how strong it seems, can only lead to an assumption. Many claims to truth are simply speculation: hypotheses based on more, or less, reliable evidence. So our leaders may tell us: "Unless checked, a trickle of asylum seekers entering the country will become a flood." They may claim it is a certainty but of course it remains only one amongst a number of quite different hypotheses.

Ayer argues that all other propositions are literally senseless, in that they cannot be tested by an appeal either to analysis or to a sense experience. A judgement like "This painting has great beauty" is really only an unsubstantiated expression of approbation and has no more sense in it than the statement: "This painting—hurray." Many claims to truth are expressions of approval or disapproval. They are simply opinions, no more true or false than other, entirely different opinions. So someone from the big end of town may say: "Privatization improves efficiency". But is she or he saying any more than: "I prefer private over public enterprise"? And when someone in authority says: "Rapid executive response to a perceived terrorist threat is a necessary evil," is she or he in reality saying "Summary execution—hurray!"

And a moral proposition such as "Murder is bad" is not just an expression of opinion but an injunction. The statement can be interpreted both as "Murder—ugh!" and "Do not commit murder!" Many claims to truth are simply straightforward injunctions. So when a politician says of the opposing political party: "They have no experience and no fiscal responsibility" she or he is in all likelihood really saying: "Do not vote for them!" And when our leaders told us: "Iraq has weapons of mass destruction," were they really saying: "Invade Iraq!"?

Using these categories of statement, speculation, opinion, and injunction means that we can critically examine the "knowledge" we acquire and the "knowledge" we are presented with. We can tidy, and sharpen up, our minds.

We can help ourselves and others think clearly by teaching and learning various forms of problem solving or decision making. We may have to overcome skepticism in some of our learners. People find it normal to go to a tennis coach or a driving instructor but sometimes assume that analyzing problems and coming to decisions are capabilities we acquire "naturally" in the way we do basic speech. They may point to the fact that they solve problems every day of their lives, be they minor ones like finding the best route to an address they have never visited before, or major ones like deciding, mutually or separately, on a divorce. People resist the idea that problem solving is a skill that can be taught, and we may have to persist in order to prove our point, encouraging people to reflect honestly on their own experiences as problem solvers, and providing new experiences for them through role-plays and other structured exercises. We may have to find ways of making the point that problem solving can be ad hoc and messy or elegant, effective, and creative, and that it makes sense to teach and learn how to achieve the latter.

I like using and teaching a straightforward problem-solving model based on the three questions "What's wrong?," "What can we do?," and "What will we do?". In response to the question "What's wrong?" we examine the knowledge we have and the knowledge we need to acquire, and the way that knowledge is expressed as statements, speculations, opinions, and injunctions. Once we have established what we consider are the "facts" of the matter, we can tease out the meanings that issue from each of those facts, and then rank those issues. In response to the question "What can we do?" we can canvass the various options open to us to address the most significant issues. And in response to the question "What will we do?" we will choose the option we feel most likely to succeed, and decide on the action we will take. The model can be described in shorthand as "facts, issues, options, and action."

If we teach and learn how to categorize and manage knowledge and how to analyze and address problems, then we are in effect teaching a form of critical thinking. But we need to be careful in our use of the phrase since over the past two or three decades critical thinking has lost its edge and become domesticated. It has become a skill, competency, or capability to be taught at school, in HRD courses, in the office, or on the shop floor alongside project planning, the ability to work in a team, and the desire to produce high quality products.

We need to give back to critical thinking its political purpose. We need to go back to critical theory from which critical thinking, in its modern form at least, derives. Critical theory implies a philosophy, a state of mind, a stance, of constant and continual critique. It helps us resist being hoodwinked. It helps us combat a Gramscian kind of hegemony. It enables us to make up our own minds. Critical theory is not "neutral." It requires us to locate our thinking within an analysis of power, and it argues that a genuine communication is made and a problem solved only when there has been an adjustment in the distribution of that power and a move toward the establishment of equity. Critical thinking deriving from critical theory is constructed upon a commitment to social justice.

Central to critical theory is the idea that we change our thinking by examining the *history* of our thinking (Rasmussen, 1996, p. 12). We do not just categorize and analyze the knowledge we acquire; we subject to critical scrutiny the *sources* of that knowledge. So we adopt the habit of saying: "Where does that thought (or opinion, idea, belief, or value) come from? Our education? Our culture? Our parents? Our peers? Our leaders? But how reliable are those sources? And, while we are at it, to whose benefit is it if we believe it?"

Here we can draw on Jürgen Habermas's (1984, pp. 99–100) ideas on the validity claims of truth, rightness, and truthfulness. Habermas argued that whenever people, be they teachers, salespeople, our next-door neighbor, or the prime minister, make an utterance, whether they are aware of it or not, they are claiming that what they are saying is true, that they have a right to say it, and that they are sincere in saying it. To test what they say, therefore, we can examine the extent to which they are redeeming each of these validity claims. For truth we can ask: Is what they are saying accurate? Have they told the whole story? Have they revealed their sources and are those sources reliable? Have they revealed aspects that may not be to their advantage as well as those that are? For rightness, we can ask: Are the speakers in a position to say this? Have they the accord of the people on whose behalf they are speaking? Do they have the necessary experience, knowledge, and background? Do they have the authority? And for sincerity, we can ask: Are the speakers being consistent? Have they disclosed all interests and all responsibilities to other parties? Have they been open and frank about their motives, feelings, beliefs, and values?

Teaching People to Think Imaginatively

Thinking clearly is not enough. Rational, enlightened thought gave us extraordinary scientific and technological advances, but it also gave us the means to exploit people, squander resources, and manufacture the weapons of war. Some of the critical theorists looked to aesthetics and the less strictly rational forms of discourse as a redress (Rasmussen, 1996, p. 23) and I suggest that activist educators can follow suit. We can look at ways in which we can encourage ourselves and others to think imaginatively, to take intellectual risks, to think, as they say, "outside the box." We can examine ways in which we can encourage insight.

Insight is both an intellectual and an affective phenomenon. It is intellectual in that it is a sudden understanding, a sudden realization, a sudden falling into place of things, or a sudden completion of a half-guessed-at schema. But insight is equally an affective experience. It is a sudden elation flowing into satisfaction, or a sudden horror flowing into resignation or resistance. Whether intellectual or affective, insight is that mysterious experience in which we come across the answer without asking the question. It is the conclusion without the argument.

Some argue that insight can also be a gradual process, as in the case of a person undergoing analysis and gradually gaining insight into their troubled childhood. But this is a use (or misuse) of the word "insight" as a synonym for understanding through the process of rational reflection and discourse. Here I am talking about insight as a *non-rational* intellectual and affective experience.

Sometimes, once we have had this non-rational kind of insight, we cannot understand how the insight has not happened before. It all seems so obvious now! What was in the background and unnoticed becomes all enveloping foreground. Something we took for granted and never questioned suddenly becomes starkly evident. The familiar becomes explicit (Segal, 1999, pp. 75–76).

Since insight is more an event than a process it will be impossible to teach. But we can establish the conditions, and help others learn how to establish the conditions, that may encourage insight. We can use literature. We can use metaphor analysis, critical incident exercises, mind mapping, and the other tools of the transformative educator. We can use a dialogic form of enquiry. We can use physical activity such as body sculpture. We can use games. We can use role-play. And we can use forms of playback or forum theater. All of these in their different ways create situations or "climates" in which people may experience insight, in which they may suddenly understand some significant element of their world intuitively, spontaneously, even mystically.

In all these processes we are abandoning rational discourse and encouraging ourselves and others to indulge in non-rational or even willfully irrational, discourse. We are abandoning Habermas's validity claims and going in search of a kind of supertruth. This is the "truth" of literature and dreams, the sense that the events described on the page or seen in the theater or experienced in the poem or dream have their own kind of significance, their own kind of meaning, and their own kind of reality. They may not actually have happened but they are nonetheless true.

Teaching People to Act

If we have helped people learn how to think clearly and imaginatively, we can then help them learn how to take action based on that thinking. Looking again to the critical theorists we can see our being taking shape concurrently in our objective world made up of tangible and physical phenomena, our social world made up of relationships, organizations, and collective experience, and our subjective world made up of values, assumptions, prejudices, predilections, and ideologies. In the objective world we act as subjects to objects, in the social world as subjects to other subjects, and in the subjective world as subjects to ourselves. And so we engage and make meaning through physical action, through our interaction with others, and through study and reflection (Habermas, 1972; Dallmayr, 1996, pp. 85–87).

In our role as activist educators, we can help ourselves and others choose actions that "fit" the three worlds. Since the worlds exist concurrently the fit will rarely be neat, but there will be times when direct physical, that is, objective, action such as organizing a picket line predominates, when social action such as holding a meeting predominates, or when subjective action such as a period of reflection and investigation predominates.

We can help people choose roles that "fit." So there will be "front line activists" who engage primarily in direct physical action, putting themselves, their careers, their bodies, and even their lives at risk. There will be "strategic activists" who organize groups, forge alliances between different organizations, mobilize, lobby, and make use of the law and the institutions of the state. And there will be "activists of the mind" who develop ideas, write, argue, and persuade, and make themselves and others think.

Using this threefold concept of action, we can teach and learn how to analyze, plan, and manage campaigns, altering the mix of the different kinds of action in order to meet changing circumstances as the campaign progresses. So in the campaign against the treatment of asylum seekers and their children here in Australia, activists engaged in physical action at the detention centers and in demonstrations in the cities, directly confronting authorities and their representatives. They engaged in a whole host of social action, including organizing, developing, and managing various kinds of action groups, lobbying, petitioning and meeting with political representatives, coordinating meetings and discussions, and forming alliances with other organizations. And they engaged in activism of the mind, researching, writing and publishing, organizing information campaigns, performances, conferences and public meetings, and making and showing films.

Teaching People to Act Wisely

Once we act on our world in order to change it we impinge on the lives of others. All but the most isolated of acts have an impact on other people and so have a moral dimension to them. If we are to help people make critical decisions, form understandings and then take action on those decisions and understandings, it is incumbent upon us help them make decisions they believe to be good and right. It is incumbent upon us to teach morality, not in the form of some established code but by helping ourselves and our learners examine and review the principles upon which we judge an action to be good or right.

We can do this through story-telling. We can tell stories of people who have been confronted by moral dilemmas and have made difficult moral decisions. I have often used the story of the maverick activists in a campaign to save a rainforest who went against the will of the other campaigners and escalated their action from peaceful resistance to a form of potentially very dangerous action. They drove metal spikes into the felled trees lying deep in the forest. This put the loggers, the frontline workers using chainsaws, at risk of serious injury. All work stopped when the loggers discovered the spikes, and it can be argued that the maverick activists' action actually turned the tide and saved the forest. This raises the age-old question: "Does the end justify the means?" As luck would have it no one, frontline worker, boardroom decision maker, or activist, was injured but what if someone had been? Just what means justify what ends? The story is from the 1970s (Foley, 1991) and is sufficiently long ago to allow for a reasonably dispassionate discussion, but it can also lay the ground for a discussion of the means and the justification of those means in more recent events.

We can encourage our learners to find other stories of people who have faced moral dilemmas, and we can discuss the decisions made by the people in the stories and ask if they were morally good ones. And if the climate is right we can encourage our learners to tell their own stories, and ask the same question of their own decisions and actions.

Since no two moral dilemmas will be exactly the same we cannot offer hard and fast rules to use in order to respond. But by telling stories we can build up a stock of experience, both personal and vicarious, upon which we and our learners can draw when confronted by moral challenges in the future. Decisions taken in the light of a rich and varied experience have a better chance of being the right ones.

A Democracy

Carl Rogers (1983) talked of "a fully functioning person": an autonomous person, open to change and new experience, intellectually curious and emotionally adventurous, in control of her or his own life. Paulo Freire (1972) talked of a "conscientized population" in which citizens and leaders were equally liberated by their capacity to think and act critically, and in which the only language used was the language of truth. And in 1990 Nelson Mandela walked free from his years of imprisonment carrying with him a vision of a society he had articulated twenty-six years earlier at his trial when he said: "I have cherished the ideal of a democratic and free society in which all people live together in harmony and with equal opportunities" (Mandela, 1994, p. 181). From the day of his release—he addressed his first mass rally that same evening—Mandela worked to achieve his ideal. He eschewed revenge or revolution. The white minority had oppressed the black and "colored" majority for decades and the temptation could have been to crush and expel the whites. But Mandela sought to sublate the dominant white minority, both subduing their power and influence yet preserving them, reducing their domination yet drawing them as active and willing participants into another, newer kind of social and political system, which Archbishop Desmond Tutu hailed as "the rainbow nation."

Activist educators cannot cure all the world's ills but in the course of our work we can hold in our minds the ideal of a democracy in which all citizens are fully functioning people, in which the population as a whole is conscientized, and where, through universal franchise and the democratic institutions and principles that go with it, the forces of domination and selfishness are continually subdued and drawn back into a fair and egalitarian society. It may be a dream, but David Deshler, an American adult educator, once said to a group of learners I was working with: "Just because the challenges are big does not mean we give up the struggle."

My proposals in this chapter are doable. As activist educators we can take every opportunity to help ourselves and others think clearly, think imaginatively, act effectively, and act morally. And if we do this we will be better able to defy unwanted futures planned for us by others, to take control of our own lives, and to work toward the kind of democratic and sustainable future we want.

References

Ayer, A. J. (1971 [1936]). *Language, truth and logic*. Harmondsworth, UK: Penguin.
Dallmayr, F. (1996). The discourse of modernity: Hegel, Nietzsche, Heidegger and Habermas. In M. Passerin d'Entreves & S. Benhabib (Eds.), *Habermas and the unfinished project of modernity* (pp. 59–96). Cambridge: Polity Press.
Foley, G. (1991). Terania Creek: learning in a green campaign. *Australian Journal of Adult and Community Education*, *31*(3), 160–176.
Freire, P. (1972). *Pedagogy of the oppressed*. Harmondsworth, UK: Penguin.
Habermas, J. (1972). *Knowledge and human interests*, Trans. J. J. Shapiro. London: Heinemann Educational.
Habermas, J. (1984). *The theory of communicative action* (Vol. 1). Trans. T. McCarthy. Cambridge: Polity Press.
Mandela, N. (1994). *The struggle is my life*. Belville: Mayibuye Books, University of Western Cape.
Newman, M. (2006a). *Teaching defiance: stories and strategies for activist educators*. San Fransisco: Jossey-Bass.

Newman, M. (2006b). *Throwing out balance with the bathwater*. Address at the annual conference of the Commission of Professors of Adult Education, Milwaukee, USA, November.
Rasmussen, D. (Ed.) (1996). *The handbook of critical theory*. Oxford: Blackwell Publishers.
Rogers, C. (1983).*Freedom to learn for the 80s*. Columbus, OH: Charles E. Merrill.
Segal, S. (1999). The existential conditions of explicitness: an Heideggarian perspective. *Studies in Continuing Education*, *21*(1), 73–89.

Chapter 7
Transformative Learning and AVE for Social Sustainability

Patricia Cranton

Abstract Transformative learning theory is founded on Habermas's three kinds of knowledge: instrumental, communicative, and emancipatory. Adult and vocational education emphasizes instrumental knowledge in meeting its goals of transmitting technical knowledge and developing specific skill sets and competencies. Yet when individuals acquire new technical skills this knowledge easily spirals into the communicative and emancipatory domains. In this chapter, I explore five approaches to transformative learning and examine the implications of each for promoting social sustainability. (1) The traditional cognitive approach is centered on critical reflection, which leads to revised habits of mind about the self and the world. (2) The extrarational perspective on transformation is concerned with imaginal and emotional learning. (3) Those theorists who favor connected knowing over autonomous knowing pay attention to the role of relationships in learning and understanding others' points of view. (4) Critics of the individualistic understanding of transformation advise us to pay attention to the role of social change, both as a precursor to and a product of transformation. (5) Finally, some writers propose a global, holistic, and ecological understanding of transformation.

Introduction

In this chapter, I first discuss the meaning of social sustainability and attempt to untangle some of the many different definitions I encountered in preparing to write this chapter. I then explore five overlapping and interdependent perspectives on transformative learning and consider how each illuminates our understanding of how we acquire knowledge for social sustainability. Finally, I examine the implications of this discussion for adult educators who wish to promote knowledge for social sustainability in their practice.

P. Cranton (✉)
Penn State University, Harrisburg, Pennsylvania

Social Sustainability

A dictionary definition of sustainability includes: from the verb "to sustain," meaning to hold up, to bear, to support, to provide for, to maintain, to sanction, to keep going, to keep up, to prolong, to support the life of (*Chambers concise dictionary*). In the literature we find, for example, biological sustainability (preservation of individual life), economic sustainability (the efficient use of resources so as to maintain the system), sustainable agriculture (a system that can evolve indefinitely through efficient use of resources and healthy environmental practices), sustainable development (a system that ensures that incomes rise and the general quality of life is improved without compromising the future), and ecological sustainability (where the demands placed on the environment can be met while still providing for the future).

Moore (2005), in writing about sustainability education, describes sustainability as a concept, a goal, and a strategy. The concept includes social justice, ecological integrity, and the well-being of all living systems. The goal is to create an ecologically and socially just world without compromising the future. The strategy is to move toward a sustainable future, and this is what Moore means by sustainability education.

Social sustainability is mentioned less often in the literature, and when it is, it is usually interrelated with environmental sustainability or sustainable development. The Hawke Research Institute for Sustainable Societies of the University of South Australia proposes that social sustainability must be developed as an independent field of study (independent of environmental or economic concerns) before examining its interplay with other facets of sustainability. They see social sustainability as "a positive condition created by social institutions and policies" (HRISS, 2004, para 8). Characteristics of that positive condition include: equity of access to key services (health, education, and so forth), equity between generations (future generations will not be disadvantaged by current activities), a valuing and integration of disparate cultures, and participation of citizens in political activity.

Although he does not use the phrase "social sustainability," it was Daloz (2000) who was the most helpful in my understanding of the concept. He writes that we first become encultured within our family, then to the broader culture, and finally to a larger sense of self, one that "identifies with all people and ultimately with all of life" (p. 105). As we "grow ever more deeply in love with the world" (p. 120), we care about safety, social justice, and a healthy environment for others, and deliberately injuring others becomes unthinkable. We work for the common good and realize our "fundamental interdependence with one another and the world" (p. 120).

For the purposes of this chapter, I define social sustainability as a commitment to humanity in which social justice for all is the goal, so as to preserve the future of the human race. This commitment involves an identification with and love for all of humanity, a recognition of our interdependence, and a breaking down of the self–other dualism.

Perspectives on Transformative Learning

Transformative learning theory has its origins in Mezirow's (1975, 1978) study of women returning to college in adulthood. Mezirow (2000) contrasts transformative learning with learning that is not transformative by delineating four kinds of learning: the acquisition of new knowledge or skill, elaboration on existing knowledge or skill, the revision of assumptions, and the revision of a meaning perspective or frame of reference. Only the latter two kinds of learning are transformative. Transformative learning is stimulated when we encounter a point of view that is different from our own and when we pay enough attention to that point of view to consider revising how we see things. This can occur in formal learning settings when educators challenge learners' perspectives, as is discussed in this chapter, but also in everyday life, without the intervention of an educator. Most adults do engage in critical thinking and challenge assumptions, and many take action for social justice though they may not have the language to describe it; our role as educators is to set up an environment where this type of learning is encouraged and supported.

Over the decades, the theory of transformative learning evolved into a complex and comprehensive explanation of how adults revise their perspectives on themselves and the world around them. Mezirow (2003) continued to expand his thinking, and simultaneously encouraged others in the field to contribute to a "theory in progress" (2000). We now have several ways of thinking about transformative learning—points of view that need not be seen as being in competition with each other but rather as different and potentially complementary facets of the same phenomenon. Following my previous writing in part (Cranton, 2006), I integrate these approaches and define transformative learning as a deep shift in beliefs and assumptions about self, others, and the world around us that occurs through critical reflection, relational learning, and intuition. Here, however, I describe five of these perspectives separately in order to consider how each may contribute to our understanding of how we acquire knowledge for social sustainability.

Cognitive Perspective

Mezirow's (2003) perspective on transformative learning is largely cognitive and rational. It is based on the underlying assumption that we develop meaning from our experience and validate it through communication with others. We articulate, question, and revise our perspectives. Mezirow puts it this way:

> Transformative learning is learning that transforms problematic frames of reference—sets of fixed assumptions and expectations (habits of mind, meaning perspectives, mindsets)—to make them more inclusive, discriminating, open, reflective, and emotionally able to change. Such frames of reference are better than others because they are more likely to generate beliefs and opinions and will prove more true or justified to guide action. (2003, pp. 58–59)

Transformative learning can occur when an individual encounters an alternative perspective that calls into question prior habits of mind. This can be a single event or, more likely, a gradual cumulative process. Critical reflection and critical self-reflection are at the core of the process, as is rational discourse. Critical reflection involves questioning the content, process, and premises of our beliefs and assumptions. Discourse is a kind of dialogue in which we assess our beliefs, assumptions, and values. Reflective learning becomes transformative when the person finds prior habits of mind to be distorted, inauthentic, or invalid.

Our habits of mind can be epistemic (related to knowledge and the way we acquire knowledge), sociolinguistic (based on social norms and the way we use language), psychological (how we see ourselves), moral-ethical (incorporating conscience and morality), philosophical (worldview, philosophy, or religious doctrine), or aesthetic (taste and standards about beauty). Habits of mind are uncritically absorbed from our family, community, and culture, and remain unexamined until we encounter a discrepant perspective that leads us into the reflective process.

It is clear how engagement in this process of transformation can work toward social sustainability. Uncritically assimilated habits of mind about cultural differences, for example, could lead us to be fearful of or antagonistic toward diversity, thereby limiting the possibility of social justice. Uncritically assimilated habits of mind about the resources in our environment could lead us to wasting or destroying the world's resources, thereby diminishing the possibility of there being energy, food, and shelter for all in the present and in the future. Through questioning habits of mind that lead to oppression, poverty, and abuse, we can work toward sustainability. As Moore puts it, "learning about sustainability should include discussions of ethics, worldviews, the role of humans within ecosystems, and ultimately a discussion of what matters" (2005, p. 88). And in describing her study of transformative learning for revitalizing citizen action toward a sustainable society, Lange comments that, as her participants "recovered suppressed values/ethics and forgotten relations (restoration), they engaged in a critique of dominant cultural values and embraced new values related to the concept of sustainability (transformation)" (2004, p. 135).

Extrarational Perspective

Many contributors to the literature on transformative learning object to the primarily cognitive process outlined in Mezirow's work. Early on, Boyd and Myers (1988; Boyd, 1991) described a transformative process in which symbols, images, and archetypes played a role. They see transformation as a fundamental change in personality that resolves a personal dilemma and expands consciousness. Boyd (1991) suggests that transformative learning occurs through discernment of the psychic structures that make up our unique nature.

More recently, it is Dirkx (1997, 2001) who has worked to extend transformative learning theory beyond the rational approach. He suggests that transformative learning involves personal, emotional, spiritual, and imaginative ways of knowing—facets of knowing that we see in symbols, images, stories, and myths. From this perspective, transformative learning is a holistic, whole-person process that involves the small everyday occurrences of life. It is soul work, a process in which we become aware of and consider the psychic structures of anima, animus, ego, shadow, and the collective unconscious.

How does this perspective contribute to our understanding of acquiring knowledge for social sustainability? Logical, scientific, objective, and modernistic thinking, once thought to be capable of curing the ills of society, has obviously failed. A quick look at the newspaper confirms this. We need to move beyond the rational, while not abandoning that which is good about it. Daloz (2000) is helpful here. He says that emancipatory learning is "not about *escape from* but rather about a deeper *immersion into* the rough-and-tumble of human relationship" and "our responsibility is to work to bring about transformation at the individual and societal level that will enable us to realize our fundamental interdependence with one another and the world" (p. 120). Drawing on interviews he and his colleagues conducted (Daloz, Keen, Keen, & Parks, 1996), Daloz describes how people feel a sense of inevitability in their commitment to working toward a just society. It is not a rational decision: people say they cannot not act.

Relational Perspective

There has recently been a slight shift away from the value placed on independent, autonomous learning, though most of our educational practices still focus on the individual. Gardner's inclusion of interpersonal intelligence in his work on multiple intelligences (Gardner, Kornhaber, & Wake, 1996) and Goleman's (1998) work on emotional intelligence drew attention to the importance of relational knowing and learning. Belenky and Stanton (2000) brought the idea of connected knowing to transformative learning theory. They describe six developmental stages of knowing for women: silenced, received knowers, subjective knowers, separate knowers, connected knowers, and constructivist knowers. It is the distinction between separate knowing and connected knowing that Belenky and Stanton use to critique Mezirow's (2000) cognitive, rational, and individualistic approach to transformative learning.

Unlike separate or rational knowers, who use logic and weigh evidence in their learning process, connected knowers try to understand others' points of view from their perspective. Belenky and Stanton write: "The more Connected Knowers disagree with another person the harder they will try to understand how that person could imagine such a thing, using empathy, imagination and story-telling as tools for entering into another's frame of mind" (2000, p. 87).

It goes against Belenky and Stanton's conceptualization of connected knowing as a holistic way of seeing the world to set it up as a dualism (connected *versus* separate knowing), which they unfortunately have a tendency to do (including associating connected knowing with women's knowing and autonomous knowing with men's knowing). However, Belenky and Stanton provide practical suggestions for engaging in transformative learning in this perspective, using a midwife-teacher and midwife-leader metaphor. The midwife "draws out" and "raises up," helping students deliver their words to the world (p. 92). Learners are active constructors of knowledge; connected discussion focuses on finding the sources of differences and reconciling different opinions. People work hard to understand each other.

In relation to acquiring knowledge for social sustainability, the relational perspective serves us well. Social sustainability involves a commitment to social justice for all (present and future) through identification with and love for humanity, recognition of our interdependence, and breaking down the self–other dualism. We need to work hard to understand each other, across culture, class, race, geography, gender, religion, and other seemingly insurmountable political, social, and economic barriers. Working toward this goal is a transformative process. It is a collective habit of mind of humanity to separate self from other along any of these lines. Our social structures are arranged into "us and them" factions; we continually function on these uncritically assimilated assumptions. As Daloz says, "In a world that ruthlessly offers greater material incentives and a bombardment of encouragement to place one's welfare before that of the larger community, to care for the larger good seems almost an act of civil disobedience," and "deep change takes time, strategic care, patience, the conviction we are not working alone" (2000, p. 121). We need to "create mentoring communities where socially responsible commitments can be formed and sustained" (p. 121).

Social Change Perspective

Historically, social reform has been a goal of adult education, exemplified through the Highlander Folk School in the United States and the Antigonish Movement in Canada. Following his early publications on transformative learning, Mezirow was criticized for his inattention to social change (for example, see Collard & Law, 1989). Mezirow (2000) defended his point of view by distinguishing between educational tasks (helping people become aware of oppressive structures and how to change them) and political tasks, which force economic change. However, according to those who advocate for transformative learning as social action, transformation includes not only change in an individual's way of seeing the world, but also structural change in the social world that provides the context for the individual's life. This school of thought builds on Freire's (1970) work. According to Brookfield (2000), without social action critical reflection is self-indulgent and makes no real difference to anything. Newman (1994) suggests that we should study oppression, not the individual who is oppressed. He argues that we need to look outside of ourselves to define the enemy and only then should we study ourselves in relation to the struggles confronting us (Newman, 2006). Torres (2003) clearly situates transformative learning as an instrument for social justice. He says that "transformative social justice should be based on unveiling the conditions of alienation and exploitation in society, thereby creating the basis for the understanding and comprehension of the roots of social behavior" (p. 429).

Clearly, this perspective on transformative learning is directly related to the acquisition of knowledge for social sustainability. The goal of social justice requires structural changes in the social world, and that is also the goal of transformation for social change. What is less clear is how to go about this in our role as adult educators. Belenky and Stanton (2000) draw on Freire (1970) to say that in order for people who have been excluded and treated unjustly to question authority and tradition, they must be listened to with great care. Their visions and struggles must be documented, critiques taken forward, and action projects must be developed that have the potential to transform communities. However, as Torres (2003) notes, people need to be educated in democratic participation, but knowing how to exercise democratic rights and obligations is both a precondition of and a product of democratic participation, so we have a catch-22 situation.

Ecological Perspective

The ecological perspective is the most recent of those surveyed here. It is a holistic vision, spanning individual, relational, social, and global perspectives on transformative learning. O'Sullivan and his colleagues describe it this way:

> Transformative learning involves experiencing a deep, structural shift in basic premises of thought, feelings and actions. It is a shift of consciousness that dramatically and permanently alters our way of being in the world. This shift includes our understanding of ourselves and our self-locations and our relationships with other humans and with the natural world. It also involves our understanding of relations of power in interlocking structures of class, race and gender, our body awareness, our visions of alternative approaches to living, and our sense of possibilities for social justice, peace and personal joy. (Transformative Learning Centre n.d., paras 3–4)

Central to this perspective is a focus on the individual as a part of the whole of humanity (O'Sullivan, 2003).

As in social sustainability, the goal is to create a planetary community that will be there for future generations of humanity. Transformative learning within this perspective is learning that would lead to the acquisition of knowledge for social sustainability. Gunnlaugson (2003) illustrates how this occurs in practice in the Holma College of Integral Studies. The college offers an intensive program in personal and global well-being that is intended to be transformative at the individual and collective level.

Implications for Adult Educators

For the past 25 years, I have been teaching in a program (called the Instructor Development Program) designed to help people from the trades (primarily) to become teachers of their trade at the community college level. Certification through the program is a condition of employment, and most participants have no previous experience in higher education beyond their trades training. Some participants go on to apply the credits earned to a Bachelor's degree in Adult Education, but upon entry into the Instructor Development Program most do not have this as a goal. They merely want to "get through" this mandated time "at school." They mostly resent giving up a part of their summer and are prepared to count the days and hours until they are finished. The course I teach is six hours a day, five days a week, over three weeks. Somewhere in the process, many participants experience transformative learning as they revise their perspective on their identity—from tradesperson to teacher. These participants leave the program with a different point of view as to their role in the world and their place in the various systems that support the training and functioning of their trade.

The program takes place in eastern Canada, in a small province that is sparsely populated and primarily working class (fishing, forestry, and farming). There is little racial or cultural diversity in the province. Most people are white. There are First Nations communities in the province, and the university has a center for First Nations teacher education, but there has never been a First Nations person in the Instructor Development Program. There are very few people of color in the province and in the program. The majority of program participants are males (approximately 80%). Overall, people in the province are family-oriented, church goers (both Protestant and Catholic), and conservative in their values.

In discussing the implications of using transformative learning as a framework for acquiring knowledge for social sustainability, I draw on my experience in this program. I also draw on twelve interviews with six participants from the previous three years of the Instructor Development Program. The interviews were conducted as a part of a larger research study on how educators develop a sense of authenticity in teaching and how that is a transformative experience.

What should adult educators who wish to promote knowledge for social sustainability in their practice do? How does using transformative learning as a framework for acquiring that knowledge contribute to practice? I organize my suggestions around the five perspectives on transformative learning described in the previous section of this chapter.

Cognitive Perspective

Critical reflection, critical self-reflection, and rational discourse are central to the cognitive perspective on transformative learning. Educators use strategies such as critical questioning, asking learners to keep reflective journals, and consciousness-raising activities (role play, debate, critical debate, and simulations, to name a few). The goal is to help learners break free from one-dimensional thought, to see alternative points of view, and come to question their formerly unquestioned habits of mind.

Frank, a young plumbing instructor, describes how he uses his own mistakes to jar people out of their habits of mind:

> I find that's one of the biggest things I am trying to achieve in teaching, to get them to actually be able to apply that knowledge, not just know the books and be able to answer a multiple choice question or a fill-in-the-blank question, but to actually apply that when you're out working, and I always try to give an example of something I did. I'll often use a mistake I made. There's lots of people in the class who would have done the same thing, but wouldn't mention it, and once I mention it, then everyone gets talking.

Students learn to think things through critically, to look at problems from different angles, to turn something upside down and see it from a new perspective. These cognitive processes, including "thinking about their thinking," serve well to promote social sustainability.

Extrarational Perspective

The extrarational perspective on transformative learning centers on the use of images and symbols. Educators use arts-based activities such as painting, drawing, sculpting, collage, scrapbooks, photography, and writing poetry and fiction. Watching films, listening to music, reading fiction, and going to the theater can encourage people to see themselves and the world around them in new ways. One summer day in the Instructor Development Program, when folks seemed weary of being in the classroom, we decided to go on an outing. After some debate, we chose a trip to the art gallery. Almost no one in the group had been to an art gallery, and we chose a general goal of "finding something relevant to our practice" for the excursion. The afternoon felt miraculous. People wandered alone or gathered in small groups in front of a painting trying to "make sense" of it through conversation. Everyone found some image that expressed an insight into their practice.

Here is an Instructor Development Program participant describing how he would represent his teaching in a painting:

> Well, I think I would probably not make, like, a "picture of me" type of thing. It would probably be something in nature's colors, but the abstract would be things that don't belong. Like if you see water and sunset, well, in my sunset, you would probably see, if you looked, like that big thing he's got there, oh what's his name, the horse, and when you look closely it's all angels? So it would be kind of like that, so you would see things that are important to me, like music notes, or some quotes, or you know, things like that, just plain words like "honesty," "trust," but you'd have to look into it. It would be kind of weird, because you would look and there would be something in there, but then when you see it, "ah, ok," you get it. Whatever forms who I am.

Letting ourselves go with images and fantasy can lead to a vision of how things could be, to an integration of self and other and humanity, and to perspectives that could not be created through rational thought.

Relational Perspective

Collaborative learning is at the core of the relational perspective on transformative learning. Group work and discussion are common strategies in adult education, but the kind of collaboration that promotes relational transformative learning goes beyond cooperative work to solve problems or discuss issues. Learners work together to create new knowledge through story-telling, sharing experiences, careful listening to each other's points of view, and a drawing out of each person's thoughts and feelings. Underlying these strategies is the need for non-judgmental acceptance of others and what they bring to the knowledge construction.

Evelyn talks about herself as a learner in a way that captures the essence of the relational learning perspective.

> I've been misjudged pretty much my whole adult life, and people who do then get to know me, they're "I had no idea you were that nice, or that you were like this, or ... didn't know you even had anything to do with music," and that bothers me because I'm thinking well, "why did you judge in the first place?" But I think it's a human thing for a lot of people; it's hard for them not to do it. We all judge at one point, but I'm the type, because I've been treated that way, I like to get to know people first ... Everybody's got good. Sometimes it's deep inside.

Knowledge for social sustainability is predicated on understanding ourselves, others, and the collective of humanity. Accepting, respecting and deeply listening to people across culture, race, class, gender, and sexual orientation is essential.

Social Change Perspective

At the heart of the social change perspective on transformative learning is exposing the conditions of alienation, oppression, and exploitation in society. People who are marginalized and excluded must be listened to, and their views must be documented. The adult educator working for social change works directly with those who are oppressed in order to develop action projects for community and social development. The great work done in the Antigonish Movement in Canada and the Highlander Folk School in the United States illustrates this kind of process. Study circles, kitchen meetings, protests, cooperatives, and environmental projects are examples of the kinds of strategies educators develop in this context.

Mark, an automobile mechanic instructor, has become involved in union work at his college. Within the college context, he works for social change.

> I'm also a union activist where I work, and oh my Lord, Patricia, this year, it's unbelievable the amount of work I'm getting from departments throughout the school. Well, we're undergoing academic renewal, and we're revisiting old vehicles with new faces on them, and that makes it difficult because it puts so much strain on instructors. The academic renewal—they're juggling numbers around and they're not bringing in the extra bodies that we require to meet the needs of the quality that a lot of our staff members have grown accustomed to. As you know, teachers are very conscientious about the quality of what we do, and because of these added strains and this new look, this new vision, it's causing a lot of undue stress in the lives of teachers that are having to go out there under the guise of academic renewal. It

sounds like we're breathing fresh air into some things, but in fact what we're doing, we're just putting, we're really reducing the quality of what we do.

Those educators who work toward transformative social change are directly addressing the acquisition of knowledge for social sustainability. They are deliberately and consciously helping others become free of exploitation and oppression by changing the social structures that are oppressive. They challenge the status quo and recruit the exploited to share their vision.

Ecological Perspective

In the ecological perspective on transformative learning, educators work to help others understand themselves, their relationships with others, and their relationship with the world. What that means in practice is less clear. We need to contemplate our collective destiny within the context of the history of our planet. It seems that strategies from each of the preceding perspectives would have the potential to meet this general and integrative goal. Collaborative learning, the use of images and symbols, critical questioning of our current positions in the world, and community action projects all seem to be relevant practices for the ecological perspective.

The ecological perspective is represented in this quotation where the instructor is describing how he engages students in integrative thinking:

> but after twenty minutes they're really either getting restless or they're not. I mean often they're engaged but I feel that a break would be good. And I'll often do it between giving, presenting a theory but before doing an example that sort of gives a practical use for that theory. So in between I will say "okay who's got the fun fluids fact for today?" And it can be anything from the driest place on earth to the wettest place on earth to the fact that you know X number of children die each year in the world because of water-borne disease or it takes X liters of water to make a shoe, you know. They have all, they find all sorts of different facts, it's great ... They find them, yeah. I do the first one usually, just to give them an example and I tell them about the wettest place on earth which is actually a place in India, so that really surprised me and it surprises the students and so they get an idea from that.

Making unusual connections, bringing surprising ideas together, helping learners see the global perspective on ordinary issues—this is what forms the ecological perspective and also what informs social sustainability.

In Conclusion

I entered into this writing with trepidation. I was unsure of the meaning of social sustainability and less sure of how to connect it to transformative learning. I read; I hesitated; I almost abandoned the project. Now, in conclusion, I can no longer see how I could not see the connections that seemed so elusive a few weeks ago. Considering transformative learning in the light of social sustainability has given me a deeper understanding of both concepts, but it was especially worthwhile to frame the writing within each of five perspectives on transformative learning. Though I have often argued for the integration of perspectives in my writing, I have, in practice, remained mostly rooted in the cognitive perspective (a way of thinking that suits my nature). I do encourage arts-based activities in my teaching, but they have not been as well integrated as I would like. The writing of this chapter may have changed that.

The acquisition of knowledge for social sustainability must, almost always, I think, be transformative. And how we get there, whether it is cognitive, extra-rational, relational, social, or ecological or (hopefully) a combination of all five, hardly matters as long as we do get there.

References

Belenky, M. F., & Stanton, A. (2000). Inequality, development, and connected knowing. In J. Mezirow & Associates (Eds.), *Learning as transformation: critical perspectives on a theory in progress* (pp. 71–103). San Francisco: Jossey-Bass.
Boyd, R. D. (1991). *Personal transformation in small groups: a Jungian perspective*. London: Routledge.
Boyd, R. D., & Myers, J. B. (1988). Transformative education. *International Journal of Lifelong Education*, 7, 261–284.
Brookfield, S. (2000). Transformative learning as ideology critique. In J. Mezirow and Associates (Eds.), *Learning as transformation: critical perspectives on a theory in progress* (pp. 125–150). San Francisco: Jossey-Bass.
Collard, S., & Law, M. (1989). The limits of perspective transformation: a critique of Mezirow's theory. *Adult Education Quarterly*, 39, 99–107.
Cranton, P. (2006). *Understanding and promoting transformative learning: a guide for educators of adults*. San Francisco: Jossey-Bass.
Daloz, L. (2000). Transformative learning for the common good. In J. Mezirow & Associates (Eds.), *Learning as transformation: critical perspectives on a theory in progress* (pp. 103–124). San Francisco: Jossey-Bass.
Daloz, L., Keen, C., Keen, J., & Parks, S. (1996). *Common fire: leading lives of commitment in a complex world*. Boston: Beacon Press.
Dirkx, J. (1997). Nurturing soul in adult education. In P. Cranton (Ed.), *Transformative learning in action: insights from practice* (pp. 79–87). New Directions for Adult and Continuing Education, no. 74. San Francisco: Jossey-Bass.
Dirkx, J. (2001). The power of feelings: emotion, imagination, and the construction of meaning in adult learning. In S. Merriam (Ed.), *The new update on adult learning theory* (pp. 63–72). New Directions for Adult and Continuing Education, no. 89. San Francisco: Jossey-Bass.
Freire, P. (1970). *Pedagogy of the oppressed*. New York: Herder and Herder.
Gardner, H., Kornhaber, M. L., & Wake, W. K. (1996). *Intelligence: multiple perspectives*. New York: Harcourt Brace.
Goleman, D. (1998). *Working with emotional intelligence*. New York: Bantam Books.
Gunnlaugson, O. (2003). Toward an integral education for the ecozoic era: a case study in transforming the global learning community of Holma College of Integral Studies. *Journal of Transformative Education*, 2(4), 313–335.
Hawke Research Institute for Sustainable Societies (2004). *Eco-social sustainability of the Murray-Darling Basin. Position paper: redefining social sustainability*. http://www.unisa.edu.au/hawkeinstitute/research/ecosocial/eco-position.as p. Accessed 3 April 2008.
Lange, E. (2004). Transformative and restorative learning. *Adult Education Quarterly*, 54(2), 121–139.

Mezirow, J. (1975). *Education for perspective transformation: women's reentry programs in community colleges.* New York: Center for Adult Education, Teachers College, Columbia University.
Mezirow, J. (1978). Perspective transformation. *Adult Education, 28,* 100–110.
Mezirow, J. (2000). Learning to think like an adult. In J. Mezirow & Associates (Eds.), *Learning as transformation: critical perspectives on a theory in progress*(pp. 3–33). San Francisco: Jossey-Bass.
Mezirow, J. (2003). Transformative learning as discourse. *Journal of Transformative Education,* 1(1), 58–63.
Moore, J. (2005). Is higher education ready for transformative learning? A question explored in the study of sustainability. *Journal of Transformative Education, 3*(1), 76–91.
Newman, M. (1994). *Defining the enemy: adult education in social action.* Sydney: Victor Stewart.
Newman, M. (2006). *Teaching defiance: stories and strategies for activist educators.* San Francisco: Jossey-Bass.
O'Sullivan, E. (2003). The ecological terrain of transformative learning: a vision statement. In C. A. Wiessner, S. R. Meyer, N. Pfhal, & P. Newman (Eds.), *Transformative learning in action: building bridges across contexts and disciplines. Proceedings of the Fifth International Conference on Transformative Learning* (pp. 336–340). New York: Teachers College, Columbia University.
Torres, C. A. (2003). Paulo Freire, education, and transformative social justice learning. In C. A. Wiessner, S. R. Meyer, N. Pfhal, & P. Newman (Eds.), *Transformative learning in action: building bridges across contexts and disciplines. Proceedings of the Fifth International Conference on Transformative Learning* (pp. 427–430). New York: Teachers College, Columbia University.
Transformative Learning Centre (n.d.). *About the TLC.* http://tlc.oise.utoronto.ca/wordpress/about/. Accessed 3 April 2008.

Chapter 8
Education, Religion, Sustainability, and Dialogue

Chris Provis

Abstract Social sustainability requires adult and vocational education to equip people for constructive dialogue with others who have different religious commitments. To equip people for such dialogue requires understanding of how it differs from scientific discussion, on the one hand, and from bargaining over interests, on the other hand. It is possible to understand religious difference as a sort of cognitive difference that resembles different ways of seeing, or different decision frames. If we understand religious difference in that way, it may be possible to develop educational tools that are as simple and straightforward as others that have been developed to equip people for bargaining over interests.

Introduction

Various writers have noted the changing and increasing demands that globalization makes on adult and vocational education (see, e.g., Kell, Shore, & Singh, 2004; Velde, 2001). It is clear that the changes create a wide variety of needs, in terms of curriculum, technology, organization, and professional development of educators. Meeting these needs requires an equally diverse range of initiatives. This chapter offers just one modest suggestion about a way to meet one clear need: the need for education in dealing with religious difference.

There are three basic premises behind the suggestion. One is that social change and development will continue to highlight differences amongst people who have divergent religious views. The second is that social development will only be sustainable if educators have simple, accessible tools to use with learners to build strategies to deal with those religious differences. The third is that such a tool can be provided by clear understanding and a statement of how people may differ in religious belief without one of them being in error. The next section will amplify the first of those premises. The later sections explore several issues related to the other two premises.

C. Provis (✉)
University of South Australia, South Australia, Australia

Diversity, Work, and Education

Why is religious difference relevant to adult and vocational education? If we focus initially on vocational education, the point emerges from the UNESCO-UNEVOC answer to the question "What is VET?":

> The current focus is increasingly upon preparing knowledge workers to meet the challenges posed during the transition from the Industrial Age to the Information Age, with its concomitant post-industrial human resource requirements and the changing world of work. (UNESCO-UNEVOC International Centre for Technical and Vocational Education and Training, 2006, para. 5)

Post-industrial human resource requirements and the changing world of work are inextricably bound up with religious diversity. Toepfer comments that "intercultural competence in dealing with clients and partners from or in other countries is basic know-how in a globalized world" (2004, p. 25), and that is important. However, such intercultural competence is increasingly needed not just in dealing with people across national borders; it is also important to cope with increasing diversity at individual workplaces. In either case, whether across borders or within a single workplace, such diversity includes diversity in respect of not only gender, ethnicity, and disability, but also of culture and religion. Ball and Haque (2003) have noted the significance of religious diversity in US workplaces, while Ogbonna and Harris have recently published a detailed case study of one UK firm, noting the intermingling of religion with other factors:

> The ethnic mix in the company has had some ramifications for religious issues. Of particular significance is that most of the ethnic minority staff are practising Muslims with strong religious beliefs and outwardly apparent manifestations (e.g. headwear) and practices (e.g. prayer traditions). The consequences can be profound where religion is fused with culture. (Ogbonna and Harris, 2006, p. 392)

During an induction session attended by one of the researchers, "Debbie, the Personnel Officer, highlighted religious sensitivity as an important issue which should be observed by all the new recruits" (Ogbonna and Harris, 2006, pp. 392–393). Sensitivity is tied to understanding and dialogue, and it seems likely that education for work will increasingly have to develop competencies in these areas.

However, "the changing world of work" is separated only narrowly from the changing wider world. Tensions that we see in the wider world carry across to the workplace, and the need for dialogue in the workplace is mirrored by the need for dialogue in the wider world. Dialogue is important in a variety of contexts, but has become especially salient in connection with worldwide concerns about terrorism since September 11, 2001. Mojab (2004) has argued that adult education has an important role to play in countering the neo-conservative developments that have been widespread since the 2001 attacks on the New York World Trade Center. Nevertheless, how to do that, in concrete terms remains an open question. It is unlikely that mere exhortation will be enough. Specific initiatives are needed. One direction for such initiatives to pursue is the development of tools for religious dialogue. One sociologist argued soon after September 2001 that "it would be an error for sociologists and political analysts to concentrate on revisions of economic and political theory while not paying equal attention to the moral tensions between Islamic and Western cultures," and suggested a need for "bilateral studies of Western and Islamic conceptions of morality and standards of right and wrong" (Davetian, 2001, p. 1). His point has been borne out subsequently. We have seen a variety of events that have shown such a need. Highly publicized cases have included controversy in Italy when a Muslim objected to the display of crucifixes in schools (Smith, 2003), international incidents resulting from Danish publication of cartoons of Muhammad (see, e.g., Reynolds, 2006), and others. Recently, many of the religious tensions we have seen have involved Islam, but other religions are no strangers to conflict, as European history bears ample testimony.

Certainly, it is not always clear to what extent a particular episode of conflict is rooted specifically in religion. All too often, religious differences go together with differences of ethnicity, class, and culture. That is true of recent conflicts and others, both broadly in the community, and within specific workplaces, like the one described by Ogbonna and Harris (2006, p. 395). We know that differences of group identity can lead to conflict, and that such differences can be grounded in the slightest of factors (Brown, 1988, pp. 223–224). It is often hard to say to what extent it is differences in religious belief and commitment that are directly responsible for episodes of conflict, as opposed to other differences that go along with those religious differences. However, differences in religious belief certainly play a significant part in some cases. If so, it is important to consider how to approach such differences, and to consider ways to foster dialogue amongst people separated by religious differences: in particular, what basis there is for education to foster such dialogue.

This chapter focuses on the area of religious dialogue, and in particular on tools by which constructive dialogue and understanding can be fostered by educational processes. It seems clear that, despite some limitations, education can have some effects in promoting intercultural tolerance, as well as overcoming other barriers to workplace diversity (e.g., Probst, 2003). If we can facilitate dialogue amongst people who are separated by religious differences, that will be one building block in the process of mitigating or resolving such conflict, and if we can identify a theoretical basis for such dialogue then that in turn will support education for such dialogue. Even then facilitating dialogue will only be one building block in resolving conflict, and others will be necessary.

Forms of Dialogue

Of course, the significance of dialogue is well accepted. A number of prominent theorists have recognized the general importance of dialogue in social and political processes, and I need not try to discuss all the important work that has been done (for some discussion and references, see Thompson, 1998). What this chapter will do is offer a classification of forms of dialogue. This does not seem to have been put forward by others, and it may be useful in approaching education for dialogue.

This classification revolves around the idea that some dialogue is essentially to do with people's different cognitions. Cognition has to do with perception, understanding, thought, and knowledge (Solso, 1995, p. 2), to be distinguished from desire, motivation, preference, and the like, even though the boundaries between cognition and other psychological functions are vague and sometimes contentious. As we shall note further below, some definitions of cognition have focused just on the association with "knowledge," but processes of thought and interpretation do not always involve knowledge, at least not in the common sense of the term.

The fact that some dialogue has to deal with different people's divergent cognitions is important because the point has been obscured by the dominant western liberal tradition. Historically, in the West, literature about religious dialogue has often been labeled discussion of religious "toleration." So identified, it figured significantly in early liberal writings, such as Locke's *A letter concerning toleration* (1963). However, later liberal thought has tended to drift away from its concern with religious toleration and dialogue, and subsequent liberal writers have focused on other aspects of socioeconomic arrangements, emphasizing desire and preference more strongly than belief and cognition. In particular, classical liberalism has been associated with *laissez-faire* economic arrangements, and the hope that free markets would resolve clashes of individual preferences (Macpherson, 1962). This emphasis has created a tendency to analyze all conflicts in terms of conflicts of preferences and interests. Thus, for example, it is suggested that if market arrangements fail to reconcile differences initially it may be possible to negotiate with a focus on "interests," not "positions" (Fisher & Ury, 1981). "Positions," unlike preferences or interests, have a strong connotation of interpretation and perception, as implied in reference to people's "religious position." Differences in people's religious positions have a significant cognitive element, obscured by the liberal emphasis on *laissez-faire* economic arrangements and their ability to manage people's divergent preferences.

A focus on preferences and interests implies a certain sort of dialogue. We have reasonably well-established ways of approaching dialogue about matters of preferences and interests: rules that apply to market transactions, ideas of compromise and fairness, the idea of focusing on interests and seeking win-win outcomes, all these are quite well established. There are some well-established principles and standards to govern processes of bargaining and exchange, and quite well-developed ideas about fairness, even if we often fail to implement those principles and standards in contexts where different parties have varying advantages and power.

Because there are some well-established principles and standards that can be applied to that sort of dialogue, we also understand how to educate people in these processes. Adult education requires "ideas that are practical, easy to use, and 'ready to wear'" (Fogarty & Pete, 2004, p. 8), and so adult and vocational education students are receptive to straightforward, usable techniques like those that Fisher and Ury provide in *Getting to YES* (1981), not only such techniques as "Focus on interests, not positions" (p. 41), but "Separate the people from the problem" (p. 17), or "Invent options for mutual gain" (p. 58). These are straightforward, but have theoretical foundations in areas like game theory, which analyze conflict processes that revolve around opposed preferences and interests.

However, the sort of dialogue that is required to deal with religious differences must go far beyond the exploration of one another's preferences and interests; it has to get to grips with others' positions as well (Provis, 1996). In many of the sorts of conflicts we are concerned with, what are important are the concerns people have, the decisions they make, and the actions they carry out that emerge from values and ethical commitments, and there is evidence that these are bound up with people's positions and social identities (see, e.g., Monroe, 2003; Harré & van Langenhove, 1999). The sort of group-based conflict that is especially salient and problematic in the world at present seems to be associated to a significant extent not just with divergence of interests and preferences, but with divergence of cognitions. Such divergence seems to be important in group conflicts that have a significant religious element. In this context, the need for dialogue seems especially apparent, and we have to consider what the pre-requisites are for educating people to engage in dialogue. But this means identifying some important things about the nature of dialogue: we cannot plan for education in dialogue if we have inadequate ideas about dialogue itself.

In particular, for example, the sort of dialogue required cannot stand on extreme relativism, as though matters of cognition are similar to matters of preference or mere inclination. Some postmodern views seem to suggest that sort of relativism, promulgating scepticism about any sort of claim at all, whether aesthetic, moral, scientific, or otherwise. This approach is fraught with both practical and logical difficulty. Practical difficulty, because we cannot in fact avoid making some belief commitments; logical difficulty, because it invites questions about its own status, and disappears into paradox. Some dialogue, at least, is about matters where we need to assume that it is possible to be mistaken, and to have false views.

We have well-established approaches to dialogue regarding some such matters, just as we have reasonably well-established ways to approach dialogue about divergent preferences and interests. Scientific enquiry and its norms, rules, and guidelines for argument, even a good deal of courtroom procedure, have evolved to deal with differences of opinion about matters where there is putatively some right and wrong answer. If we are considering dialogue in the form of argument, for example, we have some established criteria that rule out some processes as unacceptable, and to a large extent we justify these criteria by reference to the fact that they affect the likelihood of the dialogue resulting in people accepting true positions or beliefs and rejecting false positions or beliefs.

What we have developed less well are processes for dialogue where there are differences amongst people that are cognitive differences rather than differences of preference or interests, but where the issue does not centrally revolve around truth or falsity (Schick, 1992). This may be the sort of dialogue required where people are separated by religious differences. It seems unlikely that the sort of dialogue required here can assume that there is a single correct solution to be unearthed by processes of technical or scientific enquiry. To accept this, we do not have to believe that there is a supernatural realm accessible only through processes of faith or mystical revelation. We know quite uncontroversially that there are "ways of seeing" that reflect cognitive differences amongst individuals which nonetheless are not distinguished by the fact that some are true and others false. Wittgenstein

Fig. 8.1 The duck-rabbit

(1958, p. 194) drew our attention to the "duck-rabbit" picture that can be seen either as a duck or as a rabbit (Fig. 8.1).

Traceable earlier to Jastrow (1899), the idea has subsequently been the subject of extensive and detailed investigation by cognitive psychologists, and some of this investigation has used the concept of "framing" for a related family of ideas. They revolve around the idea of a "decision frame": "a decision-maker's 'conception of the acts, outcomes, and contingencies associated with a particular choice' " (Solso, 1995, p. 428, quoting Tversky & Kahneman, 1981). For our purposes an important feature of framing was clearly identified in empirical study by Kahneman and Tversky, where they showed that different cognitive decision frames can significantly affect people's behavior, even though the differences between the different frames—or "ways of seeing"—cannot be distinguished on the basis that one is true and the other false. One classic experiment showed that people's attitude to risk was significantly affected by whether they were led to frame a decision as letting some people die or as saving the remainder:

A group of subjects was presented with the following problem.

> The United States is preparing for the outbreak of an unusual Asian disease that is expected to kill 600 people. Two alternative programs are being considered. Which would you favor?
>
> 1. If program A is adopted, 200 will be saved.
> 2. If program B is adopted, there is one-third probability that all will be saved and a two-thirds probability that none will be saved.
>
> Of 158 respondents, 76% chose Program A, whereas only 24% chose Program B. The prospect of being able to save 200 lives for certain was more valued by most of the subjects than a risky prospect of equal expected value. Thus, most subjects were risk averse.
>
> A second group of subjects received the same cover story and the following two choices:
>
> 1. If program A is adopted, 400 people will die.
> 2. If program B is adopted, there is one-third probability that no one will die and a two-thirds probability that 600 people will die.
>
> Out of the 169 respondents in the second group, only 13% chose Program A, whereas 87% chose Program B. The prospect of 400 people dying was less acceptable to most of the subjects than a two-thirds probability that 600 will die. Thus, most subjects were risk seeking to the second set of choices.

> Careful examination of two problems finds them to be *objectively* identical. However, changing the description of outcomes from lives saved (gains) to lives lost (losses) was sufficient to shift the majority of subjects from a risk-averse to a risk-seeking orientation.
> (Neale & Bazerman, 1985, p. 42; from Tversky & Kahneman, 1981)

Cases where people differ in their cognitions in these sorts of ways are now well researched, but without clear recognition of the fact that such differences may call for forms of dialogue beyond those we are most familiar with.

Cognition and Religious Difference

There are three key elements to these cases where people see things differently, in the sorts of examples shown by Wittgenstein and by Tversky and Kahneman: (1) the differences are cognitive differences, not differences of taste or preference; (2) nevertheless, the differences do not correspond to factual differences in objects of cognition; and (3) despite the fact that they are not about factual differences in objects of cognition, nevertheless they can lead to marked differences in behavior.

The significance of such differences has been noted and built upon in some areas: for example, the idea of "cognitive reappraisal" is used as an approach to management of stress and anxiety (e.g., Lazarus & Folkman, 1984). However, the ideas of framing and "seeing as" do not seem to have been taken up so widely as one might have expected in the philosophy of religion (although Hick has touched on it: see Hick, 2004; Scott, 1998).

Kellenberger (1985) gives a good discussion of the more general issue about the extent to which religious belief commitment may be construed as a "cognitive" state. That is not a perfectly straightforward matter partly because the definition of "cognitive" is not perfectly straightforward. We noted earlier that some definitions of cognition tie the idea to "knowledge." For example, at the outset of his 1976 book, Ulric Neisser said that "cognition is the activity of knowing: the acquisition, organization, and use of knowledge" (Neisser, 1976, p. 1). He is not alone in offering such a definition (cf. Gregory, 1987, p. 149). That definition would rule out phenomena like framing from the realm of cognition, if we accept the widely used definition of knowledge as justified true belief, or some other similar, plausible definition (see, e.g., Honderich, 1995, p. 447). But twenty years later, Robert Solso gave a much broader definition at the start of the second edition of his textbook, commenting that "cognition touches all parts of the perceptual, memory, and thinking processes" (Solso, 1995, p. 2).

The definitional difficulty is to some extent reflected in Kellenberger's discussion, as he sets it in the context of two opposed views about religion that he refers to as "two very different religious intuitions about the place of knowledge in religion," adding further that "these opposed intuitions extend as well to the cognates of knowledge, including rationality" (Kellenberger, 1985, p. ix). To a significant extent, the difference amongst religious writers who represent the two opposed views he identifies revolves around the issue of rationality, with some writers like Kierkegaard being "highly suspicious of rationality in religion" (Kellenberger, 1985, p. 6), while for others like those in the Thomist tradition "the value of rationality is axiomatic" (Kellenberger, 1985, p. 13).

It may be that to some extent the opposition between such points of view hinges on a specific view of rationality, and in particular on the idea that for a position or belief to be rational there must be reasons that support it. In epistemology, this harks back to the Cartesian approach, which sees beliefs as reasonably just, if they are based on other reasonable beliefs, until finally we reach basic beliefs that are reasonable in themselves (Quinton, 1966). Kellenberger identifies various thinkers in the second tradition whose approach to rationality is along those lines: "They are sympathetic toward the idea that we all should hold our beliefs with a firmness proportionate to the weight of the evidence, and until there is support we should try to withhold belief" (Kellenberger, 1985, p. 19).

Both approaches to religion create substantial difficulties for dialogue. If we take it that religious commitment is somehow beyond rationality, then we seem to lose criteria for how to conduct dialogue: it is not clear what the dialogue is about, and if we are confronted with believers who have a different faith commitment than our own, it is difficult to know how to engage with them. We may exhort toleration, but we then tend to downgrade the commitment and are also without a place to stand with respect to belief commitments tied to action that we condemn. On the other hand, if we contend that we hold our own belief commitment because of the evidence and reasons that underpin it, then we seem committed to saying "I am right and you are wrong," without room for allowing different ultimate commitments in the long run. Dialogue is possible, as it is in science, but as in science it must be oriented toward showing that one view is correct and the other not. Either approach can end in religious fundamentalism. The first, because religious commitment is avowedly impervious to rational dialogue; the second, because such commitment purports to be grounded in evidence, but can often explain away any specific counter-evidence.

Kellenberger aims to show that there is a third possibility, a middle way, and he identifies a number of thinkers who are oriented to some such third perspective. My aim here is to suggest that the idea of framing, or "seeing as," can offer such a middle way, and do so clearly enough to be a basis for education in processes of dialogue about religious difference. It is enough to make sense of the idea that dialogue amongst people of different religious commitments may be dialogue amongst people who share real differences in how they see the world, but differences where there is no fact of the matter that could even in principle be used as a basis for investigation and enquiry to aim for ultimate agreement. If I see a glass as half full, and you see it as half empty, our different ways of seeing it may be real and may significantly affect our behavior, even though there is no way to say that one of us has a true belief and the other a false belief. What is more, however, this kind of phenomenon is familiar and accessible enough to us all, teachers and students alike, to function as a basis for developing ideas about religious dialogue.

Implications

The point that differences in religious commitments are like differences in seeing things one way rather than another is important for dialogue amongst people with different religious or value commitments. What are the implications for education?

The clearest implication is just that we need to become clearer about the sorts of dialogue that may be needed about differences that are cognitive differences and not just matters of preference, but where we cannot evaluate dialogue by whether it will arrive at true conclusions. We cannot hope to deal with this sort of dialogue just by acquainting students with the standard principles that apply to enquiry and argument, important though they are, because these are oriented toward attainment of true conclusions. On the other hand, however, we cannot afford to leave students with the impression that such differences are the same as matters of preference. For one thing, in such matters the fact that there is more than one legitimate way to see things does not mean that all ways of seeing things are legitimate. There may be no fact of the matter to determine whether it is better for me to see my glass as half full rather than half empty, but it would still be incorrect to see it as a jar of honey.

It seems very important not to confuse this case with either of the other two. When people have opposed religious views, they may be seeing things differently, and it may be that neither of them is wrong. On the other hand, however, their difference is not just one of preference or interest. The different sorts of conflict may become bound up with one another, and make those conflicts that much harder to deal with, but one thing we can do is educate people to distinguish amongst the different sorts of issues that can divide us, and to be wary of using means to solve one sort of conflict that are more appropriate for another. In education, we can show how to distinguish various sorts of differences amongst people, including those differences where what is at issue is a different way of seeing or framing the same things. We can display this latter sort of difference in simple ways, free from threats to personal identity and values, by referring to uncontroversial cases, and then move toward cases of religious difference. The process of developing curriculum and educational resources does not immediately become easy, but the fact that it has a clear theoretical basis may give us hope that it can be done.

So much is a programmatic statement. It still leaves the concrete work to be done to develop curriculum and teaching materials. Ideally, perhaps, what we might aim for would be something like the book *Getting to YES*, but a version that dealt with dialogue about religious difference rather than bargaining over interests and preferences. If it were possible to give equally straightforward examples and guidelines, it might be possible to draw learners nearer to a "Yes" of religious understanding with others.

References

Ball, C., & Haque, A. (2003). Diversity in religious practice: implications of Islamic values in the public workplace. *Public Personnel Management, 32*(3), 315–330.
Brown, R. J. (1988). *Group processes: dynamics within and between groups.* Oxford: Blackwell.
Davetian, B. (2001). Moral tensions between western and Islamic cultures: the need for additional sociological studies of dissonance in the wake of September 11. *Sociological Research Online, 6*(3). http://www.socresonline.org.uk/6/3/davetian.html. Accessed 23 April 2008.
Fisher, R., & Ury, W. L. (1981). *Getting to YES: negotiating agreement without giving in.* Boston: Houghton Mifflin.
Fogarty, R. J., & Pete, B. M. (2004). *The adult learner: some things we know.* Melbourne: Hawker Brownlow.
Gregory, R. L. (Ed.) (1987). *The Oxford companion to the mind.* Oxford: Oxford University Press.
Harré, R., & van Langenhove, L. (Eds) (1999). *Positioning theory.* Oxford: Blackwell.
Hick, J. (2004). *An interpretation of religion: human responses to the transcendent.* (2nd edn.). London: Palgrave Macmillan.
Honderich, T. (Ed.) (1995). *The Oxford companion to philosophy.* Oxford: Oxford University Press.
Jastrow, J. (1899). The mind's eye. *Popular Science Monthly, 54,* 299–312.
Kell, P., Shore, S., & Singh, M. (Eds) (2004). *Adult education @ 21st century.* New York: Peter Lang.
Kellenberger, J. (1985). *The cognitivity of religion.* Berkeley, CA: University of California Press.
Lazarus, R. S., & Folkman, S. (1984). *Stress, appraisal and coping.* New York: Springer.
Locke, J. (1963 [1689]). *A letter concerning toleration.* M. Montuori (Ed.), The Hague: Nijhoff.
Macpherson, C. B. (1962). *The political theory of possessive individualism.* Oxford: Oxford University Press.
Mojab, S. (2004). From the "Wall of Shame" to September 11: whither adult education? In P. Kell, S. Shore, & M. Singh (Eds.), *Adult Education @ 21st Century* (pp. 3–19). New York: Peter Lang.
Monroe, K. (2003). How identity and perspective constrain moral choice. *International Political Science Review, 24*(4), 405–425.
Neale, M. A., & Bazerman, M. H. (1985). Perspectives for understanding negotiation. *Journal of Conflict Resolution, 29*(1), 33–55.
Neisser, U. (1976). *Cognition and reality.* San Francisco: W.H. Freeman and Co.
Ogbonna, E., & Harris, L. C. (2006). The dynamics of employee relationships in an ethnically diverse workforce. *Human Relations, 59*(3), 379–407.
Probst, T. M. (2003). Changing attitudes over time. *Teaching of Psychology, 30*(3), 236–239.
Provis, C. (1996). Interests vs positions: a critique of the distinction. *Negotiation Journal, 12*(4), 305–323.
Quinton, A. (1966). The foundations of knowledge. In B. Williams & A. Montefiore (Eds.), *British analytical philosophy* (pp. 55–86). London: Routledge and Kegan Paul.
Reynolds, P. (2006). *Cartoons: divisions and inconsistencies.* BBC News, 13 February. http://news.bbc.co.uk/1/hi/world/asia-pacific/4708216.stm. Accessed 24 July 2006.
Schick, F. (1992). Allowing for understandings. *Journal of Philosophy, 89*(1), 30–41.
Scott, M. (1998). Seeing aspects. *International Journal for Philosophy of Religion, 44*(2), 93–108.
Smith, T. (2003). Italian Muslims fear "crucifix" fallout. BBC News, 28 October. http://news.bbc.co.uk/1/hi/world/europe/3219551.stm. Accessed 24 July 2006.
Solso, R. L. (1995). *Cognitive psychology.* (4th edn.). Boston: Allyn and Bacon.
Thompson, J. (1998). *Discourse and knowledge: defence of a collectivist ethics.* London: Routledge.
Toepfer, B. (2004). Global/local education for adults: why is it a must for the twenty-first century? In P. Kell, S. Shore, & M. Singh (Eds.), *Adult education @ 21st century* (pp. 21–35). New York: Peter Lang.

Tversky, A., & Kahneman, D. (1981). The framing of decisions and the psychology of choice. *Science, 211*, 453–458.
UNESCO-UNEVOC International Centre for Technical and Vocational Education and Training (2006). *What is TVET?* Bonn: UNESCO. http://www.unevoc.unesco.org/publications/. Accessed 24 July 2006.
Velde, C. (Ed.) (2001). *International perspectives on competence in the workplace.* Dordrecht: Kluwer.
Wittgenstein, L. (1958). *Philosophical investigations.* (2nd ed.), trans. G. E. M. Anscombe. Oxford: Basil Blackwell.

Chapter 9
The Role of Religion in Education for Social Sustainability

Heather Foster

Abstract Religion and sustainability are not terms often used together, despite religion having a role in sustaining communities for centuries. Religions are rarely static, but adapt and change with the differing needs of the environments in which they operate. It is this process of change and adaptation that enables them to sustain communities, as well as to be sustained as living systems. Religions do this by creating symbolic systems of shared meaning that adapt to reflect, and alternatively are reflected in, lived experiences. I will explore the manner in which religions create symbolism, meaning, and values, while facilitating interaction with different religious systems by connecting through similar values. This will form a basis for understanding the assumptions and values of communities, both overtly and nominally connected with religious traditions and cultures, and the manner in which interaction with individuals and groups from different traditions can occur. How does this relate to adult and vocational education? Through an understanding of the connection between religion and the creation of meaning and values within communities, strategies can be developed for workplace education, incorporating education on religion, religious assumptions, and cultural difference, thus leading to a more harmonious functioning of multicultural workplaces and global networks.

Introduction

In the mid 1980s, I travelled to a remote village in the north-west of Thailand to work on an archaeological dig. As I arrived in the village in the late afternoon, an exorcism was taking place. One of the young women from Australia had cut her foot and, although she had been prescribed antibiotics, an exorcist had been brought in by the female cook for the dig, in order to exorcise from the swollen foot the spirit that the villages believed was responsible for the infection. This set off an extraordinary chain of events.

H. Foster (✉)
University of South Australia, South Australia, Australia

The exorcist demanded a bottle of whisky for his efforts but also announced that the exorcism was a three-stage process, with the same payment for each stage. At this point the leader of the dig, who came from a conservative Christian background in rural South Australia, and had agreed to the exorcism as a piece of entertainment, declared it was all "stuff and nonsense" and banned the return of the exorcist. This was countered by the exorcist declaring the cook's grandmother would die if the treatment was not completed. After a standoff that lasted a week, a distraught cook, and a distracted local workforce, the situation was resolved through an intermediary who negotiated a payment without the treatment. The foot, in the meantime, healed nicely. This was an interesting example of the problems that can occur with a lack of understanding and appreciation of different religious/cultural meanings in the workplace. If adult and vocational education (AVE) is to succeed in sustaining societies, it is important that it incorporates an understanding of religions and cultures.

Within this chapter I will outline the manner in which religion creates meaning for individuals and communities, and provide examples of the ways in which commonalities can be tapped into in order to connect different groups. An understanding of this process can assist in finding points of commonality as well as appreciating and respecting difference. By understanding the processes, strategies and programs can be developed to avoid the clashes that occur, not only in a global context, but also where different systems of meaning interact locally.

Most work on religion and sustainability has focused on the development of a global ethic. This ecumenical endeavor, laudable in its own right, looks at commonalities across religions that can be emphasized in order to unify diverse religions and cultures. One of the best known examples of this can be found in "A Global Ethic," the Declaration of the 1993 Parliament of the World's Religions (see O'Connor, 1994). This document has been criticized for failing to incorporate a realistic understanding and engagement with diversity, just presenting a construction of unity, or homogenization and "an expression of power-over by ecumenical religious elites" (O'Connor, 1994, p. 163)

Many of the more difficult and contradictory issues are glossed over in the search for commonalities. O'Connor suggests that the complexity of religions and the specific context in which they arose produces particular attitudes toward such issues as abortion, the role of women within religious hierarchy, euthanasia and divorce, as well as religious "beliefs, symbols, and ceremonial practices where differences among the traditions loom large" (O'Connor, 1994, p. 161), and these are glossed over. The example I used at the beginning of this chapter may well be placed in this category.

In spite of this criticism, there does seem to be an acknowledgment of a "shared moral space" (Schweiker, 2004, p. 28) which can be used to sustain societies, whist understanding the diversity within this "shared space." If there is an effort to identify a global ethic, there is an assumption that religious systems create meaning, and ethical systems, for their adherents. In this chapter it is my intention not only to look at the way commonalities can be found, specifically using examples from the Hindu diaspora, but also to understand the construction of meaning underpinning the search for a global ethic.

Generally, debates about social sustainability not only ignore the topic of religion but also often shy away from any mention of it. It almost seems that acknowledging religion is "politically incorrect" or, at the very least, a source of discomfort for scholars. Religion is often associated with an unscientific or anti-intellectual view of the world and therefore is ignored in scholarly debates outside selected areas such as religion studies and anthropology. Even these have come under attack from other disciplines. However, by ignoring religion and its sphere of influence, scholars are in danger of undervaluing core assumptions and practices with their roots in systems of belief. Indeed, an examination of the most recent available statistics from the Australian Bureau of Statistics demonstrates that only 19 per cent of the Australian population do not affiliate themselves with a religion. A staggering 64 per cent of the Australian population identify themselves as Christian, although only a minority of these are reflected in church attendance records (ABS, 2006).

Whether scholars wish to acknowledge it or not, religion, religious teachings, values, and ethics do play a role in underpinning the values and assumptions of acceptable ways of operating in relationship to others within social and physical environments, and they form part of the culture within which individuals operate. As such, their influence in fostering social sustainability should not be undervalued and may be utilized toward this end. McKenzie suggests that the goal of social sustainability is not just to "maintain our current society just as it is, but to alter it so that it may become worth sustaining" (2005, p. 5); so too religious systems themselves are not static, but change along with their communities and, therefore, I am not discussing a static concept of religion, but religion as a dynamic system.

It is important to understand the way in which religion creates and sustains communities with, and through, shared values. Only by understanding this process can scholars comprehend the formation of social networks with shared value systems. It can also be argued that communities with positive shared values create communities that are worth maintaining. Additionally, it is important to understand the multiple values systems that operate within and across geographical boundaries. If values are linked to the foundational religious assumptions then, in order to understand other groups, it is important to gain knowledge of the basis for the assumption on which they operate. After all, religion is intricately linked to, and underpins, cultural assumptions and values. Education that includes the study of fundamental religious teachings, values, ethics, and culture is needed to foster an awareness of common links within social and workplace settings.

Culture and Religion

Clifford Geertz defines culture as

> an historically transmitted pattern of meaning embodied in symbols, a system of inherited conceptions expressed in symbolic forms by means of which men communicate, perpetuate, and develop their knowledge about and attitudes towards life. (Geertz, 1973, p. 89)

He further suggests that "Culture is the fabric of meaning in terms of which human beings interpret their experience and guide their actions" (Geertz, 1973, p. 145). In other words, for Geertz, culture is the pattern or fabric of meaning that is inherited and influences actions and practices. Geertz describes culture as something that is cognitive and psychological, as the "socially established structure of meaning" exists within the mind (Geertz, 1973, p. 1). This influences the responses that individuals will have to particular situations. Culture is established meaning through which the world is viewed. This meaning is expressed or articulated within symbolism which forms part of a symbolic system. This symbolic system can be seen within beliefs and practices and, in turn, represents the pattern of meaning or "webs of significance" (Geertz, 1973, p. 5). As Geertz states,

> man is an animal suspended in webs of significance he himself has spun, I take culture to be those webs, and the analysis of it to be therefore not an experimental science in search of law but an interpretive one in search of meaning. (Geertz, 1973, p. 5)

As the webs of significance or patterns of meaning are socially constituted, they form part of a greater or wider pattern of meaning, forming cultural systems. These systems involve some common basis or "degree of coherence" (Geertz, 1973, p. 17) which constitutes them as systems.

As I am suggesting, it is important to acknowledge religious assumptions within cultures and therefore necessary to look at religious culture. Geertz defines religion as:

> (1) a system of symbols which act to (2) establish powerful, pervasive, and long-lasting moods and motivations in men by (3) formulating conceptions of a general order of existence and (4) clothing these conceptions with such an aura of factuality that (5) the moods and motivations seem uniquely realistic. (Geertz, 1973, p. 90)

Religion provides meaning through which the inconsistencies of the world are rendered consistent and meaningful. It is this meaning that

> the symbolic activities of religion as a cultural system are devoted to producing, intensifying, and, so far as possible, rendering inviolable by the discordant revelations of secular experience. (Geertz, 1973, p. 112)

For Geertz, a religious culture is a system of meaning or webs of significance that provide meaning for what occurs on the human plane. This meaning, which incorporates a specific notion of cosmic order, is seen within symbolic systems that are, in turn, used in ritual activity, thus bringing the ideal or cosmic and the natural world into harmony.

To suggest that there is "a culture" that can be described as a Hindu culture, a Christian culture, or Muslim culture is, of course, a gross over-simplification, and not what Geertz is suggesting. To reduce any group of people to a particular stereotype or common denominator overlooks the individual differences that exist, such as language groups, gender, age, place of birth, and family experience. As Roger Keesing states when discussing Asian culture:

> There is no Asian "culture" we can characterise without oversimplifying the picture: exaggerating the boundedness, discreteness, and homogeneity of a way of life, glossing

over internal cleavages of class and gender (and usually ethnicity as well); camouflaging conflicting interests and silencing dissenting voices; and essentialising and eternalising, then disguising radical changes that have differently affected rural communities and urban settings. (Keesing, 1991, p. 46)

The same can be said of a Hindu, Buddhist, Christian, or Muslim culture, as many of the same problems exist. However, with these constraints in mind, it is still important to note that Geertz states that

Cultural systems must have a minimal degree of coherence, else we would not call them systems, and, by observation they normally have a great deal more. (Geertz, 1973, p. 17)

There have been theorists who refute any concept of culture (Kahn, 1991; Clifford, 1997). Clifford suggests that "Culture is contested, temporal, and emergent" (Clifford, 1986, p. 19) and any attempt to describe culture, according to him, will only result in a partial truth. However, it is still an operative concept for many. Roger Keesing, although warning against constructions of an Asian culture, goes on to state that

it would be vain to imagine that by some wave of an academic wand we could eliminate "culture" from either popular or scholarly discourse about Asia. It is not only that these usages are now too deeply ingrained to be magically sanded away they also become incorporated in Asian people's discourse about themselves and their collective identities. (Keesing, 1991, p. 47)

Keesing concludes that common roots and shared traditions do exist and that "There are contexts where the violence we commit in characterising 'Japanese culture' or 'Balinese culture' may be worth the cost" (Keesing, 1991, p. 47). Although anthropologists have been accused of perpetrating the concept that culture is fixed and determinative (Bottomley, 1991, p. 304), they have, in fact, provided many examples of the "historical specificity and fluidity of cultural practices and beliefs" (Bottomley, 1991, p. 304).

The concept of culture has indeed changed over the years and can no longer be seen as a fixed, unchanging entity, nor does Geertz himself interpret culture as a static entity, for he states that "human life takes shape within a moving and diversified frame of socially constructed meanings worked out in time and reworked there as well" (Geertz, 1984, p. 513).

Religion, according to Geertz, creates circles of meaning, a shared symbolic system and shared boundaries for individuals and groups, and provides a sense of belonging—a commonality. To share in the symbolic system and gain meaning from it does not necessarily depend upon a religious conviction. Religious assumptions tend to be an intrinsic rather than extrinsic part of culture. Religions and the meanings constructed through them are organic, changing and adapting with the community. Religion provides a symbolic system that sustains societies, although religious commitment does not need to be active in order for this symbolic system to have meaning for individuals.

By providing meaning and a space for individuals, these shared symbolic systems can also provide a point from which interaction with others from the different communities can occur. It can provide a basis for interaction with others outside the main group. Points of similarity and shared values, for example, can be a starting point for establishing dialogue with others in different systems.

Shared meaning locates individuals and provides a place for them within a wider community. These circles of meaning can make available a point from which negotiations with other circles of meaning can occur. Individuals belong to a number of different circles simultaneously. For example, someone from India may identify themselves with a nation, religion, region/language, caste, or family or, alternatively, as part of an Australian community, council, school, or workplace, at differing times. Some of these configurations provide more meaning than others but all or most may provide some point of intersection. By utilizing shared meaning, individuals become part of a community, forming and reforming with different groups in different contexts but still sharing in symbolism, ideals and values that retain meaning for them at some level.

Social sustainability occurs when meaning is shared and diverse views respected. With education, points of commonality can be identified and highlighted in order to develop other webs of significance where meaning overlaps. Contemporaneously, it is important to develop respect for difference through an understanding of the meaning religion and culture has for others. For this reason AVE needs to incorporate education into religion and religious diversity, in order to cater for a diverse workforce.

Education

Education incorporating the study of different religions is currently being undertaken in several sectors. In Australian universities, courses that introduce students to religious and cultural diversity are offered as part of a variety of degrees. This includes religion studies courses such as those offered by the University of South Australia, in which students can undertake one-off broadening undergraduate courses as part of their degree or, indeed, they can study a major or minor sequence of religion courses for a deeper understanding of the topics. Courses include studies of specific religions, a comparison of different religions through their components, and religious issues such as ethical debates. At Australian universities, religion is taught under a variety of different disciplines such as anthropology, sociology, and philosophy, as well as theology.

Some universities are beginning to introduce courses that deal with religious and cultural issues for practitioners in particular fields. For example, as part of a teaching program, Flinders University in South Australia has introduced "Teaching in a multi-religious society." These courses, however, form part of the formal tertiary education process and do not provide access to continuing adult education for those working in the field. Universities have in recent years entered the area of continuing education with non-award courses, although religion is not well represented as a topic. Where it is included, it does not provide the focus required for understanding religious culture and diversity. The TAFE (technical and further education) sector throughout Australia does not include topics related to religion under its umbrella, as it appears that it does not consider this part of its portfolio.

Although the University of the Third Age across Australia, designed for older students to continue their learning, does incorporate numerous courses on different religions, and religious topics, other areas of the informal adult education sector do not incorporate substantial courses on religion. The WEA (Workers' Education Association)—and its counterparts such as the CAE (Council of Adult Education) in Victoria—do provide some courses that touch on religious themes but often with a "popular" religion focus. Hunter WEA in NSW teaches "Vipassana meditation" but also has classes on "Reiki" and "Reading Tea Leaves." These examples seem to indicate that the study of religion is something taken purely for interest rather than being a key to understanding the workplace.

Individual religious groups provide education sessions directed toward educating both their members and the general public, one example being the Jewish Museum, which provides continuing education classes. These fulfill a need in the community but do not provide the direction for the education I am suggesting is required.

There are centers that focus on multiculturalism and diversity, including the Centre for Multicultural and Community Development at the University of the Sunshine Coast. As part of a suite of services, the center delivers training in cross-cultural communication. However, there is not a specific emphasis on religion within the center's activities.

The most significant development in this area of religious/cultural diversity education has been undertaken by Griffith University in Brisbane. Their Multi-faith Centre was established in 2002 and, along with interfaith dialogue, its vision includes education. As part of this, it provides talks and symposia with a specific focus on religious traditions. This is indeed a very positive step in raising awareness of the importance of religion in intercultural understanding.

In spite of the new interest and courses that currently exist, John May from Trinity College Dublin, in a paper delivered at Griffith University, has warned that the study of religion in universities generally is tenuous as

> it has long been regarded as a luxury, if not a danger. Worse: far from being assumed to contain solutions to the problems posed by violent conflict, the religions are held to be themselves the problem, one of the main causes of such conflict. (May, 2005, p. 1)

May outlines the conditions under which the study of religions can make a positive contribution to dialogue within a multicultural society and be an acceptable academic discipline. He suggests that the study of religion needs to

> combine content and concern, information and formation, the discovery "that" religious traditions are the way they are, an understanding "why" one becomes religious by belonging to them, and an appreciation of "how" this can make a difference to life, both individually and social. (May, 2005, p. 6)

There is a need for further development to cater for the adult education sector, including courses directed toward the requirements of vocational education. Although advancements have been made within the tertiary sector, the study of religion is not in a secure position and needs to expand into non-tertiary areas to cater for different requirements in both continuing education and adult vocational education.

Methods

There are two different approaches that could be used specifically for understanding religions and cultural diversity. The first is the approach I currently take with students studying a broad range of religious diversity in the Australian context at the University of South Australia. This could be readily adapted to the AVE context for those working with religious and ethnic diversity in the workplace and the community. The second approach, a deliberative method, is more specifically suited to enhancing an understanding of one particular religious or ethnic group.

The first approach to teaching about religious diversity comprises three stages. Initially, it places the individual students, and their religious, ethnic, and migration history, into the wider Australian context in order for them to understand themselves as one piece of the jigsaw of what it is to be an Australian. The second stage involves teaching the beliefs and practices of a selection of different religions in their more theoretical form followed by an examination of their manifestation in the Australian context. The third stage of the process involves the students visiting different religious sites, and speaking with Australians with a different religion and perhaps ethnic heritage in order to ascertain the challenges and constraints they face in the Australian environment.

Over the years, I discovered that many students who fit into the profile of the dominant or host community have little concept of their own history. They tend to understand themselves and their families as pre-existing and therefore the "norm" from which others, who are not like them, differ. Initially, I was shocked at the lack of a sense of history in their construction of their identities. Without this understanding of the individual as being "constructed" through their own and their families' history and experiences, students are unable to move on to a better understanding and appreciation of difference. They need, in a sense, to decenter themselves as the "norm" from which everything else deviates. Students from minority traditions often have a much greater understanding of themselves, and this is often constructed in relationship to the dominant community.

A young woman who had migrated to Australia from Italy once commented that she had not known she was Catholic until she came to Australia: as everyone was the same in Italy, it did not need to be named, and was not. It is important for students to be able to name themselves in order to understand their constructed nature. Due to the constraints of the course, it is difficult to undertake this process in any depth; however, within AVE this process could be undertaken in considerably more depth. It not only throws light on the individual, as it places them into the Australian landscape, it also enables them to engage with Australian history.

Sharing experiences within the group, in the first stage, is also an important aspect of the process, as it enables commonalities to be built on one level, and difference uncovered at other levels. As previously suggested, as there are multiple sites of commonality, the group process is an important aspect of building one particular bond.

In the central stage of the process, teaching involves providing information in lectures and reading material; however, the religions, ethnicities, or topics selected as the focus for the program could reflect the diversity in the workplace or the community in which it operates.

The final stage of the process is important as it enables students to understand the way in which others' lives differ from their own. Students from the host community are often oblivious to the assumptions from which they operate. It is by understanding the way in which others have dilemmas and challenges living within the host community that an appreciation of difference occurs. Difficulties about food, rituals, festivals, commensality, dress, or family expectations can be highlighted though this process.

In my own research with the Hindu community (Foster, 2001), a number of workplace incidences were reported that demonstrate the difficulties in keeping up religious or cultural practices. For example, Hindu women often perform fasts for the health of their families and they found it difficult to organize their working lives around these requirements, especially when extended periods of time were involved. Other women reported that traditional dress and religious markings became the butt of jokes. Even on social occasions connected with work, vegetarianism was not always appreciated.

Students have often been shocked at some of the constraints facing others. One young Bangladeshi Muslim student reported that his employer was constantly trying to convert him to Christianity, while another Muslim student expressed her great relief once her daughter started attending a Muslim school and therefore was able to eat anything from the school canteen. Taking the time to speak with others, along with a deeper understanding of the different religions, enabled empathy to develop.

An alternative approach that could be used in order to gain a better understanding of one particular ethnic or religious group is deliberative method. This is particularly useful for the adult sector and can be offered as a workshop over the course of a few days. The concept has been used in deliberative polling in order to change attitudes toward civic issues. Most recently, it was used in Australia in order to look at Muslims and non-Muslims in Australia (Ida, 2006). It has been remarkably effective in changing attitudes and, in the most recent example, changing the attitudes of non-Muslims in Australia toward Muslims in a positive way.

Workshops consist of mixed groups, ideally with, although not necessarily involving, members of the ethnic groups/religions under consideration. Relevant material on the topic needs to be prepared for the workshop participants to read prior to its commencement. Facilitators work within the groups while the workshop itself involves a combination of group work interspersed with panel sessions where groups formulate questions to be put to a panel or an expert in the area.

When writing on deliberative workshops, White suggested, they function in order to "explore people's attitudes and beliefs and then provide them with information and arguments to reach an informed position" (2003, para. 8). Through the workshop process, the group members gain access to information, challenge each other's and their own assumptions, and direct questions toward "experts," in order to reach this informed position. It commences from the knowledge individuals bring to the workshop and uses this to refine or change their understanding of others.

Not only have deliberative methods been used successfully to educate adults and change attitudes, they also have a bonding effect amongst the participants. An experience of "communitas," or a sense of community, is developed amongst the group through the process of sharing their thoughts and beliefs.

Conclusion

Communities are often formed, sustained, and linked through religious assumptions that are part of a specific culture or cultures. Sharing in webs of significance enables communities to be sustained within changing physical and social environments. All these various systems of significance provide meaning for individuals and link them to a community, thus providing the mechanisms for the maintenance of communities. I would further suggest that communities are only sustainable where shared meaning exists at some level.

How could an understanding of the creation of webs of significance and the variety of circles and webs to which individuals and groups belong assist in the Thai workplace I described at the beginning of the chapter? Individuals from Adelaide came to the village to work on the archaeological dig. They worked together with Thais who provided the manual workforce and support services as well as archaeological expertise. Although some of the Thais shared a great deal with each other, coming from the same village, the Thai professional staff shared common aspects with both the Thai villages and the Australian team. These professional Thais understood the villagers' beliefs in the presence of spirits and the process of exorcism even if they did not share in these beliefs. These people often took on a negotiating role in the workplace as they understood the different systems of meaning operating for the different groups. The Australian scientist who acted as an intermediary had been studying Thai language and culture and had made an effort to understand the different groups within the Thai worksite.

The clash between the exorcist and the Australian excavation leader occurred due to a lack of understanding or desire to understand or acknowledge the meaning that the incident had for the Thai villagers. There was no point at which shared meaning or an understanding of the depth of belief behind the practice of spirit exorcism intersected. What was significant to the villagers, and understood by the Thai professionals and the Australian intermediary, was not considered valid by the Australian in charge. The dig as a whole experienced ongoing problems due to similar conflicts, many of which could have been avoided through an effort to understand the manner in which religion and culture provided meaning and structure for the people in the village and the Thai professionals.

Where there is not only a lack of shared meaning but also a lack of understanding of cultural difference, difficulties occur, affecting individuals, communities and workplaces. This was evident in the Thai example and was highlighted recently through the comments on the inquest results from Palm Island after the death of a young indigenous man in police custody where there was a call for people working with indigenous people to receive education in their culture in order to avoid such disastrous consequences.

There are a number of ways in which education can occur. I have only outlined two examples of these. The knowledge and understanding of other cultures acquired through education fosters an appreciation of the meaning behind the difference between groups, thus enabling a greater appreciation of this difference.

Religious assumptions are an integral aspect of culture and can not be ignored when attempts are made to work within communities. If we identify what creates and sustains groups and communities, and highlight shared assumptions and points where systems of significance coincide and values interlock then wider communities can develop within the workplace based on a better understanding of difference and commonality. It is important in any effort to locate commonalities, those aspects that may lead to a global ethic, that the aspects and differences that make religious traditions individual—the beliefs, ceremonies, and practices—are not devalued. They, after all, form the basis of religious and cultural assumptions.

References

Australian Bureau of Statistics (2006). *Census tables*. Cat. No. 2068.0. http://www.censusdata.abs.gov.au/ABSNavigation/prenav/ViewData?action=404&documentpr-ductno=0&documenttype=Details&order=1&tabname=Details&areacode=0&issue=2006&producttype=Census%20Tables&javascript=true&textversion=false&navmapdisplayed=true&breadcrumb=TLPD&&collection=Census&period=2006&productlabel=Religious%20Affiliation%20by%20Sex&producttype=Census%20Tables&method=Place%20of%20Usual%20Residence&topic=Religion&.Accessed22August2007.
Bottomley, G. (1991). Culture, ethnicity, and the politics/poetics of representation, *Diaspora, 1*(3), 303–320.
Clifford, J. (1986). Introduction: partial truths. In J. Clifford & G. E. Marcus (Eds.), *Writing culture* (pp. 1–26). Berkeley: University of California Press.
Clifford, J. (1997). *Routes: travel and translation in the late twentieth century*. Cambridge, MA: Harvard University Press.
Geertz, C. (1973). *The interpretation of cultures*. New York: Basic Books.
Geertz, C. (1984). Culture and social change: the Indonesian case. *Man, 19*(4), 511–532.
Issues Deliberation Australia/America (2006). *Australia deliberates: Muslims and non-Muslims in Australia*. http://www.ida.org.au/content.php?p=overview_of_the_dp. Accessed 13 August 2007.
Kahn, J. S. (1991). Constructing culture: toward an anthropology of the middle classes in Southeast Asia. *Asian Studies Review, 15*(2), 50–56.
Keesing, R. M. (1991). Asian cultures? *Asian Studies Review, 15*(2), 43–49.
Foster, H. A. (2001). *Accommodating difference: the cultural construction of the Hindu women of South Australia*. PhD thesis, University of South Australia.
McKenzie, S. (2005). *Social sustainability, religious belief and global ethics: outlines for research*. Hawke Research Institute Working Paper Series No. 30. Magill, SA: HRISS, University of South Australia.

May, J. D. (2005). Interreligious studies in the university: help or hindrance to peace? Paper presented at the international symposium Cultivating wisdom, harvesting peace. Griffith University Multi-Faith Centre, 10–13 August.

O'Connor, J. (1994). Does a global village warrant a global ethic?*Religion, 24,* 155–164.

Schweiker, W. (2004). A preface to ethics: global dynamics and the integrity of life. *Journal of Religious Ethics, 32*(1), 13–37.

White, S. (2003).*New politics of ownership: policy options and public opinion.* http://government.politics.ox.ac.uk/projects/new%20politics%20of%20ownership.asp. Accessed 13 August 2007.

Part III
Creating Spaces for Social Sustainability in Adult and Vocational Education

Chapter 10
Claiming Sustainable Space: Families, Communities, and Learning, an Auto/Biographical Perspective

Linden West

Abstract Using auto/biographical research, this chapter explores notions of sustainability in the context of the development of family "support" projects, like Sure Start, in the United Kingdom. Space was created in some of these projects for access to the much needed specialist services but also for parents as well as children to engage in a range of non-formal and informal learning in highly sustaining ways. Transactional space was also created to facilitate democratic involvement and practices within particular programs. I suggest that building social sustainability has to encompass long-term investment in community capacity building as well as an awareness of the subtle interplay of family life and the quality of the social fabric; and also the extent to which the delivery of public services and professional behaviors are grounded in more democratized and respectful social relationships. Notions of learning—in a holistic, life-wide sense—lie at the heart of the struggle for sustainability, beyond current narrow preoccupations with education for employability.

Introduction

I want, in this chapter, to weave some possible connections between, on the one hand, the well-being of families living in marginalized communities, the extent and quality of public service interventions, alongside opportunities for adult and community learning, with, on the other, notions of sustainability: personal, social, as well as democratic. The idea of social sustainability informing the chapter is broad in scope, connecting the most intimate of struggles for health, well-being, and meaningful lives with the quality of relationships and wider socio-cultural contexts in which we are embedded. The debate about social sustainability, I suggest, also needs to encompass issues of social justice and a more equitable distribution of resources: deeply unequal societies, or communities, like a deeply unjust world more generally, can spawn deep-seated, intractable resentments, conflicts, repression, "disease," and destructiveness. Processes of adult and community learning—in non-formal, informal, as well as democratic senses, beyond the narrow obsession

L. West (✉)
Canterbury Christ Church University, Canterbury, Kent, UK

with training the marginalized for employability—are similarly important. There is evidence from auto/biographical and other research that building more inclusive learning communities helps strengthen families, the social fabric, and the capacity of communities to sustain themselves.

The paper derives from in-depth, "auto/biographical" research among diverse groups of parents and children (as well as professionals) involved in what are termed family support and learning programs in various marginalized communities in the United Kingdom. In the research we sought to chronicle and illuminate the meaning and impact of particular programs through parents' eyes, as well as from the perspectives of the workers on the ground, in what is deeply contested territory. Are these programs for empowerment, individually and collectively, or an intrusive form of social control and disciplining for the labor market (Ecclestone, 2004)? Two projects in particular serve as case studies in how to create sustaining space, in fragmented, problem-ridden communities. They spawned positive changes in the quality of intimate relationships between parents and children, and between parents themselves, strengthening the social fabric in small but significant ways. More surprisingly, perhaps, they facilitated new forms of community activism, despite the tendency for such programs to become de-politicized and individualized when in the hands of mainstream bodies (Thompson, 2000). There may be lessons here in thinking about the politics and pedagogy of building more sustainable, inclusive societies. Rather than a narrow preoccupation with education for the labor market or with property and wealth for the nuclear family, we need to focus on the links between care for families and concern for communities, and on equity and sustainable development, with opportunities for collective and more dialogical forms of learning (Booth, 2005).

The research was informed by values of social justice and by methodological assumptions shaped by feminist epistemology: not least the importance of giving voice to marginalized peoples and creating enquiring spaces in which people feel respected, listened to, and encouraged to share stories and think new thoughts, working collaboratively with researchers. The intention was to create a kind of transitional space—in the language of psychologist Donald Winnicott (1971)—for story-telling and reflexivity, one relatively free from what may be the normalizing, disciplinary gaze of government and its agendas (Foucault, 1977. 1988). At the heart of such research is a more attentive, caring gaze, building on the insights of writers such as Simone Weil (2003) and Iris Murdoch (2003) as well as psychodynamics (West, 2007). This is a research space in which narrative risks can be taken, and stories developed as well as collaboratively interrogated, over time.

The Family

But first, some background to the research: especially the preoccupation in the Anglo-Saxon world, and perhaps more widely, with the state of the family, particularly in marginalized communities. If, as the British Home Office (1998) maintains, the family, for a range of reasons, is an institution under stress—because of high levels of divorce, for instance—this seems greatest among families living in economically fragile communities. Neo-liberal economic policies and ideology, including the retreat of the welfare state, and structural changes in patterns of employment, can impact most strongly on the poorer sections of society. Divorce rates for unskilled manual workers are double the average rate and over half of lone parents in the United Kingdom live in poverty (Ranson & Rutledge, 2005). Alongside this is growing evidence of increased mental health problems across society, with, according to one estimate, one in six families affected, rising to one in three in marginalized communities (LSE, 2006). It should be noted that families living in poorer communities tend to be the target for myriad social and educational initiatives, including education for employability, no doubt derived, in part, from fear of the marginal other as well as "efficiency" imperatives in welfare provision (Ecclestone, 2004).

Programs such as Sure Start, building on the American Head Start program (and there are similar programs in Australia) are designed to break cycles of disadvantage and exclusion (Eisenstadt, 2002). Sure Start was established in some 600 areas in England identified as having high levels of deprivation. It is a multi-agency initiative involving diverse professionals working collaboratively to support "vulnerable" families and to tackle "disadvantage," so that every child could go to school more able to learn while parents themselves were encouraged to participate in various forms of adult learning. Sure Start can vary considerably but may offer diverse services: child support, creche, and access to specialist services such as speech and language therapy or child and mental health. There can also be varied opportunities for informal and non-formal adult and family learning, ranging from "training" to broader notions. But getting parents into paid work—as a means to tackle poverty and social exclusion—is often a powerful driving force in the funding of such initiatives (Ranson & Rutledge, 2005). Levitas (1998) has chronicled a shift in social policy rhetoric around social inclusion from the need for redistribution toward notions of deficit and making people more employable. Deficit models of families and the individualization of responsibility pervade social and educational policy rhetoric.

Yet, government rhetoric can also vary while the lived experience of parental support programs (and many other community initiatives) is not simply shaped from on high. New Labour concepts often cry out for and support experimentation with more personalized approaches, even if there is also a mania for control (Apitzsch, Bornat, & Chamberlayne, 2004). There are a number of players as well as agendas occupying the space represented by these initiatives: including diverse professionals who may bring their own distinct values and practices into play, despite pressures from on high. They may exploit government rhetoric—on the need to strengthen community capacity building, or improve service delivery via partnership arrangements, or to nourish new forms of sustainable local development (Home Office, 2004)—to justify more participatory approaches to project management and community regeneration alongside more diverse and questioning forms of learning (Coare & Johnston, 2003).

The Research

Our study of family support programs is unique in its longitudinal, auto/biographical, in-depth design. It is quite different, for instance, to the design and methodological assumptions of the national evaluation of Sure Start (NESS, 2005). Some differences are obvious: this paper draws on research in a small number of communities, rather than a big national sample (West, 2007). Our opportunistic sample of 100 parents in a Sure Start program is very small (and there were only 10 parents in a second project in East London, described below) compared to the 16,502 families living in Sure Start areas in the national study, as well as the 2610 families in 50 comparison communities that were shortly to have a Sure Start project (NESS, 2005). But we spent many hours with individual families (as well as staff), and the auto/biographical design of our research enabled us to explore the meaning of experience narratively, in depth and over time, in ways that other kinds of research can barely get near. We spent time too visiting a range of courses and meetings—formal and informal—across five years.

Researchers in the national study have yet to find any discernable developmental, behavioral, or language differences between children living in Sure Start areas and those living outside, but we were able to chronicle small but significant changes over time. The methodology used in the national study did not allow for any dynamic, sustained, and in-depth exploration of underlying changes and of the meanings attached to them. We spent many hours with individual families (as well as staff) in different communities, exploring their experiences, in up to seven research cycles. The auto/biographical design of the study enabled us to locate stories within wider life histories and life worlds. We frequently touched on painful experiences, including psychological problems and abusive relationships in families but also in interactions with authority. We worked collaboratively with our research subjects, encouraging people to interpret material with us, derived from feminist research values and the constructivist idea that the social is not simply internalized but is actively experienced and given meaning to, which can sometimes help change it (Chamberlayne, Bornat, & Apitzsch, 2004).

Rapport and deeper forms of listening are at the heart of such creative research, building, as suggested, on both feminist epistemology (Fine, 1992; Hartsock, 1987) as well as psychodynamic insights (Hunt & West, 2006). Our capacity as researchers to feel, identify, and empathize with our subjects is crucial, as is the ability to contain anxieties generated in the process and to maintain an open, reflexive stance toward material (rather than seeming judgmental) and to feed back what is said, and our interpretations, in digestible form, paralleling processes in psychotherapeutic contexts (Hunt & West, 2006). We also describe our research as auto/biographical: such research seeks to be open, reflexive, and explicit about the researcher's influence—including power and even unconscious processes—and to question the notion of researchers as detached biographers of others' histories in the name of "objective" science (Stanley, 1992; Miller, 2007; West, 2001). As Roper (2003) notes, research is not simply a matter of generating words but involves a relationship, which, as well as producing evidence of life outside itself, is, in its own right, a dynamic process, shaping, consciously and unconsciously, the enquiry and the development of understanding. Moreover, other people's stories of family life can evoke strong, even disturbing, feelings in researchers, in what is termed the counter-transference (West, 2001; West & Carlson, 2006). (Transference refers to how significant others, including researchers, can represent, to greater and lesser extents, perhaps unconsciously, powerful others from a person's past, while the counter-transference is concerned with what this induces, in turn, in the other.) Listening to experiences of difficult relationships, of breakdown and divorce, of children and their suffering can directly touch the experiences of researchers. This can become, reflexively, a resource for more fully empathizing with and understanding the other, as well as self, rather than being seen, more negatively, as a source of bias. But such research processes need to be grounded in self-awareness and intersubjective understanding.

Sustaining Space

The meaning of programs like Sure Start, we noted, could change for many parents, especially for the women in our sample: from uncertain, even threatening spaces to more sustaining ones. Parents were initially suspicious and in some cases paranoid: "was this social worker checking up on us?" Yet over time most of our sample came to see the projects as an important resource. Joe, Heidi, and their children were, for example, involved in a local Sure Start project and their experience illustrates its potentially sustaining role in highly personal terms. We wanted to know the extent to which parents like Joe and Heidi felt supported or threatened, empowered or disempowered, by the project. Heidi was involved in Sure Start in several ways, such as attending parent support sessions, a playgroup (with the children), and adult classes. She was also given access to specialist psychological services. She and Joe were understandably cautious about seeing us, as researchers, and were initially very reticent about talking. They eventually shared experiences, over time and in some depth. The two of them had known each other since childhood. They had both been abandoned by parents, and went into residential homes followed by periods in foster care. The material poured out as Heidi described being moved from one foster family to another. She had never been able to talk to anyone about her life history before, she said. It was hard to explain, and she did "not really understand myself why the things that had happened had happened, and not knowing how or where to start."

She told us that the adult courses "gave me more confidence to know what to do with my two children." She suffered from mental health problems, she explained, and began to talk about being upset with her children "when they laugh at me." Sure Start had been very threatening at first: they were afraid that people might be "checking" on them and "that was going through our heads all the time." They were frightened of their children being put in care, like they were. They filled the fridge with food and bought new clothes for the children whenever a Sure Start worker came near, even if they could not afford it. Yet the quality of their relationship to

Sure Start shifted, however contingently—as did their relationship to the research—from suspicion to some trust.

Heidi talked about the importance of contact with other mothers and physical relief at getting out of the house and having access to adult conversations, and of the positive effects of realizing that other mums also struggled with their children, in controlling them or dealing with their own irritation and anger. We asked Joe and Heidi, at the end of a second interview, about the research and they said it was "good" to be able to share their stories and to weave strands together, in ways they had not done previously, as they linked their own histories of abandonment with intense suspicion of authority at all levels. And they felt listened to and valued by us—as they did with particular project workers—even when talking about disturbing things. The research became, however briefly, a meaning-making and even therapeutic process. Being involved in a range of activities, including adult education, as Tom Schuller and others (2007) have noted, can provide a crucial and "sustaining" effect for mothers like Heidi. Schuller and colleagues observed, like us, how taking part gave mothers a temporal structure and a new rhythm to the week, access to adult conversations, new friendships, and senses of purpose. These processes are not to be judged simply in individualistic terms: self-confidence was being built on a collective basis and the social fabric was being strengthened in small but important ways.

There was a strong auto/biographical aspect to our study, as Heidi and Joe made a big impression on us. We (there were two of us involved) sat in the car quietly after the interviews and relived their narratives. We felt a mix of humility and admiration, given their resilience, but also concern for them and their future. We mused about how much they had to teach—about coping with distressing personal histories, for instance—and contrasted their resilience with deficit models of families and communities. We talked of our own family histories and senses of failure and inadequacy. I, Linden, had been preoccupied with a public career and I had correspondingly neglected family, relationships, and interiority. A painful divorce followed and difficult feelings of abandoning children came alive in the research. Memories of childhood were evoked too and we recorded this in our field notes. Childhood had been difficult for both of us—nothing in comparison to Heidi and Joe, but difficult nonetheless. Relationships between parents were fraught, at times, and we both felt responsible and wanted to make things better. We wrote extensively about how we were using others' stories to make sense of our own, as well as vice versa.

Claiming Space

But there was more to particular programs than creating some sustaining space: two programs, in particular, were committed to claiming space for parents to talk back to power, including to some of the agencies represented in projects. There was passionate conviction among key project staff—derived from principles of social justice—that top-down models of service delivery and decision making alienated local people while parents had much to offer, if the space provided was good enough. The aim was to celebrate parents' skills and strengths rather than identify their deficiencies. There was careful attention to detail and support, in highly sensitive and dialogical ways, in one Sure Start project, for example, as parents were included in interview panels, on the management board, in debating policies with professionals (in relation to child abuse, for instance), in running creche and nursery programs, as well as in devising opportunities for early and adult learning. In fact the entire exercise was a laboratory for informal yet deeply significant collective forms of learning and community development.

We asked parents about the factors that enabled them to take risks in such ways. Relationships and the role and personalities of particular workers were essential, we were told, time and again: "like good parents really." Two of these projects enabled nervous, diffident, poorly educated, and often self-disparaging people to challenge, collectively, others' agendas and take on new roles, as well as find individual sustenance. If local people initially entered this space on others' terms, some, at least, made it more their own (Coare & Johnston, 2003). They had learned, however provisionally, a new grammar of community activism. Space was created for what Bauman terms the *agora*: a transactional place in which people learn to translate private problems into a more collective language of public issues and potential solutions, and where, ways forward are sought and negotiated and the social fabric is correspondingly strengthened (Bauman, 2000).

A Case in Point

Gina, from a different project, provides a further case in point. She is a young single mother who lives on a run-down, fragmented public housing estate in East London but participated in a creative arts project, which was part of a broader parenting support program for single parents. Her material helps us to understand how artistic and symbolic activity can represent a transitional space in which anxieties and defensiveness in learning may lessen, and there can be movement toward greater creativity, risk taking, and even transformational learning as well as political agency. The idea of transitional space, as noted, derives from the work of psychologist Donald Winnicott (1971). This has to do with the quality of space between people, a mixture of the subjectively experienced, the objectively perceived and the relational. The experience of space can change, in early but also subsequent experience, via art, for instance: as we may project messy and even painful feelings into painting or sculpture, work on them, experience them in new ways, and come to perceive both them and self differently. These changes, at a primitive emotional level, are partly born out of the responses of significant others and of experiencing self, through their eyes, in new ways.

Gina is black and was living on her own with her young baby. She has a past riddled with pain, rejection, and hard drugs. I interviewed her early in the project and toward the end, and spent much time with her in the group over many weeks. Her relationship to the research, rather like the project itself, evolved from suspicion to a more open, committed participation. She told me she felt pressured to participate in education and to get a job but that a sympathetic Health Visitor had introduced her to the project. She was suffering from depression at the time. At first she was upset at leaving her daughter in the creche and resisted involvement. But she changed as a result of the program in different ways, she said, including in her relationship with her daughter (Gina talked of learning to play for the first time in her own life). Moreover, she became an advocate for young single mums with a local housing authority over accommodation issues, as well as getting involved in peer sex education programs in schools. There was a time when she would never have imagined herself doing such things, just as she could not tolerate mess in the home or anywhere else. Everything had to be kept in order, she said. She had never let her baby play on the floor, in case she got dirty, just as she, Gina, resisted letting herself go in creative ways. She changed, over time, although resisting the process too, often aggressively.

Gina was working on a sculpture, when we talked, near the end of the research:

> When I was pregnant and I didn't really get very big, I made myself a little pregnant belly from a washing basket to put your washing in. I used chicken wire and plaster of Paris and painted it up funny colors. They kind of expressed my mood when I was pregnant, bit dark, dull colors, bit cold. Yes ... I don't know, people who are looking at it probably won't get it, but to me it's a hangover for anger.

Her pregnancy was hard and troubling and she felt unreal, she said, since she did not look pregnant and sought to deny it. She was depressed and "really ill throughout." Her mood was translated into the sculpture. She was trying, she said, "to get across that, the darkness." There was no head on the sculpture, which was "deliberate," since she felt disconnected from her bodily experience. Gina found sculpting to be therapeutic and moved, in effect, from the edge of a community of practice into beginning to think of herself as an artist for the first time in her life. And she became a political activist too, as she became a more confident advocate for single mothers with a range of public bodies. She was perpetually anxious and uncertain but took risks, mainly because, as she put it, she felt understood and supported by particular youth leaders and tutors while her art had been a powerful experience. She liked talking to me too, she said, because I listened and was interested in her and her work, rather than being judgemental.

A young woman like Gina could continue to act out, on her own admission, in highly destructive ways. She could retreat defiantly to the edge of the group. In Melanie Klein's depth psychology there is a never fully resolved struggle between our capacity for love (that is to give ourselves openly and fully to another or to symbolic activity) but also for hate, resistance, and even the destruction of new possibility; alongside the capacity for reparation—to try again—and to make good the damage we do (Klein, 1997; Froggett, 2002). Art can serve as a transitional space for reparative work. For this to happen, however, and for a person's anxieties and defensiveness to decrease, requires significant others—tutors, youth leaders, or for that matter researchers—to come alongside and listen attentively as well as to cope with some of the ambivalence at the heart of any serious learning and identity experiment. These people need sufficient psychological resilience themselves, as well as sufficient reliability, consistency, and to an extent self-knowledge. Such emotionally attuned capabilities may, sometimes, not easily be won and ask much of professionals: including knowledge of self in action as well as an auto/biographical sensitivity to the emotional dimensions of our own struggle to learn, or for that matter to be a parent. My auto/biographical study of family doctors and the role of subjective and cultural learning in becoming a more effective practitioner illustrate much the same point (West, 2001). Connections are also being made, in a case study such as Gina's, between the most intimate of human experience, the potentially creative and empowering spaces of adult learning, and wider issues of social and democratic vitality.

Claiming Space for Parents and Professionals

Understanding the need for such connectedness may also require an interdisciplinary imagination in research. Struggles to become more of an active subject in such contexts are to be understood, in part, as profoundly social. Risk taking and biographical experiment do not take place exclusively "inside" the heads of individual parents, but depend on communication and interaction with others and in relation to a social context. We are all enmeshed in relationships, which can encourage or stifle. The new social spaces created by particular projects enabled some oppressive and demeaning scripts to be questioned. Yet building such social and cultural space—for parents, children, and communities—involves the most intimate of inter-subjective processes, which requires a psychological as well as sociological sensitivity. The capacity to resist abuse, to struggle for new ways of being, and to question and change oppressive scripts depends on becoming a more confident "I," a desiring subject who may be in tension with a "me," who may well have been the object of others' frequently demeaning prescriptions. From what may be termed a "psychosocial" perspective, there is a defended as well as a social subject in learning and social interaction. Anxiety is ubiquitous in learning and human experience more widely, grounded, in part, on our utter initial vulnerability and dependence on others. Such anxiety surrounds threats to the self, whether in relationships, in diverse social settings, in meetings, or in challenging authority. It has to do with whether we will feel accepted or are acceptable, are or can be good enough, or deserve to be taken seriously. Past and present can often elide, at the deepest and most primitive psychological level, when moving into unfamiliar space and in taking a risk with who we are.

To claim space, in earliest as well as subsequent experience, depends on others, whether parents or authority figures more widely: the capacity of particular workers intuitively to appreciate anxiety, to care, encourage yet also challenge—rather than being rigid or despairing—was crucial. Such loving, facilitating behaviors—the capacity for empathy and respect alongside the ability to maintain some distance from raw experience, and to think about why a person like Gina might act as she does—are analogous to processes in psychotherapy. They are in fact also central to good professional practice in diverse settings, although rarely considered in any depth (West, 2001; Hunt & West, 2006). We noted time and again in the research how frequently professional workers also drew on their own experiences of marginality, and even abuse, to work effectively with others. Such auto/biographical learning lay at the heart of good and effective practice: at a time when instrumentalism and evidence-based practice easily impoverish the language of self-understanding, of feeling and relationship in diverse professional contexts (Froggett, 2002). Building good and sustainable relationships and spaces requires, echoing C. Wright Mills (1970), an auto/biographical imagination in diverse settings.

Some of the processes described in this paper, however—to do with strengthening families, spaces for informal learning and access to specialist services, and enriching the social fabric—are deeply fragile. The need for sustained relationships and long-term investment in community capacity building is easily sacrificed on the altar of short-termism, while the preoccupation of policy makers with getting parents into the labor market can obscure a bigger picture (Glass, 2005). And while governments may recognize, at least rhetorically, the interdependence of the individual, family, and community triadic relationship, little attention is paid to the need for attentive, sustained, and reflexive care, grounded in awareness of shared vulnerability and human interdependence (Ranson & Rutledge, 2005; Dean, 2004). Fundamentally, building sustainable communities, or for that matter a sustainable world, has to do, in quite basic ways, with qualities of relationship: with self, between people, in communities, and with the natural world. This depends, in turn, on the extent to which families, communities, and whole cultures encourage mutual respect, caring, and inclusivity. Social sustainability requires a perspective on human beings and social development that is ethical, pedagogic, political, psychosocial, (spiritual too?) as well as material, which includes thinking of learning for a broader purpose than employment or employability, as important as these may be. The perspective needs to encompass space for new kinds of citizenship as lived practice at a time of deep alienation from conventional politics (Pattie, Seyd, & Whiteley, 2004). Citizenship becomes reconfigured as a dynamic, relational, learning process, forged in the actual practices that make up people's lives (Wyn & Dwyer 1999). Yet such experiments in building new forms of citizenship and, connectedly, personal and social sustainability in projects like Sure Start are now under pressure from top-down bureaucratic control and decision making (Glass, 2005). Space is being lost as well as gained; lessons lost rather than learned.

References

Apitzsch, U., Bornat, J., & Chamberlayne, P. (2004). Introduction. In P. Chamberlayne, J. Bornat, & U. Apitzsch (Eds), *Biographical methods and professional practice* (pp. 1–16). Bristol: Policy Press.

Bauman, Z. (2000). *Liquid modernity.* Bristol: Policy Press.
Booth, T. (2005). Keeping the future alive: putting inclusive values into action. *Forum, 47*(2/3), 151–158.
Chamberlayne, P., Bornat, J., & Apitzsch, U. (2004). *Biographical methods and professional practice.* Bristol: Policy Press.
Coare, P., & Johnston, R. (2003), *Adult learning, citizenship and community learning.* Leicester: NIACE.
Dean, H. (2004). Human rights and welfare rights: contextualising dependency and responsibility. In H. Dean (Ed.), *The ethics of welfare* (pp. 7–28). Bristol: Policy Press.
Ecclestone, K. (2004). Therapeutic stories in adult education: the demoralisation of critical pedagogy. In C. Hunt (Ed.), *Whose story now? (Re)generating research in adult learning and teaching, Proceedings of the 34th SCUTREA Conference* (pp. 55–62). Exeter: SCUTREA.
Eisenstadt, N. (2002). Sure Start: key principles and ethos. *Child Care, Health and Development,28*(1), 3–4.
Fine, M. (1992). Passion, politics and power. In M. Fine (Ed.), *Disruptive voices, the possibilities of feminist research* (pp. 205–232). Michigan: Michigan University Press.
Foucault, M. (1977). *Discipline and punish: the birth of the prison.* London: Penguin.
Foucault, M. (1988). Technologies of the self. In L. Martin, H. Gutman, & P. Hutton (Eds.), *Technologies of the self: a seminar with Michel Foucault* (pp. 16–49). Armhurst: University of Massachusetts Press.
Froggett, L. (2002). *Love, hate and welfare.* Bristol: Policy Press.
Glass, N. (2005). Surely some mistake? *The Guardian,* 5 January, p. 2.
Hartsock, N. (1987). The feminist standpoint: developing the ground for a specifically feminist historical materialism. In S. Harding (Ed.), *Feminism and methodology: social science issues* (pp. 157–180). Bloomington: Indiana University Press.
Home Office (1998). *Supporting families: a consultation document.* London: HMSO.
Home Office (2004). *Firm foundations.* London: HMSO.
Hunt, C., & West, L. (2006) Learning in a border country: using psychodynamic ideas in teaching and research. *Studies in the Education of Adults,38*(2), 160–177.
Klein, M. (1997). *Love, gratitude and other works, 1921–1945.* London: Virago.
Levitas, R. (1998). *The inclusive society: social exclusion and New Labour.* London: Macmillan.
London School of Economics (2006). *The depression report: a new deal for depression and anxiety disorders, a report by the Centre for Economic Performance's Mental Health Policy Group, chaired by Lord Layard.* London: LSE.
Miller, N. (2007). Developing an auto/biographical imagination. In L. West, P. Alheit, A. Anderson, & B. Merrill (Eds), *Using biographical and life history methods in the study of adult and lifelong learning: European perspectives* (pp. 167–186). Hamburg: Peter Lang/ESREA.
Murdoch, I. (2003 [1970]). *The sovereignty of good.* London: Routledge.
NESS (2005). *Early impacts of Sure Start programmes on children and families: research report NESS/2005/FR/013.* London: HMSO.
Pattie, C., Seyd, P., & Whiteley, P. (2004). *Citizenship in Britain: values, participation and democracy.* Cambridge: Cambridge University Press.
Ranson, S., & Rutledge, H. (2005). *Including families in the learning community: family centres and the expansion of learning.* York: Joseph Rowntree Foundation.
Roper, M. (2003). Analysing the analysed: transference and counter-transference in the oral history encounter. *Oral History,21,* 20–32.
Schuller, T., Preston, J., & Hammond, C. (2007). Mixing methods to measure learning benefits. In L. West, P. Alheit, A. S. Anderson, & B. Merrill (Eds.), *The uses of biographical and life history methods in the study of adult and lifelong learning: European perspectives* (pp. 255–278). Munich: Peter Lang.
Stanley, L. (1992). *The auto/biographical I.* Manchester: Manchester University Press.
Thompson, J. (2000). *Women, class and education.* London: Routledge.
Weil, S. (2003 [1951]). *Waiting for God.* New York: Perennial.

West, L. (2001). *Doctors on the edge: general practitioners, health and learning in the inner-city*. London: FABooks.
West, L. (2007). An auto/biographical imagination and the radical challenge of families and their learning. In L. West, P. Alheit, A. S. Anderson, & B. Merrill (Eds), *The uses of biographical and life history methods in the study of adult and lifelong learning: European perspectives* (pp. 221–239). Munich: Peter Lang.
West, L., & Carlson, A. (2006). Claiming and sustaining space? Sure Start and the auto/biographical imagination. *Auto/Biography*, 14(2), 359–380.
Winnicott, D. (1971). *Playing and reality*. London: Routledge.
Wright Mills, C. (1970 [1959]). *The sociological imagination*. London: Penguin.
Wyn, J., & Dwyer, P. (1999). New directions in research on youth in transition. *Journal of Youth Studies*,2(1), 5–21.

Chapter 11
Health Literacy and AVE for Social Sustainability

Kay Price

Abstract The position taken in this chapter is that healthy living is a lifelong learning project. What follows is a "critical reading" of how health education activities offered through Australia's adult and vocational education (AVE) competency-based model can contribute to this lifelong learning project. I bring forward for debate whether AVE as a workplace and an academic learning environment should/ could/can require and support educators and students to be health literate and whether AVE can achieve the aims of the Bonn Declaration on Learning for Work, Citizenship and Sustainability. I question the extent to which an AVE setting can enable educators and students to engage in interactions, conversations, and activities that challenge participants to critique what they think or the decisions/choices they have made about their health. There is a need to debate what responsibility AVE has to ensure both educators and students are health literate, to ensure that AVE educators and in turn students are capable of making choices for, rather than against, health, so as to support healthy living.

Introduction

The United Nations Educational, Scientific and Cultural Organization (UNESCO) considers that "schools should act not only as centres for academic learning, but also as supportive venues for the provision of health education and services" (UNESCO, 2006, p. 7). The position taken in this chapter is that healthy living is a lifelong learning project. Consequently, health education that focuses on educators and students learning how to live a healthy life is worth consideration within any academic learning context. In this chapter, I explore how health education activities offered through adult and vocational education (AVE) can contribute to this lifelong learning project. I specifically refer to Australia's AVE competency-based model, acknowledging that not all AVE systems are competency-based to the extent of the Australian model.

K. Price (✉)
University of South Australia, South Australia, Australia

The position I proceed from in this paper is that health is a contested term. I acknowledge the World Health Organization (1986) understanding, which suggests that health is created in the context of everyday life thus alluding to the social dimensions of health. Underpinning UNESCO's understandings is the concept of sustainability. UNESCO asserts that "A healthy population and safe environments are important pre-conditions for sustainable development" (UNESCO, 2006, p. 7). If a healthy population is needed before sustainable development can even be considered possible, then I argue that an AVE focus on health education contributing to healthy living becomes even more important.

I agree with Kickbusch who says: "Every choice in daily life potentially becomes a choice for or against health" (2007, p. 152, her emphasis). For AVE to contribute to a sustainable society, choices about how health education is delivered have the potential to influence personal choices made by AVE educators and students in relation to their own health. If, as suggested in the Introduction to this volume, social sustainability refers to "a positive and long-term condition within communities, and a process within communities that can achieve and maintain that condition," then AVE's social sustainability role in terms of health is to ensure that participants are capable of making choices for, rather than against, health, so as to support healthy living. In other words, AVE has a role to play in "health literacy."

Nutbeam comments that health literacy is a concept "that is both new and old" (2000, p. 265). He argues that it is a composite term to describe a range of outcomes and, as such, the role of health education should be directed toward improving health literacy. While acknowledging that "the field of literacy studies is alive with debate about different 'types' of literacy" (2000, p. 263), Nutbeam discusses approaches to classification that identify various types of health literacy "in terms of what it is that literacy enables us to do" (p. 263) rather than measures of achievement. Citing work by Freebody and Luke (1990), Nutbeam refers to basic/functional literacy, communicative/interactive literacy, and critical literacy. Nutbeam elaborates upon what he describes as the three levels of health literacy: functional, interactive, and critical (see Nutbeam, 2000, p. 266). Functional health literacy is defined as having the sufficient skills in reading, writing, and numeracy to be able to comprehend health information. Interactive health literacy is directed toward improving personal capacity to act independently on knowledge (Nutbeam, 2000, p. 265). I urge readers to review a critical paper by Cuban (2006) who raises criticisms about functional health literacy. A broader or more critical understanding of health literacy, says Nutbeam (2000), is offered by the World Health Organization, which views health literacy as

> the cognitive and social skills which determine the motivation and ability of individuals to gain access to, understand and use information in ways which promote and maintain good health. (WHO, 1998, p. 10)

UNESCO argues that AVE settings need to be healthy settings, and that literacies other than reading, writing, and numeracy are needed. UNESCO states:

> The wider skills of scientific and social literacy are also important ... The application of such literacies to the world of work and active citizenship need to become core dimensions of TVET if it is to respond to the imperatives of social sustainability. (UNESCO, 2006, p. 18)

The purpose of this chapter is not to present a review of literature on health literacy or debate what health literacy is (for which the reader is directed to Nutbeam, 2000). My intent is to present a "critical reading" of the notion of social sustainability through AVE in relation to health. I want to bring forward for debate whether AVE as a workplace and an academic learning environment should/could/can require and support educators and students to be health literate: a key competence in a healthy population (Kickbusch, 2005). I question whether AVE can achieve the aims of the Bonn Declaration on Learning for Work, Citizenship and Sustainability, which states:

> Preparation for work should equip people with the knowledge, competencies, skills, values and attitudes to become productive and responsible citizens who appreciate the dignity of work and contribute to sustainable societies. (UNESCO, 2004, para. 3)

However, before discussing the links between AVE, social sustainability, and health literacy, I briefly explain what I mean by a "critical reading."

A Critical Reading

My approach to critical reading is influenced by the works of Derrida (e.g., 1976, 1978, 1981, 1987, 1988, 1991a, 1991b) and by secondary readings which use his works. I premise my critical reading of collated literature relating to health literacy and AVE on the understanding that these collective resources tell a story of how a particular object or focus is given meaning. Collated literature is positioned as products of writing that inscribe organization and order (Cooper, 1989) and are a representation of a particular viewpoint produced within a particular context or way of thinking. As Cooper says about Derrida's critique of writing, "Writing, for Derrida, is primarily a form of control: its communicative function comes second to this" (Cooper, 1989, p. 492). For me, a critical reading is much more than the sense-making work an individual performs when reviewing literature. Critical reading can be likened to a pause or a reflective moment that seeks to make what has become invisible and taken for granted, visible, destabilizing, and discursive (Jacobsen & Jacques, 1997). It is destabilizing as it moves from what is presumed to be true or known about an object or focus of attention, toward uncovering a different meaning. It is discursive as it explores how certain ways of thinking construct understandings of any reality and exclude other ways of thinking about the same reality. A critical reading does not privilege that which is written as the truth.

I do not propose that the selection of literature I collated includes all that has been published in relation to AVE, social sustainability, lifelong learning, health, and health literacy. I produce *a* reading, as opposed to *the* reading of literature and I agree with Jones when she writes: "Different persons, with different perspectives and different curiosities about the area of investigation will inevitably find different categories with which to structure and make sense of the data" (1985, pp. 58–59). From my understanding of Derrida, language is a structure upon which meaning has to be imposed onto words, rather than meaning being implied within words.

The opportunity provided to me to write this chapter affirms that it is timely for a debate about whether AVE should/could/can implement health education in such a way as to support staff and students not only to learn how best to make choices for healthy living, but also how to enact choices "for" rather than "against" health. Questions emerging from my critical reading include: Within a competency-based approach such as that in Australia, is it feasible, even possible, for AVE to implement core competencies in all courses to ensure that health literacy learning activities focus on understanding health information in a way that the information is retained, believed, critiqued, and put into action? And if a competency-based approach to health literacy were to be implemented, how could educators and trainers structure assessments to determine if a student were competent and not just being obedient and complicit to pass? If assessments were structured to include measurements of the health literacy skills of students, to what extent would the educator or trainer need to demonstrate this competency themselves in order to assess it? To what extent would the school or institutional setting take responsibility for ensuring educators and students were health literate? How should/could/can AVE contribute to educators and students being health literate so that they themselves, through both their personal and work-specific roles, ensure the social sustainability of our communities through healthy living?

Making Choices *for* Health

Occupational health and safety legislation in Australia clearly places significant emphasis on ensuring that employees take reasonable care to protect their own health and safety at work (see for example South Australia's *Occupational Health, Safety and Welfare Act 1986*, Part 3, sec. 21: Duties of workers). AVE settings are both a workplace and an academic learning environment, and the delivery of a socially sustainable AVE requires workplace learning for all staff to be in concert with the modification of work processes, "as the two are inseparable" (UNESCO, 2006, p. 11). AVE educators and AVE work processes have the potential to influence student learning. This understanding focuses attention on the supportive strategies in place for sound decision making for health within AVE settings by all participants.

While literacy and numeracy skills are said to be vital for AVE (UNESCO, 2006, p. 18), the extent to which current AVE policy and practice in Australia requires and supports AVE educators as employees and students as potential employees, to protect their health and to be health literate, is debatable. It is also debatable whether AVE policy and practice requires and supports educators/trainers as employees within AVE (or any setting) to be health literate, and for educators/trainers to accept that they have a responsibility to be health literate before engaging with students in learning activities that should/could/can make an active contribution to improving students' "healthy living." Recently, it was reported that around 77 per cent of Australians (Australian Institute of Health and Welfare, 2006) and 80 per cent of Americans (Centers for Disease Control and Prevention, and Merck Company

Foundation, 2007) claim they have at least one non-communicable or chronic condition which had lasted or was expected to last for at least six months. Indeed, WHO (2005a, 2005b) warns that the number of people, families, and communities that are "afflicted" by deaths from chronic disease is increasing, and that this causes poverty and hinders the economic development of many countries. WHO has produced evidence in post-industrial nations that non-communicable or chronic diseases have associated lifestyle risk factors named as smoking, poor nutrition, risky alcohol use, physical inactivity, and being overweight. If these risk factors affecting the post-industrial nations count as evidence that people do make choices "against" their health, an issue for me is whether they make this choice intentionally, well aware of the consequences of their decisions.

Competing sources of "health" information and the diversity of lifestyle choices now available to consumers in western societies intensify the need for consumers' improved health literacy. Having the cognitive and social skills to gain access to, understand, and use information to promote and maintain healthy living over a lifetime is no easy task.

Harris (2003) describes different ways in which the word "choice" can be used. A choice, according to Harris, can be the process by which people come to a conclusion (individually or collectively) regarding different courses of actions they perceive to be available; or a performative action, which expresses a decision in a social setting; or a perceived range of available options. However, government policies and strategies in relation to health are increasingly focusing attention at the individual level on people "making good choices, only good choices and even better choices" (Bauman, 1992, p. 4). Pre-conditions for understanding how AVE can contribute to sustainable development of communities include understanding how AVE settings contribute to the process by which people

- come to a conclusion (individually and/or collectively) regarding different courses of action they perceive to be available in relation to healthy living; and
- learn the range of available options to them in relation to healthy living.

The concept of a socially sustainable AVE has links with the WHO concept of "healthy settings" (WHO, 2006; Dooris, 2005). The "healthy settings" concept is about integrating a commitment to health within the structures, processes, and routines of life in different settings and focuses on interactions and interdependencies between all persons. The approach acknowledges that each setting (for example, school, workplace, or AVE site) is part of a greater whole, and functions as an open system in synergistic interchange with the wider environment (Dooris, 2005). For example, in the school setting, health-promoting school projects have been developed that aim to raise students' literacy, though criticisms have been made about the lack of rigorous research and evaluation to enable the development of a strong evidence base for policy and practice (Dooris, 2005). These criticisms have emerged because the focus of evaluation of healthy settings has been on discrete projects within settings rather than an evaluation of the effectiveness of the settings approach as a whole (Dooris, 2005). There has been minimal discussion about healthy settings as a theoretical construct. The extent to which social sustainability through AVE has been developed theoretically, like the WHO concept of a healthy setting, is questionable. Social sustainability through AVE as a focus of research may be able to produce evaluation studies to show that staff and students engage in learning activities that make a contribution to them learning how to improve the health and well-being of others but how social sustainability through AVE improves their personal ability and capability to protect their own health is also questionable.

I have argued elsewhere (Price, 2006) that in a buying and selling marketplace, rather than *producing* health by returning the body to a healthy state (as is the approach within a sickness model of care), being in good health (preventing sickness) has become a common expectation (see also Bauman, 2000). Given the breadth and depth of biomedical knowledge and the scope of health protection and maintenance strategies available, changing people's lifestyle behaviors is often needed but difficult to achieve. Adapting from Bauman (2000), we may think we can make human beings competent so that they will follow prescriptions, specific lifestyle approaches, even research findings, management plans, and follow routines (doing what they are told in the way they are told). However, as Bauman (1993) also points out, there are no hard-and-fast principles that one can memorize and deploy in order to escape the "messiness" of the human world, as "messiness" will stay whatever we do or know. In a competency-based approach to AVE, where there is an expressed "right" way to think/act/write, it is difficult to imagine how this "messiness" can be accommodated so as to enable understanding amongst educators and students about healthy living within the different contexts of their lives.

Effective communication, cooperation, and synergy between all involved are critical to attempts to change behavior in a population as is also the need to welcome conflict as an opportunity for negotiation. This is particularly important when considering the need for people to learn new information and unlearn outdated information continually so that they can maintain good health (Kickbusch, 2005). For AVE, or indeed any institution, to contribute to a sustainable society is an enormous challenge, which focuses attention on the appropriateness and effectiveness of a competency-based approach.

Questioning the Contribution of Competency-Based Education to Social Sustainability

Wheelan and Carter state: "Australia has constructed a VET system that ... is a rigid system that is narrowly focused on work-related competencies" (2001, p. 303). It is not my intent to engage in a debate about competency development. I do want to bring forward for debate the view that the "basic building blocks" that describe the outcomes of the functions that people perform in a particular work role, and the performance criteria or statements to show what is to be assessed to determine competency (ANTA, 1999, p. 16), are not focused on sustainable development. It is clear, I argue, that they are focused on industry development.

I agree with Flax, who writes:

> We adopt the knowledge that fits our uses. Humans are very good at creating rational reasons for rejecting knowledge that does not fit our purposes or would make us doubt them. (Flax, 1993, p. 31)

Individuals, precisely because they can create rational reasons for rejecting knowledge, are more likely to be inherently conservative as a consequence to reduce confusion and stress, and to seek certainty and security. Developing competencies to reduce confusion and to work toward a specific outcome may be suitable for specific industry work roles but must be questionable for contributing to healthy living as a lifelong learning project.

Focusing on AVE as pre-determined strategies (competencies) to be implemented/disseminated where the focus is on the specific choice that is made, rather than the process of negotiating how choices are made, perpetuates expert expectations of obedience and conformity while failing to negotiate the complexity of choice confronting consumers in the context of their own individual understanding, life context, resources, and approach to survival. AVE strategies based on imparting expertise on healthy behaviors reproduce the conditions for domination as they impose as many restrictive rules as possible on the conduct of others in a context where individual freedom is recognized as a removal of the rules constraining one's own freedom of choice (Bauman, 2001). Midgley (2000) asserts that conservative people tend to move into new ways of thinking/doing only when there is a good reason and an associated emotional benefit for doing so. Within the competency-based model of AVE, it is questionable how "good reasons" can be made evident within the competency being assessed.

I argue that the emphasis in the competency-based approach currently seems to be on attracting the attention of educators and students to be obedient and conform to pre-determined health promotion strategies. Educators and students may not be able to portray an understanding of how this demand will not necessarily result in people being health literate. If AVE policy and practice becomes preoccupied with ensuring certainty of behavior, the potential exists to demand obedience and conformity from people (educators and students) who are the target of pre-determined strategies.

If AVE is to contribute to social sustainability by promoting healthy living, I argue that it requires a shift away from a competency-based approach to a setting where educators and students are enabled to engage in interactions, conversations, and activities that challenge participants to critique what they think or decisions/choices they have made about their health. That is, they should challenge themselves and each other about what they consider are "truths" or certainties in relation to health, and to be supported to work against the polarization of positions that may emerge within these interactions (see, for example Scott, 1991). Educators and students need to be able to participate in interactions, conversations, and activities that seek to make collective sense of decisions/choices they have made about health, to learn how to participate in making choices within the different contexts that make up their lives, and to explore what makes some choices more important than others (see, for example, Harris, 2003).

In acknowledging that adults are subject to an explosion of information and knowledge, Edwards, Raggatt, Harrison, McCollum, and Calder (1998) emphasize the ongoing process of learning rather than the content of learning, content they say is likely to go out of date. These authors have suggested that it is through guidance and counseling that students learn about themselves as lifelong learners. Healthy living is a lifelong learning project and knowing what you do not know is a critical factor in staying healthy. As Candy says, "It seems that the acknowledgement of one's ignorance is actually the beginning of a lifelong journey of continuing education" (2000, p. 122). Learning activities need to focus on how staff and students can acknowledge their ignorance, to understand what it means to be able to accept that they do not know, and can never know, all that there is to know when making choices for healthy living. This acknowledgement enables AVE and lifelong learning to contribute to social sustainability by focusing on learning activities that explore how people can learn to remain as healthy as possible, and how to make decisions given the different and changing contexts they exist within, and given all the challenges individuals will confront in their lives. The skills needed for this require AVE educators to be more than functionally health literate.

AVE educators need to be critically health literate—having the cognitive and skills development outcomes that are oriented toward supporting effective social and political action as well as individual action (Nutbeam, 2000). The feasibility of this requirement needs ongoing debate. However, there seems little likelihood of AVE contributing to social sustainability unless AVE staff can be critically health literate and for they themselves to be knowingly contributing to healthy living. This requirement emphasizes AVE as a workplace having the appropriate policies and practices to support AVE staff to explore and understand healthy living as a lifelong learning project. It also places an emphasis on AVE as an academic learning environment to create learning situations that contribute to lifelong learning, including a shift away from concentrating on measuring pre-determined outcomes.

In Summary

I agree with Bauman who says that many consumers want the freedom to make their own lifestyle choices and at the same time to have the "freedom from bearing the consequences of wrong choices" (Bauman, 2000, p. 89). But many people make these choices having no education to assist them in understanding the implications the choices have on their health. Galvin (2002) has written about health and individual responsibility for healthy living, raising concerns about "victim blaming" and moves by government to place "being in good health" as an individual responsibility and a moral imperative. In contrast, UNESCO considers sustainable development "more a *moral precept* than a *scientific concept*" (2006, p. 5, their emphasis). One of the "common themes" (UNESCO, 2006, p. 6) of sustainable development according to UNESCO is:

Governance: at local, national and international levels, sustainable development will best be promoted where governance structures enable transparency, full expression of opinion, free debate and broad input into policy formulation. (UNESCO, 2006, p. 7)

What about AVE governance structures as a workplace and an academic learning environment? At a minimum, AVE involves different people in health, social care, and other complementary courses to prepare them to work in a variety of health and social care related roles. While AVE may be delivered in different venues by different people I have presented this chapter based on a view that there is a need to debate what responsibility AVE has to ensure both educators and students are health literate.

I restate here my earlier comment. If social sustainability refers to a positive and long-term condition that can be achieved and maintained over time then AVE's social sustainability role in relation to health needs to ensure that AVE educators and in turn students are capable of making choices for, rather than against, health, so as to support healthy living. How best to achieve this requires at a minimum ensuring AVE participants in the western world learn how personally to be critically health literate rather than teaching them about health literacy and measuring their level of functional health literacy.

References

Australian Institute of Health and Welfare (2006). *Australia's health 2006*, cat. no. AUS 73. Canberra: AIHW.
Australian National Training Authority (1999). *Training packages development handbook*. Brisbane: Australian National Training Authority.
Centers for Disease Control and Prevention, & Merck Company Foundation (2007). *The state of aging and health in America 2007*. Whitehouse Station, NJ: Merck Company Foundation.
Bauman, Z. (1992). Survival as a social construct. *Theory, Culture and Society, 9*(1), 1–36.
Bauman, Z. (1993). *Postmodern ethics*. Oxford: Blackwell.
Bauman, Z. (2000). *Liquid modernity*. Cambridge: Polity Press.
Bauman, Z. (2001). *The individualized society*. Oxford: Blackwell.
Candy, P. C. (2000). Reaffirming a proud tradition: universities and lifelong learning. *Active Learning in Higher Education, 1*(2), 101–125.
Cooper, R. (1989). Modernism, postmodernism and organizational analysis 3: the contribution of Jacques Derrida. *Organization Studies, 10*(4), 479–502.
Cuban, S. (2006) Following the physician's recommendations faithfully and accurately: functional health literacy, compliance, and the knowledge-based economy. *Journal for Critical Education Policy Studies, 4*(2). http://www.jceps.com/?pageID=article&articleID=74. Accessed 16 April 2008.
Derrida, J. (1976). *Of grammatology*, Trans. G. C. Spivak. Baltimore, MD: John Hopkins University Press.
Derrida, J. (1978). *Writing and difference*, Trans. A. Bass. Chicago: University of Chicago Press.
Derrida, J. (1981). *Dissemination*, Trans. B. Johnson. Chicago: University of Chicago Press.
Derrida, J. (1987). *The post card*, Trans. A. Bass. Chicago: University of Chicago Press.
Derrida, J. (1988). *Limited Inc*, Trans. S. Weber. Evanston IL: Northwestern University Press.
Derrida, J. (1991a). Difference, Trans. A. Bass. In P. Kamuf (Ed.), *A Derrida reader: between the blinds* (pp. 59–79). New York: Columbia University Press.

Derrida, J. (1991b). Speech and phenomena and other essays on Husserl's theory of signs, Trans. D. B. Allison. In P. Kamuf (Ed.), *A Derrida reader: between the blinds* (pp. 8–30). New York: Columbia University Press.

Dooris, M. (2005). Healthy settings: challenges to generating evidence of effectiveness. *Health Promotion International*, *21*(1), 55–65.

Edwards, R., Raggatt, P., Harrison, R., McCollum, A., & Calder J. (1998). *Recent thinking in lifelong learning: a review of literature*. Research Brief No 80. Nottingham, UK: Department for Education and Employment.

Flax, J. (1993). *Disputed subjects: essays on psychoanalysis, politics and philosophy*. New York: Routledge.

Freebody, P., & Luke, A. (1990). "Literacies" programs: debates and demands in cultural context. *Prospect*, *5*, 7–16.

Galvin, R. (2002). Disturbing notions of chronic illness and individual responsibility: toward a genealogy of morals. *Health*, *6*(2), 107–137.

Harris, J. (2003). Time to make up your mind: why choosing is difficult. *British Journal of Learning Difficulties*, *31*, 3–8.

Jacobsen, S. W., & Jacques, R. (1997) Destabilizing the field: poststructuralist knowledge making strategies in a postindustrial era. *Journal of Management Inquiry*, *6*(1), 42–59.

Jones, S. (1985) The analysis of depth interviews. In R. Walker (Ed.), *Applied qualitative research* (pp. 56–70). Aldershot: Gower.

Kickbusch, I. (2005). The health society: importance of the new policy proposal by the EU Commission on Health and Consumer Affairs. *Health Promotion International*, *20*(2), 101–103.

Kickbusch, I. (2007). Health governance: the health society. In D. V. McQueen & I. Kickbusch (Eds.), *Health and modernity: the role of theory in health promotion* (pp. 144–161). New York: Springer.

Midgely, G. (2000). *Systemic intervention: philosophy, methodology and practice*. New York: Kluwer/Plenum Publishers.

Nutbeam, D. (2000). Health literacy as a public health goal: a challenge for contemporary health education and communication strategies for the 21st century. *Health Promotion International*, *15*(3), 259–267.

Price, K. (2006). Health promotion and some implications of consumer choice. *Journal of Nursing Management*, *14*, 494–501.

Scott, J. W. (1991). The evidence of experience. *Critical Inquiry*, *17*(4), 773–797.

United Nations Educational, Scientific and Cultural Organization (2004). *The Bonn Declaration on Learning for Work, Citizenship and Sustainability*. http://www.unevoc.unesco.org/publications/pdf/SD_BonnDeclaration_e.pdf. Accessed 19 April 2006.

United Nations Educational, Scientific and Cultural Organization (2006). *Discussion Paper Orienting Technical and Vocational Education and Training for Sustainable Development*. http://www.unevoc.unesco.org/publications/pdf/SD_DiscussionPaper_e.pdf. Accessed 12 July 2006.

Wheelan, L., & Carter, R. (2001). National training packages: a new curriculum framework for vocational education and training in Australia. *Education + Training*, *43*(6), 303–316.

World Health Organization (1986). *Ottawa charter for health promotion*. Copenhagen: WHO Regional Office for Europe.

World Health Organization (1998). *Health promotion glossary*, Geneva: WHO.

World Health Organization (2005a). *Global health promotion scaling up for 2015: a brief review of major impacts and developments over the past 20 years and challenges for 2015*. WHO Secretariat background document for the 6th Global Conference on Health Promotion in Bangkok, Thailand, 7–11 August 2005. http://www.who.int/healthpromotion/conferences/6gchp/hpr_conference_background.pdf. Accessed 19 April 2006.

World Health Organization (2005b). *Preventing chronic diseases: a vital investment*. Geneva: WHO.

World Health Organization (2006). *Healthy settings*. http://www.wpro.who.int/health_topics/healthy_settings/. Accessed 19 April 2006.

Chapter 12
Education in Post-conflict Environments: Pathways to Sustainable Peace?

Rebecca Spence

Abstract Can formal and nonformal education processes act as a catalyst for sustainable peace? In this chapter, I explore the various roles that education, in its widest sense, can play in helping progress toward sustainable peace in conflict-affected nations. Recognizing that education, particularly adult education, is one of the main tenets of any peace-building process, I suggest how educational policy and practice could be and has been shaped to integrate key peace-building and reconciliation principles. I discuss the various approaches to education as a means to peace in conflict-affected countries and then suggest ways in which these approaches might contribute to the ongoing process of peace and nation building in Timor Leste, which has recently experienced another bout of destabilizing violence.

Introduction

> The central, primary challenge of re-building war-torn societies has to do with mending relations and with restoring dignity, trust and faith ... More than the physical, institutional or systemic destruction that war brings, it is ... the destruction of relationships ... that has the potential to undermine the solutions to all other problems. (UNRISD, 2000, p.1)

Reconciliation is one of the key ingredients in promoting social sustainability in conflict-affected nations. Two distinct approaches to reconstruction and peace building/reconciliation can be identified: institutional and relational. The former focuses primarily on (re)building institutional infrastructure and capacity, holding elections, (re)vitalizing the economy, and creating and installing a functioning governance structure. The latter (often named as reconciliation) focuses upon creating or repairing the social relationships that form the glue that holds society together. Activities that support and promote the rebuilding of trust and relationships at the community level will maximize the effectiveness of the endeavor (Fred-Mensah, 2004). Relational approaches are necessary components of any reconstruction process and these are facilitated through fostering dialogue between former parties to the conflict,

---

R. Spence (✉)
University of New England, New South Wales, Australia

conflict resolution and mediation training, joint social and economic development projects, psychosocial support and trauma counseling, and, most importantly for this chapter, through various educational initiatives.

Educating for reconciliation is a vital and necessary component of building social sustainability in conflict-affected and deeply divided societies. Alongside the political and economic endeavors that seek to right the structural inequities that conflict has perpetuated and created, the process of relationship building toward reconciliation must be given precedence, particularly in societies divided along religious or ethnic fault lines. Many relational approaches to peace building are aimed at reducing prejudice through encouraging contact around superordinate goals. To be effective, prejudice reduction education programs must not only increase contact between the opposing parties but also encourage tolerance and reduce discrimination and hostility with a view to developing empathy. If the contact process allows the groups to reassess their prejudice about each other and, in the process, reflect upon how and why stereotyping occurs, then attitudinal change can take place. Similarly, if emotional ties are built through the contact process, increasing inter-group trust and confidence, then anxieties can be reduced and empathy built.

Kreisberg's dimensions of reconciliation model offers some fresh perspectives on ways in which formal and nonformal education might be used as a conflict-mediating, relationship-building and peace-promoting tool (*see* Fig. 12.1). He defines the concept of reconciliation as those actions or initiatives that "help transform a destructive conflict or relationship and views progress toward attainment of *security* and *justice* needs (in their widest definitions) as central to any recovery process" (Kreisberg, 2004, p. 82). Furthermore, he also views mutual recognition or *regard* and the sharing of perspectives or *truth* getting as the other essentials. The rest of this chapter will focus on the ways in which this aspect of relationship building has been adopted into the educational policy and practice of conflict-affected nations and suggest how formal and nonformal educational initiatives could be utilized in Timor Leste to promote a more sustainable peace.

Fig. 12.1 Dimensions of reconciliation

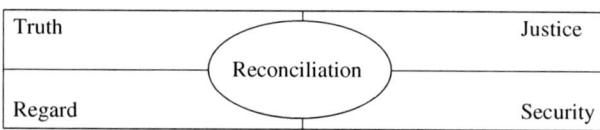

Education for Regard and Social Sustainability

Building healthy, cooperative relationships among and between sectors of society at a micro, mezzo, and macro level is essential to create the conditions for sustained peace building. In the Solomon Islands and Aceh, adult education policies and practices that have focused upon creating opportunities for regard or mutual recognition have used school governance structures and the process of rebuilding schools destroyed by the conflict as relationship-building exercises with great success. In the Solomons one of the main requirements of a large donor peace and restoration fund (of which education was one component) was that communities concentrate on projects that were of mutual rather than individual benefit. The fund, which ran from 2000 to 2004, provided support in the form of resources and money for rebuilding the schools that had been burnt down during the fighting. These vocational projects brought different sectors of the affected community together in working relationships. The elders in the community were dependent on the youths to participate in the hard physical tasks: cutting and transporting the timber, digging the gravel, and much of the construction of the new schools. Processes were established to ensure community inclusivity, to activate labor teams to undertake the building, and to ensure that the various sectors within and across villages were involved. Community management of the projects encouraged intra- and inter-community cohesion through teamwork. In requiring that communities own and manage the implementation process, it allowed communities to reexperience working together, and kept people busy and engaged with community processes. These projects helped to rebuild trust and confidence, which had been lessened by the tensions. Many of the communities that did not experience open violence during the tensions nonetheless expressed general feelings of anxiety and fear. People were "not free to move around" during the tensions. People taking advantage of the lawlessness, for example, rekindled old grievances over land, and communities were fearful because of the potential for violence. The delivery of services and the economy had ground to a halt. Work on the rebuilding projects brought people within the community together, out from their houses during a time when there was a lack of trust, when people kept to themselves. The process of working together on the superordinate goal of the project allowed people to reengage with each other and reidentify their place in the community networks. The process of rebuilding trust was particularly relevant for the youth who were caught up in the fighting. Being included in the projects, and being given responsibilities for ensuring the success of the projects (such as leading labor teams or transporting materials) allowed the youths to regain the trust of the community. It kept them busy and out of trouble and it allowed them to experience aspects of leadership in preparation for future roles. The community could witness them working productively and constructively and were reassured (Spence & Wielders, 2005).

In Aceh, the Australia-Indonesia Partnership for Reconstruction and Development (AIPRD) has focused its relationship-building efforts through a Communities and Education Project (CEPA), which seeks to promote reconciliation and village-level democracy through the education sector at the community level. The CEPA project uses adult education principles for the whole community as a vehicle to reestablish good communication between parties to the former conflict. The vehicle for relationship building is the school governance structure. Parties to the former conflict are representatives on the school committees and make mutual decisions about school management procedures, fundraising, and resource acquisition. This process facilitates and fosters a safe environment to discuss issues related to their school, and in the process communication and cooperation between parties is reestablished. The project aims to model cooperative practice in the hope that participatory processes such as the school governance structure can be taken up by other sectors and groups active in the village. Thus CEPA is introducing a system for community participation, for the selection of representatives that could enhance local democracy processes, and ultimately could make a real contribution to peace and reconciliation (AusAID, 2006). Whilst these may not seem like typical vocational and adult educational policies they do demonstrate that education can be a successful vehicle for creating situations in which people who have had their relationships disrupted by the conflict can come together for mutual benefit.

In Timor a similar approach to educational governance has been adopted by the 100 Friendly Schools Project (100 FSP), which is a component of the UNICEF and RDTL Master Plan of Operations. According to that plan, the 100 FSP aims to "strengthen national educational policy and planning, increase the capacity of primary schools to deliver quality education, and increase enrolment and completion rates" (UNICEF, 2005, p. 9). The project has four components: teacher training, school-based management, the establishment of Parent Teacher Associations, and improving Early Childhood Education. Parents and community members have benefited from the project by gaining a greater sense of ownership of the school and their children's education, becoming aware of how they can support schooling, and having a greater say in the affairs of the school. Participation in Parent Teacher Associations has also been an experience in actively constructing and participating in democratic organizations. The success of this program suggests that Parent Teacher Associations could be a vehicle by which parties to the current conflict could come together at a village level to work on the superordinate goal of providing governance and advice to the local schools. Similarly, educating for mutual regard and relationship building could be one of the outcomes of the comprehensive rebuilding process that will have to take place in Dili. Timor Leste could adopt the Solomons' model of bringing different sectors of the affected communities together in working relationships to rebuild damaged houses and infrastructure, and make it a priority to include the youth who were instrumental in causing the violence. If it is facilitated well, the process of working together could create the space for dialogue about recent events, whilst fulfilling the primary purpose of revitalizing the damaged infrastructure.

Education for Truth and Social Sustainability

Truth commissions are becoming an increasingly common feature of post-conflict nation-building processes. The main purpose of any truth commission is to record and detail human rights violations. Its secondary purpose is to help the healing process by acknowledging people's experiences of the conflict. Truth commissions can promote healing and reconciliation in several ways. A truth commission is a moral standard bearer in that it emphasizes the prevention of further human rights violations. It can also transform the old symbols of the past and rehumanize the conflict by fostering dialogue about suffering and resilience. A truth commission is the public political face of the truth and can be duplicated at the local level; each area or community has the potential to instigate its own process of truth telling.

In Northern Ireland, the Education for Mutual Understanding Initiative, introduced in schools, aims to increase tolerance and cross-cultural understanding by educating and informing across conflict lines about the rich, cultural and historical heritage of the parties to the conflict, to promote learning about self-respect and respect for others, and to improve relationships between people of differing cultural traditions. The objectives of Education for Mutual Understanding state that as an integral part of their education pupils should learn to respect and value themselves and others; to appreciate the interdependence of people within society; to know about and understand what is shared as well as what is different about their cultural traditions; and to appreciate how conflict may be handled in nonviolent ways (Smith & Robinson, 1996). As part of this initiative, stories about experiences of the conflict are shared as part of the curricula. Likewise in South Africa, curricula are being transformed to produce education for meaningful participation in society, and the Truth and Reconciliation Commission report is being scrutinized to see how it can be made available in curricula (Enslin, 2003; Bam, 2000). Wider discussion about history in South Africa centers on how knowledge about the "history of Africa and Africans in our own country" can be used "to rewrite ourselves into world history" (Bam, 2000, p. 6). This approach recognizes that this will contribute to the recovery of dignity and confidence for those who suffered under the Apartheid regime.

Therefore, there is already a precedent for transforming the Timorese Truth Commissions' report, *Chega*, into a pedagogical tool for learning about the different perspectives on the conflict, the different roles played by parties to the conflict, the suffering caused, and the resilience of the Timorese people. Sharing stories about suffering and resilience will contribute to the recovery of dignity and confidence and will create avenues for dialogue about the past and how it pertains to the future.

Education for Security and Social Sustainability

New understandings of security reflect the idea that structural and cultural violence is as much a threat as direct violence (Spence, 2004; Galtung, 1990). Indeed breaking the current cycle of violence in conflict-affected nations depends upon recognizing and addressing the underlying structural and cultural forces pushing people toward conflict. The process of rectifying these structural and cultural inequities and meeting basic needs can be viewed as simultaneously enhancing security and building peace. Nonviolent methodologies offer peace-building educators and practitioners both an integrated analysis of violence and power and a peaceful means of transforming the structures, values, and patterns of social relations that create and sustain conflict (*see*, for example, Spence & McLeod, 2002). Unless the reality of domination and exploitation embedded in global power structures and manifested at local levels is also explicitly addressed, there will be no space for values essential for sustainable recovery and reconciliation. Whilst direct violence may be momentarily interrupted by external intervention in Timor Leste, unless the structural causes of the conflict are addressed, cooperative and participatory structures that meet human needs are created, and unless the capacity of people to use nonviolent methods to transform ongoing conflict is nurtured and supported, then violence will remain as the solution to difference. In Mozambique and Sudan, nonviolence training has been incorporated into rehabilitation programs for child soldiers, using psychological support services to help them unlearn the culture of violence that they experienced during the long years of conflict (International Alert and Women Waging Peace, 2004). In Timor, nonviolence training could be adopted for use in schools and in nonformal education processes to help people find ways to manage their trauma and anger, and to help unlearn the patterns of violence experienced under Indonesian occupation. Culturally appropriate dispute resolution and mediation processes can also be adopted at school and community level as a means for working through distrust, difference, and conflict.

Education for Justice and Social Sustainability

The approach to justice adopted by the conflict-affected society will determine the extent to which relational peace-building processes are embraced by that society. Post-conflict societies such as Rwanda, the Solomons, and South Africa have adopted a two-tiered approach to justice: the main perpetrators of violence are brought to trial and punished, but alongside this a restorative justice system also operates. Restorative justice places emphasis first and foremost on restoring the humanity of the victims. It analyzes the harm that has been done and the needs that have resulted because of it. Restorative justice highlights the need to tackle and transform those structures and systems that create exploitation, misery, and poverty. It also emphasizes the obligations that follow on from violations; it encourages society to recognize and respond to the needs of those people who have been violated. Zehr believes there are several essential aspects of restorative justice. These include

- focusing on the harms of wrongdoing more than the rules that have been broken;
- showing equal concern to the victims and offenders and involving both in the process of justice;
- working toward the restoration of victims, empowering them, and responding to their needs;
- supporting offenders while encouraging them to understand, accept, and carry out their obligations;
- providing opportunities for dialogue between victim and offender when appropriate; and
- involving and empowering the affected community through the justice process (Zehr, 1997, p. 20).

If the emphasis is placed on the transformation and upliftment of society through restorative rather than retributive processes, people will be more able to look beyond violence and revenge.

While there are calls at present in and outside Timor Leste for an international tribunal to investigate crimes against humanity during the Indonesian occupation, the geopolitical interests of Timor's neighbors will prevent this happening in the near future. Perhaps, in the absence of a full tribunal, there are cogent lessons to be learnt from the village-level reconciliation processes that have occurred since September 1999. How have these local acts of restitution been enacted? How successful have they been? Are they indicators of a Timorese system of justice and reconciliation that could be used to educate and inform in the wake of this latest conflict?

Critical Literacy as the Vehicle?

With 50–90 per cent illiteracy in the districts of Timor Leste, perhaps the most effective tool for educating for peace, justice, truth, security, and regard is the nonformal approach. Critical literacy is a tool that has been used in many conflict-affected societies (e.g., Guinea Bissau, Mozambique, Brazil) to great effect. A popular education network, Dai Popular, already exists in Timor Leste, which educates and raises the consciousness of communities using the critical literacy approach. Developing a critical literacy curriculum that incorporates education for truth, nonviolence training, culturally sensitive modes of justice, and dialogue about issues pertaining to peace building is an extremely feasible proposition.

Conclusion

The recent political unrest and conflict in Timor Leste is symptomatic of a society that is still coming to grips with the horrors of the past whilst trying to forge a way forward. Now significant emphasis will need to be placed on restoring and revitalizing the relationships again disrupted by conflict, while at the same time providing security and justice to the affected societies. If this is done in a way that fosters peace and helps unlearn old patterns of violence, then the significant gains that have been made by Timorese society since independence can continue to be built upon. This chapter has suggested some of the ways in which truth, security, mutual respect, and justice can be enhanced for the benefit of all in Timor Leste through education.

References

AusAID (2006). *CEPA program outline.* Canberra: AusAID.
Bam, J. (2000). *Negotiating history, truth and reconciliation and globalization: an analysis of the suppression of historical consciousness in South African schools as a case study.* http://www.arts.uwa. edu.au/Mots/Pluriels/MP1300jb.html. Accessed 7 July 2006.
Enslin, P. (2003). Citizenship education in post-apartheid South Africa. *Cambridge Journal of Education, 33*(1), 73–83.

Fred-Mensah, B. (2004). Social capital building as capacity for post-conflict development: the UNDP in Mozambique and Rwanda. *Global Governance, 10*(4), 437–458.

Galtung, J. (1990). Cultural violence. *Journal of Peace Research, 27*(3), 291–305.

International Alert, & Women Waging Peace (2004). *Inclusive security, sustainable peace: a toolkit for advocacy and action*. London and Washington, DC: International Alert and Women Waging Peace.

Kreisberg, L. (2004). Comparing reconciliation actions within and between countries. In Y. Bar-Siman-Tov (Ed.), *From conflict resolution to reconciliation* (pp. 81–110). Oxford: Oxford University Press.

Smith, A., & Robinson, A. (1996). *Education for mutual understanding: the initial statutory years*. Coleraine: University of Ulster.

Spence, R. (2004). Befriending the neighbors: creating common security. In G. T. Harris (Ed.), *Demilitarizing Sub-Saharan Africa*. Pretoria: Institute of Security Studies.

Spence, R., & McLeod, J. (2002). Building the road as we walk it: peacebuilding as principled and revolutionary nonviolent praxis. *Social Alternatives, 21*(2), 61–64.

Spence, R., & Wielders, I. (2005). *Community peace and restoration fund, peace and conflict impact assessment*. Canberra: AusAid.

UNICEF (2005). *100 Friendly Schools project: evaluation report*. Dili: UNICEF.

United Nations Research Institute of Social Development (2000). *Rebuilding after war: lessons from the war-torn societies project*. http://www.unrisd.org/wsp/wsp.htm. Accessed 21 June 2001.

Zehr, H. (1997). Restorative justice: when justice and healing go together. *Track Two, 6*(3), 20.

Chapter 13
Social Sustainability and Activation Strategies with Unemployed Young Adults

Danny Wildemeersch and Susan Weil

Abstract In this chapter we describe some of the main findings resulting from a research project that was set up in six European countries to investigate tensions and possibilities arising from programs focused on the "activation" of unemployed youth. The research analyzed in depth the attempts in twelve cases to enhance the labor market participation of young people who encountered important problems in finding a sustainable job. Finding a balance between biographical, social, and instrumental competencies was found to be of major importance for socially sustainable projects. In this chapter we consider the intended and unintended consequences of strategies that we term "reflexive" and "restrictive" activation. We analyze some of these findings against the backdrop of changing policy orientations in present day welfare states.

Introduction

From 1998 until 2000, we engaged in a three-year research project funded by the European Union called "Balancing competencies" (Wildemeersch, 2001). It was a comparative study in six European countries aimed at understanding practices of education, training, and guidance (ETG) of young adults (16–25 years) in order to develop an integrated pedagogical theory on activation practices. In our research we focused mainly on the micro-processes within the cases observed. After the research, we felt an urgent need to contextualize our findings against the backdrop of macro policy developments.

Therefore we studied European policy making related to vocational education and training. We interpreted this European policy scene as an arena where various antagonistic tendencies and orientations compete with each other. We analyzed how, during the last decades of the previous century, the balance between "solidarity" and "competitiveness," which was the product of the postwar welfare state model, came under attack. The neo-liberal discourse gave priority to competitiveness to the detriment of solidarity. This offensive was powerful. However, it also led to attempts

---

D. Wildemeersch (✉)
University of Leuven, Leuven, Belgium

by the social democrats to rescue the welfare state. This resulted in the construction of a new perspective called the Third Way (Giddens, 1998).

In reply to the neo-liberal critique that the welfare state made people dependent on social security benefits, that it cultivated attitudes of inactivity and helplessness, the architects of the Third Way (Rosanvallon, 1995; Giddens, 1998) emphasized that indeed a redefinition of rights and duties was needed. If people wanted to profit from the welfare benefits, which social-democrats continue to consider an important social right, they also had the duty to behave as responsible citizens and try to overcome their situation of (temporary) dependency through increased activity as job seekers and/or as citizens. This ideological debate was the backdrop for the emerging discourses of "activation". Activation increasingly came to the fore as a strategy of inclusion of long-term unemployed into society in general and into the labor market in particular. It resulted in policy measures that gave more prominence to self-help, personal responsibility, employability, flexibility, activity, and so on. It is important to highlight this ideological background of the activation discourse, because the managerial practices that operationalize it tend to obscure this reality with the help of a technical-neutral discourse.

It is also important to keep in mind that these technical measures always reflect the power relations operating in the background of the managerial scene. This will also help us to clarify in the first place the paradoxical character of the activation strategies that we have encountered in the field of education, training, and guidance of the young unemployed. We will furthermore explain how activation strategies, through over-accentuating self-responsibility and entrepreneurship, tend to problematize the socially excluded rather than social exclusion. We will also demonstrate how this type of activation discourse operates in a restrictive way. We will finally sketch "reflexive activation" as an alternative that does not conceal the ambivalences and the complexities, but rather takes them as a point of departure in view of "navigating the paradoxes" of activation.

Empowering and Disciplining Dimensions of Activation

Activation is increasingly becoming "a magic word" (Kazepov, 2002, p. 20). It gives direction to social policy in many European countries, especially the ones with a social democratic tradition. This includes most Western European countries and all countries included in our research. In various policy and research documents, it is explicitly formulated as a strategy to overcome dependency. Sometimes it is also described as a specific form of empowerment that addresses particular groups. Especially in the Third Way approach, there is a focus on "empowering individuals, families and communities to move out of poverty, unemployment and social exclusion by a combination of individual responsibility, social support, education and welfare to work initiatives" (Gamarnikow and Green, 1999, p. 50).

In the Netherlands, which in many respects takes the lead in the development of activation policies, the definition is as follows: "Activation is the enhancement of social participation and the breaking or prevention of social isolation by means of meaningful activities which can be a first step towards paid work" (Ministerie van Sociale Zaken en Werkgelegenheid, 2003, translation by D. Wildemeersch). The Finnish government has adopted "activation" as a keyword of its social policy strategy. It is all about gearing social and health policy toward improving people's ability to enter the labor market and to remain in it longer before retirement. As such, this policy discourse of activation is seen as the strategy of choice to ensure that diverse (potentially) dependent individuals are required to cope with a wide variety of challenges such as the ageing of the population, improving the effectiveness of the social services, the struggle against poverty, etc. In some cases, as in Finland, activation is predominantly connected to labor market participation, whereas in other cases it has a broader orientation and includes different kinds of participation in society. Therefore it is relevant to make a distinction, as Kazepov (2002, p. 22) does, between social activation and labor activation. Social activation is directed toward categories of people who are constructed by policy makers as having such compromised autonomy that there is no chance of "inserting" them into the labor market or "making" them achieve self-reliability. The language associated with the activation discourse can be seen as both instrumental and coercive. Labor activation focuses on recipients of social benefits whose personal capabilities are seen to be of sufficient potential value to the labor market to become involved in activation programs with the intention of giving them "tools" to improve their labor market competencies.

In many of the projects we visited in our research, labor activation was the principle objective, while elements of social activation also played an important complementary role (Weil, Wildemeersch, & Jansen, 2005). Especially in the projects that we typified as the "guidance and counseling" culture of learning, targeting the "destabilized," attempts were made to balance labor activation and social activation. Particularly in the latter projects, we described the tension between, on the one hand, the necessity of "disciplining" the participants to enhance their ability to act as responsible job seekers and citizens and, on the other hand, the humanistic ambition to increase their self-expression and personal development.

This is consistent with the way in which Kazepov (2002) describes current activation policies on the broader European scene. In his analysis of "social assistance and activation measures in Europe" he distinguished the following two goals of activation:

- getting people off the payrolls by cutting down public expenditure for social assistance and employment measures, reducing the social costs of poverty and unemployment;
- empowering people who are out of work by improving their life conditions and increasing their opportunities by giving wide social support through ad hoc designed accompanying measures (2002, pp. 20–22).

Related to these two goals are two narratives: one focuses on the "duties" of the beneficiaries, while the other emphasizes the "rights" of the beneficiary to obtain support to prevent or overcome marginalization. These two distinct narratives in their turn lead to two different logics:

- a stick and carrot logic, with a high discretionary power of social workers to evaluate the beneficiary's commitment, including the menace of reducing, suspending, or terminating income support;
- an empowerment logic, which conceives of professional workers and beneficiaries as mutually involved in the same program, whereby the beneficiaries are expected to participate actively, while the professionals commit themselves to provide "tools" for reinsertion.

This distinction between the disciplining and the empowerment objectives and logics of activation helps to clarify the "paradox of activation." It means that activation inevitably is double edged: it "empowers" while it "disempowers," or it "enables" while it "disables." We encountered this paradox in most of the projects we investigated (Weil et al., 2005). We found that the young people who are the most successful in the ETG projects are the ones who can find an adequate balance in this tension. We also found tendencies in projects with accountability for predetermined outputs to select those young people perceived as most able to complete the program and obtain work. We furthermore found that the professionals and the projects that operated in a satisfactory way were the ones that juggled in a productive way what we called "voluntaristic" and "deterministic" approaches. We found that the interpretive professional is reflexively concerned with creating opportunities for the participants, while simultaneously limiting these very opportunities.

This paradox of activation has recently been described in various studies as the "pedagogical paradox," which is basically inevitable and non-resolvable. Any relevant pedagogical intervention will always be double edged: it will enable people, while at the same time it will reduce their options and limit their freedom. As the paradox is basically non-resolvable, finding a good balance between empowerment and control is an important matter. However, a distinct mathematical equilibrium or Archimedean point is not available. Given the complexity and unpredictability of the situations in which one operates and the people with whom one works, the balance has to be reflexively invented and reinvented time and again. In the case of the activation strategies we researched, we have also observed that professionals and policy makers often have great difficulty coping with this tension. To them, the exertion of control can then emerge as an important objective. We observed that this can lead to schemes that are transformed into individualized "packages" of skills and knowledge based on assumptions that these can be mastered. This leaves little room for an environment that catches young peoples' personal imaginations, promotes their social engagement in ways that they construct as meaningful, and aligns their functional abilities to wider practices of labor and social participation. Ultimately, we found that this imbalance leads to a kind of "restrictive activation," a phenomenon that we will now analyze in more depth.

Restrictive Activation

Problematizing the Socially Excluded

Somewhat contrary to our expectations, we have found that in all activation practices that we studied a lot of attention is paid to issues of identity. Even though there are some marked differences among the projects we investigated, we have found in most cases that much attention was paid to a combined development of what we called biographical, social, and instrumental competencies. Many projects included an emphasis on creating opportunities for the young adults to learn how to navigate their various options and orientations concerning their position in the labor market and to integrate these navigations into the ongoing story of their lives.

This finding strongly suggested that ETG practices have integrated (intuitively or reflexively) some of the recent sociological insights concerning the emergence of biographical reflexivity as an overall feature of late modern societies (Beck, 1992). Rather than unequivocally conforming to traditional social norms, contemporary individuals opt instead for alternative, more fluid and entrepreneurial lifestyles designed to offer greater individual freedom from canonical time structures (Herkenhoff, 2002). In close relation to this, the notion of "reflexive biography" clarifies the extent to which traditional identities are under pressure (Stroobants, 2001). Biographies become self-reflexive. Decisions regarding education, professions, jobs, places of residence, partners, children, and so on are increasingly becoming reconstructed in dominant policy discourses as a matter of individual freedom of choice and self-determination. "In the individualized society, individual people have to learn, under the threat of permanent discrimination, to behave as the centre of action, as planning bureaus with respect to their own life courses, their competencies, their orientations, their partnerships etc." (Beck, 1992, p. 217; translation by D. Wildemeersch).

However, we have also found that the focus on biographical reflexivity often suffered from tendencies to economize, which reflects the "stick and carrot" rationale of activation. We observed that attempts to foster biographical and social reflexivity were often instrumentalized and economized to fit into the disciplining goals of activation. This meant that both professionals and participants often had to operate within highly standardized and regulated limits, with strictly predetermined and circumscribed goal definitions in a limited time setting. The disciplining character of the practices also implied in many cases a negative valuation of the identities of the participants. Elsewhere we have called this the "discourse of deficiency" (Jansen & Wildemeersch, 1996). This discourse constructs the identities of so-called disadvantaged groups, such as young unemployed adults, in such a way that deficits are accentuated. This negative valuation is the basis of the legitimization of the disciplining practices. Thereby, the problem of social exclusion is mainly connected with the socially constructed deficits of individuals, groups, and communities.

Of course it cannot be denied that particular groups lack specific competencies to participate fully in the present day context, or in particular segments of the labor market. Yet, these deficits should not be exclusively connected with the deficits of particular people, but at the same time be constructed as consequences of the transforming conditions of society, the economy, and the labor market. This would imply that the "responsibility" for the problem of social exclusion cannot exclusively be linked to the individuals who are not equipped well enough to cope with these transitions. And this brings us to the second reason why activation strategies cannot be considered neutral activities. As mentioned above, activation strategies always reflect particular relations of power between different groups, categories, and classes in society. Some groups are defined as "socially excluded" or "at risk of exclusion," who need to be activated and included, while others escape such negative definitions and consequent strategies of activation and inclusion. Yet decisions made by professionals about who fits which category are seldom seen as being determined by power relations and power mechanisms.

Focus on Human Capital

In our research, we also came to the conclusion that activation practices had a labor orientation, rather than a social orientation. We noticed that in the discourses we analyzed activation is mainly constructed as the willingness to participate in a trajectory that prepares for admission to the labor market. We furthermore found that competencies and experiences are credited if they can be classed as qualifications for the world of labor, and the self is judged in terms of its labor market assets. This discourse is clearly reminiscent of the human capital approaches to education and training. Human capital is about influencing future income "through the imbedding of resources in people" (Becker, 1962, p. 9). Theories of human capital focus on individual investment in education, on return on investment in the form of higher wages, and on return on investment for society and its economic productivity.

It is important to conclude here that the economic and labor market orientation of the activation programs is the ultimate ground for the variety of efforts undertaken. We have noticed that, in many cases, social activation was eventually legitimized by the finality of labor activation. This means that insertion into the labor market is considered to be the central medium of social integration and that the ultimate criterion for the effectiveness of activation is the extent to which it contributes to this objective. This is also confirmed by Dean (1995), who found that in many schemes for the unemployed broader orientations than just labor market orientations are welcomed, as long as they are useful in promoting job re-entry. He provided examples of a wide variety of subjects such as English language courses, linguistic and numeracy competency courses, short courses on particular skills, participation in job clubs, on-the-job training and training courses, part-time or short-term work, courses and counseling to improve confidence, motivation, and presentation, and participation in voluntary work (Dean, 1995, p. 574). Inclusion in this approach was either directly or indirectly oriented toward inclusion in the labor market, and current programs have the same criteria. The labor market as it currently functions is not questioned. Being part of it, sooner or later, and in one way or another, is what counts for every member of the active workforce.

Social Responsibility as Individual Integrity

The suggestion above that activation practices mainly focus on building human capital may downplay the observation that learning for social responsibility is also an important issue in many ETG schemes. We have repeatedly expressed our surprise about the espoused importance attached to "social competencies" and to "socially responsible behavior" in activation practices. Although we have not found many direct references to the notion of social capital in documents on activation, it goes without saying that the architects of various education, training, and guidance schemes for young unemployed adults would argue that the development of social capital is an important objective of their enterprise. They would not accept that their efforts are limited to increasing economic capital, be it on the institutional level or on the personal level. They would definitely, and rightly, claim that their efforts are also directed toward enhancing civic competence and responsibility. However, in line with our observations concerning the "management of the self," we will argue that a social capital orientation in activation philosophy and practices emphasizes "individual integrity" as the main entrance to the building of social capital.

We have argued that activation practices often take the purportedly deficient identities of their participants as a point of departure. They subsequently try to transform these identities in such a way that the project participants become responsible people who not only claim their rights to social benefits, but who know their duties as active, entrepreneurial persons who take their trajectory toward the labor market into their own hands. This approach reflects the dominant activation discourse, which conceives of social responsibility in terms of individual integrity. The main leverage to produce social capital is located in the individual.

More institutional perspectives on the creation of social capital are not very well articulated in the activation schemes that we researched. The institutional perspective gives preference to actions on the meso level that create an environment that is conducive to different forms of commitment and solidarity on the micro level. According to Gamarnikow and Green (1999), the dominance of the individual integrity discourse is also related to the way "Third Way" politics frame the problem of social exclusion. They notice a significant reluctance in this political orientation to talk about social exclusion "in terms of access to economic and other resources, as a key mediating variable" (p. 50). Hence, if this institutional and structural dimension of social exclusion receives little attention, it is quite evident that in this view building social capital should mainly result from changing the identities of individuals in the first place. Activation is then first and foremost conceived of as "building" socially responsible individual identities. And this, as we have seen, is not a neutral technical activity, but a particular manifestation of governmental ethical practices (Dean, 1995).

The Imbalances of Restrictive Activation

Above, we described the paradox of activation as an inevitable phenomenon. We furthermore argued that in activation practices it is important to find a balance between direction and empowerment. However, if we look at the way negative identities are constructed, and additionally at the extent to which practices of self-formation are over-accentuated, we fear that activation will have mainly disciplining rather than empowering effects. The activation is restrictive in the first place, because the deficiency orientation presupposes a negative identity. What other competencies and personality characteristics the unemployed young people possess is put "between brackets." Decisive action seems based on the assumption that their social identity cannot be formulated in positive terms until they have acquired the proper qualifications through ETG practices, and that this condition precedes their chances of full social participation. So, to increase their social autonomy, participants "inserted" into the categories concerned should first internalize a self-image of a "deficient identity" attributed to them by others, and then make themselves dependent on norms for useful competencies and the appropriate ways to get them, again defined by others. In an activation policy discourse, anyone who is unable or unwilling to satisfy that requirement is reconstructed as an irresponsible second-class citizen. In this way, such activation strategies keep on producing, legitimizing, and perpetuating the continued existence of social inequality.

Moreover, this inequality is individualized by linking social integration to self-help. It becomes the individual's personal responsibility and merit to "catch up" and acquire the proper qualifications through ETG practices; conversely, the individuals themselves are to blame for their lasting marginalized social position if they fail to seize the opportunities offered. As a result, the individual's self-responsibility for personal well-being not only becomes the vehicle for social integration (Van Onna, 1990), but at the same time pushes questions concerning the significance of social responsibilities into the background. We have noticed that responsibility is exclusively located at the bottom of the social fabric. In this context, the attention placed on tailor-made, individualized learning paths and self-directed learning projects cannot be interpreted unequivocally in terms of the learner's increased empowerment. This development is also part of a broader process of decontextualization of social responsibility in which the impact of social (power) relations and structures on the differences in social opportunities disappears, and the emphasis shifts to people's will and efforts to qualify for a higher social status.

We can now conclude our observations with a brief synthesis of our main insights concerning the imbalances of restrictive activation. We have argued that activation is inevitably paradoxical. Further, we have found that, in many projects, balances between control and empowerment are seldom if ever achieved. On the contrary, the activation practices tend to operate in a restrictive way for the following reasons. In the first place they emphasize negative identities as a primary step in the activation strategy. Yet this tends to reinforce and legitimize existing conditions of inequality. A second finding is that the problematic of social exclusion is increasingly individualized and associated with particular social categories seen to be at the bottom of the social ladder. This implies that the responsibilities to overcome social exclusion are mainly located within individuals seen to "belong" to these disadvantaged categories.

We will now explore how restrictive activation can be counterbalanced by concepts and practices of what we have called "reflexive activation" (Weil et al., 2005). We will argue that the notion of reflexive activation presupposes problematizing social exclusion rather than problematizing the socially excluded. We will furthermore emphasize the need to extend the responsibilities of all actors involved in ETG practices. And finally we will demonstrate the importance of "situated activation practices" rather that "decontextualized activation practices."

Reflexive Activation

Problematizing Social Exclusion

In order to develop an alternative perspective on activation, we use the notion of "reflexivity" as interpreted by authors such as Beck and Giddens. It was Michael Young (1999) who showed us how the concept of "reflexive modernization" could provide an answer to some of the shortcomings of Third Way politics in the field of education. In the previous paragraph, we referred to the critique that solutions to social exclusion were associated predominantly with young people deemed to be within specific socially disadvantaged categories. According to Young, this reflects some of the shortcomings of Third Way politics as they have been elaborated in the United Kingdom. He argued that the architects of this politics have developed a new approach to social policy, without developing a new approach to political economy. The new social policy orientations consist of the new activation strategies as a component of an attempt to rescue the welfare state. People are no longer automatically entitled to social benefits in case of misfortune. They now have the "duty" to be active, or to engage in practices of "self-formation," in order to "deserve" their "allowances" rather than their "social benefits" (Dean, 1995).

The problem with this approach is that it presents only a limited answer to a problem which is much more complex than suggested by the Third Way architects. Young suggested we interpret these complexities with the help of the theory of the "risk society" and the related notion of "reflexivity." In the risk society we are confronted with so-called "manufactured risks," which are the (unintended) outcomes of modernization itself. Manufactured risks are the product of human intervention aimed at improving life conditions with the help of science and (human) technology. Dealing with manufactured risks demands other strategies than the ones we have relied upon in previous eras of the development of modern society. In this respect, we found Beck's distinction between reflectivity and reflexivity to be relevant and useful to making sense of our research findings. Beck sees reflectivity as the scientific and technological base of classical modernization processes. However, as these processes produce unintended risks, they cannot be countered with classical forms of reflectivity. They need new forms of knowledge, which can be framed under the heading of reflexivity and which involve "the self confrontation with the effects of risk society and its autonomous modernization processes which are blind and deaf to their own effects and threats" (Beck, 1992, cited in Young, 1999, p. 217).

Young's suggestion that we consider social exclusion as a manufactured risk helps to relativize the singular focus of activation policies on the excluded. Instead, we are invited to consider social exclusion more reflexively against the backdrop of broader changes in the existing social, political, and economic context of "reflexive modernization" in a globalizing economy. This means that simple answers, like "controlling" the excluded to become more active and personally accountable, or "controlling" the output of activation schemes in terms of their successes of transfer to the labor market cannot suffice. We have shown that such measures often turn out to be counterproductive because they emphasize the negative identity of the excluded. Moreover, Young argued, the simple introduction of all kinds of measures of attainment in order to raise the standards, based on external monitoring and ranking, may have the perverse effect of polarizing the distinction between the excluded and the included rather than promoting social integration.

Reflexive Activation and Extended Responsibilities

While linking the problem of social exclusion to the broader context of reflexive modernity, it becomes clear that the challenge of young employed people demands that we evolve more sophisticated strategies rather than merely technocratic answers. However, it was the latter that we found to be prominent in many of the activation schemes we investigated. However, "sophisticated answers" are not just simply available. They need to be the result of the mobilization of different forms of reflexivity which are present on various levels within the activation policies and practices themselves. Elsewhere, we have emphasized that the answers to the dilemmas the professionals and the participants cope with cannot be pre-given (Wildemeersch, 2000). They are the result of a continuous and careful interpretation of, on one hand, the structural demands that direct the activities of the actors involved and, on the other hand, the biographical and social dynamics that come into play when professionals and participants meet each other in the context of an activation program. We have described this encounter of structures and dynamics in terms of "action space" (Weil et al., 2005; Kemmis, 2001). While putting forward the notion of action space, we have insisted that professionals and unemployed are both determined by and determining the structures within which they operate. Following insights from structuration theory (Giddens, 1984), which emphasizes the interplay of structure and agency, we have observed that all actors actively (re)produce the structural context in which their meeting takes place, thereby permanently (re)creating the starting conditions of their encounter. This observation is reminiscent of other considerations in literature that emphasize that, because of the unpredictability and insecurity of the conditions in which professionals operate today, "engagement with contradictions and paradoxes" has become an inevitable feature of professional action. They therefore have to commit themselves to "an ongoing negotiation of the complexity and ambivalence of lifelong learning policies and practices and their effects" (Edwards, Armstrong, & Miller, 2001, p. 427).

In line with this, we would argue that the creation of a "negotiated action space" is an important characteristic of reflexive activation.

Yet while these observations may be theoretically very valid and relevant, we have noticed that in the policies and the practices we researched, there is an overall tendency to introduce standardized activation models that give both policy makers and practitioners the illusion of controllability and predictability of the outcomes of the process. The general atmosphere of insecurity, both with respect to the perceived characteristics of the participants and external (labor market) conditions, seems to provoke a dynamic that could be at the same time counterproductive and stigmatizing. The ministers' and government obsession with standardized and quantifiable strategies, outcomes, and targets may further limit the responsibility of the actors involved. For example, motivation may decrease when specified targets are not met, both among the professionals and the participants. Moreover, recurring patterns of "failure" within the restrictions of the discourse may eventually result in a deskilling of the professionals, because their responsibility for the "activation process" is often limited to applying pre-structured ETG instruments. Therefore, it is important to extend the responsibilities of the different actors involved in the activation projects in such a way that they may themselves negotiate meaningful balances between external challenges, as expressed in the specified outcomes, and internal demands emanating from giving meaning to principles that we would associate with a reflexive process. The following suggestions will illustrate what we mean by the principles of extended responsibilities.

A first important principle is valuing competence and diversity. Above, we have argued that the participants in activation projects are often defined as deficient or deviant, thereby constructing implicit standards of normality. Valuing competence and diversity implies that these standards of normality are not just taken for granted, but are questioned while scrutinizing the value and power frameworks that underpin them. When exclusion is at stake, it is important to investigate the multiple interacting mechanisms of exclusion and to "engage in a struggle of the criteria of in/exclusion" (Edwards et al., 2001, p. 425). It is therefore vital that activation processes also pay attention to learning about and enhancing traits and capabilities that the participants already possess and that can contribute to their own meaning making about social responsibility. These must not be limited to the criticism and resistance of school leavers, ethnic minorities, unskilled laborers, and so on regarding the social relationships and rationalities they have encountered and stored as part of their experience and knowledge. They also involve competencies developed by young unemployed people both because of and despite labels ascribed to them: inventiveness, self-will, perseverance, courage, risk. Acknowledging the strength of their knowledge, experiences, and competencies can offer fertile ground for raising their critical awareness of the socially constructed and debatable character of a negative identity ascribed to them, as well as for clarifying the desirability and value of particular learning and training pathways. This allows options of self-help and development to be weighed consciously against the significance of the social integration that, according to the qualification model, must be achieved. And only then will it become possible to reflect on the (im)possibilities of coupling self-realization to socially responsible action and the contexts that encourage this to a greater or smaller degree: these include labor organizations, living and housing conditions, (voluntary) work in community organizations, and social movements.

Connective inquiry is the second principle related to the extension of responsibility. This principle emanates from the complexity, the unpredictability, the messiness, and the value-laden character of the activation process. It entails the continuous involvement of the different partners, both external and internal to the project, in defining dilemmas and paradoxes, in formulating objectives and in the design and follow-up of trajectories. It includes a dialogical attitude that enables co-inquiry and co-learning and the negotiation and exploration of different meanings and interpretations. It implies valuing reflection-in-action, which allows for more appropriate ways of dealing with instability and complexity. Yet it is too demanding and too ambitious to try to embody all of the mentioned roles into one individual professional. In an interpretive practice, therefore, flexibility should be more than the attitude of individual professionals. Rather it is a strategy of professional practice in which different functions and roles in relationship to the participants are distributed over the team as whole, in a well-balanced and dynamic rather than fixed way. Fostering teamwork is not necessarily at odds with specialized action of the professionals nor with establishing links with the external world. On the contrary, activation teams could attempt to realize what Michael Young calls "connective specialization" (1999, p. 221), which involves new kinds of links between specialized partners and processes both within and outside learning institutions.

The third principle of extended responsibility in a reflexive activation approach concerns the development of a social capital orientation into activation strategies. Social capital is a concept that highlights the importance of connectedness among people on the level of social institutions such as families, social networks, associations, communities, and labor organizations. The better people are integrated into these institutions, the more they will feel comfortable in their daily lives and develop feelings of trust with respect to wider societal issues, even in conditions that we described before as insecure and unpredictable. Here is an important reason why activation projects should try to do more than just building individual integrity among their participants, while trying to turn them into active entrepreneurs of their professional careers. As mentioned before, Gamarnikow and Green (1999) distinguished two orientations toward the development of social capital. The first one emphasizes individual responsibility as a starting point for the creation of trust on an institutional level. The second one accentuates the institutional pre-conditions for building social capital, while pointing to the importance of institutional action for collective goods. Our research presents quite explicit evidence that supports the second orientation. We have found that the projects that were the most effective in creating an atmosphere of connectedness and hence of trust among the participants and the professionals were the ones that had a manifest ambition to embed their ETG activities in the context of wider institutional action for community building or community development. Projects that were rather weak in this respect exclusively emphasized individual competency development without paying much attention to the social fabric that either enhances or limits the emergence of trust and confidence among the participants. Of course this does not mean that fostering individual integrity should be neglected. We also found much evidence that this is still very important, especially in the case of young adolescents. The conclusion therefore is that institutional action for collective goods and enhancing individual integrity should be balanced carefully.

Reflexive Activation and Situated Activation Practices

The latter observation also has a relevant, more explicit, pedagogical consequence. In traditional pedagogical conceptions, learning of different kinds of competencies is exclusively located in the individual. Little attention is paid, both in theory and in practice, to how learning can be located on an institutional or social level. As the individual learning trajectory is overemphasized, there are no conceptual notions or practical tools with which to understand the importance of the social dimension of learning in the activation projects. We have noticed that the diverse terrain of activation "schemelands" (MacDonald, 1997, p. 170) too often lacks the relevant theory-practice and social learning connections or focuses mainly on individualized packages aimed at fostering the development of an entrepreneurial self. In short, the learning often takes place in the context of decontextualized activation practices. In opposition to this, recent research on learning brings to the fore the importance of "situated learning" embedded in "communities of practice" (Lave & Wenger, 1991; Wenger, 1998). These orientations accentuate the active participation of the learners in relevant everyday practices. Such social theories of learning present quite a few clues about how activation practices could obtain more relevance for participation and for learning, while embedding them into contexts that are closely linked to real life situations.

The activation project that we valued most in this respect, the cultural mediation project in Lisbon, strongly resembled initiatives that are nowadays being developed in the social economy such as community services or in French Services de Proximité (Gilain, Jadoul, Nyssens, & Petrella, 2001; Mathijssen & Wildemeersch, 2005). This concept covers an ensemble of provisions operating at the community level and delivering a variety of services to community dwellers or to external clients such as home support for old aged people, kindergarten services, environmental management of public spaces, and social restaurants. The development of these services has in the past been closely linked to the creation of employment for people who have difficulty finding jobs in the regular labor market. However, in an interesting critique on the narrow economical focus to which these initiatives are geared nowadays, Gilain et al. (2001) present a multidimensional concept of activation (insertion) through community services, which integrates some of the ambitions of labor activation, social activation, institutional action for collective good, and situated activation practices. In the first place, the community services establish a relevant connection with the socioeconomic environment while offering particular services that have an economic function. In the second place they create a relevant "community of practice" that brings together workers/trainees, volunteers, and clients of the services. This is the context of a situated practice, which is part of an institutional action aimed at integrating labor market functions (employment and training), social functions (integration of volunteers), and consumption functions (clients using the services). Third, the community services combine strategies of activation (insertion) at three different levels: vocational integration through employment activities, social integration through embedment in social networks, and civic integration through participation in projects of societal relevance.

The framework of community services helps us to consider activation policies and practices on multiple levels, including a plurality of actors and aiming at a plurality of effects. This is in sharp contrast to young people on U.K. New Start programs being required to do the "community service" slot, which they soon learned was the category where the least likely to succeed were directed. Although it is not applicable in all circumstances where ETG practices are developed, it may inspire us to consider the quality of the embeddedness of different activation practices. It locates the solution to problems of social exclusion not exclusively on the level of the individual unemployed, but rather on the level of collective action and of public responsibility. These forms of collective action also have the potential to trigger social learning processes, which are an important prerequisite to deal with issues of social exclusion and activation in a profound way. Such an approach corresponds with forms of social and public learning that could be characteristic of reflexive modernity coping with manufactured risks.

The notions of public or social learning, when related to experiences in communities of practice, accentuate the need to integrate activation projects at various levels. First, there should be an integration of the inner project activities and the world "out there." Projects as a whole should be meaningfully linked to the environment, so as to transcend the limitations of isolated schemeland (MacDonald, 1997). Second, there should be an integration of different actors involved, both within and outside the project, expressing the need to develop solutions to social exclusion as a shared responsibility. As the projects are primarily about finding and creating employment for young people who are currently excluded from the labor market, various actors who can influence the conditions of employment in differential ways should be interconnected and should engage in a joint process of critically reflexive collaborative action inquiry (Weil, 1998). However, as the projects are basically social projects that are geared toward social integration, actors from civil society have proved to be highly relevant in creating integrative initiatives. Third, there should be an integration of the different competencies needed. In our research the idea of balancing competencies has been a leading idea from the very beginning of the project. It has proven to be relevant in many ways.

Let us conclude this final consideration about situated activation practices with a recollection of some of the major intuitions formulated at the beginning of the research project on education, training, and guidance of unemployed youth (Wildemeersch, 2001). Balancing competencies implies that participants are encouraged to explore the meaning of the knowledge, skills, and practices they learn with respect to their personal life course—in the short and in the long term, for example, to look at both present dreams and future options (imagination). Furthermore, their commitment should be evoked by situating learning in a joint practice of common goals and shared responsibilities, and embedded in a safe and supportive atmosphere (engagement). Finally, they should be provided with the relevant know-how, skills, and hands-on experiences to give them an adequate sense of taking part in the wider world of real life labor (alignment). These findings confirm, deepen, and nuance the basic argument of this book about the value and the necessity of social sustainability with regard to activation practices for the unemployed.

References

Beck, U. (1992). *Risk society: towards a new modernity*. London: Sage.
Becker, G. (1962). Investment in human capital: a theoretical analysis. *Journal of Political Economy, 70*(5), 9–49.
Dean, M. (1995). Governing the unemployed self in an active society. *Economy and Society, 24*(4), 559–583.
Edwards, R., Armstrong, P., & Miller, N. (2001). Include me out: critical readings of social exclusion, social inclusion and lifelong learning. *International Journal of Lifelong Education, 20*(5), 417–428.
Gamarnikow, E., & Green, A. (1999). Developing social capital: dilemmas, possibilities and limitations in education. In A. Hayton (Ed.), *Tackling disaffection and social exclusion: education perspectives and policies* (pp. 47–64). London: Kogan Page.
Giddens, A. (1984). *The constitution of society: outline of a theory of structuration*. Cambridge: Polity.
Giddens, A. (1998). *The Third Way: the renewal of social democracy*. Cambridge: Polity Press.
Gilain, B., Jadoul, P., Nyssens, M., & Petrella, F. (2001). Les services de proximité: une pluralité d'acteurs et d'effets sur l'insertion. In G. Liénard (Ed.),*L'insertion: défi pour l'analyse, enjeu pour l'action* (pp. 241–268). Sprimont: Mardaga.
Herkenhoff, P. (Ed.) (2002). *Tempo. Publication of the Tempo Exhibition, 29 June to 9 September*. New York: MoMa QNS (Museum of Modern Art Queens). http://www.moma.org/exhibitions/2002/tempo/index.html. Accessed 29 April 2008.
Jansen, T., & Wildemeersch, D. (1996). Adult education and critical identity development: from a deficiency orientation towards a competency orientation. *International Journal of Lifelong Education, 15*(5), 325–340.
Kazepov, Y. (2002). Social assistance and activation measures in Europe. Paper presented at the Cost 15 Conference, Oslo, 5–6 April.
Kemmis, S. (2001). Exploring the relevance of critical theory for action research: emancipatory action research in the footsteps of Jürgen Habermas. In P. Reason & H. Bradbury (Eds.), *The handbook of action research: participative inquiry and practice* (pp. 91–102). London: Sage.
Lave, J., & Wenger, E. (1991). *Situated learning: legitimate peripheral participation*. Cambridge: Cambridge University Press.
MacDonald, R. (1997). *Youth, the "underclass" and social exclusion*. London: Routledge.
Mathijssen, C., & Wildemeersch, D. (2005). *Participation in community services*. Paper presented at the Conference on Democratic Practices as Learning Opportunities, New York Teachers College, 5–6 November.
Ministerie van Sociale Zaken en Werkgelegenheid (2003). Nationaal actieplan ter bestrijding van armoede en sociale uitsluiting 2003. *Nieuwsbank*, 3 July. http://www.nieuwsbank.nl/inp/2003/07/03/e111.htm. Accessed 29 April 2008.
Rosanvallon, P. (1995). *La nouvelle question sociale: repenser l'état providence*. Paris: Seuil.
Stroobants, V. (2001). *Baanbrekend leren—een levenswerk. (Pathbreaking learning—a lifetime work*. PhD thesis, Department of Educational Sciences, Katholieke Universiteit Leuven, Leuven.

Van Onna, B. (1990). Individualisering en sociale interventie. *Tijdschrift voor Agologie, 19*(2), 88–101.
Weil, S. (1998). Rhetorics and realities in public service organizations: systemic practice and organizational learning as critically reflexive action research (CRAR). *Systemic Practice and Action Research, 11*(1), 37–62.
Weil, S., Wildemeersch, D., & Jansen, T. (2005). *Unemployed youth and social exclusion in Europe: learning for inclusion?* Aldershot: Ashgate.
Wenger, E. (1998). *Communities of practice: learning, meaning and identity.* Cambridge: Cambridge University Press.
Wildemeersch, D. (2000). The interpretive professional. In K. Illeris (Ed.), *Adult education in the perspective of the learner* (pp. 157–176). Roskilde: Roskilde University Press.
Wildemeersch, D. (Ed.) (2001). *Balancing competencies: enhancing the participation of young adults in economic and social processes.* Report for the European Commission—Targeted Socio-Economic Research. Leuven: Centre for Research on Lifelong Learning and Participation, Katholieke Universiteit Leuven.
Young, M. F. D. (1999). Some reflections on the concepts of social exclusion and inclusion: beyond the Third Way. In A. Hayton (Ed.), *Tackling disaffection and social exclusion: education perspectives and policies* (pp. 210–223). London: Kogan Page.

Part IV
Adult and Vocational Education for Social Sustainability in Action

Chapter 14
Chasing the Vultures Off the Roof: AVE for Living in Sierra Leone

Astrid von Kotze

Abstract This chapter begins with a challenge to the UNESCO-UNEVOC principles of technical and vocational education, which have a narrow focus on employment and the labor market. I suggest there are three tensions: first, we need to rethink work as not just jobs/employment, but in terms of activities undertaken to maintain and create life. Second, I ask, what would a more inclusive notion of vocational education and training look like, one that is not premised on work understood as wage labor or the enhancement of professional qualifications. Third, I suggest we may want social change rather than social sustainability. The chapter outlines in some detail the construction and workings of community health clubs (CHCs) in Sierra Leone and describes how the process of learning together can build sociality and networks of social protection, which are important steps toward increased livelihood security and well-being. I propose that the principles underlying CHCs offer suggestions for a more socially just adult and vocational education, one that is people-centered, contextualized with the rhythms of life and work, supports livelihood activities, and that respects and builds on local technologies and knowledge as the basis for sustaining life.

Introduction: Sierra Leone, 2005–06

In 2002 Sierra Leone, a small country on the west coast of Africa emerged from a brutal civil war that had lasted for 11 years, claiming 20,000 lives and displacing 1 1/2 million people who either fled into neighboring Guinea or Liberia or survived in the forests, swamps, or mountains. The devastation caused by rebel campaigns of terror destabilized rural areas, cities, and towns throughout the country and is in evidence everywhere: in the burnt-out shells of houses, old electricity wires that are no longer connected, in youth who try to sell popsicles from cooler boxes suspended in wheelchairs donated for amputees, in the disease-infested slum areas of Freetown, and in the flock of vultures that perch on the roof of the local hospital in Kabala.

A. von Kotze (✉)
University of KwaZulu-Natal, South Africa

Sierra Leone's ranking as last in the world in the Human Development Index had remained unchanged by mid 2004. The conditions of extreme poverty and oppression that had given rise to the dissatisfaction particularly of young people have not altered. For decades, young people had hoped for a chance to participate in the life of their communities as respected human beings whose voices are heard. Although the youth have now committed to peace this must translate into more than the end of armed conflict. Many feel betrayed as they experience the continued lack of educational opportunities, health care, and employment while the same people still enrich themselves and plunder the country's resources.

Addressing the root causes of the war and poverty must, therefore, be a priority, including creating livelihood security and a human rights culture in which every person enjoys respect and is able to realize her/his right to live with dignity. I arrived in the northern district of Koinaduku, the poorest province of Sierra Leone, in January 2005 to help draft a curriculum and develop health education and promotion materials to be used by "community health clubs" (CHCs). I was extremely daunted by the task because I was skeptical whether even the best possible curriculum could really contribute to addressing what seemed to be essentially socio-political and structural problems. Over the next 10 months I collaborated with community development practitioners to develop and test "a participatory toolkit for field agents" entitled *Communicating health, communicating rights* (Care International in Sierra Leone, 2005). As the title indicates, the materials combine a focus on health and sanitation with a focus on human rights. The format attempts to make education an integrated part of the routine of daily livelihood activities, builds on local knowledge and culture, and does not assume literacy. In the process I had to abandon theory in order to learn. Alternatives that are sensitive to local conditions have to emerge in a seriously dialogic way. Since January 2006 the materials have been used within the context of the CHC approach by field agents of numerous international and local NGOs and government employees in Sierra Leone.

This health program does not fit prevalent notions of what constitutes adult and vocational education (AVE) or technical and vocational education and training (TVET) as it supports strategies for life rather than jobs. Yet it offers ideas that should be integral to any planning of education and training for/in the majority world. In particular, I came to think that it is the organization of people in community health clubs that is the most important lesson for education for social sustainability.

This chapter is in three parts: I begin by drawing on crucial definitions and assertions from UNESCO-UNEVOC principles and documents. I argue that despite good intentions the commitment expressed in sections of the documents is soon lost in the retreat into what is commonly understood as TVET for employment and the labor market. The second part of this chapter attempts to show how the health curriculum responds to the issues articulated by UNESCO-UNEVOC. Thirdly, I ask what lessons can be learnt from this model for AVE for social sustainability generally. I end by proposing a set of considerations that may guide the search for more equitable policy and provision in the future.

UNESCO-UNEVOC Intentions

In 2003, the UNESCO-UNEVOC International Centre for Technical and Vocational Education and Training was set up in order to

> provide technical backstopping to strengthen and upgrade TVET. Its primary focus is on least developed and developing countries, those in a post-conflict situation and those going through a period of transition. Special attention is given to meeting the specific needs of women and girls, and disadvantaged groups such as those in remote areas, the poor, minority groups and demobilised soldiers in a post-conflict situation. (UNESCO-UNEVOC, 2003, p. 7)

The center's summary document claims that the center is committed to "sustainable human development by strengthening education for the changing world of work" and one would have hoped that this might translate into programs that serve people like those in Senekaduku village in Sierra Leone. However, beyond the initial statement the document soon slips back to a conventional understanding of "workplace" and reasserts the link to "the needs of the labour market" (UNESCO-UNEVOC, 2003, p. 11) even if this, clearly, is ill-defined and barely existent in a place like Koinaduku.

The UNESCO-UNEVOC discussion paper of 2006 draws on the Seoul Congress report of 1999, which was confident about future contributions of technical and vocational education to sustainable development. Not only was TVET to

> prepare individuals for employment in the information society, but also make them responsible citizens who give due consideration to preserving the integrity of their environment and the welfare of others. (UNESCO-UNEVOC, 2006, p. 2)

Since then, further meetings have concerned themselves with the role of education and training for sustainable development, defined here as a dynamic concept,

> a culturally-directed search for a dynamic balance in the relationship between social, economic and natural systems, a balance that seeks to promote equity between the present and the future, and equity between countries, races, social classes and genders. (p. 5)

Realizing the fallacy of a "one size fits all" solution, the document asserts that "Appropriate sustainable strategies must be developed for both rich and poor nations" because sustainable development is "more a *moral precept* than a *scientific concept*," linking notions of peace and human rights with theories of ecology, and concerning itself "with the values people cherish and with the ways in which we perceive our relationship with others and with the natural world" (p. 5).

Furthermore, work is conceptualized more broadly to embrace different livelihood activities:

> The concept of sustainable livelihoods embraces existing concepts of work and employment but widens them to include the multiple forms of economic and non-economic activities through which people create opportunities to sustain themselves, their families and their communities. (UNESCO-UNEVOC, 2006, p. 18)

Yet, despite such good intentions, the rest of the discussion paper does not conceptualize TVET as linked to livelihood activities outside the formal economy, and work is not defined inclusively as also embracing activities like care taking and community mobilization. Issues of risk and social safety are dealt with in terms of providing facilities and technical equipment not social protection as the main means for reducing vulnerability, including risk in the face of emergencies and disasters.

We need to seriously reconceptualize work. It has been well established that unlike their wealthier counterparts in the West people in the South diversify their activities, combining and integrating activities necessary for sustaining life, such as fetching and carrying water and wood-fuel and cooking, with activities aimed at building social relations and generating income, such as plaiting ropes while participating in a community meeting. Yet only those activities that are built on a labor relationship of domination and subordination and that have a price attached to them are recognized as work.

Let us begin by defining work less as paid work, nor the work arising from the "need to act, to strive, to test oneself against others and be appreciated by them" (Gorz, 1999, p. 72), but as comprising all the daily activities undertaken to sustain life. If we were to draw on the writings of Bennholdt-Thomsen and Mies (1999) on subsistence production and Hart's (2002) insights regarding motherwork our curricula would address the context of "work that is expended in the creation, recreation and maintenance of immediate life" (Bennholdt-Thomsen & Mies, 1999, p. 20).

The Sierra Leone health program retains the focus on people most at risk, such as poor women and youth in a postwar situation, and it defines work as livelihood activities. In the following I outline some aspects of this program, with particular reference to (1) building community organization as the basis for social sustainability, peace, and transformation, (2) the format of TVET as community education that fits into the rhythms of work, and (3) a holistic approach that respects local technologies, renewable resources, and indigenous knowledge while challenging old ideas that threaten participation in democratic processes.

Building Sociality: Community Health Clubs

The Primary Orientation Toward Organization for Social Protection

The notion that people constitute a community just because they live within the same physical space is wrong, especially in a postwar situation. CHC members have common experiences of sickness and disease, of heavy rainfalls, of young girls dying in childbirth, and of young men becoming depressed or aggressive on account of punitive fines imposed for comparatively small misdemeanors. Yet, if these experiences are common, they are not shared. Across and even within households there is often distrust and suspicion both as a legacy of the war and as people compete for scarce resources. The first task, therefore, is to build the basis for trust and respect.

Health education and promotion is a useful beginning point for creating a form of sociality because well-being is close to everybody's daily life and unlike housing or sanitation there are no material subsidies that could lead to rivalry for gain

(Waterkeyn, 1999). CHCs are voluntary non-exclusive associations of men and women, young and old, from the same area, who get together on a regular basis in order to learn and make practical suggestions about issues of individual and collective health. Members enter into a social contract and establish a system of accountability and transparency through membership cards, regular attendance at meetings, dialogue, and common projects.

At weekly health club meetings neighbors get to know each other: they exchange news and laugh together and they express concerns about the weather, the lack of public facilities, and the condition of their crops. Given the high-risk lives of the poor, who depend to a large degree on their social and natural surroundings, who have no savings or security systems, and who have limited access to goods and services from outside their immediate vicinity, they spend a lot of energy on building relations of care and mutual support, both for immediate practical needs and for times of increased stress due to sickness or death (Lund & Nicholsen, 2003). When social links have been shattered due to war and displacement they need to be rebuilt. CHCs help to forge networks of social protection and thus improve livelihood security and a sense of well-being about belonging to a community.

Through education sessions, members get to know each other's strengths and weaknesses and they begin to identify emerging leaders. When it comes to the selection of committee members they can therefore vote with some confidence. Not surprisingly, village development committees often include many of the leading CHC members. Increasingly, women also take on public roles and responsibilities beyond that of "mammy queen." Strong structures are important to ensure democratic governance and projects for mutual benefits; they are also crucial as a basis for lasting peace.

Questions and group tasks within CHC sessions aim to shift participants away from individualism toward solidarity and toward realizing that what they perceived of as their private troubles are public issues (Wright Mills, 1970). When participants make broader connections between symptoms of sickness and human actions, social taboos, and cultural habits and conditions such as the lack of health care provision and other services they realize that their vulnerability is tied to powerful decisions and interests elsewhere. Some villages with established health clubs demonstrate how they can bring about change through organizing and mobilizing with a sense of common purpose. From there it is just another step toward affirming how their collective resolve can exert pressure on local authorities and eventually the state.

Format and Curriculum Design

Program design has to be responsive to the particular conditions of a place and its people. The main economic and survival activity of Senekaduku residents is mixed farming; however, both men and women also spend a significant amount of time in the bush collecting thatch, timber, and wild foods or harvesting forest products such as palm oil and palm wine which, once processed, can be sold for precious cash (Care Sierra Leone, 2003). While all community members are free to collect and use natural resources they have different levels of accessibility depending on fitness, health status, and the existence and condition of their tools.

The changing rhythm of diversified livelihood activities impacts on the provision of AVE for social sustainability in two ways: with regard to resource management, and in terms of the format of sessions. First, it is important to acknowledge how physical capacity, limited market opportunities, and knowledge about local resources have guided people in sustainable resource management. Imported notions of what constitutes development in the name of progress and economic growth are often based on ruthless exploitation of natural resources. The UNESCO-UNEVOC document stresses that "environmental sustainability requires a change from the 'business-as-usual' approach to development" (2006, p. 15). Without global pressures local populations tend only to take from nature what they need for their own consumption in cash or kind and this attitude and knowledge needs to be affirmed (Shiva, 2000).

Second, the format of the CHC sessions had to be mindful of seasonally changing livelihood activities with regard to time, place, and content of meetings. All these were negotiated and agreed upon collectively before the course and often required renegotiation in response to weather and other constraints. This was critical to creating a sense of ownership of the program and hence commitment to regular attendance during its initial lifespan of six months and beyond. Furthermore, sessions had to be designed to be highly participatory.

Participants give up valuable time and in a sense "trade" one form of livelihood security—through growing produce or collecting wild resources—for another—through building knowledge and skills for improving health. Since access to health experts is expensive and often impossible, membership of health clubs must provide the capacity for wise and skilful emergency responses—whether this is recognizing the urgent need for a trip to a health clinic, or locally available treatment. The confidence to act decisively is crucial, as Mrs. Shaw described:

> When I took my son to the barber to shave his head the barber took an old used razor blade but since we have been told during our weekly sessions that not only unprotected sex can transmit HIV/AIDS but also the use of used sharp instruments. So I went to the shop to get a new razor blade for the barber to use, and I went further to explain to the barber the reason why I bought the new blade.

Each session ends with a discussion and resolution about practical steps to be taken in the week to come. This may involve collecting items for a "first aid" kit for each home, organizing a children's rights day or washing all the bed clothes to avoid the spread of ringworm and scabies. Participation in processes of consensus building toward the decisions has allowed every member to be fully informed not just about *what* a proposed action involves but *why* it would be useful and necessary.

A participatory approach also recognizes that the drudgery of daily livelihood activities saps the energies of all, particularly women, and that there are few educational opportunities for adults. CHC sessions can offer welcome intellectual stimulation, and they must allow everyone to be recognized as knowing subjects able to contribute to the process of exploration and sense making by having access to the same information.

In all this, the facilitators have a responsibility to steer discussions so they go beyond "sharing as airing" (von Kotze, 1998) and a mere recycling of the already known. This also demands the courage and sensitivity to guide the exploration of prevailing relations of power and interest especially with regard to gender, age, status, and affiliation to tribes or societies. Using pictures as codes and tokens for playful experimentation I observed field agents skillfully raising contentious issues and handing over "the talking stick" to elders and leaders to ensure they were included in the process. If we want to ensure active commitment to discussions, role plays, games, and story-telling participants need to feel safe to question and have a clear sense of useful outcomes from what may be experienced as a difficult and painful examination of experience, accepted beliefs, and cultural norms.

Holistic Approach

A brief description of some moments during a weekly session of a relatively newly formed CHC best illustrates how teaching, learning, and development action are integrated with boosting self-esteem and confidence and building community. Early in the morning in Senekaduku village people gather in the communal meeting space opposite the mosque and next to the central water pump. They are excited to be together but also anxious to get to the fields before the sun gets too hot. About 15 well-dressed teenage mothers, older women and the women leaders sit on benches on the one side, babies on their laps, toddlers tugging at their skirts. Men sit on stools and benches on the other side and the rice husks laid out to dry on the hardened surface in the middle are pushed aside to create a free space. The majority of households in the village are represented here. The imam and preacher lead the assembled participants in short prayers and after a brief introduction the session begins with a review of the previous sessions. The new topic is introduced with reference to personal experience: who has experienced malaria and how do you get it? Taking turns, participants describe the symptoms and causes of malaria, a significant cause of death here. The facilitator initiates questioning of some of the prevailing myths about catching malaria and with much laughter these are explored, corrected, and dismissed: malaria is not caused by locally brewed beer, even though you may be more exposed to mosquitoes and hence infection if you sit in open drinking houses until late at night.

Referring to the monitoring chart that is publicly displayed and collectively updated weekly, the facilitator asks: Why are young breastfeeding mothers still getting infected despite having access to free insecticide-treated bed nets? Some women are surprised and briefly check with their neighbors about the availability of such nets. An older woman raises the problem that husbands want to claim the nets even when it is their turn to be with one of the other wives who may not have a net. There is some laughter behind hands from the women, some visible embarrassment from men as old habits and beliefs about men's status are questioned, and some assertive insistence that as head of a household it is a man's right to claim such comforts. The "mammy queen" makes a little speech about respect and after some cautious but heated discussion there is agreement that this practice is against the human rights of women. The matter will need further discussion, but at least it has been brought into the open and is likely to become a topic of conversation in informal chats as a practice that reinforces male privilege while endangering the lives of young women and babies.

With the help of flashcards participants construct the cycle of malaria and identify points at which the cycle might be broken. Other forms of prevention are suggested and participants demonstrate wrapping up themselves and their children, and exchange "recipes" for burning locally available plants and fruits to repel mosquitoes. Finally, they suggest both individual and collective action to be undertaken to reduce the rate of malaria infection in the future. Suggestions do not involve measures that require expensive outside resources; instead, they involve behavior changes and environmental courses of action such as covering water sources and filling in potholes that serve as mosquito breeding places.

The session illustrates a holistic approach that works by highlighting connections and interrelations instead of setting up binaries that create impossible choices. The attitude to knowledge production and dissemination is dialogic: recognizing the link between different knowledge discourses and the value and importance of local indigenous knowledge, between ways of generating understanding and the role of culture, religion, and tradition, and focusing particularly on gender and power dynamics, the meeting does not simply deal with a particular disease as an individual problem but links the personal with social and environmental dimensions and thus reinforces health and well-being as a concern for all. Human rights issues are raised not as abstractions but in terms of the impact they have on daily relations and relationships. In this way, old ideas that serve to dominate or oppress particular sections of the community can be challenged without the holders of such ideas feeling disrespected and undermined. This opens the way for change.

Sessions on health give way to action that does not just improve individual and household attitudes and behavior around preventable diseases. Discussions on sanitation and hygiene also lead to a demand for improved water and sanitation facilities and eventually other development initiatives that might improve household food security. The CHC committee will form sub-groups to address the need for water wells, latrines, drainage systems, and the like and the same structure of weekly meetings is used to plan and implement projects. One week, agricultural extension officers may run a food processing or palm-wine production session, the next week the focus on economic enterprise will investigate saving and lending schemes, or introduce honey marketing.

Beyond the CHCs: Some Ideas for a more Socially Just AVE

If we ask: what should be the curriculum for an education and training program that serves the most vulnerable in the majority world we cannot answer with a list of subjects and a generic curriculum. A Zulu proverb reminds us that "Amanqe akakuboni, intuthwane isikubonile" (the vultures cannot see what the ant has seen). The answer to what is the most appropriate and useful form of AVE for social sustainability will be very different depending on whether we ask the powerful "vultures" or the "ants," the people who are the workers on the ground and who live with and within the environment on which they depend for their survival. We require a much better understanding of the constraints and strengths that affect people's decisions and how these are less deliberative in terms of preferred options than in terms of available alternatives within the context of vulnerability, threats, and capabilities. Before embarking on another prescriptive round of policy we need to listen and observe; we need to learn from the very people who have never lived with safety nets provided by state-led social security systems but always had to construct their own networks of social protection.

Is it not time we faced up to the fact that international capital will not invest in the poorest countries of the world and, while training in information technologies, job sharing, and the like may be appropriate for industrialized countries, they are not a priority for the global South? The African continent is trying to recover from histories of colonialism, neo-colonialism, and civil strife and its reconstruction offers an opportunity to rediscover or redefine the values, institutions, and mechanisms that will be the foundation of the future. There are some useful lessons to draw from the CHC model for the design and provision of education for social sustainability, lessons for education and training that aims to develop productive sociality built on social and economic justice for all rather than an adult and vocational education for a few. I want to suggest three lessons.

First, adult and vocational education should become people-centered rather than job-oriented. Fundamentally, community health clubs are about people: building relationships and trust, introducing a culture of transparency and accountability, inculcating the values of reciprocity, solidarity, and mutual responsibility, transforming power relations, and encouraging a questioning orientation that welcomes critical analysis and challenges as vehicles for dynamic change. Williamson suggests that

> there is no greater challenge in the modern world than to find the ways to enable the underlying mutualities and interdependence of all communities to be acknowledged, understood and acted upon in ways which enable people to live together in a sustainable way in peace. (1998, p. 98)

He believes that

> communities which strengthen their capacity to think, to plan, to organise, to acquire the resources they need and if necessary, to protest are the ones most likely to combat exclusion and improve their opportunities. (1998, p. 105)

A reorientation toward collective rather than individualistic forms of education and training might be a first commitment to a political agenda beyond self-interest and competitive individualism, beyond the market and profitability, beyond the exploitation of environments and people, and toward community as shared forms of living with strong ties and emotional security.

Second, education and training should be clearly contextualized with the rhythms of life where work is understood as livelihood activities consisting of different types of paid and unpaid work. The relationship between the two sheds light on the dynamics of poverty and gender inequality (Chen et al., 2006, p. 29) and AVE for social sustainability must consider the impact of women's unpaid care work on their ability to participate in programs and sustain such participation.

Third, the first 't' in TVET refers implicitly and explicitly to (male) western technologies and thus reinforces the disciplining dominating western knowledge system and by implication the message that salvation of the global South can only happen through the knowledge and technologies of the wealthier nations. Local technologies are specially adapted to particular conditions and use and are based on indigenous knowledge and skills and available resources. Where appropriate they should form the basis of education and training rather than being replaced by inaccessible, unaffordable, and often environmentally unsustainable ones.

Finally, let us put education and training in its place. AVE and TVET are not some magical injection: if only the right medicine could be found, the patient could be fortified against all evils and not only would the economy become healthier but "the poor" would benefit all around. A person whose immune system is already compromised (by poverty-related diseases) can be further at risk if subjected to such vaccination policies. Poverty eradication primarily requires a radical redistribution of wealth, not amelioration through skills development projects. While workshops that explain markets and marketing may be very useful, they do not replace the necessity of creating fair access to markets. A training program might explain how different interests are protected or negotiated, but it does not replace having a voice at the negotiation table when favorable trade agreements are forged.

If we want to chase the vultures off the roof in Kabala the best we can do with education and training is to help people to organize, mobilize, and devise plans for effecting change through dialogue and alternative visions.

References

Bennholdt-Thomsen, V., & Mies, M. (1999). *The subsistence perspective: beyond the globalised economy.* London: ZED Books.
Care Sierra Leone (2003). *Household livelihood security assessment: synthesis document.* Freetown: Care Sierra Leone.
Care International in Sierra Leone (2005). *Communicating health, communicating rights: a participatory toolkit for field agents.* Freetown: Care Sierra Leone.
Chen, M., Vanek, J., Lund, F., Heintz, J., Jhanvala, R., & Bonner, C. (2006). *The progress of the world's women 2005: women, work and poverty.* New York: UNIFEM.
Gorz, A. (1999). *Reclaiming work: beyond the wage-based society.* Cambridge: Polity Press.
Hart, M. (2002). *The poverty of life-affirming work: motherwork, education, and social change.* Westport, CT: Greenwood Press.
Lund, F., & Nicholsen, J. (2003). *Chains of production, ladders of protection: social protection for workers in the informal economy.* Durban: School of Development Studies.
Shiva, V. (2000). *Stolen harvests.* London: Zed Books.
UNESCO-UNEVOC International Centre for Technical and Vocational Education and Training (2003). *UNESCO-UNEVOC in brief.* Bonn: UNESCO.
UNESCO-UNEVOC International Centre for Technical and Vocational Education and Training (2006). *Orienting technical and vocational education and training for sustainable development.* Bonn: UNESCO.

von Kotze, A. (1998). Monologues or dialogues? Missed learning opportunities in participatory rural appraisal. *Convergence*, *32*(4), 17–55.
Waterkeyn, J. (1999). Structured participation in community health clubs. Paper presented at the 25th WEDC Conference: Integrated development for water supply and sanitation, Addis Ababa, September.
Williamson, B. (1998). *Lifeworlds and learning: essays in the theory, philosophy, and practice of lifelong learning*. Leicester: NIACE.
Wright Mills, C. (1970). *The sociological imagination*. Harmondsworth: Penguin Books.

Chapter 15
The Contribution of Non-formal Adult Education to Social Sustainability: Policy Implications from Case Studies in the Asia-Pacific Region

Richard G. Bagnall

Abstract In this chapter I examine, from a policy perspective, the contribution of non-formal adult education (NFAE) to social sustainability through its contribution to vocational learning. I draw on five country case studies of NFAE in the Asia-Pacific region: Australia, Fiji, India, the Philippines, and Thailand. Vocational learning can enhance social sustainability because it facilitates the development of individual capacity for meaningful, productive, and competitive engagement in income generation. The case studies highlight a number of common qualities in the contribution of NFAE to vocational learning. NFAE was found in each of the countries to be an important provider of vocational education and a contributor more broadly to vocational learning outcomes. That contribution was facilitated by the low capital overheads and the high situational responsiveness and cost effectiveness of provision in the NFAE sector. The sector's involvement in vocational education also raised a number of tensions, which need to be considered in policy initiatives and reviews. The democratic, participative, community-based, and humanistic nature of NFAE provision, and its commitment to social justice, also benefit its promotion of informed, active, and responsible citizenship, which itself encourages productive self-employment or cooperative enterprise. These findings suggest the value of the sector in carrying forward the social sustainability learning agenda.

Introduction

In this chapter I consider the contribution of non-formal adult education (NFAE) to social sustainability through its impact on vocational learning outcomes. Let us define social sustainability as "ensuring that the basic needs of all people are satisfied and that all, regardless of gender, ethnicity or geography, have an opportunity to develop and utilise their talents in ways that enable them to live happy, healthy and fulfilling lives" (UNESCO-UNEVOC International Centre for Technical and Vocational Education and Training , 2004, p. 18). If we then take vocational learning outcomes as being those learning outcomes that contribute directly to enhancing

R.G. Bagnall (✉)
Hong Kong Institute of Education, Tai Po, Hong Kong, China

vocational capacity or performance, it is evident that they may contribute to social sustainability most directly by raising individual, family, or community capacity to attain and maintain economic self-sufficiency within their cultural contexts (Bagnall, 1999). Such vocational learning will include skills, practical understanding, values, and commitments to engage in work that is culturally valued and demanded: work, variously, through employment by others, through cooperative enterprise, or through self-employment.

Vocational learning, then, may be facilitated directly through vocational education (Winch, 2000)—or what UNESCO terms "technical and vocational education and training" (TVET) (UNESCO, 1999). It may also, though, be enhanced by other categories of educational provision and engagement, especially those recognized less on the basis of their educational goals (as is the case in vocational education) than on the basis of their formal (procedural) properties, such as the nature of their learners, their accreditation status, their centrality to education as an institution, and the extent of their regulation by the state. The formal schooling, higher education, and NFAE sectors each contribute in important, and importantly different, ways to vocational learning outcomes (Abrahamsson, 1999). NFAE, then, may be seen as contributing to vocational learning outcomes primarily in two ways: through the provision of vocational education programs and through the contribution of other—general or non-vocational—NFAE programs (Moore, 1998).

To return, then, to the beginning, this chapter focuses on the contribution of NFAE to social sustainability through its impact on vocational learning outcomes. It outlines a comparative study undertaken by the Asian South Pacific Bureau of Adult Education (ASPBAE). The study sought to identify, in different countries, the policies impacting on the contribution of NFAE to vocational learning outcomes. It sought thereby to identify policy alternatives across the countries, focusing on the influence of those alternatives on the impact of NFAE on vocational learning, and on the issues arising through those alternatives in the different national contexts. The study was driven by a desire to foreground the contribution that NFAE makes to vocational learning and to identify policy alternatives that may be used to inform policy review in countries within the Asia-South Pacific region in order to enhance the quality and impact of that contribution. It was seen also as providing insight into the policy alternatives through which NFAE may be used in different political contexts in the Asia-South Pacific region to enhance sustainability through vocational education.[1]

In this chapter, then, I outline the study and those implications. Following a brief outline of the genesis of the project, I describe the way in which the project was undertaken. I then outline prominent characteristics of the contribution of NFAE to vocational learning in each of the country case studies as a context to the following articulation of common features of the NFAE provision, engagement, and vocational learning impact that emerged across the case studies. These common features raise a number of issues that are important in understanding, assessing, or initiating policy. In the following section, then, I articulate the more important of those issues. Finally,

---

[1] A full report of the original study (Bagnall, 2003) is available from the publisher or ASPBAE.

15 The Contribution of Non-formal Adult Education to Social Sustainability   195

I examine important features of the alternatives described in the country case studies on the impact of NFAE on vocational learning outcomes as a contribution toward our understanding of how NFAE may be used to enhance sustainable work practices.

Background to the Project

The study was conceived at a regional consultative meeting, convened by ASP-BAE and the Department of Non-formal Education, Ministry of Education, Thailand (DNFE), at Jomtien, in 1998. That meeting recommended that ASPBAE initiate a program of advocacy, policy research, and knowledge exchange, focusing on vocational education within the NFAE sector. The comparative study reported here was identified by ASPBAE as the first major project to be undertaken in that program. It was designed to inform ASPBAE and its member NGOs of the part played in achieving vocational learning by the NFAE sector across the Asia-South Pacific region, as a basis for ASPBAE's future policy advocacy and leadership training in vocational education. The study was placed under the academic leadership of the present author, with Mr. Bobby Garcia providing the executive leadership.

The Project Methodology

Five countries were selected for the study: Australia, Fiji, India, the Philippines, and Thailand. The selection sought to include and represent a diversity of national and developmental contexts and policy responses across the Asia-South Pacific region. Therein it was hoped that policy similarities, differences, and alternatives would be revealed—providing the comparative information with which to meet the purpose of the study, within the limited resources available to it. Each country study was made the responsibility of a within-country expert. In Fiji it was Mr. Joseph Veramu; in India it was Dr. Vandana Chakrabarti; in the Philippines, Ms. Rachel (Che) Aquino-Elogada; in Thailand, Dr. Wisanee Siltragool; with the present author assuming responsibility for the Australian case study.

The drafting of the case study reports was guided by a concept paper that I prepared with critical input from participants in the Jomtien consultative meeting. Resource limitations restricted data for the case studies largely to existing documentation—government reports and legislation, policy reviews, program evaluations, and published research—although the authors were also encouraged to draw upon their own experience and contacts in preparing the case study reports. The case studies were drawn together between June 1999 and June 2000.

Draft reports from the country studies were subject to comparative critique at a week-long workshop held in Cebu (the Philippines) in June 2000. Commonalities, differences, and policy implications evident in and across the cases were also teased out as part of that workshop, and in the course of subsequent work on the case studies, through Internet-mediated exchanges between the academic leader and the country-study researchers. I drew together the final report of the study in a similar manner, and I assumed responsibility for cross-study consistency and the overall quality of the research.

This process was undertaken with a view to finding an appropriate middle ground in the tension between, on the one hand, uniformity for the sake of comparability and, on the other hand, individuality for the sake of faithful representation. The concept paper sought to create a common conceptual framework within which the country studies would be undertaken. It suggested an overall structure for the case study reports and included, within that structure, a list of possible questions from which each researcher was encouraged to select those that were most meaningful and important in the context of their study. The researchers were encouraged to write case study reports that reflected the particular features of culture, policy, and provision pertaining to their country, as well as the academic traditions that they took to the task. When I edited the case studies I sought to preserve the individuality of each case study report, without sacrificing the comparability that comes from a shared structure and informing conceptual framework.

The conceptualization of both "vocational education" and "NFAE" were seen in the study as being matters specific to each of the case studies. Nevertheless, a broad understanding and a range of nuances of these concepts were articulated and discussed in the concept paper as a way of informing each individual case study. Vocational education was thus conceptualized as learning provision or engagements directed primarily to enhancing the economic potential of individual learners. Economic potential was seen as including employment potential: the potential to obtain paid employment, or to obtain better paid employment than that which a learner currently has. Employment potential in this sense thus clearly pertains to working for others on a remunerative basis: piecework, wages, contract, salary, or such like. Economic potential, though, while encompassing employment potential, was seen as being broader, including also the potential to engage successfully, or more successfully, in self-employment or in cooperative enterprise, in the production and marketing of commodities (goods or services) from which economic return is produced, but only after successful sales have been concluded, and then only if and to the extent that there is an economic return after production costs have been met. Economic potential therefore also included the potential to engage in the *informal* economic sector as well as the formal.

What we excluded from vocational education was education and training for ends other than those of economic return: voluntary work, unpaid domestic work, and educational outcomes such as civic, health, recreation, leisure, individual or social development, and so on. The term "general education" may be used to differentiate such education from the more strictly vocational (Hager, 1993). This distinction is not, though, intended to imply that general education does not contribute importantly to vocational learning or development. The distinction made between vocational education and general education is, rather, that between broad categories of provision and engagement, on the basis of the *primary purpose* informing the design, management, and evaluation of a given educational program.

The notion of NFAE was taken in the study, broadly, as referring to educational provision and engagements that are intended, designed, managed, and evaluated particularly for adults, and that are outside the mainstream of formal, for-credit educational provision (Bagnall, 1994, p. 1). We acknowledged that the usage of the notion, and the standard term used to name it (whether "non-formal," "adult," "community," "popular," or whatever), varies greatly from country to country. Generally, though, as is implied in the above definition, we understood the field to exclude adult enrolment in mainstream formal education courses, whether in the primary, secondary, tertiary, or higher education sectors (Davies, 1985).

In this study we recognized vocational education and NFAE as traditional but overlapping "sectors" of educational provision and engagement in the sense that they are both recognized as such in respective government policies and commonly by practitioners and scholars (Moodie, 2002; Senate Standing Committee on Employment, Education and Training, 1991). That recognition, though, in no way denies the vagueness and permeability of their sectoral boundaries and the lack of clarity or agreement on the defining sectoral qualities. Importantly, the two sectors overlap to the extent that vocational education may be provided in what is normally regarded as the NFAE sector.

The study was intended to focus attention on policy alternatives impacting on the contribution of NFAE practice to vocational learning outcomes. That focus, though, was understood as being expressed in and through the concrete forms of NFAE provision and engagement. The case studies thus primarily examined the forms of that provision and engagement in each of the participating countries. Impacting policy was understood to be not just the policies that are articulated in government legislation or official policy documents, but also those that are established and maintained through management practice. The latter becomes a part of departmental, organizational, or more broadly cultural practice, even though its origins and maintenance are dependent entirely or largely upon management decisions or interpretations, rather than on clearly articulated and gazetted policy statements. The notion of policy here thus incorporated both that of policy as text and that of policy as discourse (Ball, 1999). The study may thus be characterized as a form of policy review (Weimer & Vining, 1989).

The Country Case Studies

NFAE in each of the five country case studies took different forms and exhibited different emphases and outcomes in relation to vocational learning. In this section, important features of those profiles are outlined, to give a sense of the cultural contexts in which the subsequent analysis was grounded.

Australia

In Australia NFAE has historically been provided by a diversity of public bodies, including universities (generally through designated outreach units), evening colleges, community-based organizations, technical and further education (TAFE) colleges, public libraries, museums, and such like. The traditional role of the NFAE sector—or "adult and community education" (ACE) as it is known in Australia—was that of providing second-chance education to adults and communities who were unable or failed to benefit from formal education to the extent that they were in a position of being socially or economically disadvantaged. ACE was the sector that provided educational opportunities to develop basic skills, understanding, and confidence to progress further through more formal education. It also provided continuing educational opportunities in professional, academic, and artistic fields and has traditionally been home to active individuals and groups interested in social change for social justice.

From the 1980s, the progressive and pervasive marketization, vocationalization, and privatization of NFAE have changed that profile beyond recognition. To some extent, the traditional role of the ACE sector in providing second-chance education has been taken over by the upper secondary and higher education sectors, through policies of mass, open, flexible, publicly supported formal education provision. Government funding for ACE is otherwise limited to designated target programs for particular categories of adults recognized as disadvantaged—largely contracted out by government agencies to private providers. Such programs are strongly vocationally oriented and focused on developing basic or generic social and work skills. Indeed, the profile of ACE provision is now importantly constrained by the priorities of the vocational education and training (VET) sector, including its outcomes-driven and competency-based nature, its qualifications framework, and its preoccupation with the labor market demands of industry. Programs of general ACE persist through Workers' Educational Associations, universities, colleges, community-based organizations, and private agencies. They are, though, largely or entirely self-funded, as is the flourishing field of continuing professional education (CPE). ACE for democratic change and empowerment is marginalized by the highly centrist policy agenda that now characterizes both VET and ACE.

Fiji

Government policy in Fiji sees NFE as benefiting the population directly and indirectly through the provision of education for personal development and vocational skills training. It has historically focused on providing skills for working in the informal economic sector. School-based vocationally directed NFE programs are run through a large number of government secondary schools throughout the Fiji islands. A large number of NGOs are also involved in a range of non-formal education programs, many of which have economic outcomes for the learners involved. However, NFE in Fiji suffers an image problem, with many learners preferring more formal general education, even though such education demonstrably fails to deliver the economic outcomes demonstrated by NFE.

The contribution of NFE to vocational learning outcomes has been given a boost in recent years through the development of partnerships involving government NFE providers, NGOs, employers, trade unions, VET providers, and other stakeholders. NFE-based VET providers—such as Montfort Boys Town, the Nadave Centre for Appropriate Technology, and the Chevalier Training School—are benefiting from international support to modernize infrastructure and curriculum and from developing links with vocational accreditation bodies. Recent policy directives in NFE have clarified programming priorities, including that of providing vocational learning for youth employment and of encouraging the development of employment-related programs with stakeholders. Reforms to NFE curricula from the 1990s have seen a strong emphasis on environmental and economic considerations and on social sustainability. These reforms have revitalized NFE and enhanced its vocational significance and impact in Fiji.

India

India has a vast non-formal NFAE—there termed "adult education"—program, with vocational skills development as one of its important objectives. Provision is dispersed across a number of different government departments and agencies, as well as the polytechnics, engineering colleges, and other vocational and technical training institutions. The focus of adult education is strongly on addressing the very high illiteracy rate among adults, as literacy is recognized as an important part of the skills needed for generating income. "Income generating programs" are thus a major feature of adult literacy education and are promoted and implemented in the context of both national and local community development. Illiteracy and its associated economic and social disadvantage are heavily concentrated among women, lower socioeconomic (caste) groups, and ethnic minorities. Adult literacy programs are thus targeted to those groups, using a diversity of models of provision and engagement to ensure curriculum responsiveness to local needs and situations.

The National Open School of India provides a wide range of vocational and general education courses and opportunities for learning assessment, as a much-needed alternative for those who are unable to gain access to or benefit from mainstream schooling. It works in affiliation with a wide range of NGOs and government agencies to provide vocational education that is accessible in local communities. A network of Continuing Education Centres provides non-formal educational opportunities, resources, and study centers for neo-literates. These centers are intended to be contextualized in their curriculum, encouraging vocational learning. Similarly local in their orientation are Institutes of People's Education, which are intended to develop vocationally linked literacy, primarily in migrant laborers.

NFAE in India is characterized by the magnitude and complexity of the educational needs that it seeks to address and by the magnitude and the diversity of programs designed to address those needs. It thus provides a great array of experiments in alternative approaches to using NFAE in addressing individual, social, and economic challenges, most of which have an important vocational dimension.

Philippines

NFE in the Philippines is largely provided through the Bureau of Non-Formal Education (BNFE) of the Department of Education, Culture and Sports, although NGOs also account for an important, although lesser, proportion of the provision. The work of the BNFE is directed toward meeting the learning needs of individuals in any of three designated age bands, with priority being given to the youngest (15–39 years). Government NFE provision is strongly geared toward enhancing basic literacy, including marketable work skills, while NGO provision is more strongly directed toward developing social and political consciousness raising, leadership, and organizational skills. A competency-based Accreditation and Equivalency System framework (KAVS) provides assessment of core competencies learned through NFE, parallel to the formal accreditation system, allowing the recognition of learning through NFE and its transfer to the formal system. Its focus is on basic skills.

The main provider of formal TVET is the Government Technical Education and Skills Development Authority (TESDA). Its focus is on formal, technical skill development, to enhance the international competitiveness of Philippine industry. However, non-formal TVET, especially that through apprenticeships, has in recent years been more integrated with the formal, in what has become known as the "Dual Training System." There has also been a shift to a greater focus on the development of self-employment skills—entrepreneurship, marketing, and skills for developing micro enterprises—in both urban and rural areas.

NGOs in the Philippines work with People's Organizations (POs) and communities on a wide range of issues and development programs. They flourish in responding to the widespread social and economic marginalization, particularly in rural areas, where the incidence of poverty and illiteracy is high. Another important approach to non-formal education in the Philippines is "popular education" (pop-ed)—regarded as being an alternative to formal, mainstream academic education, in its focus on contextualized learning. Its main target is disadvantaged groups and communities, especially in rural but also urban areas. For these groups it contributes importantly to vocational learning, especially for cooperative and self-employment.

Thailand

NFAE in Thailand is a major provider of vocational education and a major contributor to vocational learning. Since 1979, the country has had a Department of Non-formal Education (in the Ministry of Education), with programming strongly directed to vocational learning. Other government departments and ministries, though, are also major providers, especially the Departments of Vocational Education, Skill Development, and Community Development. The Department of NFE runs a national network of provincial and regional NFE centers, running programs at community and district levels. NFE for self-employment and job employment are both important—and in both rural and urban areas. The curriculum is well articulated and developed, both by educational level and by intended vocational outcomes.

In its educational policy, Thailand recognizes formal, non-formal, and informal education as three major fields of educational provision and engagement. That explicit recognition has made it possible also to promote the transfer of learning and qualifications across the boundaries between these fields. NFE provision in Thailand is focused strongly on those sectors of the population that are in greatest economic and social need, and this applies no less to vocationally directed NFE than to other areas.

Although Thailand is formally a democracy, its constitutional monarch plays an important role in promoting national development programs, all of which have a strong NFE component directed to vocational learning. The current unifying philosophy of these programs is that of the "Sufficiency Economy"—a well-articulated framework for individual and social development, grounded in values of sustainability, self-reliance, respect, and risk minimization.

Emergent Commonalities

The patterns of educational involvement and vocational learning varied across the five case studies, as did the policy alternatives to which these patterns gave expression. However a number of features were shared in some form or other and to different degrees. They raise important issues for policy studies or policy initiatives intended to enhance or assess the contribution of NFAE to vocational learning outcomes. I endeavor here to articulate the more significant of these commonalities.

First, and most importantly, each of the case studies exemplifies the considerable importance of NFAE, both in the provision of vocational education and, more broadly, to vocational learning outcomes. Those contributions include not only specific work skills, but also generic work skills and, even more broadly, generic life capabilities.

Importantly, this contribution is part of a general trend toward the vocationalization of education, particularly NFAE. In each of the case studies there is evidence of a heightening preoccupation with vocational learning outcomes in the policy initiatives impacting on NFAE. This trend is strongest in the Australian case study, but is evident also in each of the others.

NFAE is particularly responsive to global, regional, and national pressures for change. This is most notably so with respect to the contribution of NFAE to vocational learning outcomes. It may be seen as one of the major strengths of the NFAE sector in relation to vocational learning outcomes, in that it gives that sector's educational provision an immediacy and relevance unmatched by any other sector. On the other hand, it makes the sector's programs and providers highly vulnerable to the whims of cultural change, and there is a danger of providers vacuously responding to contextual demands, regardless of the value of the demands or of what is lost in the process of change.

One consequence of that responsiveness is in the increasing tendency of NFAE to focus on labor market demands. In each of the case study sites the sector is making a major contribution to vocational learning outcomes. It could also be seen, though, in the context of contemporary labor market reforms, as unduly serving the interests of big business, multinational companies, and the advance of globalization more generally. From this latter perspective, the NFAE sector is arguably compromising its commitment to enhancing social justice.

Another consequence of the responsiveness is the common shift to a competency-based approach to education. This is pervasive in the Australian case study, strongly evident in the Philippines, acknowledged in Thailand, but still being considered and evaluated in Fiji and India. Competency-based education is a notable feature of contemporary vocational education reform agendas. Its impact on the NFAE sector is therefore an expression of that sector's responsiveness to those reform agendas.

The attractiveness of competency-based education to policy makers in the vocational education sector underlines an important differentiation that is made across all of the case studies. This differentiation is between vocational education as the province of work-specific skills and aptitudes of a technical nature, and general education as the province of humane values, understandings, and complex capabilities. This distinction in itself ensures the relatively lower cultural value and standing of vocational education relative to non-vocational education in each of the countries studied. Competency-based approaches further sharpen this distinction, in their association with vocational education and their reductionist, technical approach.

Interestingly, across the diversity in policy frameworks that give substance to this responsiveness, and in spite of the parallel diversity of cultural contexts in the countries studied, there is a *convergence* of the issues being faced and the educational approaches being adopted to address those issues. The common issues include those of educational, social, and economic disadvantage; the exploitation of women, immigrant groups, indigenous peoples, and ethnic minorities; and the marginalization of groups such as incarcerated, elderly, and handicapped persons. The common approaches to those issues are underpinned by a strongly humanistic set of values, which may be seen as the core of the common culture of NFAE as a field of practice.

That set of humane values is expressed in a general concern for social justice. Across the case studies, policies, practices, and practitioners are strongly influenced by a commitment to use NFAE to improve social equity. Given the focus of the case studies on vocational learning, that commitment is focused strongly on enhancing the opportunities for disadvantaged persons to engage productively in work to enhance their economic potential.

Correspondingly, perhaps, in all of the case studies voluntary contributions are important in the provision of NFAE opportunities. In no other sector of education is voluntary work such a major feature.

Much of the programming is also undertaken with limited, often minimal infrastructure. This keeps overhead costs low. It enhances the responsiveness of programming to contextual learning needs and interests. Together with the voluntary nature of much of the contributing work, it also enhances the apparent efficiency of the educational activities involved.

The experience of NFAE engagement in vocational education provision, with its emphasis on vocational learning for self-employment or cooperative enterprise, has highlighted the importance of entrepreneurial skills as learning outcomes. The experience of many programs in Thailand and the Philippines, for example, may serve as models for practice in this regard.

In times and areas of high unemployment, the focus tends to be more on the development of individual capacity for self-employment or cooperative enterprise—as is strongly evidenced in the Thai and Indian case studies. In times or areas of lower unemployment, and when government policy is directed strongly at achieving structural change in the labor market, the policy emphasis is more on the development of skills for the labor market—as is evidenced here in the Australian and the Philippine case studies.

Nevertheless, in all of the case studies, non-vocational education provision—programs of general NFAE, recreational and hobby programs, for example—make an important contribution to vocational learning outcomes. That contribution includes general skill development, enhanced self-confidence and self-awareness, and the development of effective study and work capabilities and routines.

The case studies also reveal a relationship between the level of social disadvantage through cultural marginalization and the strength of the NGO sector in NFAE. The NGO sector is strongest and most important in providing NFAE under conditions of, and with societal groups most adversely affected by, serious social disadvantage. This relationship is strongly evidenced, for example, in the Philippine case study, where state provision tends to be concentrated on mainstream provision, while a strong NGO sector focuses on disadvantaged groups.

Issues Arising

Those commonalities across the five country case studies give rise to a number of significant policy issues. These issues will importantly influence the impact and success of any policy initiative directed to enhancing the impact of NFAE on vocational learning outcomes. They should also, therefore, be considered in any assessment of policy impacting on the form of NFAE and its impact on vocational learning outcomes. I endeavor in this section to identify the more significant of those issues.

One important issue was the lower cultural value and acceptability of NFAE provision in comparison with more formal provision. In spite of the quality of vocational learning outcomes through the NFAE sector, its location on the policy fringes seems to ensure its second-class status. The irony here is that its marginal positioning is clearly essential to the responsiveness, efficiency, and effectiveness of its contribution, but it also ensures its lower status. To address the problem of status would be to diminish if not to deny the quality of the provision and engagement.

In vocational education programming, this status difference is heightened by the lower cultural value of vocational education itself, relative to more general education. In all of the case studies, there is evidence of the greater cultural value, and hence the attractiveness, of general over vocational education. It contributes to anomalies such as the oversupply of job seekers with high levels of general or professional education, and the under supply of job seekers with sought-after vocational capabilities and aptitudes. This pattern is strongly evident in India, but in the other case studies as well. This value differential derives from the tendency in all cases for vocational education to be associated with particular vocational skills and propensities, while general education is accepted as the province of more general, humane values and understandings. The valuing of the latter over particular vocational skills and propensities is fundamental to the value frameworks in all of the otherwise diverse societies examined in the case studies. The standing of vocational education in the NFAE sector is thus doubly diminished: on the one hand through its association with NFAE, on the other through its being vocational education.

The competency-based approach to vocational education that is evident in all of the case studies to some degree contributes further to the devaluing of vocational education. As an approach to learning, it is based entirely on those values that ensure that vocational education as a whole is of lesser value than general education. It seeks to sharpen the focus on the learning of particular vocational skills (competencies) in the most efficient manner. It therein heightens the status differential between vocational and general education. This effect is most marked in the case of Australia, where by government decree all vocational education must be competency based. It is least marked in India, where more general approaches to vocational education continue to be used and advocated.

That sharpened focus in competency-based approaches on the efficient achievement of particular vocational skills is in tension with the democratic, participative, and humanistic values that are central to NFAE culture. From the perspective of the latter set of values, the exclusive emphasis on skill development that tends to characterize competency-based educational ideology leads to the de-humanization and robotization of human beings. Competency-based approaches to vocational education—so important in Australia and increasingly so in the other case study countries—are thus incorporated with some reluctance into the NFAE sector. They tend to sit there as part of the pluralism that characterizes NFAE provision and engagement, without becoming a central and fully accepted part of it. They serve undoubtedly as a major barrier to the greater involvement of the NFAE sector in vocational education provision, at least to the extent that policy in the vocational education sector is driven by a competency-based approach to vocational learning.

A related tension emerges from the fact that the introduction of competency-based approaches to vocational education tends to be driven by government policy initiatives. It thus tends to be imposed authoritatively and often manipulatively on vocational education providers, including those in the NFAE sector. This is entirely at odds with the democratically grounded approach to educational planning, engagement, and assessment that characterizes NFAE and its providing agencies.

Competency-based approaches also tend to serve national (and international) industrial demands for workplace reform and skill development. They tend, therefore, to be in conflict with the more grounded, local, community, and individual learning needs identified through traditional approaches to vocational learning in NFAE. They effectively diminish the value of people and their situated learning needs and interests and so are in direct and fundamental conflict with NFAE culture.

This conflict highlights a more general tension between vocational education for the labor market and vocational education for self-employment or cooperative enterprise. The case studies suggest that government policy may be increasingly concerned with legislating in favor of vocational education for labor market reform. From a NFAE perspective, though, the evidence suggests that vocational outcomes among disadvantaged sectors of society are most often achieved through vocational education for self-employment and for cooperative enterprise.

Relatedly, vocational education provision in the NFAE sector raises the issue of maintaining independence from formal sector control. Government-driven vocational education reform tends to be associated with formal systems to monitor and ensure compliance and accountability. Those systems inevitably, by their very nature, erode provider autonomy: a value that tends to be of paramount concern particularly to NGO providers of NFAE.

The conflict between centrally driven and grounded approaches to educational provision and engagement is also evidenced in the tension among different interests in the setting of competency standards. In countries such as Australia and the Philippines, where penetration of competency-based ideology is more advanced, there is a continuing debate about whether competency standards should be set by industry, by vocational education professionals, or by government.

An associated concern is the commodification of learning (and of knowledge more generally) that tends to accompany vocational education provision that is driven by labor market interests. Vocational knowledge tends to be constructed increasingly as a marketable commodity rather than a public good. Vocational learning and education, correspondingly, tend to be privatized and commodified. More general and public educational values tend to be diminished or lost. It is just these latter values, though, that are most strongly and traditionally associated with the NFAE sector.

The involvement of NFAE providers in vocational education tends to be limited by the high equipment costs in some areas of vocational education. The generally low levels of capitalization of NFAE providers, and their general dependence on short-term funding, limit the possibilities for their involvement in such areas. On the other hand, the generally good record of the NFAE sector in establishing collaborative links with industry can be used to offset this limitation. Such links can also be used to enhance its responsiveness to labor market demands, and to facilitate the incorporation of meaningful workplace experience into vocational education courses, while also providing enhanced opportunities for job placement after course completion.

In the vocational education sector, a tension is evident in the case studies over the sort of values informing engagement as a provider. That tension is expressed in disagreement about the relative value of private (for-profit) vocational education provision, increasingly common in Australia, and that of NGO (not-for-profit) and government agency provision—traditionally important in all countries studied here.

The NFAE and vocational education sectors are shown in the case studies to share a concern for social integration. There emerges, though, a tension between social integration with social justice, to which the NFAE sector is strongly committed, and social integration with learner compliance, to which many of the recent vocational education policy reforms are directed. This applies particularly to reforms that are labor market and employer driven. In these cases, policy may seem to have lost sight of learning (and its contributing educational interventions) as an ongoing, lifelong process of engagement. In embracing vocational education, NFAE needs to ensure that it does not fail learners in this regard.

A related concern is whether vocational education should focus on short-term learning needs or longer-term development needs. Community-based NFAE has traditionally focused on the progressive, integrated, longer-term development of individuals through whole-of-community or community-integrated approaches. More recent vocational education reforms tend to place primary or sole emphasis on immediate vocational learning (generally skill) demands, which tend to be ephemeral and changing. The value of the vocational learning achieved in the latter situation may emerge to be no less ephemeral. Again, there is a tension here between the NFAE sector and the direction of contemporary vocational education policy reforms.

Another related tension commonly emerges between vocational education for individual advancement and NFAE for collective community advancement and for the correction of social and educational injustice. These constructions of vocational education and NFAE respectively are clearly over-simplifications. Nevertheless, there is certainly a tendency for recent vocational education policy to focus on individual opportunity, just as there is a strong community development tradition in NFAE.

That tradition is, perhaps, strongest in rural NFAE, and it contributes to the difficulty in finding a proper balance between vocational education for rural development and that for urban development. Policy emphasis on employer and labor market interests tends to favor urban development, labor mobility, and flexibility, and these have characterized much recently instituted vocational education policy in the countries studied. The community-based tradition in NFAE, however, places more emphasis on providing vocational education for local community development, relying on and developmentally enhancing the economic potential of existing community members. It therefore is opposed to any undue emphasis on urban development that may lead to skilled migration from rural to urban areas, or from disadvantaged to more advantaged urban areas.

Underlying this issue is a desire to integrate NFAE and vocational education policy with other aspects of social and economic development. The extent to which this is evident across the case studies is limited, although variable. As a general rule, it seems that vocational education and NFAE policy initiatives are most often each (and often separately) driven by particular and unfortunately singular social concerns, whether these be to enhance labor flexibility, reduce unemployment, diminish gender discrimination, or whatever. Policy integration would seem to be limited to attempts to take into account the impact of related policies on the particular reform being proposed on the occasion.

A consequence of this lack of adequate policy integration in recent vocational education reform agendas is their perceived tendency to create newly marginalized sectors of society, while addressing their specific programmatic target concerns. Variously in the countries studied we see concern for the increasing marginalization of older adults made redundant by workplace reform, of individuals who do not fit the formal definitions of disadvantage or sectoral responsibility that are used in operationalizing the reforms, of adults who are not responsive to the contemporary individualization of teaching and learning, and of other groups as well. In embracing vocational education reform agendas, NFAE providers need to be alert to their potential complicity in the creation of new or enhanced sectors of educational and social disadvantage.

Frequently overlooked or marginalized in the enthusiasm for vocational education reform has been its impact on gender equity. Recent policy reforms may actually be regressive in their effects, particularly on women and their access to vocational education and to work on a non-discriminatory basis.

Another concern is the general failure of vocational education reforms to give adequate (or any) recognition to indigenous knowledge systems. All too often, the interests that seem to be driving recent vocational education reforms are those of the dominant culture, or even of transnational corporations. The diversity of cultures that constitute countries such as India and the Philippines is not being given due recognition in any of the policy initiatives noted. And this would seem to be a feature of vocational education reform in all the countries studied.

A problem that emerges from the case studies, in the present climate of rapid cultural change, is the tendency to over-promote the potential of both vocational education and NFAE to be effective instruments of cultural change. This has characterized the political processes of educational reform, and it is an enthusiasm to which we as educational practitioners are easily persuaded. Its unfortunate and inevitable consequence is a perception of these educational sectors as failures when they unavoidably fall short of the inflated educational outcomes and social consequences that were expected of them.

The case studies also demonstrate the need for enhanced performance in the NFAE sector on a number of fronts. Support for continuing learning after initial vocational education needs to be improved. There is a need for stronger linkages with employers offering potential job placements. And micro-enterprise investment support needs to be associated with vocational education provision, so that self-employment and cooperative enterprise learning outcomes can be put into effect.

Finally, here, we might note the evident need for much more exploration and refinement of the respective responsibilities of civil society, private providers, and the state for different aspects or types of NFAE and vocational education. There is no well-grounded understanding of how these different sectors may best work together in either NFAE or vocational education. The effectiveness of these sectors in contributing to vocational learning outcomes may be greatly enhanced by better informed policies in this regard.

Policy Implications

The foregoing issues arising in the case studies serve to underpin the nature and extent of the impact that NFAE is having on vocational learning. That impact is important in all of the case studies, although our attempts to quantify it have not been satisfactory. The impact arises partly from the direct and explicit involvement of NFAE providers in the provision of vocational education courses. It arises also, though, from the less direct and non-explicit contributions of non-vocational education to vocational learning. NFAE thus emerges as an important consideration in any policy initiatives or assessments focusing on vocational education or learning.

Whatever the nature of the course or the programs, that contribution is underpinned by the responsiveness of NFAE providers to the different cultural backgrounds of client groups. The field is thus characterized by its responsiveness to emerging, contextually specific, and often ephemeral vocational learning needs. Providers are able to respond in a timely manner to the gaps left by more formal provision and to the latter's inadequacies and failings. They can do so without necessarily waiting for the ponderously slow adjustments to educational policy that tend to characterize more formal provision. The NFAE sector should be understood particularly in this light in any policy initiatives in vocational education or learning.

Indeed, an important part of programmatic activity in the NFAE sector is its positioning outside any educational policy framework. It operates on the margins of formal policy, tapping expediently into whatever policy initiatives may be used in support of its social and educational mission. Of course, some NFAE programming is driven by and dependent upon formal policy. This is particularly so with programming by state departments and agencies. It is also the case with major national initiatives, such as the national adult literacy programs in India. It is thus important to consider the policy effects of social and economic policy much more broadly in any policy initiative or assessment.

Further underpinning the contribution of NFAE to vocational learning is its humanistic approach to teaching and learning. Through this approach it achieves levels of learner involvement in, identification with, ownership of, and commitment to the educational engagement that are the frequent envy of educators in more formal sectors. This enhances not only the quality, the meaningfulness, and the relevance of the learning outcomes, but also the efficiency of the engagements in terms of learning outcomes.

Relatedly and integrally, the contribution of NFAE to vocational learning outcomes is underpinned by its democratic and participative approach to educational provision and engagement. In working on the fringes of formal educational policy, NFAE is able, openly and honestly, to engage its clients and learners in contextualizing, planning, undertaking, and evaluating its educational programs. It is free to exercise its democratic and humanistic imperatives without fear of contradiction with overarching policy.

NFAE provision thereby tends naturally to be more community based than more formal provision. It seeks generation from within communities, rather than creating artificial learning communities. It seeks learning through those communities, as an integral part of their being. It is thus more naturally educational in form than is more formal provision.

Through the foregoing features, NFAE provision tends to be more efficient than its more formal counterparts in achieving learning outcomes. The enhanced quality, meaningfulness, and relevance of learning ensure greater returns on investment in vocational education provision through the non-formal than through the formal sectors.

It is also evident from the case studies that NFAE makes an important contribution to vocational learning through the learning that comes directly from the democratic, participative, and humanistic nature of its engagements. Through engaging in structured educational experiences that are essentially informed by democratic, participative, and humane values, clients and learners refine their own tacit understanding of those values, they hone their capacities to act according to them, and they enhance their commitment to doing so. They become, in other words, essentially more fully human in the process of educational engagement, regardless of its particular educational objectives. These understandings, capabilities, and commitments are not only essential learning outcomes for a fuller and more satisfying and meaningful life. They are important *vocational* learning outcomes—in themselves enhancing the economic potential of the individuals involved. They may include collaborative capabilities, associations, and models through which learners can become productively self-employed or engaged in cooperative enterprise—and therefore less likely to become migrant labor in search of work elsewhere. The impoverishment of disadvantaged regions through the emigration of skilled labor may thus be diminished through the use of NFAE in the search for vocational learning outcomes.

A notable and related feature of the sector that underpins its contribution to vocational learning outcomes is the importance of NGOs as providing agencies. NGOs tend to capture and give organizational substance to the democratic, participative, and humane values that inform the distinctive qualities of the sector. It may, indeed, be argued on the basis of the evidence in these case studies that the NGO sector is *essential* for the fuller realization of those qualities. The ineradicable formality of the government sector and the unavoidable commitment to the efficient through-put of students that characterizes private provision are, in themselves, antithetical to highly democratic, participative, and humane structures and relationships.

Each of these implications calls for consideration in the development or assessment of policy in vocational education. They suggest ways in which issues of sustainability may be integrated strongly into the provision of vocational learning opportunities through the NFAE sector. The importance of the sector in achieving vocational learning outcomes, and the efficiency and effectiveness with which it is able to do so, suggest that it should be an important sector in policy developments to enhance sustainability. Its relatively high embeddedness in the communities of its generation and concern and the relatively highly democratic, participative, and humanistic nature of its educational engagement suggest that it is ideally constituted to take a major role in carrying forward the sustainability agenda.

Across the diversity of cultural and policy contexts studied here, NFAE clearly plays an important role in poverty alleviation and economic development through learning for employability, for self-employment, for cooperative enterprise, and for citizenship. In each of these ways, it contributes significantly to social sustainability.

References

Abrahamsson, K. (1999). Bridging the gap between education and work: the balance between core curriculum and vocationalism in Swedish recurrent education. In F. van Wieringen & G. Attwell (Eds), *Vocational and adult education in Europe* (pp. 317–342). Dordrecht: Kluwer Academic.

Bagnall, R. G. (1994). *Conceptualizing adult education for research and development: selected critiques*. Brisbane: Centre for Skill Formation Research and Development, Griffith University.

Bagnall, R. G. (1999). Ethical implications of contemporary trends in work and adult vocational learning. In M. Singh (Ed.), *Adult learning and the future of work* (pp. 69–85). Hamburg: UNESCO Institute for Education.

Bagnall, R. G. (2003). *Enhancing income generation through adult education: a comparative study*. Brisbane: Australian Academic Press.

Ball, S. (1999). What is policy? Texts, trajectories and toolboxes. In J. Marshall & M. Peters (Eds), *Education policy* (pp. 3–18). Cheltenham, UK: Edward Elgar.

Davies, A. (1985). Defining nonformal education. *Asian South Pacific Bureau of Adult Education Courier, 34*, 23–26.

Hager, P. (1993). Education vs. training: implications for post-compulsory education in the 21st century. In Centre for Skill Formation Research and Development (Ed.), *After competence: the future of post-compulsory education and training. Conference papers Vol. 1.* (pp. 172–179). Brisbane: Centre for Skill Formation Research and Development, Griffith University.

Moodie, G. (2002). Identifying vocational education and training. *Journal of Vocational Education and Training, 54*(2), 249–265.

Moore, A. (1998). ACE and adding value to the training market. In C. Robinson & R. Kenyon (Eds), *The market for vocational education and training* (pp. 85–90). Leabrook, South Australia: National Centre for Vocational Education Research.

Senate Standing Committee on Employment, Education and Training (1991). *Come in Cinderella: the emergence of adult and community education*. Canberra: Parliament of the Commonwealth of Australia.

UNESCO (1999). *Second international congress on technical and vocational education. Lifelong learning and training: a bridge to the future. Final report*. Paris: UNESCO.

UNESCO-UNEVOC International Centre for Technical and Vocational Education and Training (2004). *Orienting technical and vocational education and training (YVET) for sustainable development*. Bonn: UNESCO-UNEVOC.

Weimer, D. L., & Vining, A. R. (1989). *Policy analysis: concepts and practice*. Englewood Cliffs, NJ: Prentice-Hall.

Winch, C. (2000). *Education, work and social capital: toward a new conception of vocational education*. London: Routledge.

Chapter 16
Community Adult Learning Contributions to Social Sustainability in the Asia-South Pacific Region: The Role of ASPBAE

Bernie Lovegrove and Anne Morrison

Abstract The Asian South Pacific Bureau of Adult Education (ASPBAE) is a non-government organization committed to promoting adult education throughout the Asia-South Pacific region. Many countries within this region are characterized by striking contrasts in access to, and distribution of, basic education and training opportunities. In partnership with regional and global educational and civic bodies, ASPBAE promotes social sustainability by advocating for the right of *all* individuals to an education that assists them to combat poverty and inequality, and that facilitates empowerment and transformation of individuals, groups, and communities. In this chapter, we provide an overview of ASPBAE's activities followed by a case study, in order to highlight the organization's contribution to social sustainability in the Asia-South Pacific region.

Introduction

The Asian South Pacific Bureau of Adult Education (ASPBAE) is a non-government organization that promotes adult education throughout the Asia-South Pacific region. Covering a vast area extending from Mongolia and Japan in the north, to Australia and New Zealand in the south, and from the Kiribati and Cook Islands in the east, and beyond Pakistan in the west, the Asia-South Pacific region is characterized by tremendous ethnic, cultural, linguistic, and socioeconomic diversity. In many nations, access to key services is uneven, with marginalized groups, and in particular women and rural populations, unable to realize fully the benefits of formal and non-formal education and vocational training. This chapter focuses on the role played by ASPBAE in promoting access to education and training across the region, especially for marginalized groups.

This chapter is inspired by the presentations of ASPBAE members who shared their perspectives on adult and vocational education and social sustainability at the AVE for Social Sustainability conference held in Adelaide during April 2006. The chapter is divided into three sections. The first section gives an overview of

---

B. Lovegrove (✉)
Asian South Pacific Bureau of Adult Education (ASPBAE), Colaba, Maharashtra, India

ASPBAE and its mission in the Asia-South Pacific region. The second section provides a case study of ASPBAE's efforts to document and promote sustainable adult literacy innovations in India. The chapter finishes with a brief conclusion.

About ASPBAE

Formed over forty years ago, the Asian South Pacific Bureau of Adult Education (ASPBAE) is a nonprofit association of organizations, networks, and individuals engaged in formal and non-formal adult education. Currently, ASPBAE has a membership of approximately 240 organizations and 100 individuals operating in 30 Asia-South Pacific countries.

ASPBAE's approach to adult education is based on four core principles

1. Education is a fundamental right of all.
2. Governments are primarily responsible for ensuring education for all their citizens.
3. Gender justice is integral to education.
4. Adult education is critical to enabling all citizens to cope with, transform and improve their life and work conditions, fight all forms of discrimination and exclusion, and participate meaningfully and decisively in decisions that impact on their lives.

These principles are advanced through policy advocacy, strategic partnerships, capacity building, and resource mobilization. ASPBAE aims to activate and support community, regional, and national bodies as they endeavor to hold governments accountable for the provision of education to all citizens. ASPBAE acts both with and through civil society organizations (CSOs) and various government agencies. ASPBAE's focus on educational policy advocacy is extended by seven priority themes:

- adult literacy for social justice and empowerment
- education for women's empowerment
- indigenous people's education
- HIV/AIDS education
- education for active citizenship and good governance
- education for peace and conflict prevention
- education for displaced peoples.

Although the concept of social sustainability is not specifically articulated in ASPBAE's mission statement, it is clear that the organization's aims are closely aligned with the visions of social equity, civic participation, and self-determination outlined in the introduction to this volume. ASPBAE is convinced that adult education, both formal and non-formal, makes a vital contribution to social sustainability. Conventionally, community-based adult education tends to be marginalized in favor of formal educational interventions. However, many CSOs are able to impart a holistic approach to learning that includes values and citizenship education, community-building ethics, and education about traditional cultures and practices, while at the same time imparting skills useful for income generation.

ASPBAE has been involved in capacity building of CSOs so that they can engage more effectively with governments in relation to education policy. Capacity building has included training in policy research, data collection, report writing, policy analysis, campaign design, and policy advocacy. Much more needs to be done to research and document the contribution of CSOs toward social sustainability and to argue for more substantial and secure funding so that they can expand their work.

As a contribution to this task, in 2003 ASPBAE undertook a comparative study of five countries (Australia, Fiji, India, Philippines, Thailand), examining policies that impact the contribution of non-formal adult education to vocational education outcomes. This study, *Enhancing income generation through adult education*, was edited by Dr. Richard Bagnall (2003), Griffith University, Brisbane.

ASPBAE has worked with member organizations to promote holistic education for social sustainability, dealing with various issues such as educating for increased citizens' participation in governance, values education, and respect for traditions and cultures. For example, in 2002 in Vanuatu, ASPBAE produced a Learning Circles Kit on Democracy and Citizens' Participation in Governance. Training was provided for key CSOs and offered in various communities and also at Rural Training Centres as part of the curriculum. The Vanuatu Education Department has expressed interest in incorporating aspects of this kit into the school curriculum.

In 2005, on behalf of the Commonwealth Foundation, ASPBAE produced a Citizens Education Action Learning Guide for CSO trainers to promote citizens' participation in governance. The guide has been well received and a series of training courses is being planned in Africa, Asia, the Pacific, and Latin America.

In Samoa, ASPBAE has supported a member organization, METI (Matuaileoo Environment Trust Inc.) in conducting values education and life skills education including training life skills coaches. Over the past two years ASPBAE has also worked with members of indigenous organizations to develop a community action tool to enable indigenous communities to reflect on issues relating to sustainable livelihood, and strategies for poverty alleviation in their communities. The tool is currently being piloted in indigenous communities in Nepal, Malaysia, India, and Indonesia.

These examples are small efforts in the larger scheme of things, but they nonetheless show potential for broader application and relevance. One of the key challenges for ASPBAE is to develop the pool of community adult vocational educators, and to promote within this constituency (and beyond) a strong advocacy capacity so that they can call upon donors and government leaders to meet the educational needs of all people.

A Case Study of Adult Literacy in India

Referring to literacy, UNESCO states the following:

A person is functionally literate who can engage in all those activities in which literacy is required for effective functioning of his [or her] group and community and also for enabling him [or her] to continue to use reading, writing and calculation for his [or her] own and the community's development. (UNESCO, 2005, p. 30)

Although many people throughout the world have been able to lead successful lives without being literate (Hildebrand & Hinzen, 2004, pp. 52–53), literacy can nevertheless act as a catalyst in the fight against poverty, oppression, exploitation, inequality, disease, and infant mortality, thus advancing the long-term sustainability of groups and communities. As Roy argues

> Adult education, with adult literacy at the core, can assist and enable people and communities to deal with these many challenges. It can provide people with the necessary skills, information, awareness and creative competencies to cope with as well as transform their conditions. The right to learning and education opportunities is the right that enables people to best exercise and advance their other rights. (2004a, p. 119)

Yet the interrelationship between education, literacy, and social transformation may be far more complex than has previously been assumed. As Archer notes,

> ... there is dramatic evidence, particularly from [literacy] programmes using participatory approaches, of a whole range of impacts on people's confidence, on people's capacity to participate in wider development processes, on gender equity and women's empowerment, on the education of children, on changing attitudes and behaviours (for example, in relation to HIV/AIDS) on improving health and, on strengthening people's capacity to access government services or assert their basic rights. The list could go on and on. However, most of these outcomes are often more closely attributable to the learning process than to literacy in itself. (2004, p. 67)

Indeed, the quality of the learning process and its responsiveness to learners' own priorities are crucial variables in any literacy intervention. Here, we consider ASPBAE's role in monitoring, evaluating, and critiquing adult literacy interventions in India.

The National Approach to Adult Literacy

In the 60 years since India attained independence there have been significant advancements in literacy levels. In 1951, the national literacy rate was approximately 18% of a population of 361 million. Today, with the population exceeding 1027 million, the literacy rate stands at 65% (Kohli, 2003, p. 8). Despite this significant improvement, much further work is needed before "total literacy" is a reality for all Indian people, regardless of gender, caste, ethnicity, region, and age. The last decadal census in 2001 revealed significant gaps in literacy between men and women (76% versus 54%), between urban and rural populations (80% versus 59%), and between states (Kerala: 91% versus Bihar: 47%), (National Literacy Mission, 2008). Furthermore, as many as 300 million adults who were classified as "literate" for the purposes of the census may in fact have very tenuous reading, writing, and numeracy skills (Kothari, 2003, pp. 17, 19).

India is one of 164 nations committed to the UNESCO-sponsored worldwide Education for All (EFA) campaign, which was launched in 1990 and reaffirmed a decade later at Dakar. The campaign is currently focused on achieving six educational goals globally by the year 2015:

1. expanding and improving comprehensive early childhood care and education;
2. ensuring that by 2015 all children have access to, and complete, free and compulsory primary education of good quality;
3. ensuring that the learning needs of all young people and adults are met through equitable access to appropriate learning and life-skills programs;
4. achieving a 50% improvement in levels of adult literacy by 2015, and equitable access to basic and continuing education for all adults;
5. eliminating gender disparities in primary and secondary education by 2005, and achieving gender equality in education by 2015;
6. improving all aspects of the quality of education and ensuring excellence of all so that recognized and measurable learning outcomes are achieved by all, especially in literacy, numeracy, and essential life skills.

ASPBAE is an active partner in UNESCO's EFA campaign, and is one of several bodies monitoring and reporting on the progress of participant countries in achieving the six goals. It is becoming apparent that many governments are targeting some goals at the expense of others, with adult learning and literacy faring poorly in comparison to the target of widespread childhood schooling (Hildebrand & Hinzen, 2004, pp. 53–53; Rogers, 2004, p. 3; Petersen, 2007, p. 446; Archer & Fry, 2005, p. 2). ASPBAE joins the call for *all* the EFA goals to be returned to the global education agenda.

In India, the government has prioritized two strategies in order to meet the EFA objectives. The first strategy is directed toward the universal elementary schooling of all children, and especially those children from historically marginalized groups. The second strategy focuses on the adult literacy component of EFA and falls under the umbrella of the government's National Literacy Mission. Currently, however, EFA in India is increasingly being associated with elementary education (Kohli, 2003, p. 13).

Although literacy movements have a long history in several districts of India (Saxena, 2004, p. 179), the implementation of the National Literacy Mission (NLM) in 1987 focused attention on literacy across the country. After experimenting with alternative models, the NLM adopted the "Total Literacy Campaign" (TLC) as its principal mechanism for tackling widespread adult illiteracy (Paul, 2004, p. 57). Each TLC is conducted in a delineated area and within a specified time frame, usually over a period of 6–18 months (Bhola, 2002, p. 284). Although early campaigns were implemented by NGOs, the Indian government has been increasingly involved in the process. Various activities, including house-to-house surveys, media drives, and "cultural caravans" (*kalajathas*), are used to raise awareness of literacy, enroll learners, and recruit volunteer teachers *en masse*. Under the guidance of the volunteer teachers, classes of up to 10 learners work though a graded series of three literacy primers. Classes are conducted out of hours at a mutually accessible location, often in the home of the volunteer teacher. It is expected that within a time frame of 200 hours learners will be able to read from unknown texts such as newspapers and road signs, compute simple problems involving multiplication and division, and apply the skills of writing and numeracy in their daily lives (Chakrabarti, 2004, p. 10).

In recent years, National Literacy Mission has introduced post-literacy and continuing education initiatives that are launched on a region-by-region basis after the completion of the TLC. The post-literacy phase is described by Chakrabarti as follows:

> Post-literacy specifically aims at remediation and the retention and consolidation of literacy skills. It comprises providing post literacy primers of graded textual materials to the learners for guided study with the help of a volunteer instructor. In a second phase, the learners are provided with a variety of unstructured learning opportunities to practice their literacy skills through supplementary reading materials and library services, thereby helping them to continue learning through self-directed processes. (2004, p. 11)

According to Chakrabarti (2004), the main element of the CE phase is the establishment of Continuing Education Centres, with the ideal of one per village serving a population of 2000–2500. The center acts as a hub for reading, training, information, discussion groups, development and cultural activities, sports and other programs, as well as providing linkages with other learning institutions such as schools, colleges, and universities. As of 2001, 112 districts had entered the continuing education phase (Chakrabarti, 2004, pp. 11–12).

The effectiveness of the literacy intervention is measured by the administration of standardized tests to a sample of learners. Both internal and external evaluations are conducted and the results reported to the government. Amending earlier goals that proved overly optimistic, the NLM is currently targeting a functional literacy rate of 85% in the 15–35 age group, and a reduction in the gender gap to 10% (National Literacy Mission, 2008). Since 1988, when the first campaign was held in the city of Kerala, TLCs or other literacy interventions have been conducted in 597 of India's 600 districts, "and nearly 124 million people are reported to have been made literate so far" (National Literacy Mission, 2008). In 1999, the NLM received the UNESCO Noma Literacy Prize in acknowledgement of its achievements in both adult literacy and childhood schooling. The NLM's spirit of mass mobilization is enthusiastically captured by Bhola

> an entire district or State taken up in one go; total coverage—no member of society, literate or illiterate, to be left un-enrolled and uninvolved; transformation of literacy work from an avenue of employment to a duty/obligation, tinged with pride and patriotism; meticulous and spatial planning, as in a war, for mobilization and deployment of human resources; integration of people's enthusiasm with the ingenuity of the administrative machinery, on the one hand, and creation of a professional project implementation machinery on the other; de-linking the implementation machinery from governmental bureaucracy to increase dynamism and flexibility, and at the same time ensuring accountability by stringent monitoring by the people themselves. (2002, pp. 282–283)

However, despite the rhetoric, it is important to consider the long-term sustainability of the NLM's strategies, and to focus not just on the numbers "made literate" but also on the contexts in which literacy may or may not make a tangible difference in the lives of individuals. ASPBAE and other non-government organizations are well positioned to offer more sensitive analyses of the NLM than is possible from "official" quantitative evaluations.

As Khan and Rao note, "Most evaluation studies of the literacy campaigns have not taken into consideration the social parameters, the historical and contextual differences in the different districts and states, but followed a standard quantitative format" (2004, p. 14). In order to better understand the impact of the campaign from multiple perspectives, ASPBAE studied six Indian districts that have been through the total literacy and post-literacy phases of the campaign. The studies, published in Karlekar (2004), are based on field trips, interviews, and focus groups with stakeholders (learners, volunteer teachers, and administrators), and on district and state-level workshops involving learners, adult education practitioners, researchers, and policy makers. These studies offer insights into the campaign experience that are not readily discernable in official quantitative reports.

Positive outcomes of the TLC reported across these studies include

- strong demand from parents for the education of their children
- high levels of initial commitment and enthusiasm
- high levels of community participation, particularly amongst marginalized groups, including women, indigenous people, and those from lower castes.

Common problems reported include

- limitations due to the programmatic and time-bound nature of the TLC
- loss of campaign momentum in the post-literacy and continuing education phases
- significant gaps in time between the TLC and later phases
- unrealistic expectations of volunteerism
- lack of ownership of literacy initiatives by the learners
- skill erosion, particularly in marginalized groups
- political and/or administrative discontinuities.

The target-orientated nature of the campaign, while successful in creating momentum, has had unwelcome repercussions in some regions. For example, Saxena describes the competitive atmosphere generated as result of the intervention in Ajmer district:

> The expectation was to somehow get your district declared totally literate. So much so that the people who dared to express their doubts with the method or the achievements in the light of their own experiences of limited successes and innumerable hurdles, were at best silenced or at worst reprimanded for their "inefficiency." (2004, p. 215)

In Ganjam district Roy reports

> I was told that many of those involved in the TLC did whatever they could to ensure that the [External Evaluation] team met the right people ... The [External Evaluation] report lists so many shortcomings and failings in the teaching-learning process, and incidents of widespread falsification of statistics, that it is surprising that the team did not question its own conclusions! (2004c, p. 250)

In several regions there have been significant success stories, whether in terms of initial literacy levels achieved (e.g. Ernakulam district), social impact (e.g. Nellore district), or both (e.g. Pudukkottai district). On the other hand, reports of low literacy attainment are common. In a study of the Dumka region, Kanjula found

> Most of [the learners] learnt to sign their names and more than half of them had forgotten even that as they did not sign their names in their daily lives. The VTs [volunteer teachers] said that out of 10 learners, two on average learnt to read and write. (2004, p. 291)

In one impoverished region, people found it difficult even to recall the TLC campaign completed only a few years earlier (Roy, 2004c, p. 224). In Ajmer

> most of the people [interviewed for the study] insist that the literacy campaign was reduced to a campaign to teach the illiterate just how to write their names. People, especially the workers, were given the message that in order to get their wages, rations, kerosene or work under the food-for-work programme during the famine, they would have to learn to write their names. So, people used to come to classes to learn to sign their names. (Saxena, 2004, p. 193)

Nevertheless, in this district the TLC "stirred up a whole lot of social and economic issues, which none of the evaluations, internal or external, have been able to capture or record so far" (Saxena, 2004, p. 207).

Skill erosion is identified as a ubiquitous problem, even in Ernakulam, which was the first region declared totally literate in India and the impetus for all subsequent campaigns. In Ajmer, where the target learners were preoccupied with day-to-day survival, "people did not see any obvious relationship between literacy and their wellbeing" (Saxena, 2004, p. 202). In Dumka district, many learners "were genuinely not convinced that they should become literate" (Kanjula, 2004, p. 286). Furthermore, "[a]s they did not exercise their literacy skills in their day-to-day lives, they failed to retain whatever was learnt" (Kanjula, 2004, p. 291). One of the recurring findings of these studies is that literacy must be linked to the social and economic lives of people in order for it to be meaningful to them (Rao & Govinda, 2004, p. 325). Overall, "the poorest populations in all six districts were least able to benefit from the TLC, and were most likely to be unable to retain or sustain the skills developed" (Roy, 2004b, pp. 342–343).

The NLM definition of functional literacy extends beyond the basic skills of reading, writing, and numeracy to include "Becoming aware of the causes of deprivation and moving towards amelioration of their condition by participating in the process of development." Awareness messages are conveyed via the literacy primers themselves. Although the TLC primers are translated into local languages and may contain approved local innovations, the overall format and content is governed centrally. Referring to primers in the Pudokkottai district, Saraswathi comments the following:

> The present study shows that the primers served as a powerful tool for messages imbibed by the learners ... In general, these primers provide information on development to learners. The learners are considered to be uninformed individuals regarding issues of development. The individuals are blamed if they are poor, non-literate, unhealthy and landless and hardly any attempt is made to develop a critical understanding among the learners, linking the problems of development with structural reality or an unjust social system. (2004, p. 149).

This analysis echoes Dighe's earlier study of primers in seven states, which found that

> illiteracy is posed as a problem due to the attitude of the illiterate adult. It is the individual's lack of initiative and absence of motivation that is considered to be responsible for the problem of illiteracy. Illiterates are regarded as uninformed, as lacking in knowledge and literacy is regarded as the panacea for their ignorance. There are no attempts to understand why certain sections of the community have no access to education in the first place. The larger structural issues are not even recognised, much less addressed. (1995, p. 1559)

Thus, while the National Literacy Mission promotes the goal of "awareness," many of the primers present a specific worldview and understanding, which is disseminated throughout the country via the literacy classes (Saxena, 2000).

In terms of "empowerment," one of the outcomes often claimed for literacy, the studies yield mixed results. In Pudukkottai district, the literacy campaign was coupled with the innovative strategy of teaching women to ride bicycles, an activity conventionally associated in that region with men. This resulted in "women's perception of independence in terms of all their roles in the household and the community" (Saraswathi, 2004, pp. 145–146). In Nellore, the campaign attracted the participation of many marginalized groups and facilitated a joint community effort to address significant socio-political issues. However, as Archer and Fry stress elsewhere, "Just teaching people to read and write alone does not empower people" (2005, p. 17). In regions where survival itself is fragile, "empowerment" may be particularly elusive:

> People remain illiterate due to a variety of reasons. There are fundamental structural hindrances related to their social, economic and political status, and there are practical problems as well. The question that needs to be asked is if the issue of illiteracy can be addressed overlooking or ignoring the basic problems related to hunger, poverty, unemployment, exploitation, low wages and social oppression. And without addressing these issues, can literacy lead to empowerment? (Saxena, 2004, p. 200)

Even where literacy interventions do lead to new opportunities, it should not be assumed that these opportunities are equally empowering for everyone:

> For instance, the formation of women's groups for income generation could be empowering or could turn into a merely profit making enterprise, where those who are already advantaged, such as the literate women in the group, take on leadership and simultaneously get greater exposure and training. (ASPBAE, 2006, p. 4)

Ultimately, as Saxena points out, literacy "is neither a neutral nor an isolated or autonomous variable. It is an ideological construct, a double-edged sword that could help in reinforcing or reducing the inequality or inequity" (2004, p. 179).

It is clear from these analyses that, for literacy to lead to empowerment and social sustainability, the training and learning approach needs to take each context seriously and needs to see literacy as part of a broader education and awareness program.

Alternative Approaches to Adult Literacy

With a commitment to quality adult education becoming less visible on government agendas, some practitioners are concerned that the spirit of EFA is being co-opted to serve market forces:

> Education for All is being increasingly driven by the requirements of economic growth, preparing an economic instrument, a worker, a producer, a manager; education to create a human, a humanist person, a human being has been marginalized in most systems of education. (Tandon, 2003, para. 8)

In India, "Some grassroots education groups ... oppose initiatives like the Dakar [EFA] Framework because they believe that it compels governments to pursue unrealistic targets" (Roy & Khan, 2003, p. 4). While campaigns and targets are highly visible, their long-term sustainability and effectiveness is problematic. As Archer and Fry report, "Almost all of the effective literacy work now going on around the world is designed as a programme, not as a campaign" (2005, p. 19).

While literacy is undeniably the responsibility of governments, civil society organizations can play a valuable role in designing, implementing, and evaluating education programs. ASPBAE has been monitoring and reporting on successful literacy innovations throughout the Asia-Pacific region.

In India, ASPBAE has documented the work of one of its member organizations, Laya, a non-governmental organization working with tribal communities in Andhra Pradesh. In this context, Laya's stated objectives are

- to empower tribal communities to secure access and control of their land, forest, and water resources;
- to sustain and promote sustainable alternatives for security of livelihood; and
- to ensure self-governance, recognizing their cultural identity and value systems (D'Souza, 2003, p. 8).

For Laya, education plays a powerful role in achieving these objectives; however their vision of education is much broader than literacy alone. "Empowerment" for tribal people must include the capacity to deal with significant local issues, to understand national and state laws that affect their communities, to engage with government representatives, and to assert their legal rights in the face of powerful vested interest groups. An empowering education for tribal communities must incorporate community history and a critical appreciation of traditional knowledge systems (D'Souza, 2003, p. 12).

Laya's education program has evolved over time and primarily targets the young men and women who will steer the future of tribal societies. Workshops, short-term and long-term training courses, and both intensive and non-intensive education programs are offered. Training is designed to help learners gain deeper understandings of the social, environmental, and political context in which they live, and to develop confidence and skills to advocate for their communities in a variety of ways. In addition to core topics, "interest area workshops" enable trainees to focus on themes of particular interest or relevance to them. The training is offered via discussions, lectures, role-plays, field trips, audio-visual aids, simulation activities, and games.

Although Laya reports an increase in literacy skills amongst their trainees, literacy is not the primary measure of the success of these programs.

ASPBAE has also documented the activities of another member organization, MARG (Multiple Action Research Group), which is an NGO involved in the socio-legal rights of disadvantaged people. MARG's early fieldwork centered on Madhya Pradesh, where many villages were to be submerged after the construction of a large dam. Unaware of their rights, people were at the mercy of exploitative landlords, their agents, or corrupt government officials (Monga, 2000, p. 3). MARG developed a series of manuals to help these people understand their legal rights and obligations. This work has ultimately led to the development of legal literacy manuals covering 23 significant laws that affect the daily lives of millions of Indian citizens.

MARG's current legal literacy program is designed for both literate and non-literate participants. "In the process, some of the participants may develop certain literacy skills, but the main purpose of the programme is to help people to understand [the law] and to use their new understanding to enhance the quality of their lives" (Monga, 2000, p. 1). The program is offered via workshops lasting about three days, during which participants learn about the relevant laws through interactive games, discussions, role-plays, songs, posters, and films. The legal literacy manuals, which are distributed to everyone in the workshop, are carefully designed to be useful to literate and non-literate participants.

> Each of the legal manuals is colour coded ... Participants learn, for example, that the red coloured manual is on marriage laws, the blue is on citizen's rights viz-à-viz the police, the yellow on contract labour and so on. During the workshops, the non-literate participants learn key points of the laws through posters. The posters are enlarged copies of the more than 200 illustrations appearing in the manuals. In this way, the participants become knowledgeable about the materials in the manual and recognise it when they see the illustrations. (Monga, 2000, p. 9)

The illustrations include simple icons, such as a cross or a tick, to distinguish between legal and illegal procedures and practices. Should the need arise in their daily lives, non-literate participants can produce the books as evidence in order to argue for their rights.

MARG's philosophy implicitly challenges many of the assumptions underpinning the NLM's literacy program. For example, MARG's educational program is based on the concept that literacy itself is no guarantee of "empowerment." After all, "people may be able to read and write, and yet lead a life of indignity or oppression" (Monga, 2000, p. 17). At the same time, "Non-literate persons, like literate persons, are not ignorant. They have often built up a large amount of experience, which they can use for their own purposes" (Monga, 2000, p. 5). For example,

> During one legal literacy workshop in a remote village, a non-literate woman assisted MARG Resource Persons (all lawyers) unfamiliar with the local land laws and explained them in minute details to the other workshop participants. She did not need reading and writing skills to know the procedures of the land laws; she had had to go through them for her own personal needs, and after tackling them, she went on to help many others in her village. (Monga, 2000, p. 6)

The work of Laya and MARG demonstrate that literacy does not need to be the only focus of effective and meaningful adult learning. In fact, Rogers (2000, p. 8) argues, as do many other practitioners, that literacy on its own is not enough: literacy must be linked to learning that is contextualized in the lives of learners. A "one-size-fits-all" approach is increasingly identified as a recipe for failure (ASPBAE, 2006, p. 6). "Urban, rural, nomadic, tribal, linguistic, dairy or arable farming, young and older men and women, different caste, class, racial and ethnic communities call for their own learning programmes; even within the same community different individuals will have different priorities" (ASPBAE, 2006, p. 6).

Conclusion

In multiple contexts, CSOs and NGOs play a significant role in the Asia-South Pacific region in terms of strengthening education for social sustainability. However, the outreach of each organization is bounded by location, language, funding, and human resources. By forging links between and across organizations via research, case studies, exchanges, and regional and sub-regional workshops, ASPBAE seeks to enhance best practice and to reinforce the capacities of member organizations so that they are better able to assist the people and communities with whom they work, and especially the marginalized and vulnerable.

ASPBAE's mission can be summarized as

- to build and strengthen an Asia-Pacific movement dedicated to advancing equitable access to relevant, quality, and empowering education and learning opportunities for all;
- to enhance the role and contribution of adult education and learning in empowering people toward creating a new global order that promotes equitable and sustainable human development, and upholds and protects the rights of all people to live in dignity and peace;
- to promote recognition of the role, contribution, and importance of community groups, people's organizations, NGOs, and other civil society organizations in education and development in the region.

By working with and through NGOs, community organizations, education campaign coalitions, universities, trade unions, indigenous peoples, women's organizations, the media, and other institutions of civil society across the Asia-Pacific region, ASPBAE is adding value to the local programs of such organizations, many of which are providing innovative and alternative approaches to education for social sustainability.

References

Archer, D. (2004). NGO perspectives on adult literacy. *Convergence, 37*(3), 65–74.
Archer, D., & Fry, L. (2005). *Writing the wrongs: international benchmarks on adult literacy.* Report based on research funded by the Education for All global monitoring report 2006 and UNESCO. London: Action Aid International.

ASPBAE (2006). *Resourcing for quality: adult literacy learning*. Paper commissioned for the EFA Global Monitoring Report 2006, Literacy for Life. Paris: UNESCO.

Bagnall, R. G. (2003). *Enhancing income generation through adult education: a comparative study*. Brisbane: Australian Academic Press.

Bhola, H. S. (2002). A model and method of evaluative accounts: development impact of the National Literacy Movement (NLM) of India. *Studies in Educational Evaluation, 28*, 273–296.

Chakrabarti, V. (2004). Introduction. In V. Chakrabarti (Ed.), *Innovations and experiments in lifelong learning* (pp. 1–18). Mumbai: Asian Pacific Bureau of Adult Education.

Dighe, A. (1995). Deconstructing literacy primers. *Economic and Political Weekly*, 1 July, 1559–1561.

D'Souza. N. G. (2003). *Empowerment and action: Laya's work in tribal education*. Mumbai: Asian Pacific Bureau of Adult Education.

Hildebrand, H., & Hinzen, H. (2004). EFA includes education and literacy for all adults everywhere. *Convergence, 37*(3), 51–63.

Kanjula, S. (2004). Total Literacy Campaign and its links with basic education: Dumka, Jharkhand. In M. Karlekar (Ed.), *Paradigms of learning: the Total Literacy Campaign in India* (pp. 270–318). New Delhi: ASPBAE/Sage.

Karlekar, M. (Ed.) (2004). *Paradigms of learning: the Total Literacy Campaign in India*. New Delhi: ASPBAE/Sage.

Khan, M. L. A., & Rao, N. (2000). Foreword. In M. Karlekar (Ed.), *Paradigms of learning: the Total Literacy Campaign in India* (pp. 13–15). New Delhi: ASPBAE/Sage.

Kohli, M. (2003). *The cosmos of education: tracking the Indian experience*. Mumbai: Asian Pacific Bureau of Adult Education.

Kothari, B. (2003). Literacy in India: a tide of rising rates but low levels. In B. Kothari, P. G. Vijaya Sherry Chand, & M. Norton (Ed.),*Reading beyond the alphabet: innovations in lifelong literacy* (pp. 15–40). New Delhi: Sage.

Monga, N. (2000). *Knowing her rights: case study from India*. Mumbai: Asian South Pacific Bureau of Adult Education.

National Literacy Mission (2008). http://www.nlm.nic.in/. Accessed 17 March 2008.

Paul, S. K. (2004). Continuing education program: the way for empowering rural people. *Indian Journal of Adult Education, 65*(1–2), 56–67.

Petersen, C. (2007). Education and training out of poverty? Adult provision and the informal sector in fishing communities, South Africa. *International Journal of Educational Development, 27*, 446–457.

Rao, N., & Govinda, R. (2004). Evaluating literacy campaigns: issues and prospects. In M. Karlekar (Ed.), *Paradigms of learning: the Total Literacy Campaign in India* (pp. 321–332). New Delhi: ASPBAE/Sage.

Rogers, A. (2000). *Beyond literacy: some general thoughts*. Mumbai: Asian South Pacific Bureau of Adult Education.

Rogers, A. (2004). EFA and adult learning. *Convergence, 37*(3), 3–13.

Roy, M. (2004a). Adult learning in the Asia-Pacific region: it's time to walk the walk. *Convergence, 37*(3), 115–132.

Roy, M. (2004b). Afterword. In M. Karlekar (Ed.), *Paradigms of learning: the Total Literacy Campaign in India* (pp. 333–344). New Delhi: ASPBAE/Sage.

Roy, M. (2004c). Total literacy in Ganjam, Orissa. In M. Karlekar (Ed.), *Paradigms of learning: the Total Literacy Campaign in India* (pp. 220–269). New Delhi: ASPBAE/Sage.

Roy, M., & Khan, M. L. A. (2003). Education for all in India: going up the down staircase. Background paper commissioned for the EFA Global Monitoring Report 2003/4, The Leap to Equality. Paris: UNESCO.

Saraswathi, L. S. (2004). Total Literacy Campaign: Pudukkottai, Tamil Nadu. In M. Karlekar (Ed.), *Paradigms of learning: the Total Literacy Campaign in India* (pp. 132–176). New Delhi: ASPBAE/Sage.

Saxena, S. (2000). Looking at literacy. *Seminar*, 493. http://www.india-seminar.com/2000/493/493%20sadhna%20saxena.htm. Accessed 6 May 2008.

Saxena, S. (2004). Revisiting Ajmer Total Literacy Campaign. In M. Karlekar (Ed.), *Paradigms of learning: the Total Literacy Campaign in India* (pp. 177–219). New Delhi: ASPBAE/Sage.

Tandon, R. (2003). What color is your rainbow? Global development context and international cooperation. Paper presented at the ASPBAE-IIZ/DVV Seminar on International Cooperation for Adult Education, Beijing, 23–25 February.

UNESCO (2005). *Education for all: literacy for life (EFA Global Monitoring Report)*. Paris: UNESCO.

Chapter 17
Birds Learn to Swim and Fish Learn to Fly: Lessons from the Philippines on AVE for Social Sustainability

Edicio dela Torre

Abstract As an adult educator working in the Philippines, my understanding of social sustainability lies at the intersection of social justice, environmental protection, and sustainable development. Through the lens of my life and work in the Philippines over a period of four decades, I discuss the various tensions that I have encountered between adult and popular education and technical and vocational education, and between government, non-government organizations, and social movements, as each sector strives to realize their different visions of sustainability in the Philippines.

Introduction

Until I attended a symposium on the topic in Adelaide, I had not come across the two concepts "adult and vocational education" and "social sustainability" together. However, AVE for social sustainability provides a useful framework for weaving together the themes that I have been exploring in practice and theory in the Philippines.

My current institutional base for adult and popular education work is the Education for Life Foundation (ELF), whose core program is the formation of grassroots community leaders. ELF's philosophy and methodology is expressed in our native language as "*hango sa buhay, tungo sa buhay*"—from life, for life.

From its beginnings forty years ago, my work in adult and popular education has focused on social justice. Later, "sustainability" entered our discourse in the Philippines, linked mainly to environmental protection and sustainable development. Our community of social activists accepted the need to integrate sustainability into our vision of development, but we also insisted on combining it with the idea of "equitable development." This combination of equitable and sustainable development is what I associate with the idea of social sustainability.

E. dela Torre (✉)
Education for Life Foundation, Quezon City, Philippines

But if we want to link equitable and sustainable development to technical and vocational education and training (TVET), we have to consider the more dominant concept of development as economic growth and productivity. This has been, and remains, the main perspective of technical and vocational education and training.

Different Starting Points Toward AVE for Social Sustainability

Although the Adelaide symposium focused on AVE for social sustainability, my impression is that the symposium's starting point was technical and vocational education and training (TVET). The concept of AVE for social sustainability challenges TVET to expand its perspective by incorporating the concerns of adult community education and by acknowledging "the need for the use of ethical, philosophical and imaginal teaching styles to complement the technical and professional pedagogical modes."[1] In addition, the concept of social sustainability implies that society is not reducible to the economy, no matter how important a role the economy plays. A similar and succinct message comes from a conference on development perspectives in Denmark: "Market Economy, Yes; Market Society, No" (Nagi, 2000, p. 181).

In my case, the starting point of AVE for social sustainability is not TVET but adult and popular education, and the challenge is how to incorporate the concerns of technical and vocational education and training. My work in adult and popular education has focused on social justice, empowerment of the poor, and education about their rights. Only later did I incorporate technical/vocational skilling, but still within the perspective of empowerment.

The development of my understanding of AVE for social sustainability is similar to the process undergone by the concept of "lifelong learning." At the start, lifelong learning was defined in humanist and liberal terms. Later it was appropriated and promoted by corporations and government ministries as a factor for competitiveness and labor flexibility in a rapidly changing globalized economy. Still much later, as in the Lisbon Declaration of the European Union (2000), the understanding of lifelong learning tried to strike a balance that includes both the perspective of competitiveness and of active citizenship.

Ove Korsgaard, former president of the Association for World Education (AWE), with which I am connected, articulates this as the tension between "lifelong learning," with its bias toward flexibility and competitiveness, and "learning for life." But when he evaluated the work of the Education for Life Foundation, he also posed the challenge to us: Should we not promote education for life together with education for livelihood, given the situation and needs of the grassroots communities who are our focus?

---

[1] Introduction in symposium notes, Adult and Vocational Education and Social Sustainability, University of South Australia, Adelaide, 26–28 April 2006.

AVE for Social Sustainability in the Philippine Context

I have chosen to present my understanding of AVE for social sustainability through the lens of the different stages of my life and work in the Philippines. This is of course hindsight, in the spirit of the Danish existentialist philosopher Søren Kierkegaard's aphorism that "life can only be understood backwards, though it must be lived forwards." These stages are:

1. an adult popular educator based in non-government organizations and social movements from the late 1960s to the early 1990s.
2. Director-general of the Technical Education and Skills Development Authority (TESDA) from 1998 to 2001.
3. an advocate of alternative learning systems, particularly community-based learning systems toward Education for All (EFA 2015) and lifelong learning for all.

For almost 30 years, my understanding of adult popular education was in contradiction to my understanding of technical and vocational education. This also reflected the contradictions between NGOs and social movements (where I was based) and the government.

What to Prioritize: Justice or Productivity?

My initial involvement in adult popular education was with organized farmers fighting for land reform. In the early 1960s, rural Philippines had the double problem of low productivity and inequitable distribution of incomes. In popular language, the cake was too small and was not divided fairly. Logically, both government and NGOs advocated a twofold response: productivity and justice. We must bake a bigger cake, and divide it more fairly.

Baking a bigger cake or increasing productivity emphasized the role of inputs: hybrid seeds, fertilizers and pesticides, irrigation, credit, and technology. The education and training required was mainly technical and vocational. Dividing the cake fairly, or promoting justice, involved educating farmers about their rights and organizing them to claim their rights under the land reform law. This was the content of adult popular education. There was no disagreement about the need to promote both productivity and justice. The debate was about emphasis and priorities, including what seemed to be a petty disagreement over the sequence of words: "productivity and justice" versus "justice and productivity."

Those who pushed the primacy of productivity had a straightforward argument: we need to bake a bigger cake so that the respective shares will be bigger. It seemed obvious and logical. We cannot distribute what is not yet produced. But those who emphasized the primacy of justice retorted: Why would those who are needed to bake a bigger cake do their part if they are not satisfied with their prospective share?

To bake a bigger cake, in other words to increase rice production, farmers needed to adopt the new technologies of the "Green Revolution," aimed at increasing rice production through more capital and chemical inputs and organizing marketing cooperatives. A number of farmers did so, and total rice production did increase, but in many cases their net income did not increase, because the inputs of new technologies cost more. Hence, many more farmers refused to adopt the new technologies. Francis Madigan, a priest working in an agricultural extension program, attributed this refusal to the culture of the farmer, which he called pre-modern and resistant to change (Madigan, 1962).

Refuting Madigan's analysis, fellow activists argued that the share-tenant farmers are open to change and want to increase their harvest. But they want a change in land ownership, or at least want a fixed-rent leasehold arrangement instead of share tenancy, so that they would benefit from the increase in production from the use of new technologies that require additional work and expenses on their part.

Among our social development circles, the debate took on additional dimensions including subtle distinctions: Do we emphasize reduction of absolute poverty or relative poverty? By the late 60s the development debates intensified against the backdrop of a reviving left movement that included the threat of armed guerrillas.

Many church social action projects focused on productivity: irrigation, improved seeds, model farms, even cooperatives to cut into the middlemen's profits, and diversifying incomes. A growing minority, however, chose to turn to what we now call "rights-based education" and social justice issues. We educated farmers about the law, which we translated from its original English into the native language so that the farmers could read and understand. We also recruited lawyers to provide legal services in court. But the most important action was to bring farmers together as an organized and vocal constituency so that the politicians would find it in their interest to follow the law. That was how I learned my first lesson in politics: that it must combine the power of principle and the principle of power.

1972–1986: Deepening Contradictions

The contradictions between technical/vocational and adult popular education deepened with Ferdinand Marcos' declaration of martial law in 1972. The imposition of authoritarian rule had the twofold rationale of fighting a "right–left conspiracy" and building a new society.

Martial law paid grudging credit to the social justice tradition, partly because it was taken up by armed guerrillas who declared that the main content of the democratic revolution was the peasants' struggle for land. Marcos instituted land reform in rice and corn lands. But the bigger government program was the "Green Revolution." In addition, Marcos set up the National Manpower and Youth Council to run skills training centers for out-of-school youth as a way to channel their energies toward productivity and away from activism and delinquency.

In that context of repression and the resistance it provoked, the government-sponsored vocational education and skills training was not seen positively by the adult and popular education movements. Their focus was on resistance and democratization. A great variety of left thinking circulated in the democratic resistance movement, from social democratic to communist; what they shared was a tendency to postpone "development" until after democratization.

Church involvement in social activism did not extend to vocational education for the poor, except for some religious orders, particularly the Salesians who have a tradition of vocational education. They worked with government to provide vocational education to out-of-school youth and also with larger companies who needed a trained and disciplined workforce.

The combination of worsening economic crisis and political crisis brought about political change in 1986. The replacement of authoritarian rule by a more democratic one, ushered in new conditions and challenges to adult popular education, and technical and vocational education and training.

After 1986: Democracy Restored; What About Development?

In 1986, the "EDSA People Power"[2] revolution precipitated a change of government. I was one of many political prisoners released from detention at this time. Obviously, I had a very personal reason to welcome the change. But since I was also with the movement that sought greater and deeper changes, I could not base my judgment mainly on the fact that I had personally benefited from it.

In fact, the greater part of the left movement and leadership tended to dismiss the EDSA Revolution as a very limited change of elite leaders, or worse, as a way to defuse the clamor that had been mounting in the years of resistance to authoritarian rule for more substantive political and social change.

I used a few lines from the *Magnificat* in the Bible (Luke 1: 52, 53) to express my own appreciation of the possibilities and limits of the EDSA Revolution: "[God] has put down the mighty from their thrones, and lifted up the lowly. He has fed the hungry with good things, and sent the rich away empty." The one mighty had been put down; the dictator was deposed. But will the lowly be lifted up? Or will the one mighty be merely replaced by many competing groups of the mighty? In secular political language, will elite dictatorship be replaced by elite democracy or by a broader popular democracy?

Some of the very rich were sent away, but not empty! They took quite a lot with them. And most stayed behind, switched sides, and continued their control of power and resources. One of the political cartoons at that time portrayed a motorcade celebrating the "freedom" that the EDSA Revolution represented, and posed a question through a group of urban poor bystanders: "Does this mean we will not be hungry anymore?" That reminds me of a quip attributed to Thai activists: "We want a democracy that we can eat."

---

[2] A series of non-violent demonstrations that culminated in February 1986. EDSA refers to Epifanio de los Santos Avenue, a major thoroughfare in Metro Manila, and the convergence point of protestors in the hours leading up to the exile of Ferdinand Marcos.

With the restoration of formal democracy in 1986, both adult popular education and technical and vocational education had to adjust to a new context of democratization, and eventually of greater globalization. I was mainly involved in the processes of the first, and did not get involved in the second until I was recruited into government in 1998.

Adult popular education maintained the orientation and methods that were shaped by the struggle for democracy, but it had to adjust to the transition from what I call the "politics of resistance" during martial rule to the "politics of participation" under a formally democratic system, even if still dominated by the elite. Not everyone managed to adjust to the transition, or even wanted to. A section of the radical movement pursued their oppositionist politics, and did not want to engage with the new government or pressure it to live up to its popular mandate for more meaningful changes. For those of us who decided to pursue what I call "conjunctural possibilities within the structural limits," the discourse of democratization had to go hand in hand with the discourse of development. But how do we pursue social justice and productivity under an elite democratic regime and a globalized market economy?

Paulo Freire and N. F. S. Grundtvig are two figures whom I use to represent the two poles of resistance and participation-engagement. Although Paulo Freire's practice and theory evolved through the years, we used his influential *Pedagogy of the oppressed* (1972) mainly in the context of resistance to repression. On the other hand, I worked with the ideas of Grundtvig and the Danish *folkehojskole* (folk high school) tradition (Lawson, 1991) in the post-martial law context.

Pursuing Justice and Productivity

Among my many reasons for studying the Danish folk high school tradition is its origins in rural communities during the period of reforms which included democratization and land reform. These are two focal issues in my own work in the Philippines.

I initially thought that the farmer graduates from the folk high schools led the successful but non-violent struggle for land reform in Denmark, and hoped that we could use a similar approach in the Philippines. But my initial impression turned out to be wrong. Land reform happened first, for reasons we need not discuss here, and it was the newly independent farmers who needed and could support their education in the folk high schools.

There is a second lesson, however, that I found relevant, especially in the age of globalization. The farmer graduates were also the organizers and leaders of the cooperatives, and later of the agricultural councils. When improved productivity of wheat farms in other countries made the Danish wheat farms uncompetitive, the Danish farmers were able to make a consensual decision to shift from grains to livestock. Part of the reason they could decide together was because they had built up relationships of trust over the years, rooted in their experience in the folk high schools.

I take to heart an aphorism from El Salvador: "Learn from others. Think for ourselves." But I cannot help but wish we had that kind of lead time that Denmark had to develop many farmer leaders among the agrarian reform beneficiaries in the Philippines, especially now that there is heated debate about extending the Comprehensive Agrarian Reform Program (CARP), whose legislated funding ends in July 2008.

Landlord critics of CARP question its failure to achieve targets for land transfer after 20 years, not admitting that it is their resistance that is partly to blame. The other reasons are the bureaucracy's problems, and the weakness of the farmers' organizations. But it is legitimate to ask if, after getting ownership of their land, the farmers have also produced more, and earned more. Under the CARP, land ownership has been officially transferred to over a million farmers, organized into co-ops and agrarian reform communities (ARCs). Studies show that agrarian reform beneficiaries are better off than those who do not own their land, but the net increases in productivity and incomes are not as great as expected.

Advocates of agrarian reform admit that improved productivity is not achieved merely by a change in land ownership. There has to be improved production technology and access to markets. There is also a need to diversify sources of incomes from off-farm and non-farm activities. And owner tillers of small family-sized farms need to organize cooperatives to achieve more competitive scales.

There is a clear case for helping farmers to develop technical and business skills, in addition to the usual objectives of adult popular education. And adult popular education itself has to take on new dimensions and challenges of development.

The social justice focus of adult popular education has emphasized a "rights-based" approach to development, which seeks to empower citizens to hold the government responsible for delivering basic services and start-up opportunities for the poor. It does not have as much experience in promoting entrepreneurship and assisting in the development of community-based and household-based enterprises.

But adult popular education cannot concern itself only about public policies and programs. It must help the grassroots communities understand and cope with market forces. The expanding housing and commercial sector want to convert agricultural land; this either tempts the farmers to sell or forces them out "legally." Under global agreements, cheaper agricultural imports have an advantage over the fragmented small-scale farms. More recently the demand for increased food supplies and biofuels has put the farmers under pressure to sell or consolidate their farms.

Promoting Changes from the Top: 1998–2001

This is a minor chapter in terms of years, but a major change in learning for me. Instead of being part of a movement trying to replace government, or at least pressuring it from below to implement reforms, I accepted an appointment to serve in government as the Director-General of the Technical Education and Skills Development Authority (TESDA). It was an opportunity and a challenge to push for reforms from a position of power.

A few years earlier, social activists and government officials involved in agrarian reform had articulated their reform strategy through the metaphor of the *"bibingka"* —a Philippine rice cake which is cooked in a deep pan, with fire from below and burning coals on top of its cover. The *"bibingka* strategy" seeks to combine the efforts of "state reformers" from the top with those of their partner reform constituencies from below, in order to overcome the resistance of conservative forces and the inertia of the bureaucracy.

The field of technical and vocational education is not as politically contentious as agrarian reform, where this strategy was formulated. But the *bibingka* strategy also applied there. I was presumably part of the fire on top, but TESDA's more significant achievements happened when there was corresponding fire from below, in the form of organized constituencies and partners.

The leadership role I had to play included promoting good governance by giving example and direction. It also involved redefining the orientation and strategic perspective of technical and vocational education and training (TVET). Traditionally, TVET has an urban, industrial development perspective, based on an implicit linear conception of progress: from rural to urban, agricultural to industrial to services, and local to national to global. When I took over my post in TESDA, the key word was "global competitiveness." But when we were drafting the National TESD plan, I argued against having global competitiveness as the sole strategic perspective, and pushed for targeting TVET at rural development and social cohesion. Eventually we agreed to adopt these three strategic perspectives for TVET: global competitiveness, rural development, and social cohesion.

As Director-General, I worked closely with industry and formal education institutions to promote "quality assured" TVET, through school-based, center-based, and enterprise-based programs, including dual training modes. But the perspectives of rural development and social cohesion together with my bias for grassroots communities made me give special attention to promoting community-based TVET programs in partnership with NGOs and local governments.

This approach proved to be most useful in conflict areas and post-conflict areas. Although the government had signed a peace agreement with the Moro National Liberation Front, the former rebel leaders complained that, because government did not fulfill its commitments under the peace agreement, they were also being criticized by their members and base communities for not delivering the so-called peace dividend.

As our contribution to the government's peace agreement, TESDA invested substantial resources in programs for ex-combatants, their families, and their base communities. Since they had little or none of the formal qualifications required by other modes, we offered mainly community-based programs. Since few businesses were willing to employ ex-combatants or their relatives, the perspective of TVET had to be self-employment rather than the usual wage employment. Eventually we codified our program as "community-based training for enterprise development" or CBTED.

At one point I commented that the CBTED program is particularly useful for four groups of participants: ex-rebels, ex-prisoners, ex-soldiers, and ex-street children. We should realize that they are not unskilled. But they have honed their skills and used them in the context of war or crime. They need to learn how to adapt their skills to the context of "peace and the market," and also need to acquire other competencies they need in this new context.

In some of the programs I helped design, we borrowed methods developed by the Education for Life Foundation, like "life history workshop" and indigenous modes of conflict resolution. Other technical trainers used sports activities as a channel to release pent up energies and feelings, and a way to learn cooperation and competition.

The AVE for social sustainability framework is applicable to this approach. Without it, many TVET programs for out-of-school youth and for post-conflict situations will be less than effective. It is not enough to train for skills. We need to recognize the psychological and social adjustments required to live, survive, and move ahead in the context of "peace and market."

AVE for social sustainability is both an integrative and "generative" framework for bringing together at the micro-level of training and programs the larger themes of productivity, entrepreneurship, and citizenship.

AVE, Social Sustainability, and Alternative Learning Systems

After my short stint in national government service ended in early 2001, I resumed working with the Education for Life Foundation and other civil society networks. We re-articulated ELF's core program as "grassroots leadership formation for grassroots community empowerment."

ELF's initial understanding of grassroots community empowerment was a carryover from the social movements, and focused on community mobilization for issues like agrarian reform and environmental protection. By 2001, however, another framework for our grassroots leaders formation program emerged: participatory local governance or PLG.

The 1991 Local Government Code gave greater powers and responsibilities to local governments, starting at the *barangay* or village level. It also opened up more possibilities and channels for citizens' participation. Our partner NGOs who took up PLG as their core program, and the grassroots leader-graduates who were elected into their village councils, influenced ELF to adopt PLG as the main framework for our grassroots leadership formation program for grassroots community empowerment.

Adult popular education in the framework of PLG is directed at two groups of participants. One group is the village residents, especially the poorer households, who are educated and organized to exercise their rights as citizens. The second group is the elected and appointed village officials who are trained in the basics of governance and participatory processes.

The start-up PLG activity is a joint participatory community appraisal leading to the formulation of a *barangay* development plan. This includes listing priority projects for the allocation of the *barangay* development fund and whatever other public funds the *barangay* can access from other government agencies.

Through these processes, PLG contributes to community empowerment by enabling citizens to influence local officials to use public funds and resources in more equitable and appropriate ways. But community empowerment has to address another set of resources: wealth that is generated "privately" in a market setting.

When ELF developed a grassroots distance learning program, the first course requested by the leader-graduates was on leadership and entrepreneurship. They expressed the need to earn through household or community-based enterprises so they could continue their community leadership activities without putting undue burden on their families. In addition to learning about money and the market, they also asked to acquire specific technical and vocational skills needed for their enterprises.

AVE for social sustainability is a framework that integrates this combination of citizenship, entrepreneurship, and productivity required for grassroots community empowerment.

In our education work with the indigenous Aeta communities, the formation of Aeta leaders initially focused on indigenous people's rights and on their struggle to acquire title to their ancestral domain, so that they could manage their upland resources in a sustainable manner. For this they also needed new skills, such as organic farming and sustainable agriculture, and also skills for earning off-farm and non-farm income. They asked for training in business skills, including bookkeeping and accounting.

In our education program for child workers in sugar plantations, *Quidan Kaisahan*, our NGO partner in Negros Occidental, used PLG to mobilize local officials and selected residents to offer alternative learning systems to those who wanted to leave their work in the sugar fields. When the first group of child workers successfully secured their high school certificate after passing the government exams, they naturally asked what happens next. Most asked to enroll in TVET courses, so they could better qualify for gainful employment. For the parents who supported their children's decision to withdraw from work in the fields, the question was how to replace the lost income. *Quidan Kaisahan* offered them access to micro-credit, and of course they asked for assistance in developing various income generating projects.

Of course NGOs do not think of extending our programs to all communities and the whole country. This is not just because we have limited resources. The more important reason is that we should not take over from government the primary responsibility to provide programs to all its citizens.

That is why ELF joined more than 100 NGOs and civil society organizations to form E-Net or Education Network to campaign for the goals of Education for All (EFA), and hold the government accountable to its commitments and responsibility.

The state of Philippine education is not as bad as in many sub-Saharan African countries, but the basic figures are still unacceptable. Of every 100 children who enter Grade One, only 65 finish primary school, and only 45 finish secondary school. Hence, our campaign advocates "walking on two legs" toward EFA. One leg is to improve access to and quality of the school-based formal educational system. The other leg is to offer alternative learning systems to those who have dropped out of school or could not be reached at all by the school system.

The resources even for the formal education system are not enough, so how will alternative learning systems be developed? The resources available for alternative learning programs are not enough to cover the whole country, not just among NGOs but even in the central government. Hence we have to think of how to eat an elephant bit by bit, village by village. We need to train not just grassroots leaders, but a portion of them as educators.

That led to the metaphor of birds and fishes. Birds are intellectuals like us who can somersault in the air, shift ideas, and have an overview (theory). We look down from the heights at the fish in the waters and wonder why there is little movement.

The fish of course call on the birds to plunge into the water and feel that it is thicker than air. And also that at close quarters you can see more movement than from afar. But once birds emerge to tell how we swam with the fishes, we cannot rest. We also need to teach some of the fish to fly so that they can tell their own story and articulate their own theory.

AVE for social sustainability is a strategic partnership of birds that have learned to swim and fish that have learned to fly.

References

Freire, P. (1972). *Pedagogy of the oppressed*. London: Sheed and Ward.

Lawson, M. (Ed.) (1991) *N. F. S. Grundtvig: selected educational writings*. Elsinmore: International People's College/Association of Folk High Schools.

Madigan, F. C. (1962). *The farmer said no*. Quezon City: Community Development Research Council, University of the Philippines.

Nagi, S. (2000). Toward a global community of solution. In J. Baudot (Ed.), *Building a world community: globalization and the common good* (pp. 176–188). Seattle: University of Washington Press.

Chapter 18
Breaking the Silence: Exploring Spirituality in Secular Professional Education in Australia

Joanna Crossman

Abstract Spiritual approaches to both secular business practice and adult business education are under discussion in the literature. Drawing upon the notion of sustainable education in order to "situate" discussion, the author suggests some reasons why this may be so and explores the concept of "secular spirituality" as an appropriate paradigm for considering the implications of spiritual issues in learning and at work. Finally, some notions about possible characteristics that spiritually orientated learning organizations might have are raised by drawing upon the experience of American businesses that have trodden this path.

Introduction

Academic literature appears to indicate a growing interest in "secular spirituality" as a teaching and learning issue within the context of secular adult education, particularly in the United States and Britain. It should be stated at the outset that the terms "adult" or "professional" education in this chapter will be used broadly to refer to all forms of career and adult education including vocational and university education.

A number of reasons are suggested for the attention that spirituality seems to be receiving, including a gamut of societal problems relating to racial tension, drug cultures, family issues, and an obsession with materialism. In response to pressure from the professions and the drafting of laws and guidelines referring to spiritual issues that affect professional work (Harris & Crossman, 2005), curriculum changes have been made in some secular professional education contexts where students are being prepared for careers in education, business, engineering, the health sciences, social work, and law (Harris & Crossman, 2005). Clearly these kinds of changes require appropriate initiatives in professional development and teacher training.

J. Crossman (✉)
University of South Australia, South Australia, Australia

The notion of sustainable education provides assistance in "situating" arguments about the ways in which spiritual values need to be addressed in adult education. A framework for exploring the role of the professions and education in developing understandings of sustainability with respect to social values can be found in the 1987 report entitled *Our common future*, commissioned by the World Commission on Environment and Development. The report suggested that "sustainable development requires changes in values and attitudes towards ... society and work and home" (1987, p. 111) and subsequently indicates that spiritual pathways have a role to play in the process. However, although writers since this time do not appear to have made a direct link between social sustainability and spirituality (McKenzie, 2005, p. 5), many cited in this chapter have contributed perspectives that are useful in beginning the task of constructing one. Within this chapter two key statements emerge from an exploration of the literature. First, social sustainability requires the creation of safe spaces in which empathy, respect, tolerance, and social justice can flourish. Second, social sustainability can serve as a useful lens for thinking about the relevance of an education that prepares students for approaching spiritual issues in the workplace. Thus, my discussion relates not only to providing opportunities for students to learn *about* varied spiritual issues but also to some extent teaching and learning *with* spirituality in ways that provide a model of experience that might usefully be applied to the workplace context and ultimately perhaps make some kind of contribution to a more sustainable society.

Few obvious signs exist in the Australian context that educators involved in secular adult education have given serious attention to the part spirituality might play in professional education (Harris & Crossman, 2005, pp. 3–4). I suggest some arguments for "breaking the silence" in Australia and reviewing the existing somewhat polarized perspective on the role of spirituality and rationality in adult programs. The chapter concludes with the view that the time is indeed ripe for all stakeholders in Australia to carefully scrutinize the way in which spirituality relates to student learning, their lives, and their future careers. In doing so, some contribution might be made to the development of international understandings of social sustainability.

Interpreting Spirituality in Secular Learning Contexts

A brief development of ideas about how the concept of "secular spirituality" might be understood and how it relates to religion is necessary. References to the importance of addressing non-sectarian spiritual values in educational planning have recently appeared in academic literature and significant reports (Carr, 1999; Crossman, 2003; Rogers & Dantley, 2001). These non-sectarian spiritual values are sometimes referred to as "secular spirituality," though the term is something of an oxymoron given that the "secular" is by definition worldly in nature (Crossman, 2003, p. 505).

Some writers consider the way secular spirituality resembles religion (Marty, 2000) and others emphasize the differences between the two (Carr, 1995; Tisdell,

2001, p. xi). Nash (2003, p. 54) interprets secular spirituality as a form of resistance toward organized religion but a less contentious discourse would simply view these approaches to spirituality as alternatives available to individuals. Broadly speaking however, religion could be described as a public institution underpinned by rituals developed over time in response to sacred texts and secular spirituality as a looser, less systematic, private interpretation generated by individuals (Farmer, 2001; Halford, 1999; Rogers & Dantley, 2001). Secular spirituality therefore has a non-partisan, trans-religious quality acknowledging the contributions of major religions without undue preference (Crossman, 2003, p. 505).

Since secular ways of expressing spirituality are exceptionally diverse, writers need to be cautious about referring to the concept as though it has some kind of cohesive, homogenous existence (Harris, 2005). Spirituality may be associated in the minds of individuals with crystals, nature, and New Age beliefs (Harris, 2001, p. 50) or indeed with Maslow (1970, pp. 32–33) conceptions of self-actualization. Distinguishing secular spirituality as an individually defined phenomenon that has taken hold in the West may be connected with theories (Triandis, 1995) about how western society is individualistic (as opposed to collectivist): made up of people more inclined to be motivated by individual and personal preference (Crossman, 2003).

Various writers have associated the renewed interest in spirituality in the West with societal problems including rising crime, drug addiction, materialism, racial tensions, and stresses placed upon the family (Lantieri, 2001, cited in Huang, 2001; Fogel, 2000, cited in Farmer, 2001; Miller, 2001; Scherer, 1999; Sefa, 1999; Wilson, 1991). Other writers view these kinds of concerns as a symptom of "spiritual hypochondria" that, like the prophets of doomsday warn us of imminent moral collapse (Kaplan, 1991, p. 11). Cywinski (2001, p. 12), an engineer and academic, for example, maintains that educational sustainability in the engineering discipline must involve the creation of an appropriate spiritual base in order to balance the material aspects of the profession. In this he is not unusual, in that spirituality has historically been identified as a moral force for transforming society in response to its perceived ills and a sense of *Weltschmerz*.

Academics are also looking to the adoption of holistic teaching and learning approaches that more closely reflect the circumstances of students' future work by taking into account aspects of human interaction (Reid, Nagarajan, & Dortins, 2006, p. 85). Indeed, one of the seven assumptions Tisdell draws upon in analyzing the question of spirituality in professional education is that "spirituality is awareness and honoring of the wholeness and the interconnectedness of all things" (2001, p. xi), including presumably the diverse aspects of the individual human experience.

In largely western social, political, and educational environments where religion has long been separated from matters of state (McKenzie, 2005, p. 8) (excluding private institutions with religious affiliations), spiritual conceptions without religious affiliations may seem appropriate in their apparent neutrality. Nevertheless, the topic of secular spirituality in adult education is potentially an emotive one. It is attractive however to those concerned with equity and social justice as aspects of educational sustainability (Santone, 2003, p. 61; Tisdell, 2001, p. xii) since it encourages inclusivity, without giving undue preference to any one spiritual belief.

Developments in scientific enquiry particularly relating to quantum physics and influenced by postmodernist paradigms appear to have encouraged mystical or spiritual conceptualizations of science. As a result, discourses have been altered in ways that make it difficult to differentiate the perspectives of physicists from those of mystics (Capra, 1982, p. xviii; Capra, 1985, p. 19; Crossman, 2003, p. 506) and may have opened up new pathways for discussions previously inhibited by the positivist/constructivist impasse (Capra, 1982, p. 19). To illustrate, recent work on a phenomenon known as a spiritual quotient or "SQ" is based upon neuro-physiological theories and "new" physics as well as philosophy (McKew, 2002). Constructivist approaches also call into question scientific pragmatism based on the reasoning that individual perspectives blur the differences between theory and value (Carr, 2000).

Professional Interest in the Role of Spirituality in Diverse Workplaces

In A. J. Cronin's book *The Judas tree* (1973) a young nurse, Kathy, tries to persuade David, a doctor, to join her on a mission in Africa.

> as regards the mission, you know I'm not a religious man ... I doubt if I could surrender my mind to your spiritual convictions.
> The work you do is the best kind of religion. In time, David, you would know the meaning of grace. (p. 211)

As the excerpt illustrates, perceptions of professional practice can be entwined with the spiritual. Certainly, a number of educational documents in America, the UK, and India appear to indicate a growing academic and professional interest in spirituality (Crossman, 2003). Diverse disciplines are acknowledging that spirituality is a factor in the human interaction that takes place during the working day (Crossman, 2003, p. 507; Harris & Crossman, 2005). Literature related to the place of spirituality is found in the areas of social work (Damianakis, 2001), psychiatry (Lawrence & Duggal, 2001), tertiary education (Scott, 1998), sociology (Wilson, 1991), and engineering and manufacturing (Platts, 2003a, 2003b).

Given that most professions have developed a tradition grounded in science over the last century or more, criticisms that an interest in spiritual matters is "anti-scientific" (Levitt, 2001) are perhaps not unexpected despite the rise of "New Physics" and postmodernist influences. Nevertheless these criticisms fail to respond to the emotional and spiritual human experiences that occur in professional contexts when working with people (Crossman, 2003; Damianakis, 2001; Giorgio, 1970; Lawrence & Duggal, 2001; Scott, 1998; Wilson, 1991).

Within the field of education, the Delors Report (1996) to UNESCO titled *Learning, the treasure within* suggested that educators should be contributing to the "all round development of each individual" including their spiritual needs and values (pp. 94, 22). In Britain, recent education Acts have clearly specified that spiritual issues are to be incorporated into school learning and as a result both school inspectors and teachers have collaborated in discussing what this might mean for teaching and learning in secular government schools (Stoneman, 1997). In South Australia, Chugani's (2001) research revealed that, whilst a number of state policy documents require teachers to explore spiritual issues in student learning, teacher training programs provided no direction as to how this might be achieved. Clearly, there must be adequate support provided to training teachers via the curriculum if spiritual values are to be successfully embedded in a strategy for sustainable education (World Commission on Environment and Development, 1987, p. 158).

Evidence suggests that incorporating spiritual approaches into teaching and learning would be welcomed by some teachers at least. Reportedly, students of education have spiritual though not necessarily religious reasons for wanting to become teachers (Serow, Eaker, & Ciechalski, 1992, cited in Mayes, 2001) and Tisdell's (2001, p. xiii) work indicates that all participating teachers in her research study were motivated to teach for spiritual reasons. Other evidence indicates (Neiman, 2000; Palmer, 1999, p. 6) that qualified educators are also experiencing frustration working in environments where meaning and wisdom are neglected and where professional and personal experiences are kept separate (Neiman, 2000) in somewhat artificial ways. If, as Palmer maintains, "We teach who we are" (1999, p. 11), the separating out of subjective and objective aspects of teachers limits their potential contribution to the learning experience.

Popular media reflects a general interest in non-partisan spirituality (Thompson, 2000, p. 18), indicating that it has become "a hot topic" (Tisdell, 2001, p. 25). Some of this literature is linked to business practice. For example, the works of Stephen Covey (1989) and Deepak Chopra (1994) are highly popular and have no doubt influenced business practices in organizations around the world. Spiritual issues are receiving close attention in a number of large organizations such as Tom's of Maine (Tischler, 2005), Lucent Technologies, and Southwest Airlines (Rigoglioso, 1999). These corporations have integrated spiritual considerations into their mission statements and agendas, as has the World Economic Forum since 1999 (Harris & Crossman, 2005). For the more venally orientated, there is evidence that spiritual perspectives on business practices and decision making can influence morale, reduce stress-related conditions and staff turnover, and increase net earnings and ultimately share prices (McKew, 2002; Thompson, 2000, p. 19). Consistent with findings in education, Harris (2001, p. 45) also indicates that there is abundant evidence that business employees are seeking out spiritual meaning in their work. Curiously, it may well be that the most powerful impediment to acknowledging the role of our spiritual selves in the workplace is to be found in adult education (Mitroff and Denton, 1999, p. 16).

Is the Time Ripe for Considering Spirituality in Australian Secular Professional Learning Organizations?

Social sustainability can serve as a useful lens for thinking about the relevance of an education that prepares students in spiritual ways for professional practice, though according to Green and Reid (2004, p. 257) sustainability is a contested and complex subject. Regarded by some as a "buzz word" (Cywinski, 2001), "sustainability" has made a complicated shift from environmental to educational genres. Developing spiritual understandings is not related to the kind of environmental and educational sustainability concerned with using renewable energy or food composting in universities (Santone, 2003, p. 62) or paper recycling. It has a more general mission for social and professional environments and has an enduring quality, involving developing respect and empathy for others on a deeper level. In other words, as Hargreaves and Fink (2003, p. 694) see it, sustaining education is at heart about nourishing valued features of lifelong learning that go beyond preoccupations with test scores. Encouraging students to explore the spiritual aspects of their lives and those of others involves levels of intimacy that add enduring dimensions of meaning and relevance to human and professional relationships.

Social sustainability is about creating safe spaces. Safe spaces are those that encourage empathy, respect, tolerance, and social justice where people are able to interact on a deeper level. Safe spaces through social sustainability mean that the courage to share our innermost selves is welcomed and valued. Social sustainability embraces a broad mission of individual and societal growth in human, qualitative, and subjective terms. It acknowledges the importance of these aspects of experience in personal and professional interaction including teaching and learning contexts by accepting that the professional is also the personal and vice versa. Without it, we are left to the destructive and unsustainable forces of greed, selfishness, one-eyedness and mismanaged power.

The report *Our common future*, a seminal work on the concept and implications of sustainability, notes the importance of responding to and generating changing values in society and work and calls upon the world's religions to provide leadership and direction "in forming new values that would stress individual and joint responsibility" (WCED, 1987, p. 155). Whilst religions have something to contribute to discussions of how spirituality might be addressed in professional education in secular environments, there is a need to draw upon inclusive, ecumenical approaches. Given that Australian society is spiritually diverse, any programs preparing students for the kinds of spiritual issues they may face in the workplace must logically acknowledge the spiritual realities students are likely to find. If sustainable education includes concerns relating to the rights of groups (WCED, 1987) then no doubt these "groups" extend to those with diverse spiritual beliefs.

Set against the knowledge that Nash (2003, p. 54) discovered more than 75 academic programs in America referring in some way to religion or spirituality, less thorough internet searches of academic programs in Australia suggest far fewer references (Harris & Crossman, 2005, pp. 3–4). However more extensive research is required to investigate Australia's response to spiritual issues in professional education in order to verify these initial findings. It may be that the sensitive nature of spirituality in secular and multicultural communities leaves academics cautious about the discourse they choose. For example, some courses and programs may indeed address the role of spirituality in the workplace and/or learning but choose to describe this activity as part of an "ethics" or "values" objective. As Fornaciari and Lund Dean (2001, p. 337) suggest, it is a matter of language and "fitting" it into an acceptable and legitimized rubric of a rationalist, positivist paradigm. Another possibility is that individual teachers bring spiritual dimensions to their teaching and learning practices without needing to refer to them (Harris & Crossman, 2005, p. 5) or that teaching approaches may not be captured within course outlines. This seems to be a possibility given that Mitroff and Denton (1999, p. 9) suggest that values-based organizations supposedly guided by general philosophical values or principles are defined in implicitly spiritual ways. Whatever the reason for the near invisibility of the word "spirituality" in Australian adult education documents online, multiculturalism would surely be better served by sensitively approaching the topic of spirituality in professional and educational contexts, developing a climate of shared tolerance and understandings that contribute to building a sustainable and peaceful future.

Though many academics and educators are expressing an interest in "breaking the silence" on spirituality in adult education (Tisdell, 2001, p. 27), "baby boomer" Australians educated in the last forty years or so may well share the perception with others residing in Britain and America that spirituality is a "taboo" subject in the workplace, educational or otherwise (Tisdell, 2001, p. 3) and could well be concerned that the learning experience may be "hijacked" by those with the power to impose their own spiritual agendas (Harris & Crossman, 2005, p. 5; Mayes, 2001). Mitroff and Denton (1999, p. 6) argue that it is this very tendency of trying to build a wall between the spiritual self and the workplace, corralling spiritual impulses to personal time, that creates pressures resulting in inappropriate responses such as proselytizing a particular religion.

However, despite the challenges, it may be time to revisit the way in which Australian society, like others, has hitherto encouraged the disassociation of public and professional educational behavior from more personal value systems (Neiman, 2000). Such a review would be timely given that secularization reputedly reached its zenith in the 1970s (McKenzie, 2005, p. 5) and in education appears to have remained largely unquestioned for decades until quite recently. From a learning perspective, the separation was and is a particularly curious step given the important role that subjective aspects relating to our values play in thinking and solving problems. It is worth remembering that separating subjective and objective thinking behavior in learning does not represent a "natural" human tendency but one that has been conditioned through circumstance (De Bono, 1999). Tisdell (2001, p. xi) has also argued that the deeper aspects of self are co-contributors in constructing knowledge and meaning making with rational and cognitive approaches.

There is also a view that the potential joy of learning is in danger of being severely curtailed in educational communities that focus almost exclusively upon scientific rationality (Priest & Quaife-Ryan, 2004, p. 300) and that teachers are left feeling unconnected to their colleagues, failing to engage in the spiritual dimensions of their students or indeed their inner selves (Palmer, 1998, p. 19; Palmer, 1993, p. x). There is dysfunctionality in silence that should not be interpreted as an acceptable way of keeping order. True respect and justice is in tolerating and respecting difference, not in denying the differences altogether. Silence is not a neutral phenomenon.

Australian educators also need to review the role of spirituality in preparing students for their work as professionals quite simply because these individuals are required to comply with laws and directions that relate to spiritual aspects of professional work (Harris & Crossman, 2005, p. 6). Australian and international labor laws (ILO, 1994), for example, specify that whatever the race, creed, or gender of individuals within the workplace, they have a right to pursue their own spiritual development and there are therefore some individuals with compliance responsibilities who will need to interpret and implement these laws (Harris & Crossman, 2005, p. 6). National parks officers are obliged to respond to and appreciate aspects of Indigenous spirituality and officers of the New South Wales government involved in the development and approval of water management plans are required to show due consideration of spiritual heritage in their decision making (Harris & Crossman, 2005). If these requirements are realities in the work of professionals in diverse environments then Australian secular educational institutions need to prepare students with the understandings required not simply to carry out their work efficiently but to respond to legal and professional demands that define their responsibilities.

Evidence in the literature indicates that secular educational providers in a number of countries are exploring and implementing responses to spiritual issues in both secondary and post-secondary environments. Whilst Australia has shown less enthusiasm for taking this route, the importance of global educational relationships should provide the motivation for considering at least a more focused strategy on the part of professional bodies and educational disciplines in staging forums for discussion. Such discussions will no doubt have implications for teacher training and professional development. Teachers may indeed be conscious that their students need and desire some exploration of spiritual issues but simply do not know how to develop appropriate understandings in the learning environment "without being impositional" (Tisdell, 2001, p. 19). The 1987 report published by the World Commission on Environment and Development has emphasized the need to encourage contacts between teachers working in various cultures to develop concepts associated with educational sustainability. With this advice in mind, some intercultural initiatives with those educators in the UK, the US, or India who have trodden the same path would no doubt inform the process (Harris & Crossman, 2005, p. 6), though obviously Australian academics will need to consider the issue in their own context.

I have begun to argue elsewhere (Crossman, 2006) that in conceptualizing spiritual approaches to learning, educators may like to explore some of the literature that is emerging from otherwise secular business organizations that have become spiritually sensitized in their activities (Burack, 1999; Delbecq, 1999; Wagner-Marsh & Conley, 1999). Learning organizations will need to consider if they have a supportive leadership base ready to encourage discussions about what a spiritualized learning environment might entail. In my view, it would most likely be characterized first by a curriculum that will prepare students for interacting with culturally and spiritually diverse people in the workplace. Second, educators in spiritualized learning environments will need to model specified spiritual values in their relationships with students and colleagues. In other words, implementing a spiritualized curriculum involves making decisions around teaching *about* spirituality as well as teaching *with* spirituality. Learning organizations will also probably need to identify core values and align them with mission statements and program objectives. Finally, a spiritually sensitized learning environment in an otherwise secular context is probably only workable within a pluralist paradigm that acknowledges and respects the individual's right to embrace or question conceptualizations of spirituality in critically engaged learning contexts. In this way individuals will be better prepared to contribute to socially sustainable workplaces.

Conclusion

Creative and open minded approaches to gathering ideas, particularly from professionals in the field, will assist greatly in mapping out a way to address a need that has hitherto been neglected in secular professional education. As Santone asks, "What kind of education do we need to create the future we want?" (2003, p. 61). In answering her own question, she speaks of an ethos of education for sustainability where "caring," "compassion," and "humanity" (p. 60) have something to contribute to the long-term outcomes of effective citizenship through the curriculum and instruction. Cywinski, in an engineering context, connects sustainability with spirituality even more closely, "Sustainable development meets the holistic (spiritual and material) needs of the present without compromising the ability of future generations to meet [their own]" (2001, p. 15).

Spirituality, like religion, has much to offer in building a sustainable world. With vast numbers of adherents to give voice to these concepts, spirituality has the capacity to inspire the shaping of worldviews and guide moral behavior (Gardner, 2002, pp. 11–12). It is hard to see how Australia can continue to avoid raising discussions about the implications of what appears to be an emergent shift in paradigms that would provide a greater balance between subjectivity and objectivity in learning contexts. The time is indeed ripe for Australian adult education to "break the silence" (Tisdell, 2001, p. 27) and review spiritual issues in secular educational contexts from the perspective of enhancing learning, responding to professional needs, and fostering equity and social justice in building a sustainable future in Australian society.

References

Burack, E. (1999). Spirituality in the workplace. *Journal of Organizational Change Management, 12*(4), 280–291.
Capra, F. (1982). *The turning point: science, society and rising culture.* London: Fontana Paperbacks.
Capra, F. (1985). *The Tao of physics: an exploration of the parallels between modern physics and Eastern mysticism* (2nd ed.). Boston: New Science Library.
Carr, D. (1995). Toward a distinctive conception of spiritual education. *Oxford Review of Education, 21*, 83–98.

Carr, D. (1999). The ethical school: consequences, consistency and caring/values in education/vision of a school: the good school in the good society. *Cambridge Journal of Education, 29*(1), 147–149.
Carr, D. (2000). Moral formation, cultural attachment or social control: what's the point of values education? *Educational Theory, 50*(1), 49–63.
Chopra, D. (1994). *Seven spiritual laws of success: a practical guide to the fulfillment of your dreams.* San Raphael: Amber Allen Publishing & New World Library.
Chugani, P. (2001). *The place of spirituality in mainstream pre-service teacher education: an exploratory study of teacher educators' perceptions.* Honours thesis, Flinders University, South Australia.
Covey, S. (1989). *The seven habits of highly effective people.* London: Simon & Schuster.
Cronin, A. J. (1973). *The Judas tree.* London: New English Library.
Crossman, J. (2003). Secular spiritual development in education from international and global perspectives. *Oxford Review of Education, 29*(4), 503–519.
Crossman, J. (2006). *Taking care of spiritual business: discussing the role of spirituality in secular business and learning organisations.* Paper presented at the Pacific Employment Relations Association Conference, Adelaide, 15–17 November.
Cywinski, Z. (2001). Current philosophies of sustainability in civil engineering. *Journal of Professional Issues in Engineering Education and Practice, 127*(1), 12–16.
Damianakis, T. (2001). Postmodernism, spirituality and the creative writing process: implications for social work practice. *Families in Society, 82*(1), 23–34.
De Bono, E. (1999). *Six thinking hats.* London: Penguin Books.
Delbecq, A. (1999). Christian spirituality and contemporary business leadership. *Journal of Organizational Change Management, 12*(4), 345–349.
Delors, J. (Ed.) (1996). *Learning, the treasure within: report to UNESCO of the International Commission on Education for the Twenty-First Century* (Delors Report). Paris: UNESCO.
Farmer, D. (2001). The biospiritual awakening? *Public Performance and Management Review, 24*(4), 436–439.
Fornaciari, C., & Lund Dean, K. (2001). Making the quantum leap: lessons from physics on studying spirituality and religion in organizations. *Journal of Organizational Change Management, 14*(4), 335–351.
Gardner, G. (2002). *Invoking the spirit: religion and spirituality in the quest for a sustainable world.* Washington, DC: Worldwatch Paper.
Giorgio, A. (1970). *Psychology as a human science: a phenomenologically based approach.* New York: Harper Row.
Green, B., & Reid, J. (2004). Teacher education for rural-regional sustainability: changing agendas, challenging futures, chasing chimeras? *Asia-Pacific Journal of Teacher Education, 32*(3), 255–273.
Halford, J. (1999). Longing for the sacred: a conversation with Nel Noddings, *Educational Leadership, 56*(4), 28–32.
Hargreaves, A., & Fink, D. (2003). Sustaining leadership. *Phi Delta Kappan, 84*(9), 693–700.
Harris, H. (2001). Spirituality at work: some Australian observations. *Business and Professional Ethics Journal, 20*(1), 45–58.
Harris, H., & Crossman, J. (2005). *Getting up-close and personal: the implications of addressing spirituality in university teaching and learning for faculty and professional developers.* Group for Research in Integrity and Governance working paper. http://www.unisa.edu.au/hawkeinstitute/gig/projects/trad-virtues.asp. Accessed 14 August 2007.
Huang, S. (2001). Schools with spirit: nurturing the inner lives of children and teachers. *Library Journal, 126*(11), 4–86.
Kaplan, A. (1991). Moral values in higher education. In D. Thompson (Ed.) *Moral values and higher education: a notion at risk* (pp. 11–34). New York: Brigham Young University.
ILO (1994). *Declaration of Philadelphia.* Geneva: International Labour Organization. http://www.ilo.org/public/english/about/iloconst.htm. Accessed 20 July 2006.

Lawrence, R., & Duggal, A. (2001). Spirituality in psychiatric education and training. *Royal Society of Medicine, 94*(6), 303–305.
Levitt, N. (2001). The sources and dangers of post-modern anti-science: do these intellectual popguns matter? *Free Inquiry, 21*(2), 44–48.
Marty, M. (2000). Religion no longer gets credit on campus. *Context, 32*(22), 1–2.
Mayes, C. (2001). Cultivating spiritual reflectivity in teachers. *Teacher Education Quarterly, 28*(2), 5–22.
Maslow, A. (1970). A theory of human motivation. In V. Vroom & E. Deci (Eds), *Management and motivation* (pp. 27–41). Harmondsworth: Penguin Books.
McKenzie, S. (2005). *Social sustainability, religious belief and global ethics: outlines for research.* Working Paper No. 30. Magill, South Australia: Hawke Research Institute, University of South Australia.
McKew, M. (2002). Lunch with Maxine McKew. *The Bulletin,* 12 February, p. 42.
Miller, D. (2001). Programs in social work embrace the teaching of spirituality. *Chronicle of Higher Education, 47*(36), 12–14.
Mitroff, I., & Denton, E. (1999). *A spiritual audit of corporate America: a hard look at spirituality, religion and values in the workplace.* San Francisco: Jossey-Bass.
Nash, L. (2003). A spiritual audit of business: from tipping point to tripping point. In O. Williams (Ed.), *Business, religion and spirituality: a new synthesis* (pp. 53–78). Notre Dame, IN: University of Notre Dame Press.
Neiman, A. (2000). Democracy and the education of the heart: Nel Noddings on spiritual schooling and religious education. *Decatur, 95*(2), 216.
Palmer, P. (1993). *To know as we are known: education as a spiritual journey.* San Francisco: Harper & Row.
Palmer, P. (1998). *The courage to teach: exploring the inner landscape of a teacher's life.* San Francisco: Jossey-Bass.
Palmer, P. (1999). Evoking the spirit of public education. *Educational Leadership, 56*(4), 6–11.
Platts, J. (2003a). Developing competence and trust: maintaining the heart of a profession. *Professional Ethics, 11*(1), 3–18.
Platts, J. (2003b). *Meaningful manufacturing.* York, UK: William Sessions.
Priest, A., & Quaife-Ryan, M. (2004). Re-enchanting education: the recovery of teaching as a sacred activity. Paper presented at the Central Queensland University Conference Lifelong Learning: Whose Responsibility and What is Your Contribution?, Yeppoon, Qld, 13–16 June.
Reid, A., Nagarajan, V., & Dortins, E. (2006). The experience of becoming a legal professional. *Higher Education Research and Development, 25*(1), 5–99.
Rogers, J., & Dantley, M. (2001). Invoking the spiritual in campus life and leadership. *Journal of College Student Development, 42*(6), 589–603.
Rigoglioso, M. (1999). Spirit at work: the search for deeper meaning in the workplace. *Harvard Business School Bulletin,* April. http://www.alumni.hbs.edu/bulletin/1999/april/spirit.html. Accessed 17 April 2008.
Santone, S. (2003). Education for sustainability. *Educational Leadership, 61*(4), 60–63.
Scherer, M. (1999). Is school the place for spirituality? *Educational Leadership, 56*(4), 18–22.
Scott, D. (1998). A reconstruction of spirituality and education: re-conceptualizing spirituality. Paper presented at Connections 98, an annual conference of the Faculty of Education at the University of Victoria. http://www.educ.uvic.ca/connections/conn98/scott.html. Accessed 10 October 2001.
Sefa, G. (1999). Knowledge and politics of social change: the implication of anti-racism. *British Journal of Sociology and Education, 20*(3), 395–409.
Stoneman, C. (1997). Spiritual biology. *Journal of Biological Education,31*, 131–134. http://web.ebscohost.com/ehost/detail?vid=10&hid=105&sid=7c9c5b05-e7bd-4996-9b4f-. Accessed 14 August 2007.
Thompson, W. (2000). Can you train people to be spiritual? *Training and Development, 54*(12), 1–19.

Triandis, H. (1995). *Individualism and collectivism.* San Francisco: Western Press.
Tischler, L. (2005). God and mammon at Harvard. *Fast Company, 94,* 80.
Tisdell, E. (2001). *Exploring spirituality and culture in adult and higher education.* San Francisco: Jossey-Bass.
Wagner-Marsh, F., & Conley, J. (1999). The fourth wave: the spiritually based firm. *Journal of Organizational Change Management,12*(4), 292–301.
Wilson, B. (1991). *Religion in sociological perspective.* Oxford: Oxford University Press.
World Commission on Environment and Development (1987). *Our common future* (Brundtland Report). Oxford: Oxford University Press.

Chapter 19
Waldorf Schools as Communities of Practice for AVE and Social Sustainability

Tom Stehlik

Abstract Communities of practice are characterized by an ability to generate social or cultural capital, not necessarily through formal educational provision but through informal learning, individual transformation, and cultural change arising from the collective involvement of like-minded people in a process, association, organization, or event, often based in practice. The associated theory of situated learning also suggests that for adults learning mainly occurs by situations, not subjects, and usually associated with social interaction. In this chapter I explore these notions in the context of a community of practice identified with a Waldorf School for Rudolf Steiner Education, which provided a case study for researching and analyzing the extent to which adults as parents engage in informal, social, and transformative learning. I conclude that the role of active parenting as a vocation and as legitimate work is enhanced and informed by involvement in a school that is defined by a specific educational philosophy which, inter alia, encourages the development of a learning community.

Steiner Education and Waldorf Schools

> It is a fact that a Waldorf School provides a learning and growing situation not only for the children but for the parents and teachers as well. (Edmunds, 1979, p. 112)

The first school for Rudolf Steiner education began in 1919 as an initiative of the Waldorf-Astoria Cigarette Factory in the German city of Stuttgart for employees of that company. The unique approach to education of this "Waldorf Free School" soon attracted interest from other parts of Europe, and it was not long before the initiative spread and schools were established in other countries. From these beginnings, the term "Waldorf" school has passed into common usage, and at the time of writing there were over 950 Steiner or Waldorf schools worldwide, in over 60 different countries (Steiner Waldorf Schools Fellowship, 2007).

T. Stehlik (✉)
University of South Australia, South Australia, Australia

Waldorf schools collectively "form the largest and one of the fastest growing groups of independent private schools in the world" (Cape Ann Waldorf School, 1999, p. 1). In Australia there are now about 40 Waldorf schools, most of them primary schools, with a number having a full primary and secondary curriculum based entirely on the indications originally given by the Austrian philosopher and scientist Rudolf Steiner (1861–1925).

The schools share a common philosophical foundation, which encompasses education of the whole being—spirit, soul, and body—and follows in depth the stages of human development from birth through life in seven-year cycles: from ages 1 to 7, 8 to 14, 15 to 21 and so on. These cycles continue throughout adult life, and an underlying feature of Steiner education is the recognition of continuing education and development beyond school, with the need to incorporate an understanding of adult development in the approach to child development. The belief that education is an art and that educating the whole child means addressing the forces of their mind, heart, and will, are the guiding educational principles established in 1919 which are still vibrant and alive today.

This chapter is based on research undertaken by the author to explore the notion that Steiner schools function in a much broader sense than just pedagogical institutions (Stehlik, 2002). According to my subjective experience, a commitment to Steiner education as a parent seems to involve a subtle shift in lifestyle and values that is at once rewarding and challenging and consistent with the concepts and processes of lifelong learning, meaning making, and adult development. The central focus around which the community is formed and maintained is a commitment to a particular philosophy of education, which is underpinned by the wider system of beliefs known as "anthroposophy" (literally "the wisdom of the human being", the philosophy developed by Steiner which underpins practical applications not only in education but in areas including medicine, art, and agriculture). Individuals may choose to join and participate in this community because "it is one's commitment to any system of beliefs, rather than the beliefs themselves, that provides meaning in life" (Merriam & Heuer, 1996, p. 245). Each parent, by "buying into" this philosophy, becomes responsible for carrying the flame of Steiner education into their own homes and the wider community. Determining the extent to which parents not only actively do this but are aware of why and how they do this was one of the main questions pursued in the research. The research methodology took the form of a case study of an adult learning community in the context of Steiner education in Australia by focusing on the community associated with one particular school: the Mt Barker Waldorf School for Rudolf Steiner education in South Australia.

Easton believes that one of the major achievements of Waldorf education is "the development of the school as a learning community" (1997, p. 91), and the study set out to test this notion, as well as the statement that begins this chapter: that a Waldorf school provides a learning and growing situation for parents and teachers as well as children. The major finding as expanded and discussed throughout this chapter was that the school provided a site for community members to engage, learn, grow, and develop through practical involvement in an intentional community that both sustains its members as well as sustaining itself. It became apparent that it was a community of practice.

Situated Learning and Communities of Practice

"Situated learning" encompasses three related notions about learning: that knowledge is embedded in the circumstances of its application, that learning is a social process, and that activity is central to the organization and development of knowledge (Billett, 1994; Lave & Wenger, 1991). The term can be traced originally to the work of Dewey whose theory of experience placed situation as a central term in understanding the interaction between learning and experience (Clandinin & Connelly, 1994); and also to the influential community adult educator Eduard Lindeman who wrote as early as 1926 that "the approach to adult education will be via the route of *situations*, not subjects" (Lindeman, 1926, p. 4, original emphasis). Action learning is acknowledged as an underpinning aspect of learning organization theory, but situated learning theory foregrounds this notion by stating that activities are developed through a community of practice, which is in turn defined as "a set of relations among persons, activity and the world, over time and in relation with other tangential and overlapping communities of practice" (Lave & Wenger, 1991, p. 98).

Participation in the community of practice relates to a sense of belonging to the community and is both a condition under which learning takes place as well as a constitutive element of the content of the learning, which is in turn defined by the parameters of the practice that the community is concerned with.

> Participation here refers not just to local events of engagement in certain activities with certain people, but to a more encompassing process of being active participants in the *practices* of social communities and constructing *identities* in relation to these communities. (Wenger, 1998, p. 4, original emphasis)

Furthermore, a community of practice "provides a characteristic learning curriculum" and a field of learning resources that is based in everyday practice, not necessarily in a training package, a curriculum document, or a set of textbooks (James, 1997, p. 201). In other words, the expertise or knowledge base may reside in some or all of the group members themselves (Stamps, 1997a, p. 37), and the community itself becomes an environment that facilitates informal and incidental learning. Wilson and Ryder go so far as to attribute intentionality to such communities, which they suggest "seem to have minds of their own [and] behave as though they had intentions" (1998, p. 13). Communities of practice have also been analyzed in terms of complexity theory, as self-organizing systems that reflect the tendency in nature for patterns and order to emerge out of seeming chaos, without the need for hierarchically or externally imposed direction or a blueprint in order to function (Stamps, 1997b), and it is further suggested that "the organic, spontaneous and informal nature of communities of practice makes them resistant to supervision and interference" (Wenger & Snyder, 2000, p. 140). In this sense communities of practice actually generate social or cultural capital, not through formal educational provision but through informal learning, individual transformation, and cultural change, which are interrelated aspects of situated learning theory. Wenger and Snyder further consider that communities of practice are self-perpetuating as they continually reinforce and renew themselves through this process of generation (2000, p. 143).

The term "learning community" has been used to describe the social interaction aspect of the learning organization (Senge, 1990), but has been adopted as a more generic descriptor to encompass a wider range of learning situations. Perhaps because it is more inclusive of the idea of community, it is a preferred term in the literature on schools as learning organizations. A learning community can also develop in a temporary, nominal, or even virtual group of learners who are not associated with any formal organization and may be aiming at no other goal than to experience a learning community. Harrison and Falk define a learning community as "a specific community where learning is continuous and transforming," and distinguish this term from "community learning," which is "a broad name for those individual and group processes which not only produce but also *sustain* community development outcomes" (1997, p. 46, original emphasis).

Wilson and Ryder analyze learning communities as an "alternative metaphor to traditional instruction" (1998, p. 1), and highlight the concept of learners self-organizing to guide and control their own learning without the need for a formal "expert" leader or educator. They use the term "dynamic learning communities" to describe a situation in which control and guidance is distributed among group participants, where everyone learns and anyone can be an educator; the process being associated with transformative communication. The authors also acknowledge the emerging literature on situated cognition and state that "learning cannot be separated from action" (Wilson & Ryder, 1998, p. 2). Even though this notion can be traced as far back as Aristotle, who is credited with the aphorism "What we have to learn to do, we learn by doing," it is reinforced in the literature on communities of practice, for example by Billett (1994) in his study of workplace learning in a mining plant; by James (1997) in her study of transformative learning among mature-age beginning technology studies teachers, and by Wenger (1998) in his emphasis on active participation and engaging in practice to support learning. It would seem then that whether we talk about a learning community or a community of practice, learning in action is one of the key processes in developing and sustaining them, and situated learning is a useful way of describing and contextualizing this process. It also follows that learning in action can be situated in other contexts than just the workplace: schools, families and communities can also be sites for meaningful and transformative adult learning.

Parenting as Vocational Work

> No formal or legal requirements exist that require parents to instruct their children. However, common cultural assumptions regarding child-rearing infer that parents will guide and prepare children for life in a community. (Barbour & Barbour, 1997, p. 97)

Children experience a whole world of learning long before they encounter formal schooling and a place where adults are referred to as teachers. A child in its first three years of life learns to walk, talk, comprehend, and communicate with others all by the process of imitation and experiment, not by formal schooling. What the young child learns about the world into which it is born, it learns from its significant kinship relations—parent or parents, siblings, grandparents—and "it is important to realise that cultural learning begins at birth, is mostly non-verbal and 90% unconscious" (Khoshkhesal, 1995, p. 14). An anthroposophical perspective suggests that a young child is still incarnating into its physical body until its third year, and an awareness of the child's dreamlike consciousness at this stage may lead to a deeper understanding of the parenting process.

A popular book in Waldorf circles that explores this perspective is entitled *You are your child's first teacher* (Baldwin, 1989). The book validates the important role of parenting as real work in educating children in their pre-school years, in contrast to the dominant paradigm, which views teaching as a profession while parenting has lower status and mothers especially are often labeled "homemakers"—a role that is non-paid, non-professional, and not recognized as real work, when it is probably the single most important and responsible role an adult could have, contributing immeasurably to the social fabric.

This paradigm represents a general shift away from recognition of the family as the basic unit of socialization and placing that expectation upon schools, and to a certain extent on popular culture and the media. Barbour and Barbour, writing from a "mainstream" educational perspective, consider that child-raising practice is no longer influenced by the extended family and the wider community in a modern world where "daily lives now are more frenetic, and all too often families come close to abandoning responsibilities for a home curriculum in favor of that offered by the entertainment industry—a community force that is not always appropriate" (1997, p. 97).

Much of the literature from an anthroposophical perspective on education in general and parenting in particular calls for a renewal in thinking about the home as the place where socialization and social renewal begins, where some of the negative effects of the frenetic modern world can be balanced by a return to calmness in the home life:

> It is in the social institution of the family that we have the possibility of bringing changes that are health giving in the more immediate present. Here, we can begin to change our lives and regain some degree of sanity in a world that has so many pathological aspects. What we do within the family; the home we create, is perhaps more important than any massive reforms. (Kane, 1987, p. 12)

Creating an appropriate home environment is a recurring theme not only in the literature but in the discourse of Waldorf school communities, as parents are drawn to an understanding of the importance of supporting the ethos and environment that the teacher seeks to create in the classroom, especially in the early years. A typical Waldorf kindergarten in turn seeks to re-create the environment of the home. The kindergarten teacher—almost always a woman—represents a mother figure who does not "teach" in a formal sense but creates form and rhythm and a nurturing environment by leading activities that would also take place in the child's home: story-telling, painting, cooking, singing, playing games, and allowing the children to play freely and imaginatively. The more consistency there is between the child's world at home and in the kindergarten, the more secure they can feel about the school environment and be able to grow into an attitude that will prepare them for the more formal schooling that will begin in the child's seventh year. In the secure and almost domestic situation in the kindergarten, the "teacher" is playing out the role of "homemaker," to the extent that the distinction between the two roles is so diffuse as to be almost blended.

Schmidt-Brabant suggests that for parents the role of homemaker should be viewed not as domestic drudgery but as a spiritual task, and furthermore argues that the role of homemaker can actually be considered as a vocation—something that parents should aspire to as a vital role in making the household a starting point for social renewal, as family life "is the smallest and most basic part of our social life" (1998, p. 10). This is an interesting notion as it gives rise to the idea that, if vocational training is linked to a work-specific job role, then parenting as a vocation also requires the acquisition of work-related skills and knowledge. If we further consider the classical rather than the contemporary meaning of vocation, as "a calling ... especially a religious one" (Neufeldt & Guralnik, 1988), then we can see the connection with parenting as a spiritual task.

However, Schmidt-Brabant goes on to state that training in homemaking is an individual process, arising from life or what has just been identified as destiny learning. It is therefore not associated with formal education but "the homemaking career is a question of *self-education*. Self-education is a sign of modern humanity" (1998, p. 22, original emphasis). Self-education in this sense means more than just being an autodidact: it refers to a path of development that rests on the "self-formation of the human being" (Schmidt-Brabant, 1998, p. 22). Self-education originates with the realization by the individual that they are on a path of continual learning. "Parenting is one of the most important jobs, but perhaps the most undervalued. It really is a vocation, and one that takes constant work, both inner and outer" (Dowling, 1999, p. 1). But parenting is not recognized as a vocation or acknowledged as a skill to be taught during the compulsory years of schooling. Parenting skills are acquired through learning by experience, by repeating role models from childhood, by observing and taking advice from other parents, from books or other "expert" sources, and sometimes through non-formal educational programs—but mainly it is *learning by doing*.

A formal acknowledgment of parent education is one of the underlying aspects of Steiner education, in recognition of the need for a partnership between the aims of the school and the aspirations of parents for their children, and also in a pragmatic sense.

> An ongoing parent educational program serves the purpose of deepening their understanding of the educational aims of Waldorf Education. Parents must be nourished and sustained in order to have the stamina to make it through many years of financial and moral support that they will give to their particular school. (Mitchell, 1992, p. 81)

In other words, acknowledging the learning needs of parents serves a double purpose of maintaining the Waldorf community's core values and philosophy through a process of socialization and education; while also nourishing and sustaining the growth and development or "self-formation" of parents as human beings. The two processes are mutually supportive and interconnected, so active support by parents of a Waldorf school is at the same time a process of self-education and reflection on the task of parenting and the roles and relationships involved.

The author's research into Waldorf schools as learning communities and sites for promoting lifelong learning (Stehlik, 2002) shows how parents at the Mt Barker Waldorf School in South Australia saw this reciprocal role. Many of the respondents interviewed for the study associated their learning journey with what they perceived as their parenting role in the context of a three-way relationship with the children and their teachers. Waldorf teachers are expected to undertake a path of individual development as part of their vocation and, when asked if the same notion applied to parents, one responded:

> Well of course, even more so I would imagine. For me personally, anyway, most of the time because of my work, which as I said before is mundane and more ... it's really about transforming the basic ... you know I don't have my work and my self; my work and my self has merged. (Stehlik, 2002, p. 134)

However "work" in this sense meant domestic work, which being unpaid and generally unrecognized is harder to be objective about, hence the notion of "merging with self" to the extent that this person saw their identity as inextricably bound up with their work as a parent, and furthermore:

> being able to articulate these ideas had helped a lot in understanding and accepting her role as a mother and homemaker and the importance of this role in supporting the three-way relationship of parent, child and teacher. The key phrase this parent used was *transforming the basic*, meaning that while accepting that the role of homemaker involves a lot of basic, mundane work, she has been able to transform her perspective and elevate this work to a higher level of meaning. (Stehlik, 2002, pp. 134–135)

The study further explored the basic distinction that "parents have children; teachers have pupils" and that there are different roles and tasks associated with these differing relationships. This three-way relationship is identified in the literature on the history and background of the Waldorf movement. Schwartz for example suggests there is a conscious recognition in this system that parents are also part of the learning loop:

> The Waldorf teacher recognizes that only one-third of her "class" sits before her: the other two-thirds are the children's parents, who are no less affected by whatever is being taught and by the moral attitudes that are being formed in the classroom. (1999, p. 241)

In order to support the "moral attitudes" that are being formed in the classroom a parent must first share a belief in them and second reinforce them in the environment and daily rhythms of the home. Waldorf schools for example discourage allowing small children to watch television and encourage reading and activities by parents instead, including regular daily rituals that would reflect the types of rituals in a Waldorf classroom. Already this becomes a challenge for parents to change their own attitude to television and become more creative in occupying and entertaining their children, which in turn can become a process of learning and developing. The vocation of parenting then becomes a creative and meaningful task in addition to the more mundane activities of domestic life, but for the modern busy parent also a challenging one.

Workplace Learning Leads to a New Form of Schooling

It is worth noting that the first Waldorf school was founded through an early attempt at workplace learning that failed. Rudolf Steiner himself was more concerned with larger issues of social renewal, and in 1919 published *The threefold social order* (Steiner 1972b), a book that outlined an approach to political and social renewal that was intended as a contribution to the rebuilding of a society devastated by the turmoil of the First World War and hijacked by increasing materialist and scientific rationalist thinking. The book and the lectures that Steiner gave on this theme (published as *The social future*, 1972a) created a great impression in Europe; perhaps because people were inspired by the way the three elements of the social organism were linked to the great universal ideals of liberty (cultural, intellectual, and religious freedom), equality (political freedom and legal rights), and fraternity (the right to work creatively).

Inspired by Steiner and the frequent discussions and meetings with other likeminded social reformers, the German industrialist Emil Molt—owner of the Waldorf-Astoria Cigarette Factory—enthusiastically sought to implement the ideals of the threefold social order within the community of his large factory, beginning with a desire to liberate the workers' minds by offering them free liberal adult education classes. In Molt's words:

> Amid these activities, another branch of the Threefold Movement blossomed: the Waldorf School movement. I expressly say "movement" because, with the founding of the first Waldorf School, a model was created for many. Before I give an account of this, however, I should like to say something about the attempts at adult education made within the Waldorf Astoria factory, since these were the forerunners of the school. (cited in Murphy, 1991, p. 136)

These attempts at adult education took the form of a series of afternoon lessons in foreign languages, painting, history, and geography as an introduction to the broader questions of life and learning, generously counted as paid work time. Molt was trying to put into practice the recognition of the cultural sphere in economic life, not just for the goal of increased productivity for his business but to give an opportunity for second chance learning to the workers who had experienced very limited formal education provided by the state. However, despite the best of intentions, Molt soon found participation in these classes declining—the workers were not interested in developing themselves beyond the immediate needs of the workplace. Molt came to the realization that a predisposition for *learning how to learn* was generally lacking in the consciousness and outlook of his employees:

> What soon became apparent was that learning has to be relearned by adults ... From this I concluded that one must begin with the young if forces are to be successfully schooled and interests awakened. I became absorbed by the idea of providing for children what was no longer possible in later years, and of opening the door to education for all children, regardless of their parents' income. (cited in Murphy, 1991, pp. 136–137)

The idea for a school was born, initially as a long-term societal investment in the education of the workers' children—the future generation who could then be in a better position to "create their own social forms."

What is most important to emphasize here is the fact that the impulse for a new form of education arose from a clear striving for social renewal through the education of adults in an industrialized society. Steiner recognized the significance of this, saying at the time:

> The imprint of modern society is visible in the manner of the school's creation and in its connection with an industrial firm ... we could say that it is symbolic that this school is created in connection, in direct connection, with the industrialism that gives rise to the most important social questions of our time. (cited in Murphy, 1991, p. 74)

However it was also this very industrialism that had financed the physical body of the school, through the benevolence of Molt who purchased a building to house the school, had it refurbished, and paid for the initial teaching resources. In modern times, it is the parent body and the state who together fund the physical body of the Waldorf School, but the community alone that is responsible for its spiritual development and social sustainability.

Promoting Social Sustainability

> Community is a *creative process*. It is creative because it is a process of integrating. (Follett, 1919, p. 576, original emphasis)

Mary Parker Follett, a contemporary of Steiner who was also concerned with the social questions of the times, believed that the *process of integrating* is the key to understanding the relationship between the development of community through the collective activities of individuals who share a common purpose, and the development of those individuals through the experience of community. A *sense of community* is something different from *the community*, which can be defined in terms of tangible geographic, social, or ideological boundaries: it is a collective feeling or sense of being that arises out of the dynamic process of individuals interacting with others in a particular context.

This feeling of association or fellowship is a subjective lived experience and rather intangible; an abstract construct rather than a concrete set of objects such as a group of school buildings for example, which define the community only in a physical sense. It is however a very strong and established construct which is well known as *esprit de corps*, a term associated with the management theorist Fayol and often translated in the organizational literature and in military and sporting settings as "team spirit," but in fact literally meaning the spirit of the body, of the whole body of people. In relation to the Waldorf school, parents referred to this spirit variously as "the social community"; "the feel of the place"; "a sense of family"; "the school having a life of its own"; "a sense of feeling that the school has a wholeness."

Furthermore, if community in this sense is not a static entity but a dynamic process, it is because of the creative activities and interactions of the individuals involved. Here the word creative has two distinct meanings that are both implicit in Follett's quotation. "To create" literally means "to cause to grow, to bring into being"; while a more common use of the word "creative" is in terms of "showing imagination and artistic or intellectual inventiveness" (Neufeldt & Guralnik, 1988). Follett was therefore suggesting that we "grow" this feeling of community much as we might nurture and grow a garden or in fact offspring—activities that offer the opportunity to be creative in an imaginative or artistic sense. The discourse and philosophy of the Waldorf school community reflect both meanings in a number of ways: first in the parenting courses that are offered under titles such as "Creative Parenting" or "Creative Living with Children," and in the emphasis on creative and artistic activity not only in the curriculum but in the areas of teacher and parent self-development; and second in the way in which parents spoke of their role in helping to nurture the community, that parents are a highly active element in creating community and the richness and complexity of the environment.

A view of *community as a process* suggests a focus on the quality of the doing rather than the quantity of the outcome—in other words, it puts process before product. A focus on process also makes a link between a sense of community and adult learning, the latter concept having been established as a situated activity, associated with doing. Lindeman in fact defined adult education as "a process coterminous with life" ("coterminous" meaning to have a common boundary), and observed that "the whole of life is learning, therefore education can have no endings" (1926, p. 4). In other words, the journey is more important than getting there, for each destination becomes a starting point for another.

The literature on dynamic learning communities and communities of practice has in common this foregrounding of process over product and continuous informal learning over formal sequenced instruction. However, there is a striking difference in the contexts used to describe and analyze these two models of situated learning. While the concept of the learning community is explored in school settings, in rural and regional communities, and even within adult education programs, the emerging theory associated with communities of practice seems to have been limited to a study of workplace and organizational settings. In this literature, communities of practice are defined by comparison with other forms of work organization such as formal work groups and project teams, which are generally structured, driven, and controlled by management. Communities of practice are contrasted as informal, self-organizing networks that set their own agendas and are driven by "passion, commitment and identification with the group's expertise" (Wenger & Snyder, 2000, p. 142).

By this definition the Waldorf school can also be considered a community of practice, and it provides a sustainable context for the parents and the wider community who are drawn into the community of practice by association. While a compelling picture of parenting as a vocation and as legitimate work was expressed by parents and supported in the literature, this perspective falls outside the traditional paradigm of work as a place separate from the home life. According to this perspective the community of practice can go beyond notions of the workplace to include home life, school life, and community life. In conclusion, this integrated view of work and learning as a seamless process embedded in the variety of situations and contexts created by association and communities of practice provides a useful model for thinking about social sustainability into the twenty-first century.

References

Baldwin, R. (1989). *You are your child's first teacher*. California: Celestial Arts.
Barbour, C., & Barbour, N. (1997). *Families, schools and communities: building partnerships for educating children*. New Jersey: Prentice-Hall.
Billett, S. (1994). Situated learning: a workplace experience. *Australian Journal of Adult and Community Education, 34*(2), 112–130.
Cape Ann Waldorf School (1999). *Frequently asked questions about Waldorf education*. http://www.capeannwaldorf.org/caws-faq.html. Accessed 7 May 1999.
Clandinin, D., & Connelly, F. (1994). Personal experience methods. In Y. Denzin & N. Lincoln (Eds.), *Handbook of qualitative research* (pp. 413–427). California: Sage.
Dowling, M. (1999). *Henny Penny—Waldorf inspirations: in support of the vocation of parenting*. http://www.ozemail.com.au/~cromhale/hennypenny. Accessed 26 July 2006.
Easton, F. (1997). Educating the whole child, "head, heart and hands": learning from the Waldorf experience. *Theory into Practice, 36*(2), 87–94.
Edmunds, F. (1979). *Rudolf Steiner education: the Waldorf schools*. London: Rudolf Steiner Press.
Follett, M. P. (1919). Community is a process. *Philosophical Review, 28*(6), 576–588.
Harrison, L., & Falk, I. (1997). *"Just having a little chat": community learning and social capital*. Paper presented at 5th Annual International Conference on Post-compulsory Education and Training, Good Thinking, Good Practice: Research Perspectives on Learning and Work, Gold Coast, Queensland, December.
James, P. (1997). Transformative learning: promoting change across cultural worlds. *Journal of Vocational Education and Training, 49*(2), 197–219.
Kane, F. (1987). *Parents as people: the family as a creative process*. Edmonton, Alberta: Aurora Publishers.
Khoshkhesal, V. (1995). Grace before meals. *Education Australia, 32*, 13–15.
Lave, J., & Wenger, E. (1991). *Situated learning*. Cambridge: Cambridge University Press.
Lindeman, E. (1926). *The meaning of adult education*. New York: New Republic.
Merriam, S., & Heuer, B. (1996). Meaning-making, adult learning and development: a model with implications for practice. *International Journal of Lifelong Education, 15*(4), 243–255.
Mitchell, D. (Ed.) (1992). *The art of administration: viewpoints on professional management in Waldorf Schools*. Boulder, CO: AWSNA.
Murphy, C. (1991). *Emil Molt and the beginnings of the Waldorf school*. Edinburgh: Floris Books.
Neufeldt, V., & Guralnik, D. (Eds) (1988). *Webster's new world dictionary of American English* (3rd college ed.). New York: Webster's New World.
Schmidt-Brabant, M. (1998). *The spiritual tasks of the homemaker*. London: Temple Lodge.
Schwartz, E. (1999). *Millenial child: transforming education in the 21st century*. New York: Anthroposophic Press.
Senge, P. (1990). *The fifth discipline: the art and practice of the learning organisation*. New York: Doubleday.
Stamps, D. (1997a). Communities of practice. *Training, 34*(2), 34–42.

Stamps, D. (1997b). The self-organising system. *Training*, *34*(4), 30–36.
Stehlik. T. (2002). *Each parent carries the flame: Waldorf schools as sites for promoting lifelong learning, creating community and educating for social renewal*. Flaxton, Qld: Post Pressed.
Steiner, R. (1972a). *The social future*. New York: Anthroposophic Press.
Steiner, R. (1972b). *The threefold social order*. New York: Anthroposophic Press.
Steiner Waldorf Schools Fellowship (2007). http://www.steinerwaldorf.org.uk/. Accessed 3 July 2007.
Wenger, E. (1998). *Communities of practice: learning, meaning and identity*. Cambridge: Cambridge University Press.
Wenger, E., & Snyder, W. (2000). Communities of practice: the organizational frontier. *Harvard Business Review*, January–February, pp. 139–145.
Wilson, B., & Ryder, M. (1998). *Dynamic learning communities: an alternative to designed instructional systems*. http://www.cudenver.edu/~mryder/dlc.htm. Accessed 6 April 1999.

Chapter 20
Conclusion. AVE for Social Sustainability: Where to from Here?

Stephen McKenzie

The chapters in this book, many of which began at an international symposium of invited speakers in Adelaide, Australia in April 2006, represent considerable pooled knowledge in an overlapped, dialogic way. The twenty contributors, from Australia, Asia, Europe, North America, and Africa, writing from different disciplinary perspectives, have explored the notion of a sustainable society, the changing nature of work and vocation, and the need for the reorientation and reinvigoration of current technical and vocational education and training (TVET) to include what we began to refer to as "education for social sustainability."

Initially, "adult and vocational education for social sustainability" was simply a handy phrase for the group's key interests. After three days of discussion, however, many participants felt that there was potential for "AVE for social sustainability" to become a generative concept, a rallying point for TVET workers and adult and community educators with an interest in social justice, and we therefore determined to use "AVE for social sustainability" as the main theme for the publication of this volume.

The assembled chapters all touch in some way on the contribution (current or potential) of adult and vocational education to a sustainable society. It is clear from several of the papers that give an overview of the history or current state of TVET in particular nations or regions (Harris, Bagnall, Lovegrove and Morrison, dela Torre) that, at present, TVET practice is missing major opportunities to contribute to social sustainability, or is actively contributing to unsustainable practices. Hence our call for its reorientation: if sustainability is to become a reality, we must begin to educate people for the kind of employment that will develop a sustainable future, rather than continuing to train people for unsustainable work on the basis that it will guarantee them livelihood security in the short term.

In the Introduction, the question was put: what other areas of activity might provide us with ideas or models for reorienting TVET? A majority of the papers here point to areas outside the TVET system and speak for the inclusion within TVET of new ideas from those areas. For example, we have seen material on individual and family therapy (West), religious and spiritual education (Foster, Crossman), the role

---

S. McKenzie (✉)
University of South Australia, Adelaide, South Australia, Australia

of art and the aesthetic in enriching adult and vocational education (Willis), health education (von Kotze, Price), peace education (Spence), and ethics (Provis). Furthermore, there are suggestions for appropriate curriculum (Fien and Wilson), teaching to develop thinking, imaginative, moral beings (Newman), education for logic and rational thinking (Davison), transformative learning (Cranton), and cooperative learning communities (Stehlik). This is simply a list generated by the selection of contributors—we could have examined almost any aspect of adult and community education and development to find inspiration for a more human-centered TVET system.

The redevelopment of TVET will need to be a two-way process. On one hand, we must look outside of traditional TVET structures and practices for new ideas, and this is where the present volume makes its major contribution. On the other, we must also look within TVET settings for information on how to make these new ideas work. While we have many examples of positive practice to inspire us, we currently have few examples of such practices *within TVET settings* and we cannot expect their integration to be a straightforward process.

When our group (and others within UNESCO-UNEVOC) calls for the reorientation of TVET, we do so with the supposition that education can function as an active agent in changing workplaces and their cultures. There are many who would argue, however, that vocational and technical education simply responds to the demands of the employment marketplace; any major change to the way TVET courses are taught could jeopardize the employability of current recipients, meaning that TVET is no longer serving its primary function. Despite our calls for change within TVET, many employers will still want people trained to do the work of today, even if it is done in an unsustainable manner.

There are serious pedagogic questions as well that would create dilemmas for TVET education if it began to modify its curriculum so that, as well as providing closely linked skills and knowledge for employment, it sought to include ideas around social sustainability and appropriate action. Unless employers are involved in planning and discussing ideas of social sustainability, a modified curriculum would only contribute to conflict between learners in the TVET course and their employers.

Another dilemma for the reorientation of TVET is that learners (or trainers) may not take seriously any part of their training that does not relate to their immediate vocation. If we attempt to insert sustainability and citizenship education into standard TVET courses, we run the risk that learners will simply ignore such content unless it is made directly relevant to their core skills and job prospects. Worse, we may alienate them from our position. We need to ensure, therefore, that models for redeveloping TVET take into account the pressures on learners' time and attention, and are done in a way that positions individual livelihood security alongside social sustainability, rather than setting them up in opposition or appearing to replace one with the other.

This is where we need to return to current TVET practice in order to determine how to proceed with the integration of new ideas. We cannot expect to change the TVET system entirely from without; research within TVET on stakeholder perceptions and change management processes will be vital. There are three main ways in which such research could be undertaken.

The first is case study work in existing TVET sites in which innovative education for sustainable societies is already occurring. A resulting database of best practice in TVET for sustainability would be a valuable research tool and allow us to develop models for the integration of sustainability education into TVET that are more than simple, modular add-ons.

The second way that research could proceed is by approaching the task of integrating social sustainability into TVET as a challenge of innovation. The challenge would be to identify TVET forces and interests favorable to the innovation and those against it. Perceived *benefits* would include the perception that ecological issues around global warming are now everyone's problem and ways of ameliorating these global forces in the course of human work need to be addressed. In addition, social issues around deterioration of communities through poverty, religion, and race are being perceived by at least some as challenges involving education at every level. Perceived *potential barriers* to the acceptance of new ideas within TVET would be closely linked to the necessary modification of resistant attitudes and values of TVET practitioners and managers. How could a curriculum be redesigned to include knowledge for sustainability while maintaining learner and employer interest? Research involving current TVET recipients and trainers would help to indicate the sorts of learning activities that would inculcate knowledge for sustainability while also fitting with current TVET practice.

Third, AVE for social sustainability could be furthered through research with employer organizations, particularly those that make decisions on accreditation standards for TVET recipients. Do such organizations factor in social or environmental concerns when deciding on training standards for new employees (a decision that ultimately dictates curriculum design)? What new forms of dialogue could be established between TVET providers and employers on such an issue?

The agenda for further research in this area would therefore be around developments and recommendations.

Developments:

- of theoretical models for education for sustainability in TVET settings
- of specific curricula that incorporate knowledge for sustainability into vocational programs
- of toolkits for TVET practitioners to redevelop their own curricula.

Recommendations:

- to government bodies and accreditation groups on appropriate TVET policy for sustainable development
- to non-government organizations, charity bodies, and other community development organizations on dealing with the educational needs of their stakeholders.

The two-way process we are outlining for managing change within TVET must ultimately take the form of a balanced dialogue between new ideas and existing systems. Too much emphasis on maintaining existing TVET systems will go nowhere in terms of achieving sustainability; too many external voices and ideas will be rejected by TVET stakeholders as incompatible with current practice.

This volume, which we acknowledge is simply an invitation to participate in that dialogue, has focused on major issues and areas of concern within TVET *and* on external ideas that may in some way be appropriated to begin to address these issues and concerns. Further research and discussion will need to focus on how these ideas may connect with current TVET practice.

Name Index

A
Abrahamsson, K., 194
Adebowale, M., 27
Agyeman, J., 70
Allsop, J., 49
Anderson, D., 46, 51
Apitzsch, U., 135, 136
Archer, D., 214, 215, 219, 220
Armstrong, K., 33
Armstrong, P., 172
Aulich, T. G., 51
Ayer, A. J., 84, 85

B
Bagnall, R. G., 8, 193–210, 213, 261
Bailey, B., 49
Balatti, J., 56
Baldwin, R., 253
Ball, C., 108
Ball, S., 197
Bam, J., 159
Barbier, E. B., 67
Barbour, C., 252, 253
Barbour, N., 252, 253
Battersby, M., 22
Bauman, Z., 139, 149, 150, 151
Bazerman, M. H., 113
Beck, U., 167, 171
Becker, G., 168
Belenky, M. F., 97, 98, 99
Bennholdt-Thomsen, V., 184
Bernstein, R., 74
Bhola, H. S., 215, 216
Billett, S., 251, 252
Bone, M. H., 49
Bonnett, M., 75, 76
Booth, T., 134
Bornat, J., 135, 136
Bottomley, G., 123

Bourdieu, P., 74
Boyd, R. D., 96
Bradbeer, 30, 38
Brennan, B., 50
Brookfield, S., 98
Brown, B. L., 20
Brown, R. J., 109
Burack, E., 244
Butler, E., 56

C
Calder, J., 152
Calder, W., 69, 75
Candy, P. C., 48, 152
Capra, F., 240
Carlson, A., 137
Carr, D., 52, 238, 240
Carter, R., 150
Chakrabarti, V., 195, 216
Chamberlayne, P., 135, 136
Chapman, D., 69, 75
Chappell, C., 52
Chen, M., 190
Chopra, D., 241
Chrystalbridge, M., 69
Chugani, P., 241
Clandinin, D., 251
Clemans, A., 46, 56, 57
Clifford, J., 121, 123
Clugston, R., 69, 75
Coare, P., 135, 139
Coate, R. A., 66
Coles, R., 34
Collard, S., 98
Comyn, P., 51
Conley, J., 244
Connelly, F., 251
Connelly, S., 68
Connolly, W., 72

Cooke, K., 70, 232
Cooper, R., 147
Corbin, H., 30
Covey, S., 241
Cranton, P., 6, 93–104, 262
Cronin, A. J., 240
Crossman, J., 9, 237–245, 261–262
Crotty, M., 35, 36, 40
Crowley, R., 51
Cuban, S., 146
Cummings, S. I., 21
Cywinski, Z., 239, 242, 245

D
D'Souza, N. G., 220
Dallmayr, F., 88
Daloz, L., 94, 97, 98
Damianakis, T., 240
Dantley, M., 238, 239
Darnton, R., vii, viii
Davetian, B., 109
Davies, A., 197
Davies, M., 46
Davison, A., 5, 63–76, 262
De Bono, E., 243
Dean, H., 142
Dean, M., 168, 169, 171
dela Torre, E., 8, 225–235, 261
Delbecq, A., 244
Delors, J., 240
Denton, E., 241, 243
Derrida, J., 147
Dewey, J., 71, 251
Dighe, A., 219
Dirkx, J., 96
Dobson, A., 67
Dooris, M., 149
Dortins, E., 239
Dovers, S., 70
Dowling, M., 254
Duggal, A., 240
Dunne, J., 74
Dwyer, P., 142
Dymock, D., 49

E
Easton, F., 250
Ecclestone, K., 134, 135
Edmunds, F., 249
Edwards, R., 152, 172, 173
Eisenstadt, N., 135

F
Falk, I., 56, 57, 252
Farmer, D., 239
Fein, J., 71
Fennessy, K., 47
Ferrier, F., 51
Fien, J., 5, 13–22, 262
Fine, M., 136
Fink, D., 242
Fisher, R., 110
Flax, J., 151
Fogarty, R. J., 110
Foley, G., 47, 89
Foley, P., 56
Folkman, S., 113
Follett, M. P., 257, 258
Fornaciari, C., 242
Forsythe, D. P., 66
Foster, H., 119–129, 261–262
Foucault, M., 134
Frank, A., 34
Fred-Mensah, B., 155
Freebody, P., 146
Freire, P., 89, 99, 230
Froggett, L., 140, 142

G
Galtung, J., 159
Galvin, R., 152
Gamarnikow, E., 164, 169, 174
Gardner, G., 245
Gardner, H., 97
Geertz, C., 121–123
Giddens, A., 164, 171, 172
Gilain, B., 175
Giorgio, A., 240
Glacken, C., 63
Glass, N., 142
Golding, B., 46, 54, 56, 57
Goleman, D., 97
Gorz, A., 184
Gough, S., 75
Govinda, R., 218
Green, A., 164, 169, 174
Green, B., 242
Greene, M., 30, 31, 32, 33, 34
Gregory, R. L., 113
Gunnlaugson, O., 99
Guralnik, D., 254, 258

H
Habermas, J., 86, 88
Hager, P., 196
Halford, J., 239

Halling, S., 30
Hanna, I., 52
Haque, A., 108
Hargreaves, A., 242
Harré, R., 111
Harris, H., 56, 237, 238, 239, 240, 241, 242, 243, 244
Harris, J., 57, 149, 151
Harris, L. C., 56, 108, 109
Harris, R., 1–9, 45–58
Harrison, J. F. C., viii
Harrison, L., 252
Harrison, R., 152
Hart, M., 184
Hartley, R., 46
Hartsock, N., 136
Hawkes, J., 25–26
Herkenhoff, P., 167
Hermann, G. D., 47, 48, 50
Heron, J., 28
Heuer, B., 250
Hick, J., 113
Hildebrand, H., 214, 215
Hill, S., 26
Hillman, J., 27, 30, 35
Hinzen, H., 214, 215
Honderich, T., 113
Hopkins, C. A., 69
Huang, S., 239
Hunt, C., 136, 142
Hutchinson, E. M., 50

J
Jacobs, M., 68
Jacobsen, S. W., 147
Jacques, R., 147
Jadoul, P., 175
James, P., 251, 252
Janousek, S., 72
Jansen, T., 165, 167
Jastrow, J., 112
Jecks, N., 21
Johnston, R., 135, 139
Jones, S., 147
Jonsen, A., 75

K
Kahn, J. S., 123
Kahneman, D., 112, 113
Kane, F., 253
Kangan, M., 50–51, 52
Kanjula, S., 218
Kaplan, A., 239
Karlekar, M., 217

Karmel, T., 54
Kazepov, Y., 164, 165
Kearns, P., 56
Keen, C., 97
Keen, J., 97
Keesing, R. M., 122–123
Kell, P., 107
Kellenberger, J., 113–114
Kemmis, S., 172
Kemp, R., 68
Khan, M. L. A., 217, 220
Khoshkhesal, V., 253
Kickbusch, I., 146, 147, 150
Klein, M., 140
Klusmeyer, D. B., 22
Kohli, M., 214, 215
Kollmuss, A., 70
Kornhaber, M. L., 97
Kothari, B., 214
Kreisberg, L., 156

L
Lange, E., 96
Laurent, J., 48
Lave, J., 175, 251
Law, M., 98
Lawrence, J., 18, 19
Lawrence, K., 56
Lawrence, R., 240
Lawson, M., 230
Lazarus, R. S., 113
Lélé, S. M., 68
Levitas, R., 135
Levitt, N., 240
Lindeman, E., 251, 258
Locke, J., 110
Lovegrove, B., 8, 211–222, 261
Luke, A., 34, 146
Lund, F., 185
Lund Dean, K., 242

M
McCollum, A., 152
MacDonald, R., 175, 176
McDougall, D., vi, vii
MacIntyre, A., 74
McIntyre, J., 52
McKenzie, S., 1–9, 26, 121, 238, 239, 243, 261–264
McKeown, R., 69
McKew, M., 240, 241
McLeod, J., 159
Macpherson, C. B., 110
Macrae, H., 46

Madigan, F. C., 228
Mandela, N., 84, 90
Markandya, A., 67
Martens, P., 68
Marty, M., 238
Maslow, A., 239
Mathijssen, C., 175
May, J. D., 125
Mayes, C., 241, 243
Mayne, A., v–viii
Merleau-Ponty, M., 35, 40
Merriam, S., 250
Mezirow, J., 95, 96, 97, 98
Midgely, G., 151
Mies, M., 184
Miller, D., 239
Miller, N., 136, 172
Mitchell, D., 254
Mitroff, I., 241, 243
Mojab, S., 108
Monga, N., 221
Monroe, K., 111
Moodie, G., 197
Moore, A., 194
Moore, J., 94, 96
Morris, R., 47
Morrison, A., 8, 211–222, 261
Murdoch, I., 134
Murphy, C., 256, 257
Murray-Smith, S., 54
Myers, J. B., 96

N
Nagarajan, V., 239
Nagi, S., 226
Nash, L., 239, 242
Neale, M. A., 113
Neiman, A., 241, 243
Neisser, U., 113
Nelson, A. J. A., 49
Neufeldt, V., 254, 258
Newman, M., 6, 83–90, 98, 262
Nicholsen, J., 185
Norgaard, R., 68
Nutbeam, D., 146–147, 152
Nyssens, M., 175

O
O'Connor, J., 120
O'Riordan, T., 67
O'Sullivan, E., 99
Ogbonna, E., 108, 109
Orr, D., 71

P
Palmer, P., 241, 243
Parks, S., 97
Partridge, P. H., 53
Patrick, J. J., 22
Pattenden, R., 31
Pattie, C., 142
Paul, S. K., 215
Pearce, D., 67
Pegg, L. C., 20
Penglase, B., 48
Pete, B. M., 110
Petersen, C., 215
Petrella, F., 175
Platts, J., 240
Price, K., 7, 145–153, 262
Priest, A., 243
Probst, T. M., 109
Provis, C., 6, 107–115, 262

Q
Quaife-Ryan, M., 243
Quinton, A., 114
Quisumbing, L. R., 19

R
Raco, M., 67
Raggatt, P., 152
Rainey, L., 56
Ranson, S., 135, 142
Rao, N., 217, 218
Rasmussen, D., 86, 87
Redclift, M., 68
Reid, A., 239
Reid, J., 242
Reynolds, P., 109
Richardson, E., 47, 48, 53
Rigoglioso, M., 241
Rist, G., 66
Rizzi, R., 69
Robertson, D. S., 50
Robinson, A., 159
Rogers, A., 215, 221
Rogers, C., 89
Rogers, J., 238, 239
Roper, M., 136
Rosanvallon, P., 164
Roy, M., 214, 217, 218, 220
Rutledge, H., 135, 142
Ryder, M., 251, 252

S
Sachs, W., 68
Santone, S., 239, 242, 245

Saraswathi, L. S., 218, 219
Saunders, J., 55
Saxena, S., 215, 217, 218, 219
Scherer, M., 239
Schick, F., 111
Schmidt-Brabant, M., 254
Schofield, K., 50
Schuller, T., 138
Schwartz, E., 255
Schweiker, W., 120
Scott, D., 240
Scott, J. W., 151
Scott, M. L., 20
Scott, M., 113
Scott, W., 75
Seddon, T., 51
Sefa, G., 239
Segal, S., 87
Selby, D., 75–76
Senge, P., 252
Seyd, P., 142
Sharma, K., vii, viii
Shiva, V., 186
Shore, S., 107
Simons, M., 57
Singh, M., 107
Smith, A., 159
Smith, T., 109
Snyder, W., 251, 252, 258
Solso, R. L., 110, 112, 113
Spence, R., 7, 155–161, 262
Stamps, D., 251
Stanley, L., 136
Stanton, A., 97, 98, 99
Stehlik. T., 9, 249–259, 262
Steiner, R., 249–250, 256, 257
Stiglitz, J., v
Stoneman, C., 241
Stroobants, V., 167
Sumner, R., 56

T
Tandon, R., 220
Tate, S., 18, 19
Thompson, J., 109, 134
Thompson, W., 241
Tilbury, D., 69, 70, 71, 72
Tischler, L., 241
Tisdell, E., 238, 239, 241, 243, 244, 245
Todres, L., 26
Toepfer, B., 108
Torres, C. A., 98–99
Toulmin, S., 75

Triandis, H., 239
Tversky, A., 112, 113

U
Unwin, L., 49
Ury, W. L., 110

V
van Langenhove, L., 111
van Manen, M., 35
Van Onna, B., 170
Velde, C., 107
Vining, A. R., 197
Volkoff, V., 46
von Kotze, A., 8, 181–190

W
Wagner-Marsh, F., 244
Wake, W. K., 97
Warburton, J. W., 49
Waterkeyn, J., 185
Weil, Simone, 134
Weil, Susan, 7, 163–177
Weimer, D. L., 197
Weiss, T. G., 66
Wenger, E., 175, 251–252, 258
West, L., 7, 133–142
Wheelan, L., 150
White, S., 127–128
Whiteley, P., 142
Whitelock, D., 47, 48, 49
Wielders, I., 157
Wildemeersch, D., 163–177
Williams, B. R., 50–51, 52
Williamson, B., 189
Willis, P., 1–9, 25–42, 262
Wilson, B., 239, 240, 251, 252
Wilson, D., 5, 13–22
Wilson, L., 49
Winch, C., 194
Winnicott, D., 134, 139
Wittgenstein, L., 111, 113
Wonacott, M., 19
Woodburne, G. J., 47
Woods, D., 54
Worster, D., 63
Wright Mills, C., 142, 185
Wyn, J., 142

Y
Young, M. F. D., 171–172, 174

Z
Zehr, H., 160

Subject Index

A

"Activation", 7, 163–177
Adult and vocational education (AVE), 1–9, 25, 28, 33, 39, 42, 45, 46, 93, 107, 108, 110, 119, 120, 145, 181, 182, 189, 211–212, 225, 261–262
Aesthetic education, 26, 31–33, 34, 42
Art, 31–35, 48, 101, 139, 140, 250, 262
Australia, 2, 5, 9, 45–58, 67, 83, 88, 94, 120, 124–127, 135, 148, 150, 157–158, 193, 195, 197–198, 204–206, 211, 213, 237–245, 250, 255, 261
Auto/biographical research, 133, 134

B

Bonn Declaration, 2, 145, 147
Brundtland Report, 64, 65, 66

C

Collaborative learning, 102, 103
Communities of practice, 9, 175–177, 249–259
Competency-based education, 150–152, 202, 204
Conflict-affected communities, 7, 155–156, 159, 160, 161
Conflict resolution, 156, 233
Critical reading, 145, 147–148
Critical theory, 86
Cultural
  diversity, 19, 20, 22, 57, 100, 124–125, 126
  vitality, 5, 25–26
Culture, 14, 15, 17, 20, 32, 48, 65, 72, 86, 94, 96, 98, 102, 108, 109, 121–124, 128, 129, 160, 165, 182, 188, 189, 196, 200, 202, 204, 205, 207, 228, 253

D

Decision frames, 3, 7, 38, 57, 65, 85, 89, 97, 107, 112, 139, 142, 145, 148–149, 151–152, 157, 167, 168, 185, 186, 189, 197, 212, 230, 234, 241, 244–245, 263
Democracy, 6, 21, 72, 83–90, 157, 158, 201, 213, 229–230
Denmark, 226, 230, 231
Diversity, 18, 19–20, 22, 54, 57, 73, 96, 100, 108–109, 120, 124–127, 149, 173, 195, 197–198, 199, 202, 207, 210, 211

E

Earth Charter, 18
East Timor, 155–161
Economic
  imperative, 52
  sustainability, 2–3, 94
Education for
  All, 16, 212, 214–215, 220, 227, 234, 257
  citizenship, 2–5, 8, 13–16, 19, 21–22, 30–32, 46, 47, 55, 57, 83, 90, 94, 96, 142, 145, 146, 147, 164, 165, 170, 183, 193, 210
  insight, 6, 36, 40, 87, 101, 134, 136, 167, 170, 172, 184, 194, 217
  labor market, 50, 51–52, 134, 142, 163–177, 181, 182, 198, 202, 203, 205, 206
  moral thinking, 5, 6, 17, 19, 34, 42, 48, 63, 64, 70, 71, 73–76, 85, 89–90, 96, 109, 111, 120, 152, 158, 183, 239, 241, 245, 255–256, 262
  personal development, 9, 46, 47, 165, 198
  problem solving, 85–86
  reconciliation, 7, 27, 28, 35, 38, 39, 41, 42, 57, 155–159, 161

social sustainability, 1–9, 13–22, 25–42, 83, 93–104, 107, 119–129, 133, 142, 145–153, 155–161, 193–210
sustainable development, 1–6, 13–17, 45–46, 57, 63–72, 94, 134, 146, 149, 150, 152–153, 183, 225–226, 238, 245, 263
Environmental sustainability, 2, 14, 26, 65, 94, 186
Equity, 3, 5, 7, 13, 14, 17, 19, 26, 27, 30, 48, 50, 52, 55–56, 68, 86, 94, 134, 183, 202, 207, 212, 214, 219, 239, 245
Ethics, 8, 19, 26, 64, 70, 96, 121, 213, 242–243
Evocative portrayal, 25, 33, 34–42

F
Family support programs, 7, 134, 136–137
Fiji, 193, 195, 198–199, 202, 213
Film, 35, 38, 89, 101, 221
Finland, 165
Folk high schools, 230

G
Gender equality, 15, 20, 22, 215
Germany, 14
Globalization, 14, 19–20, 107, 202, 230
Great tradition, 47, 48

H
Health
　education, 3, 94, 145–148, 182, 184–185, 262
　literacy, 7, 145–153
Human capital approaches to education, 168–169
Human rights, 17, 20, 65, 69, 158, 182, 183, 188

I
Imaginal knowledge, 1, 5, 6, 25–42, 93, 226
Imagination, 6, 26–31, 34, 97, 141–142, 166, 176–177, 258
India, 103, 124, 193, 195, 199, 202–204, 207, 208, 211–222, 240, 244
Indigenous peoples, 19, 55, 129, 202, 212, 217, 222, 234
Indonesia, 157, 160, 161, 213
Informal economy, 196, 198
Information age, 20–21, 108
Intergenerational equity, 70
International Labour Organization (ILO), 16, 17, 244

L
Learning
　community, 249–252, 258
　culture, 15, 57
Literacy, 18–19, 55, 56, 65, 161, 182, 199, 200, 208, 213–222, 478
Livelihoods, 18, 46, 54, 183
Local knowledges, 182

M
Millennium Development Goals (MDGs), 14–15
Mozambique, 160, 161
Mythopoesis, 33, 34

N
Netherlands, 165
Non-formal
　adult education, 8, 193–210, 212, 213
　education, 7, 65, 195, 198, 199, 200–201, 211, 254
Northern Ireland, 159

P
Parenting, 9, 139, 249, 252–256, 258, 259
Participatory approach, 135, 186–187, 214
Phenomenology, 35, 36, 38, 39–40, 42
Philippines, 8, 193, 195, 200, 202, 203, 205, 207, 213, 225–235
Poetry, 32, 35, 101
Political participation, 3
Practical reason, 71–72, 74–76

R
Reconciliation, 7, 27, 28, 35, 38, 39, 41, 42, 57, 155–159, 161
Relational learning, 95, 102, 142
Religion, 6–7, 16, 98, 107–115, 119–129, 188, 238–240, 242–243, 245, 263
Religion studies, 121, 124
Religious dialogue, 108, 109, 110, 115
Restorative justice, 160
Risk society, 171

S
Safety at work, 18, 21–22, 33, 94, 148, 184, 189
Samoa, 213
Second-chance sector, 54
Self-employment, 8, 193, 194, 196, 200, 203, 205, 210, 232
Self-esteem, 55, 187
Sierra Leone, 8, 181–190
Slums, 15, 181

Subject Index

Social
- capital, 9, 56, 169, 174
- ecology, 5, 25–29, 42
- exclusion, 7, 135, 164, 167–172, 176
- inclusion, 55, 58, 135
- sustainability, 1–9, 13–22, 25–42, 83, 93–104, 107, 119–129, 133, 142, 145–153, 155–161, 163–177, 181–190, 193–210, 211–222, 225–227, 233–235, 238–239, 241–242, 249–259

Solomon Islands, 156
South Africa, 159–160
Spirituality, 4, 9, 76, 237–245
Steiner education, 249–250, 254
Story-telling, 33–34, 89, 97, 102, 134, 187, 254
Sudan, 160
Support networks, 7, 8, 26, 27, 28, 35, 56, 68, 72, 94, 100, 109, 114, 128, 133–136, 137, 145–148, 152–153, 155–158, 160, 166, 175, 185, 199, 207, 208, 212, 230, 241, 252, 254, 255

Sustainable
- development, 1–6, 13–17, 45–46, 57, 63–72, 94, 134, 146, 149, 150, 152–153, 183, 225–226, 238, 245, 263
- living, 18, 19, 46, 54, 183, 213

T

Technical education, 2, 8, 9, 49, 50, 53, 200, 227, 231, 262
Technical and vocational education and training (TVET), 1, 2, 4, 5, 14–22, 33, 45, 46, 57, 108, 182, 183, 184, 190, 193, 194, 226, 229, 232, 233, 234, 261–264
Thailand, 119, 193, 195, 200–203, 213
Third Way politics, 164, 171

Transformative learning, 6, 93–104, 249, 252, 262
Truth commissions, 158–159

U

Unemployment, 164, 165, 203, 206, 219
UNESCO, 14–17, 19, 57, 64, 69, 71, 145–147, 148, 152–153, 194, 213–216, 240
UNESCO-UNEVOC, 1, 2, 45, 46, 54, 108, 181, 182, 183–184, 186, 193–194, 262
United Kingdom, 49, 83, 133–135, 171
United Nations Development Program, 18
Unsustainability, 63, 64, 67, 69, 74
Urban development, 206
Urbanization, 66, 123, 200, 201, 206, 214, 222, 229, 232

V

Values, 1, 3–9, 13, 17–19, 26, 33, 47, 49, 53, 57, 63, 65–73, 75, 87, 88, 96, 100, 111, 115, 119, 121, 124, 129, 134–136, 147, 149, 183, 189, 194, 201–202, 204–205, 209, 212, 213, 238, 240–245, 250, 255, 263
Vanuatu, 213
Vocational
- education, 1–9, 13–22, 25, 28, 33, 39, 42, 45–47, 50–53, 56, 107–108, 110, 119, 120, 125, 181–183, 189, 193–210, 213, 225–230, 232, 261–262
- training, 4, 51, 211, 254

Voluntary work, 168, 174, 196, 202

W

Workplace relations, 20, 22
World Health Organization, 146, 149, 150

Y

Youth programs, 15, 16, 51, 140, 157–158, 163, 176, 181, 182, 184, 199, 228, 229, 233

Printed in the United States
136854LV00003B/14/P